THE CALL
OF THE WORLD

THE CALL
OF THE WORLD

A POLITICAL MEMOIR

BILL GRAHAM

a UBC Press imprint
Vancouver . Toronto

25 24 23 22 21 20 19 18 17 16   5 4 3 2 1

Printed in Canada on paper that is processed chlorine- and acid-free, with vegetable-based inks.

Library and Archives Canada Cataloguing in Publication

Graham, Bill, author
    The call of the world : a political memoir / Bill Graham.

(C.D. Howe series in Canadian political history, 2368-9080)
Includes index.
Issued in print and electronic formats.
ISBN 978-0-7748-9000-7 (hardcover). – ISBN 978-0-7748-9001-4 (pdf). –
ISBN 978-0-7748-9002-1 (epub)

    1. Graham, Bill. 2. Cabinet ministers – Canada – Biography. 3. Politicians –
Canada – Biography. 4. Canada – Politics and government – 1993-2006.
5. Canada – Foreign relations – 1945-. I. Title.

FC636.G72A3 2016   971.064'8092   C2015-908688-4
                                                             C2015-908689-2

Canadä

UBC Press, which owns the On Point Press imprint, gratefully acknowledges the financial support for our publishing program of the Government of Canada (through the Canada Book Fund), the Canada Council for the Arts, and the British Columbia Arts Council.

Printed and bound in Canada by Friesens
Set in Alternate Gothic, Perpetua Titling, and Minion
by Artegraphica Design Co. Ltd.
Copy editor: Deborah Kerr
Proofreader: Lana Okerlund
Indexer: Cheryl Lemmens

On Point Press, an imprint of UBC Press
The University of British Columbia
2029 West Mall
Vancouver, BC V6T 1Z2
www.ubcpress.ca

I believe everyone in the House carries within him or her the desire to serve our country ... Let us treat each other with the respect that thought brings. In what we bring to this place, let us respect one another and, in so doing, I believe our fellow countrymen will respect this institution and respect us for the work we do.

— BILL GRAHAM, HOUSE OF COMMONS, JUNE 17, 2007

CONTENTS

PART 1: FOREIGN EDUCATION

1   Where I Come From / 5

2   Out and About / 38

3   Trading Places / 55

4   Never Twice without a Third / 84

PART 2: FOREIGN MATTERS

5   House Duty / 121

6   Parliamentary Diplomacy / 133

7   Democratic Deficit / 156

8   Human Security / 177

9   All Geopolitics Is Local / 193

10   Marching as to War / 216

PART 3: FOREIGN AFFAIRS

11   Friends in High Places / 231

12   The Unwilling / 266

13   Picking Up the Pieces / 322

CONTENTS

PART 4: FOREIGN LEGIONS

14 Changing of the Guard / 339

15 The 3D War / 373

16 Home Fires / 403

Aftermath / 417

Acknowledgments / 437

Illustration Credits / 441

Abbreviations / 444

Index / 447

THE CALL
OF THE WORLD

PART 1:
FOREIGN EDUCATION

1

WHERE I COME FROM

I don't know where I was born. I can't even be certain when, which makes it difficult to get an accurate horoscope. According to the official birth certificate I carry in my wallet, I entered the world on March 17, 1939, at the private hospital of Sir Henry Gray in Montreal, Quebec, the son of Loring and Helen Bailey. But that document, issued five years later, turned out to be false. It's quite possible I was born, as my mother had been, in Atlantic City, New Jersey; I have no idea why Carvel is my middle name; and Loring Bailey proved not to have been my father.

When my mother divorced him in October 1938, five months before my birth, she had three children: Arthur, young Loring, and my sister, Helen. The four of us were present on June 9, 1940, or so I was told, when she married Francis Ronald Graham, a wealthy, fifty-five-year-old widower with ten children of his own, ranging in age from twenty-four to nine. Born in Burlington, Ontario, to down-and-out Protestant Irish immigrants, he had combined business acumen with a gregarious nature to rise from bank clerk to bonds salesman to stock broker to corporate financier to sugar baron, first in Toronto in the 1920s, then in Montreal in the 1930s. There, where his first wife was to die of cancer at the age of forty-nine, he met Mrs. Bailey, taller than he and more than twenty years younger, with jet-black hair, the face and figure of a Hollywood star of the period, and a personality as enchanting as her beauty. Early in 1941 they decided to start their lives afresh by moving to Vancouver, British Columbia.

Several of the older Graham children stayed behind. Mary, the eldest, who had suffered a severe nervous breakdown during her mother's fatal illness, was kept in a psychiatric hospital until a facility was found for her in Vancouver, where she remained institutionalized for the rest of her very long life. Kathleen, whom everyone called Ki, wanted to stay in Montreal to qualify as a chartered accountant and soon married a fellow student. Margie was in New York, getting a degree from the Columbia School of Journalism, after which she moved permanently to the United States to become a freelance writer and a drama professor's wife. Ronnie Jr. had married his childhood sweetheart, Mimi, before going overseas to fight with the Canadian army, following which he returned to Montreal to look after the family's investment company. Ann, Peter, Philip, John, Sheila, and Jane went west to finish their education and eventually settled there with families of their own. Arthur and Loring were packed off to board at Pickering College in Newmarket, Ontario, and Helen and I were sent to live with our mother's sister, Anna, in Toronto.

My earliest memories are of being brought up with my maternal grand-parents, Arthur and Elizabeth White – he a big-drinking, big-talking mining promoter, she kind-hearted and lovely. They had met in New York City, moved to Hamilton in Ontario, and were living at the time with Aunt Anna and Uncle Bill in the Dickies' comfortable house on Avenue Road, now a stretch of high-rise condos between St. Clair Avenue and the grounds of Upper Canada College. Mother must have visited on occasion, but I have no recollection of seeing her until I was four. Odd as that might seem now, I was too young to ask any questions. Many families were experiencing unusual and prolonged separations during the war, and I simply accepted that people grew up that way. Above all, it was a stable, loving environment infused with my grandmother's embracing warmth and the loving generosity of Anna, Bill, and their children – the eldest of whom, Carol, was more like a sister than a cousin.

Everything suddenly turned upside down in 1943, when Helen and I, aged seven and four, were put on a transcontinental train to Vancouver to go and live with these virtual strangers, our mother and her second husband, whom we soon learned to call Dad in the absence of any other. The time had come, apparently, to consolidate their two families under the same roof, prompted perhaps by the birth in July 1942 of yet another child, David, and the tragic death of young Loring in March 1943 – the result of a heart attack while playing basketball at boarding school. Seven decades later I stumbled on the fact that my good friend Hal Jackman, a leading figure in the Toronto business community and a former lieutenant-governor of Ontario, had been Loring's roommate at the time of the tragedy.

Home was now a grand Tudor Revival mansion on Selkirk Avenue, with formal gardens at the back and the chief justice living next door. As big as it was, the house still wasn't large enough for all of us, so the separate garage was converted into living quarters and connected to the main residence by an overhead walkway. This became the "nursery," where my sister Helen, baby David, and I were housed with our nanny, "Nurse" Camplin, and her helper, Mrs. Laws, whom we called "Lawsie." From time to time we were allowed into the main house for a visit with the rest of the family or for Sunday dinner, but mostly we lived a relatively independent existence in the nursery, which contained its own kitchen and play area. I attended Athlone School for Boys, a private school just up the road; I played with the chief justice's son, Haig Farris, who remains a good friend to this day; and I retain fond memories of Selkirk Avenue as a magical place to be a child.

Meanwhile, Mother and Dad came and went. He had seen their move to Vancouver as a kind of semi-retirement, at least in the sense that it re-moved him from the active business life back east. In reality, though he now had more time to watch his racehorses at the track or play golf, he never stopped making deals. He and Mother regularly travelled to Toronto, where Dad attended board meetings, or to New York City, where he met up with his many friends on Wall Street while she shopped. Such was her beauty, she turned heads in every restaurant she entered. They were away so much that I was always surprised that the dogs gravitated toward them when they were home. I was close enough to one woman who worked for our family, an Estonian named Erna, that she promised to name her son after me if she ever had one. Years later, she did indeed have a baby boy, christened him William Mart, and put me in the registry as his godfather. William Mart Laanemäe grew up to become his country's ambassador to Austria. You can imagine my surprise when, as foreign minister, I received a letter one day from the Estonian ambassador to Austria announcing that he was my godson! I had the pleasure of meeting him in Vienna during an official trip, and we have kept in touch since.

Winston Churchill's beautiful mother shone for him "like the Evening Star," he remembered in *My Early Life*. "I loved her dearly – but at a distance." That was my experience as well. In addition to her exceptional looks, Mother had a vivacious spirit, a loud laugh, and a wonderful way of reaching out to people. She was genuinely interested in them, went to great lengths to put them at ease, seemed generous with both her time and Dad's money, and was beloved by many. Any ability I might have to establish a rapport with others I attribute to her.

Not that she wasn't a handful. She loved parties, spent extravagantly, and could be feisty. Once, I remember, when I was still a boy, Grandma White and I went to New York to meet up with Mother and Dad on their arrival by ship from Europe. After a few days we returned to Vancouver by train via Chicago, with Dad and I sharing a sleeper with two berths while the women occupied the larger cabin. At one point Mother went on a rant about something or other, as was her wont, and Dad wasn't happy. "William," he said as we retired for the night, "I have to have a serious conversation with you. Whatever you do, do not drink gin. Gin is definitely your mother's worst weakness." To this day, whenever I have a martini, I think of him and of her.

Though she was smart about many things, Mother's tastes in reading ran to parapsychology and the paranormal. Most of us thought it was absolute nonsense, but somehow she got away with it as part of her charm. Less appealing, though no less irrational, was her inexplicably strident anti-Catholicism, even though (or maybe because) Dad's first wife had been a very pious believer who brought her husband and all their children to the Church of Rome. He had built an enormous stone house in Montreal during the depths of the Depression, and when he gave it to the Jesuits, it reinforced Mother's paranoia about a Catholic conspiracy – or perhaps her fear that Marguerite Phelan Graham had risen from the grave to reclaim her rightful estate. And when Pierre Trudeau was elected prime minister in 1968, Mother was convinced against all reason that it portended a papist takeover of Canada.

Dad was in many ways her complete opposite, though together they made a very effective team. Short, portly, with a cigarette forever in his hand, he resembled a dapper, distinguished W.C. Fields. Mother was the tall, glamorous woman whom everyone buzzed around at parties, but Dad gained their respect for his intelligence and quick sense of humour. Short-tempered at times and never one to suffer fools gladly, he was basically of an easygoing, non-judgmental nature, generous, warm-hearted, and philosophical. Decades after his death, his friends and family continued to recall his droll aphorisms or wise sayings, some borrowed, some original. "There are only two ways to lose money – stupidity and cupidity," he declared. "And of the two, cupidity is the worse." Or "One good investment is worth a lifetime of toil." Or "Service is remembered long after price is forgotten."

For a man of his wealth and connections, he never came across as snobbish or conceited. When Mother used to march us all down Granville Street on Sunday afternoons to hear the Vancouver Symphony play in the Sun Theatre, Dad invariably fell into a deep postprandial nap while we children squirmed in our seats, almost wishing she had taken us to church instead. Dad much preferred going out to the stables to check on his horses and chat with the grooms, forever full of questions and advice. And, having dropped out of school at the end of Grade 8 to work in a bank to help support his parents and seven siblings, he developed an autodidact's devotion to reading, particularly history and biography. That became a strong bond between us when my interest in non-fiction started to match his own. He was always curious about what I was reading and later used to read many of the texts from my university courses so that he could discuss them with me during the holidays. One time, I remember, he got quite exercised that I had been assigned Mason Wade's *The French Canadians*. "No, no, William, that's crazy," he started arguing. "That man doesn't know what he's talking about." And he gave me a list of other books he thought were better on the subject.

Until I was old enough to carry on an adult conversation, however, it was hard to get close to him. He was too old to be interested in small children, especially after raising a brood of ten. He was often absent. And even when he was home, he had so many people wanting his attention, so many responsibilities and activities to attend to, that he couldn't help but seem remote. Every morning I used to watch his butler pin a fresh rose on his lapel before the chauffeur settled him into the back seat of the big Cadillac. Then he was off again, in and out of my life.

Unlike my sister Helen, who was forever curious about Loring Bailey and anxious to make contact with her real father, I was totally indifferent about who or where he was. I never asked any questions about him and had no desire to meet him; nor did he ever want to meet with Helen or me. Though I was raised with the knowledge that Arthur, Helen, and I were Baileys, I didn't reflect on how we fit into the Graham family. Dad was the only father I knew. Helen and I took his surname from the start, though Arthur preferred not to – partly because he was old enough to have had a bond with his father, and partly because he would inherit, as Loring Bailey's eldest son, the hereditary title of Baron d'Avray that an ancestor had received for services rendered in helping restore France's Bourbon monarchy in 1815. Because of that, we were told, Arthur was the only sibling who wasn't given a stake in the family company that Dad set up in 1948 to provide for his children's well-being. In financial terms, Helen and I were treated exactly as little David. Actually, the three of us benefitted more than the other ten children when Dad set up special trust funds that gave each of us a substantial amount of money at the age of twenty-one.

Yet, despite having the Graham name and a share of the Graham fortune, Helen and I grew up with a sense of ourselves as outsiders. Compared with David, who felt entitled to all he received by virtue of being his parents' son, I felt I was there by the grace of God, on sufferance. I grew up feeling that I owed somebody something, not the least of which were dutiful behaviour and hard work.

In 1948, when I turned nine, the family moved to 6101 Northwest Marine Drive, ten kilometres from downtown Vancouver at the gates of the University of British Columbia and set amid towering conifer forests on a point jutting out into the sea. The new house made Selkirk Avenue seem dark and pokey. Built in 1915 on 1.5 hectares of gardens overlooking the Strait of Georgia, it was a huge Tudor-style mansion to which Mother and Dad added a modern annex, an indoor Olympic-size pool, a commercial-sized kitchen, two tropical solariums, and an aviary. In addition to its many bedrooms, there were two dining rooms, a music room, a recreation room with a granite bar, and a small movie theatre in the basement. We even had a private staircase down the steep cliff to a secluded expanse of beach.

David and I shared a spacious room at the opposite end of the house to Mother and Dad's. It had a breathtaking view up Howe Sound to the snow-capped Coast Range, and to this day I can hear in my head the foghorn from the Point Atkinson lighthouse, which used to sound early every morning and often through the night. With the move, I was transferred from Athlone School into Grade 5 at University Hill School, which was nearby and renowned for its high standards because of the number of professors' children who went there. Many mornings I had the thrill of being given a lift to school in the sidecar of a motorcycle driven by one of the Mounties who policed our tiny enclave, part of what was termed the Unorganized Territories of British Columbia, which consisted of only three houses: ours, Senator Stanley McKeen's next door, and the residence of the president of UBC, Norman MacKenzie. Every so often Dad got together with his two neighbours over dinner and several Scotches for a kind of municipal-council meeting, with Senator McKeen serving as "mayor" and himself as "postmaster."

In addition to the house on Marine Drive, my parents had torn down a couple of rustic shacks on Cave Avenue in Banff, Alberta, and built a holiday home large enough to accommodate twenty or more relatives, friends, and staff. Banff came to represent the only extended family time I ever had. That's where I got to know Mother and Dad best as real people. That's where I got to spend whole days with some of the older Graham children, from whom Helen, David, and I were normally separated. And the house had an atmosphere of warmth and domesticity that was very different from what we experienced in Vancouver, especially at Christmastime, when many of us, some married and with children of their own, bunked down in close quarters for a couple of weeks at a stretch. We skied together during the day, skated on the outdoor rink in the evenings, and swam at the hot springs. There were sleigh rides, festive dinners, all-night poker games, and on Christmas morning Dad showed up in a Santa Claus outfit, jingling bells and acting the merry old soul. He delighted in handing out presents for everyone from a big bag, just as much as Mother had delighted in buying them.

My brother John, who was to my mind the wittiest and most mischievous of the Grahams, used to say that living in Vancouver in the 1950s was like being a bee on a beautiful flower at the end of a long, long stem. At that time, it certainly was different from today's Pacific Rim metropolis. Yet, even though we were insulated by time zones and thousands of miles from the political and financial epicentres of the East and of Europe, I never felt isolated from the larger world. The West Coast had its own distinctive vantage point on politics and international affairs, and I was always surrounded by family and friends whose lives reflected broader horizons.

With the conclusion of the war, Mother and Dad began to travel even more widely and more frequently – to California for two or three months every winter, to Mexico and the Caribbean, to Europe and the Middle East, to Japan and India. Dad sent me postcards from Istanbul and Tokyo, Mother brought back exotic gifts, and their tales excited my imagination about foreign lands.

More significantly, whether they were at home or away, they opened our house to a constant stream of people, many of whom were complete strangers from abroad. Quite often "6101" seemed more like a small hotel than a family residence. Thousands attended fundraising events for the Vancouver Symphony and the Red Cross in the gardens. Hundreds came to the costume parties and musical soirees. Because UBC had no indoor pool of its own, the swimming team used to train in ours – and that meant I learned to swim from the head coach himself. Most Sunday nights, more than two dozen family members and friends came over to watch a current-release movie and share a spaghetti supper. You never knew who would show up at the house. A lord mayor of London one day, a former president of Lebanon another day. Sir Thomas Beecham played "Flight of the Bumblebee" on the grand piano. Louis Armstrong, Maureen Forrester, Glenn Gould, and Lawren Harris dropped by. Tony Curtis and Bob Cummings visited from Hollywood. The New Zealand rugby team trashed the basement bar in a party so wild that it made the international news. Bruce Hutchison, the distinguished editor of the *Victoria Times Colonist,* sometimes stayed with us when he was in Vancouver, and he and I had long talks about Canadian politics – quite an opportunity for a young person.

As well, out of friendship for Norman MacKenzie, Dad offered to put up any of the university's visiting academics and dignitaries who might need a place to stay within proximity of the campus. At one point we had five eminent scholars living with us for about two weeks, including the French mathematician Laurent Schwartz and Homi J. Bhabha, the world-renowned physicist who is still revered in India as the founder of its nuclear power program. He was accompanied by his companion, the wonderful Mrs. Wadia. Mother wanted to talk to them about Paracelsus and her zany parapsychological theories, but the physicists actually seemed amused. It was endlessly fascinating to hobnob with such an array of brilliant minds and diverse perspectives across the breakfast table, and I think it was a formative part of my interest in history, politics, and the world beyond Canada.

In Banff, too, all sorts of people drifted through. Jack Oakie, the comic character actor, and his wife stayed one Christmas. Ezra Taft Benson, President Eisenhower's secretary of agriculture, used the house one summer and, to the horror of Dad and his friends, turned the bar into a Mormon altar for prayer meetings. Charlie Beil, the renowned bronze sculptor, lived next door. The mayor of Calgary once presented Queen Elizabeth II with a copy of Charlie's statue of Dad riding a bucking bronco. When she visited his foundry in Banff and compared his methods to those of Benvenuto Cellini in the sixteenth century, Charlie was impressed by her knowledge. "I should know something," she replied. "I do own a collection of Italian sculpture." Senator Donald Cameron, the director of the Banff School of Fine Arts, and Nicky Grandmaison, an eccentric White Russian already renowned for his pastel portraits of Aboriginal chiefs, often dropped in to play poker with Dad or, in Nicky's case, to talk mysticism with Mother. Whenever I visited the Grandmaisons to play with their five children, I used to be intrigued by the huge painting of God that hung in their hallway above a votive candle. "How does an artist know what God looks like?" I once asked Nicky, and even he seemed flummoxed.

My childhood was a happy and very privileged one. A bit bizarre, but fun bizarre, spent among the natural beauty of the mountain peaks and ocean winds, the magnificent forests and coastal beaches, with good friends and every sport a young boy might desire. That made it all the harder when my life of luxury and freedom was unexpectedly interrupted in 1950, and I was exiled to what seemed by comparison a jail.

FROM THE AGE OF EIGHT, as was the tradition with the Graham children, I spent a couple of months each summer at Camp Ahmek on Canoe Lake in Ontario's Algonquin Park, while Helen attended the nearby Camp Wapomeo for girls. Nurse Camplin always escorted us east on the four-day train trip and then picked us up at the end of August for the return to Vancouver. The fourth time, however, Aunt Anna told me, "You're not going back, William." Instead, at age eleven, I was enrolled as a boarder at Upper Canada College (UCC), the most exclusive private school in Toronto since its founding in 1829 by Major-General Sir John Colborne for the education of the sons of the Family Compact.

Not to have been forewarned, not to have been consulted, seemed almost brutal, though not particularly unusual for children in those days. I presume my parents had decided that "6101" wasn't a healthy environment for a pre-adolescent. They were away too often to provide proper parental guidance. I was outgrowing the authority of Nurse and Lawsie. My brothers Arthur Bailey and John Graham, who shared an apartment above the garage, were leading a wild student existence, and the whole place had the aura of an ongoing party at which the booze flowed freely and for free. In retrospect, I can see that sending me to UCC was the right thing to do, though I resented it at the time and still feel I was too young.

I wasn't the happiest member of the student body. Already somewhat bookish by Grade 8, I was an above-average student all through my years at UCC but never at the top of the class. I was a house prefect, but not a head boy like the political economist Stephen Clarkson or the intellectual-turned-politician Michael Ignatieff. The highest rank I ever reached in the cadet corps was lance corporal. Though I enjoyed sports that I could do on my own, such as skiing and swimming, I never played football, didn't particularly like hockey, thought cricket a bizarre game, and wasn't good at any of the compulsory team activities – a liability at an institution founded on the British public-school model in which boys were to be made men on the rugby field. Even if I had performed well academically, the real heroes were the star athletes, and I had no interest in attaining that status at all.

Nor was I impressed by the school's colonial claptrap about the British Empire and British traditions. The principal, the Reverend Dr. C.W. Sowby, was an English import who acted the part of an Edwardian headmaster – a role that struck me as rather silly. Though there was a great deal of commendable talk about service to queen and country, social responsibility, and our duty to the less fortunate, I couldn't help but notice that many of the most illustrious Old Boys had headed lickety-split into the brokerage houses and law firms on Bay Street – as I later did too. That said, I can't entirely dismiss the values I absorbed at UCC, and they undoubtedly influenced my own decision to leave a lucrative legal practice for the challenges of teaching and, later, public life.

There were other compensating factors as well. My teacher in UCC's junior school, known as the Prep, was Alan Harris, a warm and inspirational figure who was responsible for Norval, four hundred acres of wilderness thirty miles away, where we boarders could spend most weekends, hiking through the woods, swimming in the river, cross-country skiing, planting trees, and camping out. Some of the fondest memories of my time in the Prep stem from those days at Norval. In the Upper School there were a few excellent teachers who cared about scholarship more than sports – in particular Dr. William Bassett, who taught me history – and I benefitted a great deal from the extracurricular activities, from the vigorous debating society to the model United Nations. Seaton's House, my residence, was led by two men – "Piff" Biggar and Dick Sadlier, the senior and junior housemasters, respectively – who cared deeply about our development. Best of all, I was reunited with Aunt Anna and Uncle Bill. Though my grandfather had passed away, Grandmother White was still living with the Dickies in their new house in Forest Hill, again within walking distance of UCC. I had my cousins Carol, Billy, and Susan to play with on the one weekend a month I was allowed an overnight break. Over the years the Dickies became a second family to me because of all the time we spent together, and I owe them a tremendous debt of gratitude for the generosity and love with which they took me into their home as one of their own. Surely it's no coincidence that I have made my own home in Toronto ever since.

Needless to say, their domestic life could not have been further from the one I had known in Vancouver. Aunt Anna was Mother's sane sister, solid, disciplined, and always home. Uncle Bill was highly regarded in the field of industrial relations, a job that suited his droll, easygoing temperament. In 1958 he was a vice-president of A.V. Roe when the Diefenbaker government cancelled the Avro Arrow aircraft, a political drama I lived through almost first-hand at the Dickies' dinner table. Subsequently he became an independent arbitrator for labour disputes and then assistant deputy minister of labour for the Province of Ontario. Every Sunday morning Aunt Anna and Uncle Bill went to Deer Park United Church near the corner of Avenue Road and St. Clair to hear its famous preacher deliver a fire-and-brimstone sermon for almost an hour, until I thought I would go nuts. Sunday nights they took us to the Granite Club for a swim, bowling, and dinner, which seemed a relatively sedate form of entertainment after what I had known at 6101.

Given Mother's aversion to organized religion and Dad's indifference to it, I had never been baptized in any church – a revelation that horrified Dr. Sowby when he found out. Forced to choose a denomination, I agreed at the age of fifteen to be confirmed into the Church of England. As a child, we had gone on occasional Sundays to the chapel at the Anglican Theological College because it was just around the corner from the house on Marine Drive. That, I figured, made me an Anglican by geographic proximity, if not by spiritual inclination. Moreover, UCC had Anglican prayers every morning, and every Sunday the boarders were compelled to attend an Anglican church not far from the school. My conversion wasn't, therefore, akin to St. Paul's on the road to Damascus. Though I went on to attend Trinity College at the University of Toronto, another Anglican institution, and to marry a woman who takes her Anglican faith seriously, I have never defined myself by any sect or religion. My Anglicanism, however, did prove important later in life, when I was appointed Trinity's chancellor, a position that, by statute, can only be filled by a member of the Anglican Church of Canada.

As much as I disliked being shipped off to UCC so arbitrarily, it probably changed my life for the better to have the structure of a boarding school and the grounding of a normal family at that time. I was satisfied enough with its education to send my own son there, and I never hated it as much as my brother David, who made headlines across Canada when his secretly planned escape triggered a massive police search for his possible abductors.

With hindsight, too, I can see that UCC expanded my horizons in ways I couldn't appreciate until much later. Though most of the boys enjoyed a privileged social and economic status, living and dealing with them in close and constant contact was clearly outside the comfort zone of most Canadian schoolchildren in the 1950s.

A few of my fellow boarders in the Prep were there because it was considered the proper thing for them to do, according to the ancient British upper-class custom of sending six-year-olds away to be toughened up by sadistic prefects and cold showers. Others, particularly the sons of Anglo expats in South America, were sent to UCC to get a good education in English with an infusion of British culture. To make a sweeping generalization, I would guess that a majority came either because their parents didn't feel they could bring them up or because they weren't able to do so. Though not necessarily troubled themselves, these boys seemed to have been removed for their own good from homes as dysfunctional as mine. Coming to UCC was like finding yourself cast among an unknown tribe in which you had to learn the uncodified rules of survival or be crushed. If I can't point to any great accomplishments in academics or sports at UCC, I at least survived.

Another of the side-benefits of being sent to boarding school was that I was no longer sent to camp in the summer. Instead, my parents took me on trips and encouraged me to begin my own travels. Dad, in particular, was a great believer in the educational value of travel, and he was generous in giving me whatever money and introductions I might need to get out and know the world. One Easter we went to Mexico, where we were hosted by business leaders, visited the racetrack, drove to the beaches at Acapulco, and stayed in a hotel in Cuernavaca that had once been a monastery founded by Cortez. It was the start of my lifelong fascination with that country, and I've had several vacations there with my own family and many trips as a lawyer, businessman, and politician.

When I was in my teens, I spent several weeks learning to ride a horse at a ranch that was owned by some friends of my parents near Skookumchuck, British Columbia, in the East Kootenays. While there I got to know an American family named Smith. The father, a colonel at the Air Force Academy in Boulder, Colorado, had been famous in Georgia during his youth as a football player known as Catfish Smith. Once, on a bet, he had eaten the head of a catfish. Polly, the mother, was a remarkably open, free-spirited woman, quite ahead of her time. Their daughter, Lee, became my first real girlfriend, and I visited the family in their various homes in Boulder, La Jolla, and Hawaii. This was my first exposure to the warmth and energy of a great American family. One summer a band of us roamed totally free through the hill country of Colorado on horseback, pretending to be prospectors in search of uranium. We crawled through abandoned silver mines with a Geiger counter. "You go down first, Bill," the others said, "because if the mine collapses, we don't want all of us to be killed." On the day that my pickaxe went through a rotted wooden pit prop, I realized that wasn't the smartest thing to do.

I took my first trip abroad in June 1956, when Bryn Matthews and I sailed on the *Empress of Britain* from Montreal to join about three dozen other young men and women on an extensive tour of the United Kingdom. Bryn, the grandson of a well-to-do lieutenant-governor of Ontario and the son of a distinguished major-general, was a close friend of mine at UCC. I spent many weekends at his family's grand home on Bayview Avenue and their equally impressive "cottage" on Lake Rosseau in the summers. The trip, organized by the Commonwealth Youth Movement and chaperoned by a couple of straitlaced monarchists, was obviously intended to inculcate us even more thoroughly with the glories of the British tradition – "First unto God, then to the Queen" proclaimed the enamelled pins we were given to wear – and it included several West Africans, a few Greek and Turkish Cypriots, and kids from many parts of the United Kingdom itself. All smartly dressed in maroon blazers and white shirts, the boys carefully segregated from the girls, we journeyed by coach from Liverpool to Scotland and back down to London and the south, with an extra excursion for a few of us to Spain and Gibraltar. What made it interesting was that, rather than staying in hotels, we were billeted alone or in pairs in private homes.

One night I stayed in a village with a family who had the tiniest car I have ever seen; another in an enormous castle belonging to a Scottish earl; and another with the family of a Conservative MP who also happened to be the nephew of a duke. I had been learning about rotten boroughs in my English-history textbook – the discredited custom by which landed aristocrats "gave" a parliamentary riding within their control to a friend or relative so their interests might be protected in the House of Commons – and here I encountered it alive and well. I felt as though I had stepped back in time to the nineteenth century.

"William, we're going to go out and see some of the tenants," the MP announced one morning at breakfast. So we mounted horses and rode around from house to house, and at every door we were invited inside for a glass of sherry. After a half-dozen or so, I was completely plastered. Somehow, while we were crossing a stream, the girth of my host's horse came loose and his saddle began to slip sideways, taking him with it. Abruptly I had to sober up sufficiently to prop him up until we got to the other shore. After dinner that night, the Honourable Member, his teenaged son, and I retired to the library for cigars while his wife and daughters were sent to amuse themselves in the drawing room. There they scrutinized a newspaper clipping of an aerial photograph of my parents' house in Vancouver that had somehow come into their possession. Meanwhile, we "men" began to drink ourselves numb in a desperate attempt to fathom the patriarch's opinions on the state of the British nation. Thus was I introduced to the life of the English country house and had, despite Dad's best advice, my first gin and tonic.

En route from London to Madrid, Bryn and I stopped to visit Joe Essaye, our UCC friend, at his family's elegant villa outside Paris. To celebrate our temporary release from the strictures of the Commonwealth Youth Movement, we decided to initiate ourselves into the glories of French culture by spending our evenings drinking champagne at the Moulin Rouge in Pigalle. It was the start of my lifelong attachment to Paris. Once through university, I returned there almost every year, first as a doctoral student and then as a litigation lawyer, a member of Parliament, a Cabinet minister, and eventually a grandfather of three little Parisians born to my daughter and her French husband.

I CAN'T RECALL GIVING much thought to selecting a university once I graduated from Upper Canada College in June 1957. I could have returned to Vancouver to go to the University of British Columbia, but Dad took a dim view of how easily John and Arthur had fallen into partying at home and saw me as a more serious student. I could have gone to Harvard or

Oxford, but that was less of a consideration in the 1950s than it is today. My best friends were heading to the University of Toronto, particularly Trinity College, and I simply followed the flow in September, living with Aunt Anna and Uncle Bill for the first two years and moving into residence for the last two.

This turned out to be a life-altering decision: there I fell in love with the woman who became my wife, met many of the people who remain among my closest friends, and, fifty years later, ended up becoming chancellor of the college. I took to Trinity in a way I had never taken to UCC. I did an honours BA in modern history, a four-year program focused in a chosen discipline. In my case that meant world events from the Renaissance on, supplemented by a couple of English courses, an economic history class that must have ranked among the most boring courses ever devised by mankind, and a course on religious knowledge – a Trinity prerequisite that Professor Gordon Watson turned into a wonderful survey of quasi-religious literature. It was my good fortune to have some truly inspirational teachers. Jack Saywell, J.M.S. Careless, and Donald Creighton taught history. Paul Fox was a star in the Political Science Department as well as a lovely man with an incredible ability to remember the names of his students long after they had graduated. And Elliot Rose, a legendary character, wore kilts to class and made a specialty of witchcraft and lesbianism in sixteenth-century Europe.

The classes were small enough that you could drop in and talk to anyone, and spending time with your teachers became just another way of learning. Once, for example, my friend Patrick Wootten and I were in such awe of A.P. Thornton, who had just written a brilliant book called *The Imperial Idea and Its Enemies,* that we invited him to dine with us at Trinity, and he accepted. As we discussed current affairs over dinner, the issue of the trial of Adolf Eichmann, the Nazi war criminal, came up. Patrick, in one of his iconoclastic moods, argued that the Israeli secret service had contravened international law by going into Argentina and kidnapping Eichmann. I'll never forget the expression on Professor Thornton's face when he looked across the table and said, "I was a young captain when the Allies liberated the concentration camps. My troops shot every German they saw for the next forty-eight hours – man, woman, or child – and there was nothing I could do to stop them. So if you think kidnapping Eichmann is a problem——."

Patrick was just one of the many wonderful people I met at Trinity. David Halton became a highly respected television reporter. George Butterfield, the son of a distinguished business family in Bermuda, went on to found the world's premier biking and hiking travel company with his wife, Martha, and her brother, Sidney Robinson. Tom Wilson was to serve as a key adviser when I got involved in politics and later acted as my trustee when I entered the Cabinet. John Hill joined the diplomatic corps and was still there when I was named minister of foreign affairs. Lisa Balfour became an art critic and an active promoter of the French language and culture in Canada. Pat Gossage was to gain fame as Pierre Trudeau's press secretary. One day, on a visit to St. Hilda's College, I watched an elegant young Chinese woman put six lumps of sugar in her tea and immediately went over to introduce myself. "I just have to meet someone who would put six lumps of sugar in her tea," I said. Her name was Adrienne Poy. She later married my friend Stephen Clarkson, became a media star, was appointed governor general of Canada, and remained one of my best friends from that moment on. And then there was Cathy Curry, a beautiful, sparkling young woman I had met at a party when I was in my last year at UCC and she was at St. Clement's School. Driving her home afterward, I skidded off the road into a mailbox, an inauspicious start to any relationship.

Not surprisingly, given how compact a town Toronto was in the 1950s, our families were known to each other. Cathy's father, Hugh Curry, had immigrated from Ulster in the 1930s and found work at Eaton's department store. He ended up owning a successful dairy company, just as Dad had done in the 1920s. Her uncle, Jack Barrington, was a prominent mining engineer who had been a close associate of Dad's friend C.D. Howe, the "Minister of Everything" in the St. Laurent government. Her aunt Josephine, an actor who had once performed in a hit play in London with Peter Ustinov, was a dear friend of Dad's long-time business partner, Percy Gardiner, and Percy's sister Helen. When Cathy transferred to Trinity after a year at McGill, we started going together in a serious way – and we've kept going for fifty years and counting.

Toronto was a parochial town in those days, still an outpost of the British Empire, where the annual Orange Day parade was a big event and a clique of Anglicans, Presbyterians, and Methodists set the tone. If you were an Irish Protestant, like Cathy's father, you almost had a right to be hired at

Eaton's. If you were an Irish Catholic, you had to make your own way. If you were Jewish, you kept to your own. And if you were Protestant, Catholic, or Jewish and wanted to have a good time, you went to Montreal. There certainly wasn't a lot of choice for a student looking for a swell place to bring a young lady. The Pilot Tavern was a beer joint. The King Cole Room in the Park Plaza Hotel was divided, like all the pubs in Ontario, into a men's section where no women were allowed to enter and a mixed section where no man could go unless accompanied by a woman. One little French restaurant in Yorkville had checkered tablecloths and a wine list, the very height of sophistication. A couple of Hungarian places were opening up along Bloor Street, and the Italians were starting to arrive in large numbers, but we were a long way from the gastronomic paradise that Toronto is today. One year, before Trinity's big dance, a couple of my friends and I thought it would be fun to do something different, so we took our dates – the guys in white tie, the girls in formal gowns – to a Chinese dive called Hop Sam's. The women were furious with us. But the thing was, if you asked for cold tea rather than hot, Hop Sam put rye whisky into the pot.

Many of my friends joined fraternities or sororities as a way to party, but I was steered away from them by an old hand who said, "Don't join a fraternity your first year, Bill, because Trinity will become your fraternity." He was absolutely right. By focusing on the college, I got involved in a host of different activities. I became active in the Debating Society and used to travel to Harvard and other campuses for debating competitions. I joined the Trinity College Literary Institute, which was really a mock Parliament with a prime minister, a leader of the Opposition, and a debate every Wednesday night, where I managed to hold on to the office of prime minister for almost a year until my friend Patrick Wootten organized a vote to dislodge me. In my final year I plunged into student politics and got elected as head of arts, the highest position a Trinity undergraduate could attain, in a very close race.

I was also elected scribe of Episkopon, a spring tradition at which Trinity students were able to blow off steam toward the end of the academic year. The scribe basically collected stories from people at the college and assembled them into a satiric presentation that was delivered to the other members at a black-tie dinner in early March, replete with old songs and quasi-tribal rituals. "The Divines," Trinity divinity students, performed a parody of a Black Mass. It was all silly at some level but nevertheless a popular part of campus life dating back to 1858. Archibald Lampman, the great Canadian poet, had been a scribe in 1896, and many former scribes showed up at the annual event decades later. In the 1980s, unfortunately, Episkopon fell into disrepute when some of the readings crossed the line from playful teasing to racist, sexist, and homophobic insults. In 1992, following a series of complaints, Trinity College barred Episkopon from meeting on the campus, which was understandable but also regrettable. To many Trinity students and alumni, it was a symbol of happier, more innocent times.

IN ADDITION TO MY academic studies, campus activities, and social life, I joined the Canadian navy – more precisely, the University Naval Training Division (UNTD), which trained students to become officers in the Forces or the reserve. On Tuesday nights I went in uniform to HMCS *York* for classes and drilling, and I spent part of two summers on board ship and at training facilities on the East and West Coasts. Why did I do it? Dad would have let me travel wherever I wanted during the holidays, and if I chose to get a summer job, he could have arranged for me to work for friends such as Donald Macleod at the brokerage firm of McLeod, Young, Weir or for Senator Salter Hayden at the law firm of McCarthy and McCarthy. But these opportunities seemed mundane compared to what I heard about the navy from my friend Hal Davies and others who had done the UNTD program. Two of my pals, Tom Bastedo and Charlie Gunn, also signed up. And, to be honest, I thought I needed a bit of toughening up.

The navy did not disappoint on that score. Living in a ship's close quarters for weeks at a time, sleeping in a bunk so tight that you'd bump your head if you sat up too quickly, waking at six in the morning, washing your own clothes, marching back and forth, crawling under barbed wire, painting ships, working in the engine room, competing in rowing races, and literally learning the ropes – it was unlike anything I had previously encountered in my privileged life. In my division there was an Anglo-Quebecer from Montreal, two francophones, three or four Maritimers, a couple of Westerners, and an Aboriginal from Winnipeg – Bill Shead, whom I saw frequently years later when he ran for Parliament as a Liberal. Training with fellow cadets from across Canada was a personal exercise in nation building, and I'm not sure I would ever have got to know Nova Scotia otherwise or seen so much of the Queen Charlotte Islands (now Haida Gwaii).

"By working and playing together we have got to know and understand one another's point of view," I wrote in the journal we were required to keep as a record of what we learned in class and on deck. "This is a rare principle for which I am very grateful."

These journals, which were read and critiqued by a couple of officers, were intended to develop our powers of observation and expression. I've continued the practice, jotting down random notes or writing long letters by hand, usually in a series of "black books" but often on the back of menus at official dinners or at the edges of my daily agenda sheets. Early in the naval journal, with all the authority of a nineteen-year-old university student, I digressed for several pages to reflect upon the geopolitical situation in Lebanon, Indonesia, the United Arab Republic, and France, where General Charles de Gaulle was returning to power to deal with the crisis in Algeria. Not for the last time did someone upbraid me for my inclination to "ramble," and another officer cautioned me that "more time is to be spent on service matters and less on foreign affairs."

The real eye-opener was the course on atomic, biological, and chemical warfare defence. "This is the first time that it has been brought home to us what we might have to face or do in time of war," I wrote. "After taking the ABCD course it would be difficult to think of the navy just as a nice way to spend the summer, a pleasant organization where we meet and get to know a lot of other students, a place where we learn things which might be useful if we like sailing, or for that matter a sort of useless organization. You cannot escape being impressed with the force of modern warfare and the fate which might well be ours if we relax our vigilance."

Navy life may have been hard, but it was also fun. I greatly enjoyed the mess dinners and helped organize the annual cadet ball. I got what I called a "valuable" look at the working environment of the United Nations when *La Hulloise* cruised into New York City one weekend. And one night on shore leave in San Diego, I was heading back to the *Jonquière* with Denis Lynch, a zany Irish character from Montreal, when we came across a couple of our sailors in trouble with the American Military Police. Denis went over to the police and said in his most officious voice, "We're Canadian naval officers, gentlemen. You can release these men into our custody." Our ship's captain went ballistic when he got wind of the tale, and I was sure we were going to spend the rest of our days in the brig for impersonating an officer, but I suspect he was secretly proud of what we had done because he let us off with a lecture.

Though the military discipline at first struck me as stupid, designed only to turn us into automatons ready to do the bidding of our superiors, I came to understand its value. Once during a training exercise on a destroyer, the captain ordered me off the bridge the moment he noticed I wasn't paying proper attention: I had become, he said, a danger to the others. Another time, when I was put in command of launching a whaler in a heavy sea, I stepped forward to grab one of the ropes. "Don't do that!" a lieutenant shouted. "Someone has to oversee the situation, and that's you, so step back!" One error by a single sailor, one failure of a single piece of equipment, and it could have meant serious injury.

There was also a fair amount of classroom teaching, which wasn't so different from university except for the subject matter. Navigation, as an example, though I can't say I mastered it. One time a couple of friends and I had a whim to borrow a friend's motor yacht for a cruise through the islands between Vancouver and Victoria, confident that my training as a naval officer would suffice. We came close to smashing up on some rocks. "Let's take this thing back if we can," I said, "before we kill somebody with it."

Years later, sailing off Corsica with my daughter's father-in-law, Denis Debost, I tried to navigate by shooting the sun. I stood on the deck doing my calculations and screaming them out to Denis, my crew of one, who was down below studying the charts. "So where are we now?" I asked.

"According to you," Denis replied, "we're right on top of Monte Cinto." My naval skills had apparently landed us on the highest peak in Corsica.

If I didn't come out of the navy with any particular professional skills, I did pick up a set of important life skills that someone of my background wouldn't have acquired easily. I learned how to deal with all sorts of different and sometimes difficult people, whether officers or ordinary seamen. I learned how to take orders and how to give orders. I learned how to adapt to a completely strange environment, where nothing and nobody bore any resemblance to what and who I knew at home or at university. That turned out to be of immeasurable value when I came to practise law in Africa or campaign in the rougher sections of my riding. Decades after the fact, I can still recall the pride I felt when, after helping a petty officer in some small way, he offered me a share of his daily ration of rum – a very high compliment indeed.

Nor could I have guessed how that experience would play out years later, when, in 2004, I became Canada's minister of national defence. The navy guys particularly loved it, of course. Whenever I boarded a ship, they would say, "The minister is one of ours, you know." And at the big mess dinners that the military love so much, with all the chiefs present, the bands playing regimental marches, and everyone dressed up in full uniform, I always stood, as is the custom, when the naval march "Heart of Oak" was played. The army and air force brass always yelled at me to sit down, but the admirals drowned them out by shouting, "Stand up, stand up, Minister, you're a navy man!"

IN THEORY I SHOULD have done my naval training over three summers, but I finished enough courses during the winter to earn my commission as a sub-lieutenant in Her Majesty's navy after my third year at university. (A couple of years later, I received a letter informing me that I had been promoted one grade, without having done anything in particular to deserve it.) So, with more than four carefree months until our final year began, Patrick Wootten and I concocted a plan to buy a Land Rover and drive it to India and back in time for the fall term. Crazier still, we thought we could get businesses to finance our adventure by putting their logos all over the car. It seemed like a good idea in the middle of the night after a few drinks. A lot of hustling netted just one sponsor, Rose's Lime Juice, which gave us two cases of their sweet, treacly drink to take on our journey. Dad was as supportive as usual, however, and Patrick's mother was so enthusiastic that she threatened to come along, which wasn't quite what we had in mind.

Patrick's upbringing was almost as unusual as mine. His mother was an extremely wealthy American who had met and married a British naval attaché in Washington, DC, with the classic name of Captain Patrick William Wootten-Wootten, but the marriage hadn't lasted. When we visited the captain in England at the start of our trip, he was living with an un-married sister down in Devon. The odd thing was, the two of them never spoke directly to each other. They communicated through their black Labrador, Nancy.

"Nancy thinks it's a very hot day," said Captain Wootten-Wootten.

"Nancy doesn't think it's a very hot day," his sister replied. "She thinks it has cooled off."

"Nancy says the birds are eating the raspberries."

"Well, Nancy, I suppose we'd better do something about that. What do you suggest, Nancy?" It was like a Monty Python skit or a scene out of *Alice in Wonderland*.

Patrick and I set off in May without much of a plan, except that both of us were interested in reaching India if we could. My parents had fired my imagination with their trips to Beirut and Cairo; Dad was on the board of an insurance company with interests in Lebanon, and he and Mother gave us introductions to the good friends they had made there. As well, my UCC friend Joe Essaye had filled my head with exotic images of his mother's family, who owned a highly successful business making araq, the anise-flavoured alcoholic drink, in Iraq. To prepare for the trip, I read T.E. Lawrence and Gertrude Bell, Freya Stark and Wilfred Thesiger, a biography of Atatürk, and a history of the Ottoman Empire.

We hastily crossed Europe to Slovenia, down the Dalmatian coast with a stop at the great Palace of Diocletian in Split, along the Adriatic coast to Dubrovnik, and east into Montenegro. We were winding down a narrow mountain road when we literally ran into a motorcyclist coming the other way around a sharp corner. He crashed right into the middle of our Land Rover. Fortunately we had been travelling too slowly on the bad road to do any real damage to him or to our car, but the motorcycle was a total wreck. We hoisted it into the back and drove its aggrieved owner into Cetinje, Montenegro's former capital, where he immediately laid a com-plaint with the local authorities. They impounded our car and ordered us not to leave town until we had paid to have the motorcycle repaired or replaced. Though we had insurance, we could see ourselves being stuck there for a long time. None of the hotels looked appealing, but we had learned to enjoy camping in fields by the side of the road, so we pitched our tent in the local military compound, where we were watched like prisoners in case we tried to bolt. We wasted a day trying and failing to make a phone connection to the insurance company in London. Another day was spent getting through to Dad in Vancouver to ask him to phone London. On the third day, we walked into a bar, utterly frustrated.

"Where are you boys from?" asked a guy sitting beside us.

"Vancouver," I said.

"Oh, I'm from Seattle. What the hell are you doing here?"

"Well, we were on our way to India, but we had an accident, and now it seems that we aren't going anywhere."

"That's a shame," he said. "But you seem like nice young fellows, and my brother-in-law is the chief justice of Montenegro, so let's see what we can do about things."

The next morning we went to see the chief justice. He looked over our papers, found nothing wrong, and immediately signed an authorization giving us permission to leave. We rushed back to the encampment and hastily packed up the Land Rover, pausing only at the military gas pump to fill up for the journey. When we asked what we owed, the soldier just winked and said, "We'll send the bill to Tito."

In Istanbul, where we stayed in the gloriously archaic Divan Hotel before it was ruined by a modern renovation, we sensed trouble brewing. The streets were full of Sherman tanks with rubber tracks that were clearly designed for urban conditions, and troop manoeuvres were taking place all over the city. We wanted to keep moving, however, so we headed off to Ankara. We arrived in the capital around seven in the evening on May 27, 1960, and found the situation no better. There were military and police checkpoints at every major corner. We decided to go straight to the British embassy to find out what was happening but didn't get far before we were stopped by armed soldiers. Finding someone who spoke English took a while. "You're in violation of the six o'clock curfew," he barked. "What are you stupid British kids doing driving around the streets anyway? Don't you know there's been a coup?"

"Actually, no, we don't. That's why we were heading for the British embassy."

While we were waiting for our fate to be decided, one of the soldiers invited us to drink some raki with him, and we were soon buttering up a colonel with compliments about how professionally the Turkish army behaved and how especially kind it was to young travellers from abroad. As it turned out, he had fought in the Korean War. "That was the most wonderful experience," he said. "The Americans gave us all the ammunition, and the Chinese gave us all the targets." Finally, around 11:30 p.m., there was great excitement at the news that the general himself was about to arrive.

"General who?" Patrick asked.

"General Gürsel. He's the commander of the army, and now he's going to be the leader of the country. If you stick around, you can meet him." And that's how, I always tell my Turkish friends to their utter astonishment, I got to meet General Cemal Gürsel – something very few Turks can claim. Of course, with other fish to fry that night, he didn't spend much time with us other than to say hello and promise to arrange for our release. The next day we watched a big military parade go by, and I took a picture of our colonel waving to us as he slowly passed. It was my first, but not last, coup d'état.

Once we crossed into Iran, I became aware that its situation was more complex than I had expected. I wrote Dad several long letters about what I was seeing, and what I was seeing didn't correspond with the optimistic reports he had been getting from his Iranian business contacts. "I don't think things look good here for the shah," I wrote. "The mullahs are rioting. By taking land away from them to give to the peasants, he's creating a horrendous political problem for himself." When Iran exploded in protest demonstrations a couple of years later, Dad thought I was some sort of political genius who had figured out what nobody else, not even *Time* magazine, had predicted.

My insights were hardly my own. They mostly derived from the conversations I had had in Mashhad, the famous pilgrimage city in the northeast corner of Iran, where Patrick and I were given an introduction to an old princely family. Though they had been overthrown by the shah's father and were understandably cynical about the stability of the regime, they were still highly respected landowners with a profound knowledge of the city. When we visited the exquisite museum of which they were the historic custodians, they arranged permission for us to peer into the sacred mosque next door, where Imam Reza lies buried. As Christians, of course, we weren't allowed to enter. The week before, we had been told, an American Muslim had been worshipping there when rumours spread that he was really a spy, and he had been killed on the spot.

As it happened, our visit coincided with the holy day known as the "mourning of Muharram." Patrick and I witnessed the extraordinary sight of Shia literally whipping themselves into a state of religious fervour. A parade of men flagellated themselves or were flagellated until blood soaked their backs. Suddenly a man from our hotel came running up to us. "You have to return immediately," he said breathlessly. "There's a phone call for you from North America." Puzzled and very worried, we sped back as fast as we could, only to find that there was in fact no phone call. "I felt you wouldn't listen to me otherwise," the hotelier explained, "but it's far too dangerous for you to be out on the streets at this time. I had to get you away from there before somebody decided to take a whip to you."

The next day we drove to Herat, the westernmost city of the westernmost province of Afghanistan. Patrick and I were the only guests in our hotel. At dinner, as had been the case most nights since leaving Turkey, there were only two items on the menu: chicken or lamb. "Okay," we said, "let's go for the chicken." A few minutes later I happened to look out the window and saw a guy come out the back door of the kitchen, get on a bicycle, and ride down the road. After about half an hour, he came pedalling back with a chicken tied to his bike. Lucky we hadn't ordered the lamb, I thought.

Then, as now, there was no direct route from Herat to Kabul. We had to drive deep into the southeast to Kandahar through forbidding mountain passes, stretches of empty desert, and valleys lush with fruit and nut trees, before swinging north to the capital. I don't remember much of Kandahar, because I was very ill with amoebic dysentery by the time we got there. By luck we encountered a German doctor who had some antibiotics with him, though I've been susceptible to intestinal ailments ever since. Decades later, when I returned to Kandahar as Canada's defence minister, it didn't look all that different – small, dusty, rudimentary, with a bit of a Wild West feeling. Missing, though, were the attractive wooden buildings, some lovely gardens, and the large Saturday market where gun-toting tribesmen wearing colourful turbans came to buy or sell the fat-tailed sheep. I bought a lambswool hat, which I still possess, and a sheepskin jacket that I loved and wore for years despite its increasingly foul smell.

By the time we reached Kabul, we were out of cash. Getting money from a foreign bank, if successful at all, was usually a half-day affair in those dark ages before debit cards, and something to be avoided until absolutely necessary. While waiting for the Afghani manager to figure out what to make of my letter of credit, I noticed that some of his employees were standing in a thick cloud of smoke in the courtyard, setting fire to wads of banknotes. "What are those guys doing?" I asked him.

"Oh," he said matter-of-factly, "there's an IMF inspection going on, and because there's far too much currency in circulation, the Central Bank wants us to burn some of it."

Ever since reading the *Baburnama,* the story of Babur's conquest of India, I had wanted to visit the Mughal emperor's tomb and its famous garden. He had asked to be buried in Kabul, and though his shrine wasn't as large or as elegant as the Taj Mahal, I found it very beautiful nevertheless. Indeed, when I returned to Kabul as Canada's defence minister in 2005, I insisted on taking Cathy to see it despite all the dire warnings from my security detail. It was a delight to see the progress the Aga Khan Foundation had made in restoring it to its former glory as an imaginative contribution to the peace and prosperity of the city.

From Kabul, Patrick and I drove northwest to Bamiyan to see the famous sixth century standing Buddhas, which were destroyed in 2001 by the Taliban in a shameless desecration of one of the world's greatest religious monuments. We climbed through the caves in the mountain behind them and emerged at the top of a Buddha's head. From there we enjoyed a panoramic view of the green, lush, beautifully terraced valley below, whose orchards were fed by its ancient irrigation systems. The light was dazzling; there was barely a sound except for the bleating of sheep and the shepherds' shouts. It was hard to imagine that this place had been a centre of civilization, full of traders and monks, and even harder to imagine it as a battlefield where the Mughals, the Soviets, and the Taliban had waged campaigns. Four decades later, I was to sit with President Karzai at an official event in Ottawa and lament with him the loss of those magnificent statues.

We had hoped to continue north to Samarkand and Bokhara to join the Silk Road, but we had to turn back when we learned that the Russians wouldn't let us cross the border. We hadn't gone far when the car broke down. Patrick and I flipped a coin to determine who would stay and who would hitchhike to Kabul to fetch a new carburetor. I lost the toss and soon found myself riding atop a truck piled high with animal hides. On every mountain curve, as the truck swung to the edge of a steep cliff plunging to the river far below, I thought I wasn't going to make it. Somehow I managed to get to Kabul and back alive. We continued on to the southeast through the Khyber Pass, where we came across a group of small shacks in which men were manufacturing perfect replicas of Mausers and Winchesters, right down to the detail of fake registration numbers. In Lahore, Pakistan, we were invited to dine at the old British officers' mess, now long gone, where we were served drinks on the cool, spacious veranda overlooking immaculately manicured lawns. And though we were sorely tempted to cross into India, we wouldn't be able to get home in time for classes in September if we didn't turn around, particularly if we wanted to stop in Iraq and Lebanon.

In Quetta the governor said, "You can't go through Baluchistan without an armed guard. I'll give you a mounted escort."

"But that will take us three months," we said. "We've got to get back to university." So he lent us two guys who sat on the front of our Land Rover with their guns at the ready all through Baluchistan, and he instructed Patrick and me to load up the shotguns we had brought from Canada for bird shooting in Turkey with some friends. It seemed surreal that two twenty-one-year-olds would actually be forced into a gun battle with tribesmen, as though we were still in the days of the Great Game, but we were in a different world. While having dinner in a caravanserai one night, we heard shots ringing out. Someone had been shooting at a car that had driven up. A man jumped out, furious, and turned out to be the local magistrate. It took some doing to calm him down, and I realized for the first time – but not the last – how hard it was to tell your friends from your enemies in that part of the world.

We crossed into southern Iran and headed to Yazd, a major centre of Zoroastrianism, where we watched the vultures circling the dead bodies left out on the "towers of silence," just as Dr. Bhabha, himself a Parsi, had described when he stayed with us in Vancouver. Along the road we were invited to spend the night with a gang of rough-looking characters who resembled bandits. If that's what they were, the laws of hospitality prevailed, and we drove away the next morning with our money and belongings still in our possession. We then continued north to Isfahan and Qom and encountered the next hurdle when we arrived in Iraq. The border guards discovered our shotguns and went into high alert. Unknown to us, the dictator Abd al-Karim Qasim had recently escaped an assassination attempt, and the guards were certain they had just caught two armed foreigners who had been involved in the plot. They seized our guns and the car, and we were bundled off to Baghdad and promptly thrown into jail. At least we got a cell of our own and weren't tossed to the wolves among the general prison population.

There wasn't a Canadian embassy in Iraq at that time, so Patrick used his British nationality to contact the British legation. After two days we were released from jail but still kept under surveillance in a local hotel. We spent a week in bureaucratic limbo before we got our documents stamped by a variety of ministries for permission to carry on. We were also required to have tea each day with the military governor of Baghdad, ostensibly to give the brigadier an opportunity to practise his English, though we came to suspect that his true interest lay with Patrick, a very good-looking, blond-haired, blue-eyed young man.

Baghdad was still an exotic place in 1960, with not much more than a million people. The evenings were hot, but not insufferably so, and after enjoying a meal of grilled fish fresh from the Tigris, we liked to stroll along the riverbank under the stars. If a fortune teller had stopped me then and prophesied that one day I would weigh the decision of whether to go to war against these people or that a son of mine would be living here as American bombs rained down from the night sky, I would have thought him mad.

Patrick and I drove out to see the Hanging Gardens of Babylon, but we were hugely disappointed. Formerly one of the Seven Wonders of the Ancient World, they were nothing but a depressing pile of rubble reconstructed by a German archaeologist, and it was impossible to tell what was real and what was imaginary. When finally allowed to leave Baghdad, we were provided with a guide to escort us on to the Jordanian border, no doubt with instructions to ensure that we left without making trouble. He sat on the front of the car along the truck route through the barren desert and hopped off in the middle of what looked like nowhere, directing us to head toward the setting sun. "When you reach the highway," he said, "you turn right if you want to go to Damascus or left if you want to go to Amman." We turned left.

In Amman we stayed with Andrew Watson, a Trinity College don who was working on contract with the Ford Foundation as a consultant on Jordan's first five-year plan for economic development. Andrew was generous in sharing his considerable knowledge about the history, economics, and culture of the Middle East. One night we drove with him out into the desert and came across a wedding party. "Stop the car," Andrew shouted, and we were soon invited to join the celebrations, dancing and talking until four in the morning. Another day we rode on horseback into the spectacular ruins of Petra, the fabled "rose-red city half as old as time." Then we travelled north through Damascus to Beirut, with a stop in the Beqaa Valley where some friends of my parents, the Kfourys, had a very beautiful home high in the mountains. The Kfourys, who owned bus lines in Egypt until Nasser expropriated their wealth and effectively drove them into exile, later welcomed us into their lovely apartment in Beirut. After months of the road, sleeping in a tent and looking like vagabonds, we suddenly found ourselves treated like princes, waited on by servants and fed by chefs. One night Patrick and I went to the casino and watched a sheik drop a hundred thousand dollars playing baccarat.

To our deep regret, we couldn't go into Israel. If we had received an entry stamp in our passports, neither we nor our car would have been permitted to exit into Jordan or Syria for the drive back to London. However, we did go into East Jerusalem, which hadn't yet been annexed by the Israelis, where we had lunch with Aref al-Aref, a renowned scholar and former mayor of the city. I remember he was very bitter about what he considered the betrayal of the Arabs by the British government, despite the obvious pride he felt in having held high office under the Mandate. After a long anti-British diatribe, he presented us with his business card, which read "Aref al-Aref, OBE."

If the trip didn't exactly make me an Arabist, it certainly informed me of the peoples, cultures, and issues of the Middle East. It also made me somewhat skeptical about almost everything that the Western press wrote regarding the region, not least the portrayal of Arabs as generally backward. With hindsight, of course, I regret that we had not taken more time and paid more attention to the area through which we drove so quickly. More knowledge of Afghanistan's porous borders and a better understanding of its tribal conflicts would have been useful when I became defence minister. They would have given me the context to appreciate what President Pervez Musharraf meant when he spoke to me of Pakistan's inability to control the Northwest Frontier. And I might have raised more concerns when assessing Canada's commitment to send our soldiers into an environment that was unlike anything they had encountered before.

Patrick and I returned to Trinity College in mid-September, a bit late for the beginning of our fourth and final year. The long absence had pulled Cathy and me apart, and we decided we were too young to commit to a long-term relationship. We broke off seeing each other, I graduated in the spring of 1961, and we went our separate ways. Cathy, who still had another year to complete before getting her degree, landed a summer job in London's business district and shared a flat with her lifelong friends, Linda L'Aventure and Martha Robinson, who was to marry my old pal George Butterfield. I enrolled in an intensive French course at the University of Toulouse and Bordeaux in Pau, which meant taking classes all day and living with a French family at night for several weeks. Why? Because learning a second language was considered part of a well-rounded education, and given the exciting changes taking place in Quebec with the so-called Quiet Revolution, French seemed the obvious choice.

Missing Cathy and obviously in love, I realized I had made a terrible mistake, and I journeyed regularly up to London for visits to rekindle our romance. When we met up in Paris at the end of that summer, I took her to Maxim's for dinner and proposed marriage. She turned me down flat, on the grounds that I had had too much champagne. So the next day I took her to the top of the Eiffel Tower and said, sober, "Either marry me or I'll jump." We became engaged during her final undergraduate year and my first year at the University of Toronto law school, and we were married in the Trinity College Chapel on June 9, 1962.

Mother and Dad came to Toronto for the wedding, but I could see that he wasn't well. Though he could get around all right, he lacked his usual energy and conviviality, in part because he was exhausted from the demands of having had Prince Philip as a houseguest a few days before but mainly because he was beginning to suffer from the cancer and weakened heart that would claim his life on April 6, 1963, at the age of seventy-eight. I interrupted my second-year law exams to fly to Vancouver for the funeral in Christ Church Cathedral, a grand affair attended by Dad's many friends in business, politics, the universities, the charities, and the arts, as well as an honour guard from the Fifteenth Field Artillery, in which he had served as honorary colonel. That night I sat alone with my mother at the house to comfort her in her grief, her distress made worse by the fact that my sister had not been allowed to attend. Between divorcing her first husband and marrying her second, Helen had become pregnant. Having a baby out of wedlock wouldn't raise an eyebrow today, but it was scandalous at the time. "This is God punishing me for what I did with your father," Mother sobbed.

I hadn't a clue what she was talking about.

"William," she said, "we buried your father today." And then it came out that both Helen and I were really F.R. Graham's children, conceived while both our parents were married to someone else, and in my case born in secret.

Many of the older children had known all along but been sworn to silence for the sake of their father's reputation. Arthur Bailey had even been used as an emissary between Mother and his own natural father to help establish the false paper trail concerning the births of Helen and myself. It was also common knowledge among Dad's closest business colleagues and some of Cathy's Toronto relatives who were friends of friends of my parents, yet I had been kept in the dark and Helen had to learn the truth from me.

Small mysteries now made perfect sense. One day, for example, when Dad and I were on a long walk from the hot springs to the house in Banff, his shoelace had come undone and I bent down to tie it for him. As I was doing so, he kept patting my head. "Oh, William," said Jane, one of the original ten, who was on the walk with us. "I really think you're Dad's favourite."

"Well, I don't see how that could be," I replied, "given that I'm not actually his son." And I had been puzzled by her wry smile.

I wasn't angry with Mother. I wasn't upset. I was simply too stunned to have any emotional reaction. The revelation came as such a shock that it took some time to sink in. I had always considered Dad as my only father and felt loved by him as a son, even though I grew up believing that we weren't bound by blood. It wasn't the shame or the deception that hurt. It was the regret I carry to this day that I was never given the chance to tell my true father, as my true father, how proud I am of him, how grateful I am for all he gave me, and how much I still love him.

2

OUT AND ABOUT

J ust as I had gone from Upper Canada College to the University of
Toronto without much thought or strategy, so I went from Trinity
College to the university's Faculty of Law, just across Philosopher's
Walk. It turned out to be a formative experience that changed my life ir-
revocably and for the better, thanks to the small but extremely dedicated
group of professors led by Cecil "Caesar" Wright, a towering figure in legal
education.

In 1949 he and Bora Laskin, a brilliant jurist who later became chief
justice of Canada, had quit Osgoode Hall, which was run by the Law Society
of Ontario, after a dramatic fight over academic freedom. After they walked
away to join the law school at the University of Toronto, it took almost a
decade of persistent lobbying to get the law society to permit University
of Toronto graduates to practise in Ontario. The split centred on the question of who was ultimately in charge of the curriculum: the practitioners
or the scholars. The law society wanted students to be taught the practi-
calities of law – whatever would help legal firms carry out their business.
The scholars, many of whom were social progressives like Wright and
Laskin, wanted to teach students the philosophy of law, the role of law in
helping to make a better society, and the responsibility of lawyers to craft
parliamentary legislation and judicial decisions to support democratic
institutions and the social good. That might explain why my own small
class produced a disproportionate number of politicians, including a future

prime minister, Paul Martin, Jr.; a future mayor of Toronto, John Sewell; a future leader of the Liberal Party of Newfoundland, Ed Roberts; and a future NDP MP from British Columbia, John Brewin.

The school's founding philosophy attracted highly principled and highly motivated professors who also happened to be among the finest legal minds of their generation in Canada. Ronald St. John Macdonald presided over international law; Mark MacGuigan, who subsequently became secretary of state for external affairs and a minister of justice under Pierre Trudeau, taught jurisprudence; Albert Abel, whom we called "Iowa Al, the students' pal," specialized in property law; John Willis instructed in contracts; and Bora Laskin taught land law, back to fifteenth-century England, and constitutional law, which in those pre-Charter days was mostly about the division of powers between Ottawa and the provinces under sections 91 and 92 of the British North America Act.

The law school was smaller and more informal than it is today, and the professors were accessible as well as inspirational. Students could drop in on any of them for a coffee and a talk. The day John Kennedy was assassinated, teachers and students alike piled into my car to listen to the news because there weren't any radios in the school. On one occasion, a group of us were invited to the home of Claude Bissell, the president of the university, where we ended up playing charades in the basement. The least approachable was Dean Wright, a difficult man who ran the place with an iron hand. By not letting his professors have a telephone in their office, he forced them to go through his secretary if they needed to make or receive a call, so he always knew what was going on. My most treasured friendship was with Bora Laskin. He had known my uncle Bill Dickie through their work in labour law, Cathy became close to his wife, Peggy, and in later years as I went to Ottawa on business I was fortunate to enjoy the occasional dinner with the chief justice.

The classes were confined to two old buildings, Flavelle House and Falconer Hall, and totalled only 250 students. Just a handful were women, with none at all in my year. We were a lively bunch who competed hard but also shared many good times. My apartment on Avenue Road, not far from where I had lived as a toddler, became a favourite home-away-from-home for hanging out and parties. After my marriage to Cathy, our honeymoon in Portugal, and a shorter French-language intensive in Pau during the summer, we moved into the second-floor apartment of an old house in Rosedale and later bought a house of our own nearby, on Powell Avenue.

I found law school to be a very stimulating environment, and for the first time in my academic life, I worked really hard. I had enjoyed history as an undergraduate and done well enough at Trinity, but I hadn't taken my studies all that seriously. They were constantly interrupted by the fun I was having with student politics, debating competitions, the navy, and partying. But once I discovered how much I loved law, I took a totally different approach to my education. When I got curious about something, I wanted to know why it was so, and that led me to research in the library and discussion with my professors. I also co-edited the *Law Review*. Consequently, I got better grades than ever before. I was at the top of the class in my first year, which pleased Dad enormously when he came to my wedding. I placed second in my second year, when my exams coincided with his death. And I was top again in my third and final year, winning the gold medal and the Butterworth Prize for combined academic and extra-curricular achievement. Better yet, on June 2, 1964, our daughter, Katy, was born. The *Toronto Telegram* ran a picture of us and, in the caption, called her my additional award.

IN THE SUMMER OF 1964, Cathy and I lived in The Hague while I was taking a course in international law. It was not perhaps one of my better ideas: I was still wearing a brace after breaking my foot in a ski accident in March, and the apartment was so tiny that we had to make up a bed for Katy in the bathtub. Nevertheless, I managed to learn a great deal about the importance of international law as taught by some of the world's elite practitioners.

On our return, I was required to article at a law firm if I wanted to work in the profession. The choice of firm was an important one for a budding young lawyer because it could determine the rest of your career, if not the rest of your life. In my case the obvious place to start was McCarthy and McCarthy, a venerable Bay Street firm where Senator Salter Hayden, a business partner of Dad's and the trustee of my personal affairs, was a senior partner. "Well, William," he said bluntly, "I assume you're coming to McCarthy's." But when I went there for an interview, the interviewer kept calling me "Graham," as if I were a new boy back at UCC. I was turned off, and I left thinking that McCarthy's wouldn't be the right fit for me.

I went to check out Fasken, Calvin, MacKenzie, Williston and Swackhamer, which I heard had an interesting litigation practice – the kind of law in which I wanted to specialize. Sure enough, I liked what I saw. It was small, with just seventeen lawyers, including well-known litigation lawyers of the stature of Walter Williston, future Supreme Court justice John Sopinka, Ron Rolls, Julian Porter, and in later years, Allan Rock. It also had a slightly zany atmosphere. I was one of a handful of articling students whom it hired in 1964 at twenty-five dollars a week. Because I had won the gold medal, the others figured I had the least chance of being fired for being uppity. They delegated me to speak to Ron Robertson, the lawyer in charge of students, and ask for a raise on everyone's behalf.

"Well, twenty-five dollars seems like a lot of money for you guys," Ron said in his gruff voice. "Let me phone around town and find out what the other fellows are paying." He made a few inquiries and discovered, to his shock, that the going rate was forty-five dollars a week. "What are they trying to do, break us all?" he barked. Nevertheless, we all got an 80 percent increase, and I became an accidental hero among my colleagues.

Articling students were supposed to divide their year into three equal parts: four months on real estate law, four months on commercial law, four months on litigation. However, I never spent much time in the real estate department, not only because I couldn't imagine anything more boring but also because Walter Williston was happy to keep me busy in litigation. As a result, the practical issue of searching a title has remained a bit of a mystery to me. That caused a problem when it came to the bar admission exam. At one point we had to go as a group to do a collective title search at the registry office. "So this is where the registry office is," I said as we entered. "I've never been here before."

The others looked at me, part amazed, part alarmed. "Just go and sit in that corner over there and keep your mouth shut," they said. "You'll screw up the exam for the rest of us." So they did all the work, and I shared their grade.

I got away with that sort of behaviour because I was concentrating all my efforts in litigation. Ron Robertson took me to an important trial that went on for months in London, Ontario. J.W. Swackhamer used me as his junior in a couple of high-profile cases – one featuring a hockey superstar, the other a dispute in which the American government claimed that Canada's Gut Dam had caused water levels to rise with damaging consequences for property owners on the US side of the St. Lawrence River. Walter Williston put me by his side on various files, then and subsequently, including one involving a rabbi who had gotten tangled in a real estate dispute. One afternoon, Walter had to leave me in charge while he rushed from the courtroom on another matter. The rabbi grabbed him and said with some bitterness, "I get it, you're sacrificing the rabbi to give experience to junior."

My big break as an articling student came when Bryce MacKenzie, the senior partner, called me into the office and said, "We've got a problem, Bill, and we want you to look for an answer." The problem had to do with financing the construction of the Toronto-Dominion Centre, a complex of downtown office towers designed by the great architect Ludwig Mies van der Rohe and developed by the Toronto Dominion Bank in partnership with the Fairview Corporation, a real estate developer owned by the Bronfman family. A question arose as to whether TD Bank could guarantee the bonds that were being issued to help finance its own project. A considerable amount of money rode on the answer because a guarantee from the bank would substantially reduce the cost of borrowing. Both McCarthy's and Fasken's, which were in fierce competition in those days, had been retained by TD Bank to give an opinion.

"This is a huge opportunity for us," Bryce MacKenzie told me. "McCarthy's has advised the bank that it can't be done, because it's beyond the scope of the Bank Act for a bank to guarantee these bonds. TD has asked us to come up with an opinion that it can be done. So go see what you can do, Mr. Gold Medal."

I went to the law school library and started working my way through the volumes of documents that had been prepared for the Royal Commission on Banking and Finance, led by the chief justice of the Ontario Court of Appeal, Dana Porter. After two and a half weeks of reading up on the subject, I mapped out an opinion that the bank could in fact guarantee the bonds of a building in which it intended to have its own head office. I gave it to Bryce MacKenzie, who read it and passed it on to Walter Williston.

After perusing the document carefully, Williston declared, "I can sign that opinion without having to change a word." Then, looking hard at me, he added, "This is the first time an articling student around here has actually earned any money for us."

WITH A YEAR OF ARTICLING under my belt, I did the six-month bar admission course and wrote the exams that gave me the licence to practise law in Ontario. I wasn't in a rush to settle down, however, even though on November 11, 1965, Cathy and I had the great joy of welcoming into the world our son, Patrick, born less than a year and a half after Katy. On the advice of Jean Castel, a brilliant French scholar of aristocratic manner and background who was teaching international law at Osgoode Hall, I decided to kill two birds with one stone by improving my French while pursuing a doctorate in law at the Université de Paris. Cathy shared my love of France, though she wasn't thrilled to give up our beautiful home on Powell Avenue for an apartment on the Rue de Berri. Pulling up stakes and raising a young family in a foreign culture was a gutsy move for her – a much less common decision in 1966 than it is today. The level of the family's concern was expressed by her grandmother, who asked if there would be reliable hospitals where we were going.

In some ways, studying at the Place du Panthéon was like living in the Middle Ages. Before formal lectures the professor was announced by the *hussier,* an usher wearing a white tie and a medal around his neck, and smacking a big stick. The classes and library were overcrowded, so I usually did my work in a nearby cafe. Nor could I get an appointment to discuss my thesis with the professor charged with international commercial law, who would have been the natural choice for my doctoral supervisor.

I did get a chance to talk with Berthold Goldman, however, and when I vented my frustration about not being able to get started, he allowed me to study under him. This was a stroke of good fortune. Professor Goldman, who taught European law, was recognized as a major authority in the field. He was regularly consulted by governments and the European Court of Justice. Having Goldman as my director turned out to be a wonderful personal experience as well as a great learning opportunity. His office was above a fine little restaurant called Chez André, just around the corner from the Canadian embassy, and we occasionally met there for lunch to talk about my topic. Given my background and his own interests, he suggested I compare the anti-trust laws of Canada with those of the European Economic Community (EEC).

The EEC had emerged from the European Coal and Steel Community (ECSC), a common market of six countries established by the Treaty of Paris in 1951 as a way of preventing another war in Europe. If the regulation of the means of production of coal and steel were taken away from Germany and France and assigned to an internationally controlled body, the argument ran, the two countries could never again build an independent military capability that could be used to go to war against each other. In fact, the ECSC became a supranational governing body, albeit over a narrow range of products. Before long its signatories asked themselves, "Since this arrangement works well for coal and steel, why don't we extend it to general trade?" And so, in 1957, they moved from the particular to the general with the Treaty of Rome, which created the EEC and led to the European Union in 1993. A series of subsequent treaties expanded the original framework.

The original concept was guided by a group of savvy international lawyers who drafted the terms of the Treaty of Rome in such a way that some of its rules would have the force of law in member states even if those states hadn't adopted them through local legislation. Normally when a country enters into an international treaty, the terms of that treaty must be adopted by its legislature before they have the force of domestic law. In the case of the Treaty of Rome, however, subsequent court decisions held that certain provisions had the force of domestic law without any act of the legislature being necessary. What's more, such provisions would trump local laws in the case of a conflict and could be cited in court by citizens challenging the validity of such inconsistent legislation. The Treaty of Rome went on to create institutions – a council, a commission, and the Parliament – which could adopt regulations with a similar effect or issue directives that would require the member states to legislate the necessary subject matter into their own domestic law. Since its inception, case law from the European Court of Justice and the various courts of the member states has gradually defined these powers, to the point where a legal system now exists that in many ways approximates the system in a federal state.

Europe was made by the lawyers, I later told my students, and the Treaty of Rome was a legal revolution. But most Europeans had no idea what the EEC implied when they joined it. A member of the French National Assembly once admitted to me, with deep regret, that if he had known that the Électricité de France would be forced someday to obey European rules set down by Brussels, he would never have voted for the treaty. It took decades of painstaking jurisprudence before people came to realize the extent to which European laws and the rulings of the European Court of Justice could transcend inconsistent national laws in local courts. When I was doing my graduate studies, the professors at the Université de Paris were still teaching French administrative law and the judicial structure of the French administrative system, with no reference whatsoever to European law. Today European laws permeate everywhere.

One important exception lay in the area of European anti-trust legislation, my chosen field of study, where there was already a substantive body of court rulings. The origins of European anti-trust legislation can be traced back to the Nuremberg trials at the end of the Second World War, when IG Farben and other German cartels were not only accused of using slave labour in the concentration camps but were also suspected of building up the war machine to boost their sales and profits. If this were the case, as the Americans in particular argued with their introduction of the Marshall Plan, the best way to prevent such egregious conduct in the future was to introduce North American anti-trust provisions in Europe. And that is precisely what the Treaty of Rome did with regard to trusts, combines, and mergers and acquisitions. I never imagined that the library of the University of Cairo would write me decades later to ask for a copy of my unpublished thesis, "L'Article 85 du Traité de Rome et l'Article 32 de la Loi canadienne relative aux enquétes sur les coalitions, étude comparative," or that an Egyptian student might ever need to parse the mysteries of European and Canadian anti-trust legislation. Nor could I have predicted how soon I would need to apply its theory to the practise of law.

BEFORE LEAVING TORONTO, I thought about trying to find a job I could do while pursuing my studies. Paris was expensive, I had a young family to support, and I had really enjoyed the hands-on experience of practising law. So I went to New York City to speak with a couple of large US firms that had offices in Paris. They were vaguely interested but noncommittal, to say the least, and I assumed that my proposal would come to nothing. When the senior partners at Fasken's got wind of this, however, I was summoned into Harry Macdonell's office. "What's all this about, Bill?" he inquired. "If you do that, we'll never see you back here." And he asked for a day to think about it.

The next morning he made me an extraordinary offer. "We have clients in Europe," he said. "Having somebody closer to them might not be a bad idea. So why don't you keep working for us over there? We'll pay you the same salary we'd pay you as a junior here."

The salary proved helpful, but an even greater benefit was the entrée the job gave me to people and experiences that enriched my university days in Paris. For starters, because Fasken's was the Canadian solicitor for the Rothschild family's North American investment company, I obtained an introduction to members of the famous financial dynasty who subsequently gave me an office in their grand old banking headquarters on Rue Laffitte, just behind the Stock Exchange. All sorts of important figures used to show up for the long, generous lunches to which I was sometimes invited. Strolling to my beautiful office after my morning classes, learning first-hand about French politics and society over a superb meal and an excellent bottle of wine, I found this connection invaluable for a twenty-seven-year-old student and junior lawyer.

It was also a fascinating time to be in France, especially for people with a liking for history and international affairs. President Charles de Gaulle was a giant in world history, and I had a great deal of admiration for him. I read his three-volume memoirs, and I sympathized with his frustration at how badly he had been treated by the British and the Americans during the war. Only he could have solved the problem of getting France out of Algeria, as had to happen someday, because only he could have stared down the generals and the right-wing forces who wanted to stay. I once watched him give a televised press conference that lasted about an hour. First he let the journalists ask anything they wished. Then, without referring to notes, he divided their questions into a few general areas – foreign affairs, domestic issues, political matters, and so forth – and answered them in a totally logical, classically Cartesian fashion. When he was finished he stood to his full height, said, "Thank you, gentlemen," and walked out. It was a tour de force that very few leaders, then or now, could match. Later, when he showed up in Montreal for Expo 67 and shouted "Vive le Québec libre," those of us who sympathized with France's aspirations for its culture and its language felt betrayed by a country we loved and a hero we admired. More than shock and hurt, I remember feeling almost personally insulted. For the most part, however, I followed French politics as a kind of academic exercise, closely but with no vested interest in who was winning, who was not. What especially impressed me was the intellectual quality of the French political class.

One day Fasken's called me in Paris with a European issue involving a client of ours, an international mining giant. As it happened, it owned a Canadian steel company that had bought a coal-rolling process from Japan. The machinery broke down, however, and the steel company decided to fill the orders of its European clients by shipping them Japanese steel as a temporary measure. When a customs inspector in Rotterdam opened the shipment and found supposedly Canadian steel wrapped in Japanese packaging, all hell broke loose on the eve of a major bond financing that the parent company was doing out of New York.

I spent about four months on that case, flying out on Mondays to the parent's head office in Lausanne, putting out fires around the Continent, and ending the week in London with a report to Sir Val Duncan, a war hero and influential investment broker who was the company's chairman. "What the hell are you doing?" he used to shout. "This is only $5 million. It's bee's knees, my boy, bee's knees." In fact, the European rules against importing Japanese steel were severe, the duties on Japanese steel were extreme, and the fines for smuggling it into Europe were horrendous. Instead of being bee's knees, it had turned into a $25 million nightmare. But, as one of the Rothschilds warned me, "You're too young to be taken seriously, Mr. Graham." Finally I phoned J.W. Swackhamer and said, "Listen, you'd better get your ass over here. I'm only a junior, and I'm getting steam-rolled by these high-powered Brits."

THE OTHER MAJOR CASE that landed on my desk was an early introduction to the role that international law would play in my life. By luck I became a bit player in one of the most famous cases in the evolution of a global legal system, still cited and studied to this day.

The Barcelona Traction, Light and Power Company was a Canadian-incorporated holding company that owned major hydroelectric utilities in Spain through local subsidiaries. Over time the company came to be mostly owned by Belgian shareholders, though its head office remained in Toronto, where it had been incorporated in 1911, because Canada's tax regime made it a haven for holding companies in those days. Like Brazilian Traction, Light and Power, and Mexican Light and Power, Barcelona Traction was a forerunner of the modern multinational corporations that invest in underdeveloped countries, export the profits to foreign owners, and base themselves in the most favourable tax and regulatory regime they can find. In fact, all three companies had been founded by the same American electrical engineer, Frederick Stark Pearson, who had based himself in Canada for tax reasons, received funding for his ventures from the Montreal financier James Dunn, and died in 1915, when the *Lusitania* was torpedoed off the coast of Ireland.

At an early stage in Barcelona Traction's development, it raised capital by issuing bonds that were required to pay interest not in Spanish pesetas but in British pounds. When the Spanish Civil War made that impossible, no interest was paid from 1936 to 1948, and the value of the bonds fell on the world market. In stepped Juan March, a Spanish financier who had made a fortune in tobacco smuggling, had gotten elected to the Spanish Parliament, had been arrested by the Republicans until his dramatic escape from jail, and had helped finance General Franco's Nationalists in their fight against the Republicans. March began accumulating a majority of the bonds at discount prices. He then got a provincial judge in Spain to ignore the niceties of corporate law and declare Barcelona Traction, a Canadian company, bankrupt because of its failure to service its bonds. That put the assets of the company's Spanish subsidiaries in the hands of Spanish bankruptcy trustees, who manoeuvred to sell them to March for a song. In effect, it was a "Hispanization" of the assets of Barcelona Traction, a form of nationalization by a private enterprise that probably had the blessing of the Spanish government. This process took place over many years and involved every possible layer of the Spanish judicial system, often including the Supreme Court itself.

The Canadian parent company and the Belgian investors, stymied by the arbitrary and unprecedented judgments of the local Spanish court, were slow to react. "According to accepted Anglo-Saxon private international law," they were advised by their lawyers, "a Spanish court has no jurisdiction over a company incorporated in Canada. But if you go there to defend yourselves, you would be recognizing its jurisdictional authority." That may have been a principled position to take, but it was dangerous in practice. When you go to court, you may win or you may lose, but if you aren't there at all, you have no way of influencing a decision that will be made regardless. And that's exactly what happened with Barcelona Traction.

In 1958 the dispute reached the International Court of Justice (ICJ) in The Hague. Established in 1945 by the United Nations Charter as the UN's principal judicial organ, the ICJ followed in the footsteps of the Permanent Court of International Justice as a mechanism to help settle legal disputes between countries. But an international legal system is different from a domestic legal system. For one thing, countries can choose whether they will accept it. Even Canada, despite being a huge supporter of the ICJ, insulated itself from the court's jurisdiction when the Trudeau government adopted the Arctic Waters Pollution Prevention Act in 1970, as the government wanted to prevent other countries from challenging the act's legality before the court.

In the Barcelona Traction case, the suit was between Belgium (on behalf of the Belgian investors) and Spain. In fact, though the Spanish government was the defendant, the actual defence was organized – and paid for – by the March interests under the direction of a stern ex-military jurist by the name of Dr. Antonio Rodriguez Sastre. The case turned out to be hugely complicated and extremely rewarding, both intellectually and financially.

Because the sterling bonds issued by Barcelona Traction were secured by trust deeds held by the National Trust Company of Toronto, a number of issues of Canadian law became relevant when the case crept toward the International Court of Justice. And because Juan March happened to be a long-time client of Sir Val Duncan's merchant bank, Kleinwort Benson, whenever the Spanish lawyers needed an opinion about Canadian law, Duncan passed them along to Fasken's because of the work we had done with him over the years. I had been an articling student at the time and worked on one such file, and I remember my frustration at not being told who the mysterious client was. "This is ridiculous," I protested. "Any opinion will be totally abstract without knowing more." Not long afterward, during my first summer in Paris, Dr. Sastre got wind of the fact that Fasken's had a young lawyer in Paris and asked that I be sent to him right away. And so I got a phone call from Toronto ordering me to Barcelona. "We can't tell you why – just get there as quickly as possible."

The moment I stepped off the plane, I was met by a contingent of the Guardia Civil, wearing their traditional black *tricornio* hats, and was whisked to a hotel high in the hills. There I met the Spanish government's legal counsel for the first time. In the meeting room I was bombarded by questions about the nature of "trusts" in Anglo-Saxon law in general, and in Canada in particular. Giving a mini-lecture on Canadian trust law to some of the sharpest minds in Europe was daunting enough, but I also had to do it in French and with no time to prepare. Because French was the working language, I later thought it useful to ask the librarian at the Fasken's office in Toronto to send me a French "version" of the Canadian Bankruptcy Act. Unfortunately, I dictated the letter to a secretary and didn't review her draft. "I need to get my hands as quickly as possible on a French *virgin*," it read, "but if a French *virgin* isn't available, an English one will do." The firm's librarian, a woman with a great sense of humour, posted it on the communal notice board with the comment "Our Mr. Graham is obviously enjoying his time in Paris."

Sastre had taken over the entire hotel and filled it with a host of renowned international lawyers and scholars, including the distinguished Uruguayan jurist Eduardo Jiménez de Aréchaga, who later became a president of the International Court of Justice, and Maarten Bos, a noted law professor from the University of Utrecht. "For the first two years of this case, we used to meet at an office in Barcelona," Sastre explained to me over dinner one night, "but these damn guys would go out every night and drink and have a good time. So I moved the whole bunch up here to see if we could get some actual work done."

Though we all worked closely together, at mealtimes the Spaniards ate with the Spaniards and the foreigners with the foreigners. I had been there for about a week when the sommelier came over to our table and inquired about our choice of wine with dinner. A senior member of the group requested a Marqués de Riscal. "I'm sorry, sir," said the sommelier, "but you've already finished all the Marqués de Riscal from the hotel's cellar." The wine that remained wasn't anything special, and shortly afterward – whether by coincidence or not – my European colleagues suddenly realized that they all had to return to their own offices as quickly as possible. I had no excuse to leave, or wasn't as experienced as the others in making one up, so I stayed on. As a result, I developed a close working relationship with the Spaniards, and a close friendship with some of the younger members in the group. Once I was home in Paris, Sastre began to send stacks of documents to my apartment, with a note asking me to read them and tell him what I thought.

One day he asked me about a minor issue involving the United States. I said I didn't know, but it would be easy to find the answer in the Library of Congress in Washington, DC. All that's needed, I suggested, is to retain someone there to go get it. "No, no," he said. "Go research it in Washington yourself." So I did. I'm sure if I had told him we had to research the bankruptcy laws of Japan, I could have travelled around the world in grand style on that case. In fact, hundreds of lawyers – and not a few accountants – in Europe and North America lived very well while that case lumbered on, and they were sorry to see it end after eleven years.

As it was, I spent three years of my life working on it. And when it was finally argued at the ICJ in 1969, my family and I had returned to Toronto. I spent several months in The Hague as an adviser to Spain's legal team. That was a heady experience for a thirty-year-old novice, rubbing shoulders with the likes of Paul Reuter, the Belgian counsel and one of the principal drafters of the Schuman Declaration, which led to the Treaty of Rome, and Sir Humphrey Waldock, the distinguished professor of international law at Oxford and later a president of the International Court of Justice. "Sir Humphrey," I said during dinner with him one evening, "I have something to ask you that's been bothering me for a long time. Franco was generally considered the bad guy in the Spanish Civil War. Juan March was Franco's financier. He got Barcelona Traction's assets for next to nothing. The Belgian shareholders were basically robbed. International legal opinion considered the decision of the Spanish court a travesty of justice. So how come you're working for the Spaniards?"

It turned out that March had been secretly assisting the Allies during the Second World War in all sorts of ways, including payments to high-ranking officials to keep Spain out of the war and helping to finance the operations of the British Secret Service. "So a very grateful British government made him a promise that he could have whatever he wanted once the war was over," Sir Humphrey concluded. "And when he went to them and asked for the best international lawyer in England to argue his case in the International Court, he got me."

At some point Walter Williston came over from Toronto for an important strategy meeting in Amsterdam with Sastre. Walter was well known as both a superb lawyer and a heavy drinker. He brought me a fish my young son, Patrick, had caught back home, as a memento of family life in Canada. Unfortunately, he hadn't put it in a cold box. The fish arrived wrapped in Walter's legal gowns and smelling to high heaven. I wired back to Toronto, "Walter and fish arrived: high."

One evening, after a long dinner with many glasses of wine, he and I decided to clear our heads with a brisk midnight swim in the North Sea. I was awoken at seven the next morning by a call from Walter. "Graham, you idiot," he shouted, "come to my room! What the hell were we doing last night?" He wasn't the most attractive human being at the best of times, with his frizzy hair and crazed eyes, but there he was covered in a thick layer of black goo. When I caught a glimpse of myself in the mirror, I saw that I was too. Apparently we had swum through an oil slick without realizing it. "What the hell are we going to do?" Walter said. Then he had a brainwave and phoned room service to send up a bottle of Dutch gin. It worked like a charm, and we were soon all cleaned up. The only problem was that we arrived at our meeting a couple of hours later reeking of gin!

One of the Spanish lawyers was a brilliant professor named José María Gil-Robles, a prominent social-Catholic politician who had been a minister in the Republican government before being forced into exile by the Franco regime. According to hearsay, when the Spanish government realized it needed the best minds available to counter the high-powered Belgian team, it went to Gil-Robles with a deal: he could return to Spain and his teaching position at the University of Oviedo on condition that he help argue the Spanish case. He was quite flamboyant in his red gown with lace overlay, looking almost like a cardinal, but he was also volatile. One morning he was arguing his points for hour after hour before the sixteen judges when he suddenly accused the Belgian counsel, Professor Henri Rolin, an equally distinguished academic wearing a black gown with ruffled collar and a row of war medals, of lying *(mentir)*. Rolin leapt to his feet with a great flouncing of robe and clanking of metal to protest such an insufferable indignity to his honour. The president of the court, José Luis Bustamante y Rivero, a former president of Peru, called for a fifteen-minute break.

Sastre was beside himself with fury. He could see Spain's entire case going off the rails because of this insult. "You're going to have to apologize," he hissed.

"Relax, relax," Gil-Robles replied, "I will deal with this." When we returned to the court, he addressed the judge in French. "Mr. President, the court will appreciate that I used the word *mentir* only in its dialectical sense."

Rolin muttered, "Ahh, son sens dialectique," and nodded his head. It meant nothing, of course, but apparently sufficed. That's why French is the language of diplomacy: you can do charming things with it that make no sense. Years later, when I was in the House of Commons, I kept hoping for an opportunity to use some unacceptable parliamentary language. If challenged, I was ready to respond, "But, Mr. Speaker, I was using the word only in its dialectical sense, as permitted by the International Court of Justice in The Hague." Sadly, I never got to try that on Peter Milliken – but I suspect it wouldn't have carried anyway.

The decision came down on February 5, 1970, almost eight years after Juan March had died at the age of eighty-one as the result of a car accident. Spain won the case. It was decided, however, not on its merits but on the procedural question of whether Belgium, the home of the major shareholders of Barcelona Traction, could bring an action against Spain when the company itself was not Belgian but Canadian. In essence the ICJ held that the personality of the company was the personality of the country in which the company had been incorporated – Canada. In theory, therefore, it should have been Canada that brought the action against Spain. Belgium certainly had exerted a lot of pressure to get us to do so. But, besides not having any real stake in the matter, the Canadian government had a very compelling reason not to get involved. The United States was in the middle of tricky negotiations with General Franco over air bases in Spain, and no one in NATO wanted to jeopardize the deal simply to spare a bunch of Belgians the loss on an investment. In any event, because the Belgian shareholders were in turn corporations, the real persons behind them who suffered damage may well have been of many other nationalities.

At the time and in the aftermath of their decision, the judges were criticized for dodging the substantive issues, such as the rights of shareholders who might be scattered around the world or the morality of nationalizing the operations of a foreign-controlled company. Yet in the course of its judgment, the ICJ did enunciate a principle that would substantially influence international law in the future. This concept, known by its Latin formulation as *erga omnes,* affirmed that some state obligations were by their nature owed to the entire international community and that all states had a legal interest in their protection. The ICJ cited the outlawing of genocide and protection from slavery as examples of basic human rights that give rise to such obligations. Scholars ever since have sought to define what other acts and rights are governed by this principle, as they have with the similar concept of *jus cogens,* referring to certain fundamental principles of international law from which no derogation is permitted.

When I first told Caesar Wright I was going to Paris to study international law, he thought I was wasting my life. "What on earth are you going to do that for?" he asked. "International law isn't real law. It's not a serious legal subject. It's just a lot of political posturing." This view was common among lawyers in those days. Because of Barcelona Traction and similar cases, however, I have witnessed in my lifetime the growth of a complex matrix of international norms governing international trade, human rights, the laws of war, and almost all legal domains, to the point where the line between international law and domestic law has become increasingly blurred.

3

TRADING PLACES

After two years in Paris, Cathy and I were in no great hurry to leave. I was flying all over Europe on the Barcelona Traction case; the children were not yet in school; we had befriended an attractive young Canadian couple, Fred and Vicky Wanklyn, and their three children; and we were renting a wonderful "fortified farm" in the countryside for weekends. It was an ancient stone tower with a moat near the small, pretty chateau of Maillebois just outside of Dreux. Paris proved a tough place to make French friends if you weren't family members, but here we were warmly embraced by the owner, Lionel Armand Delille, and his beautiful, vivacious, American wife, Diane – a former model. Katy, Patrick, and their daughter became friends for life; we rode horses through the surrounding woodlands and were invited on pheasant shoots; and we gained insights into French history and society over many lunches, dinners, and bottles of wine.

One night we were at a supper party in Paris when I happened to mention something Guy de Rothschild had said at the bank that week. "But M. de Rothschild isn't French," said one of the guests. "He's Jewish." Cathy and I had the same reaction: first, it was a deplorably anti-Semitic remark; second, if the Rothschilds weren't French after more than 150 years at the centre of France's commercial and cultural life, what chance did we have to fit in? As beautiful and as interesting as Paris was, if we couldn't ever fit in, why stay around? Besides, we were beginning to miss our family and friends in Canada. The remark about the Rothschilds, even though I didn't think it reflected the sentiments of most French people, simply reinforced our feeling that it was time to go home.

We arrived back in Canada toward the end of March 1968 and soon found the beautiful neo-Georgian house on Chestnut Park that became our home for the next nineteen years. Cathy plunged into volunteer activities, among them the Junior League, taking advantage of its exceptional volunteer-training opportunities and eventually serving as its vice-president. Katy and Patrick were enrolled at the Toronto French School. We transported a derelict pioneer log house to Glenariff, my in-laws' property in the Hockley Valley, an hour north of Toronto, and restored it into a cozy weekend retreat. In 1973, thanks to the Wanklyns, we maintained our links to France by joining them in buying an old house in the scenic village of Pigna, Corsica, where we usually spent several weeks a year between the end of the children's school term and the beginning of their month at camp.

As it happened, we had left Paris just ahead of the dramatic student re-bellions and labour strikes that paralyzed France in May and led to de Gaulle's downfall. The United States was also in turmoil that year, with the anti-war marches, the civil-rights protests, the assassinations of Martin Luther King and Robert Kennedy, and the decision of Lyndon Johnson not to seek another term as president. It was a time of significant change in Canadian politics as well. Pierre Elliott Trudeau, the debonair intellectual, was elected leader of the Liberal Party of Canada in April, and in June he won a majority government on a wave of adulation and hope. I had met him once at a reception in his honour at the Maison des étudiants canadiens, when he came through Paris as Lester Pearson's minister of justice. I was one of the few anglophones present among several hundred francophones, and he gave me a bit more attention than most of the other guests received. I was as impressed by his intelligence and charisma as everyone else seemed to be.

With his election, "French Power" came to Ottawa – a concerted effort to lure francophone Quebecers away from the separatist option that had been growing stronger and more credible during the 1960s. The rapid modernization and secularization of the province's Quiet Revolution, which was triggered by the victory of the Quebec Liberals in 1960, unleashed a nationalist energy in which the provincial government replaced the church as the primary guardian and promoter of the French language and culture

1 My father, F.R. Graham, ca. 1960.

2 My mother as
a young woman.

3 The future defence minister.

4 With some of the Graham clan in Banff. *Back row (left to right):* my father, Mary (Peter's wife), Peter, Joan (Philip's wife), John, Philip. *Middle row:* my mother. *Front row:* David, me, Jane, and Helen.

5   Skating in Banff. *Left to right:* me; my sisters, Helen and Jane; my mother and father.

6   At home in Vancouver.

7 At Upper Canada College.

8 "A diplomatic line": Upper Canada College, 1957.

W. C. GRAHAM, '51–'57
SEATON'S HOUSE
Vancouver, B.C.
Prefect
U.N. (Pres.), Debating Society (speaker), Travel, Curfew, Ski Clubs
Past Associate Editor, College Times, Head Librarian
Intended Profession: Law
"A diplomatic line between two points"

9 In the University Naval Training Division, with Charlie Gunn *(right)*.

10 Patrick Wootten with our Land Rover, 1960.

11 Cathy Curry
at McGill.

12 With Cathy at Trinity College.

13 Our wedding day, June 9, 1962.

14 Celebrating our honeymoon with Patrick Wootten and Martha Robinson Butterfield, Paris, 1962.

15 In Paris with the children.

16 With Patrick, Cathy, and Katy at Glenariff, 1979.

in North America. On a positive note, that change transformed the education system, increased the economic opportunities for French-speaking Quebecers, and produced a cultural renaissance of writers, musicians, and artists. On a negative note, it threatened the breakup of Canada, especially after the formation of René Lévesque's Parti Québécois in 1968.

In Paris, I well remember, Cathy and I had gone to hear the great balladeer Gilles Vigneault sing of his love for the people and landscape of Quebec. When we had a chance to meet him after the show, I said how moved I had been by his songs and how proud they made me feel to be a Canadian. "I'm not a Canadian," he replied tersely. "I'm a Quebecer." I was shaken to the core, though his answer probably wouldn't have startled me so much if I had been following the developments in Quebec more closely.

Trudeau was determined to prove that the federal government represented the legitimate aspirations of all French-speaking Canadians, not just those in Quebec. That meant appointing francophones to senior positions in the Cabinet, the civil service, the military, and every major national institution. It meant asserting the equality of French in Parliament, in the courts, and in the regulatory agencies. It meant guaranteeing French-speaking citizens, wherever their numbers warrant, the right to receive their federal services in French.

Though my primary motive for studying French hadn't been domestic politics, I now found that I had an extremely marketable asset for the development of my career. I wouldn't say I was perfectly bilingual, but I was professionally bilingual: I could plead a case in French, and I knew French law and the French legal vocabulary. On a somewhat more ethereal level, I had also picked up an understanding of the Cartesian structure of thought and argument that comes with a French education, especially a French education in France. Even a newspaper article is structured differently in French than in English. It follows rules and disciplines that foster a particular logic and a clarity of thinking. As a student in Paris, for example, I had been required to write a five-hour exam in which the questions had to be answered in a precise and rigid format. One of my fellow students, a Harvard graduate, wrote the same exam and was crushed by how poorly he did on it. "You Harvard guys," I said, "you come over here and think, one, that you don't need to learn French because you're from Harvard, and, two, you don't seem to recognize that you're in a different intellectual universe."

Even if you do recognize it, learning to operate in such a different universe isn't simple. Though I placed at the top of the twenty-five foreign students in that exam, I faced a greater challenge when it came to writing my thesis. I thought I had mastered the framework: thesis (European Community law), antithesis (Canadian law), synthesis (where they were similar and where they weren't). But when I defended it before a jury of leading scholars that included Suzanne Bastide, a major figure in international law in Europe, she said to me, "Monsieur Graham, your thesis reads more like an English textbook than a French thesis." I was devastated. Nevertheless, the jury did pass me, and I got my French doctorate.

That training had a lasting impact on the way I thought and wrote, and as I practised law, it proved helpful in enabling me to express complicated issues with a greater clarity. Because I was moving back and forth between French and English books, newspapers, and periodicals, I kept seeing the world through two very different lenses. That required a constant readjustment of my perspective, which sometimes led to confusion but often made me more sympathetic toward other points of view. It instilled in me an empathy for French-speaking Quebecers, who had to work extra hard to maintain their language while operating in the predominantly English environment of Ottawa. I knew what it felt like to flap around in French at a meeting in Montreal, where everybody speaks so quickly and colloquially. I would come home utterly exhausted and barely able to think straight.

In more practical terms, being bilingual gave me a tool that very few of my colleagues had at the time. On one of my early cases after returning to Canada, I accompanied Walter Williston to Ottawa, where Fasken's was representing Bell Canada at licence hearings of the Canadian Radio-Television Commission. When I began cross-examining witnesses and making arguments in French, the fluently bilingual commissioners were taken aback. They had never seen a Toronto lawyer do that before. My performance there led to my being invited in June 1976 to become co-counsel with Yves Fortier, a prominent young Montreal lawyer, for the Commission of Inquiry into Bilingual Air Traffic Services in Quebec. The commission had been appointed following a major political crisis that had precipitated the resignation of Jean Marchand, the minister of transport and one of Trudeau's most trusted advisers. This blow to national unity became a factor leading to the victory of the Parti Québécois in November 1976.

THE ISSUE WAS SIMPLE but loaded with controversy: Should a French-speaking pilot be allowed to fly a plane in the skies over Quebec, using French as the language of communication? The conventional wisdom outside Quebec was that English was – and should remain – the exclusive language of pilots and air-traffic controllers in Canada and around the world. This was seen as a matter of safety and common sense. Otherwise, went the argument, confusion would reign and planes would be colliding every other day in Montreal. Within Quebec, however, it was a question of justice. French-speaking Quebecers – a unilingual doctor in Rimouski, say, who wanted to fly his Cessna on weekends – were being denied access to what was perceived as the future of transportation and technology un-less they learned to speak English. And that played directly into the hands of the separatists, who used it as another reason why Quebec should break away from English Canada and make its own rules.

I spent about half my time over the next three years working with the commission, including three full months in a suite in the Windsor Hotel in Montreal. Our work left me with a tremendous respect for the three commissioners: Darrel Heald, who had been an attorney general of Sas-katchewan; Bill Sinclair, a member of the Alberta Court of Appeal; and Julien Chouinard, nicknamed Le Colonel because of his straitlaced, highly principled personality, a justice of the Quebec Court of Appeal at that time and subsequently on the Supreme Court of Canada. Yves Fortier and I worked hard together, but we also had a great deal of fun and became lifelong friends.

Basically, the commission ran a series of tests, held public hearings, conducted research, and travelled the world gathering evidence. Contrary to what the pilots' union alleged, we learned that English wasn't used ex-clusively in other jurisdictions. In fact, most pilots used a language other than English. Russian pilots flew over Russia in Russian. French pilots flew over France in French. Japan was a notable exception, perhaps because of the excessive politeness built into the Japanese language: by the time the most humble controller had finished paying his formal respects to the most revered pilot, the plane would probably have crashed on the runway. In Panama we discovered that the US military was controlling Spanish-speaking pilots flying over the Canal Zone in Spanish, because it was safer. In Texas we came across an American air-traffic controller who had to get a guy from the cleaning staff to give instructions to a Mexican pilot in Spanish. In Rio we found a linguistic free-for-all – Portuguese, English, Spanish, whatever was needed.

Yet English did serve as the default international language, especially for commercial pilots, and it was sometimes helpful as a backup language for the sake of clarity. Because I had a general pass to sit in the cockpit and listen to the communications, I was sometimes horrified to hear how bad the English commands could be. I hadn't a clue what was being said, and I feared that the controllers or the pilots didn't know either. In Paris one day, as the plane taxied toward the runway, I noticed that we weren't where the tower had told us to be. "Oh, yeah, you're right," the pilot said when I mentioned it. "Good thing we have you here with us." In São Paulo, Brazil, air-traffic control was conducted solely in English because the runways were flanked by two large apartment towers. The slightest veering to the left or right could spell disaster, and the military in charge of the airport didn't want to take any chances. I remember flying into Vancouver one stormy night, with visibility down to nothing, and hearing a controller screaming to our pilot, "Alitalia 422, where the fuck are you going?" That certainly grabbed the attention of every aircraft in the area.

Among my tasks was to keep the confidential minutes of the judges' meetings, type them up in Toronto, and send them by special post to Ottawa. One highly sensitive package never arrived. Even the Royal Canadian Mounted Police couldn't track it. When I went down to the post office to make some inquiries of my own, I was taken into a lost-and-found storage room that was full of torn boxes and old junk. "No, no," I said, "I'm looking for very important documents that have 'Top Secret' marked on the package." "Oh, top secret!" the clerk said to me. "We've got another place for that." Whereupon I was led into a room filled with government documents stamped Top Secret. I didn't find mine, but at least I never made the mistake of using the special post again.

Basing its conclusion on other jurisdictions and the Quebec experience, the commission's final report of August 1979 stated that using both French and English was safe, and maybe even safer in some cases. That had been the practice up till then, after all, and the accident rate was no worse than anywhere else. Some critics accused the commission of succumbing to political pressure, but that wasn't the way I saw it from the inside. The politics would certainly have been worse if we had reached another conclusion, and it was probably fortunate for the country that we didn't. Nevertheless, our decision was based on the evidence – which, I'm glad to say, has withstood the test of time.

IN 1977, AGAIN because of my French, I was invited by Justice David McDonald to be counsel for the RCMP in his royal commission of inquiry into a number of purported illegal activities by the RCMP Security Service. First, however, I had to be interviewed by the Mounties and given security clearance. When they asked me where I had been during the past three years, I started listing the countries, some of which were behind the Iron Curtain. "Forget it," they said. "We need someone immediately, and there's no way we can give you a security clearance in time." It was a rare case where my extensive travel actually proved a professional liability.

As my passport indicated, I was constantly on the road in the 1970s with my international work – some related to government files, some to my job with Fasken's. Usually I was working on several disparate cases at the same time, with my knowledge of international law and my ability to speak French the only points they had in common. When the Toronto Dominion Bank had trouble in Lebanon, for example, I was the one chosen to go to Beirut to assist with the file, much to my wife's dismay, as the country was then in the midst of a civil war.

One day I got a visit at the office from representatives of Pan Ocean Minerals, a Calgary-based subsidiary of Pan Ocean Oil in the United States. They wanted to begin exploration for uranium in Niger, the former French colony in sub-Saharan West Africa, but they hadn't managed to get any action on their visas from the embassy in Ottawa. A Calgary lawyer who happened to be a Trinity graduate told them I might be able to help. When they came to my office, I called the embassy, asked to speak to the ambassador, and explained to him in French what these people wanted.

"No problem," he said. "Tell them to come to me now and I'll give them their visas." A bit skeptical about how easily their problem had been solved, they asked me to go with them just to make sure. Then, while we were sitting with the ambassador, they said, "Give Mr. Graham a visa too. We're taking him with us." And that's how I came to spend a lot of the next four years in Niger, Chad, and Mali. It was a great adventure – novel, fascinating, and fun.

Niamey, the capital of Niger, is a fairly small town today, and it was even smaller then. My job primarily involved drafting contracts and dealing with the government. The issues were the usual ones of local employment, technical training, work permits for expats, royalties, and taxes. At first I was overwhelmed by how complicated and severe the regulations were until a very experienced lawyer in Paris told me, "Don't worry about most of them; just keep your eye on the depreciation rates. You can get a lot back with depreciation because nobody understands what it is."

Hamani Diori was the president when I first got to Niger, which worked out very well for our little Canadian delegation: he was a great friend and admirer of Pierre Trudeau from their time together with La Francophonie, the association of French-speaking nations that had been founded in 1970. We were often invited to the presidential palace and sometimes dealt directly with President Diori for the mining concessions. On one occasion we spread a large map of Niger on the floor of his office, and he and I got down on our hands and knees to study it. Suddenly, to my surprise and consternation, a gun fell out of the pocket of the aide who was helping us.

"You can know the language, you can know the law," I used to tell my students, "but there's more to negotiating than just professional expertise." To illustrate my point, I would recount the night in Niamey when the Americans, the Japanese, and the Canadians were invited to a dinner hosted by the minister of mines. The three national groups were competing for the concessions that the French hadn't already sewn up. In fact, wherever we went in Niger we were trailed by French agents whose assignment was to prevent any of our companies from muscling in on what France considered its own territory. As it happened, the Japanese missed their flight and didn't show up, which annoyed the minister, so it was just us and the Americans.

I found myself sitting next to one of their engineers, a pleasant enough fellow but obviously not accustomed to foreign places. "Bill, it says on this menu that we're going to be served tripes à la mode de Caen. What the hell is that?"

"It's an old French recipe made from the lining of a cow's stomach," I replied.

"Well, I'm not going to be eatin' no cow's innards in the middle of bloody Africa, for God's sake!"

I gave my client a kick under the table to get his attention. "Jim," I whispered, "we're asking for seconds of the tripe."

When we went to see the minister on business the next day, he greeted us warmly. "Ah, the Canadians, the ones who appreciate Niger's fine cuisine." From then on, we had a warm bond with the minister that certainly gave us an edge over our competitors.

In April 1974 Hamani Diori was overthrown in a coup led by Lieutenant-Colonel Seyni Kountché. "You're going to have to start from zero all over again," Niger's ambassador to Canada advised me over the phone. "You're going to have to establish credibility with the new regime." So I called up my clients in Calgary and said we had better get on a plane right away. We took the ambassador with us for good measure.

Niamey was still under curfew when we arrived. A military junta was in charge, and Kountché had yet to install himself as the new president when we went to see him at his army headquarters the next day. "Tell me more about the colonel," I asked the ambassador. "I suppose you know him."

"Oh, yes, I know him very well," he said. "One of the grievances behind the coup was that the government had prosecuted a bunch of student leaders when I was solicitor general."

"Forgive me for being blunt, Mr. Ambassador, but from what you've just said, it doesn't strike me that you're exactly a big asset to us in these negotiations. We flew you here from Canada thinking you were going to be our entrée to the colonel, but it seems we are your entrée to him."

"Quite so," he said. "I wouldn't dare go near the presidential palace without you. In fact, I'm hoping you're going to save my hide."

Everything went smoothly until Kountché accepted our invitation to learn more about the Canadian company's proposal with a visit to our office, located in the one building in Niamey that had an elevator. After the colonel, his guards, and a few of us piled into the elevator, it ascended about five feet and came to an abrupt stop. Their leader trapped, the guards panicked and started shouting. Was it a counter-coup? Out came their guns. "Oh Lord," I thought, "we're all going to be shot for sure." But then the elevator jolted back to life and we proceeded up without further ado. When the visit was over, we all chose to descend by the stairs.

On another occasion I was in Chad during their long-running civil war to meet with the minister of mines. It turned out that he was also the head of the air force. Three days earlier the rebels had shot down his plane. He survived the crash and had just returned to N'Djamena after a long hike across the desert. At the hotel we could hear machine-gun fire in the distance at night, though it wasn't as disruptive to a good night's sleep as the loud and persistent knocking up and down the hallway of the prostitutes who regularly crossed the Chari River from Kousséri, Cameroon, in search of clients. In the morning the Belgian ambassador was in a rage. "I'm so angry, I'm leaving – this town is driving me crazy," he roared. "I ordered my omelette, as usual, but my omelette never came. So I went down to the kitchen to get it, and there I found the chef screwing a girl on the floor while my omelette was getting cold. Enough's enough!"

There were reports that all the foreigners were about to be evacuated by boat downriver into Cameroon. Fortunately I had spent part of my time in N'Djamena out at the airport visiting the control tower. "I'm with the Commission of Inquiry into Bilingual Air Traffic Services in Canada," I told the rather bewildered controllers. "May I watch you at work?" I was with them about five hours, and afterward they invited me to join them for a beer. At three in the morning I was awakened by a phone call. It was one of the controllers. "A plane's come in that's on its way to Paris," he said, "and it might be the last plane out before the town falls. We told the pilots that they can't leave unless you guys are on it." Thank God for the commission of inquiry, my clients declared as we flew out of town, or we would now be paddling our way downriver.

Wherever I went in French-speaking Africa, I always felt warmly welcomed as a Canadian. I was seen as coming from a country that was wealthy, sophisticated, and a leader in the First World, but not a former colonial power like France or an economic behemoth like the United States. I rode on the good works and goodwill for which Canada was renowned in the developing nations. In Niger, for example, the primary school in central Niamey had always been run by a religious order from Quebec, and time after time I came across African political leaders or businessmen who had been educated by our priests or nuns. In the end, my clients never did find uranium in West Africa, but their exploration would never have gotten as far as it did if they had not been a Canadian company. "We want to have Canadians involved with us," was a constant refrain.

APART FROM ITS DOMESTIC significance, few assets are as important to Canada in international affairs as our bilingual heritage. It gives us more than just two working languages. It gives us two legal systems as well, English common law and French civil law, and two ways of seeing the world, which is incredibly useful when dealing with international business and international politics. As a result, we are particularly well placed to act as a bridge between the anglophone and francophone worlds. In fact, having both worlds as part of our DNA has enabled many Canadians to try to see where others are coming from. The dominance of the English language and Anglo-American law has stirred up resentments among all those, including France itself, who have to struggle to make their own languages heard, their own legal structures respected, in a new global order that is being formed without their ability to frame it. Some Chinese judges I once encountered, who had come on a study program to Canada, told me that they found Quebec particularly interesting because of its mixture of civil and common law. They were exposed not only to the two major legal systems of the Western world but also to our bilingual and bi-juridical character, which is one of our most valuable assets.

Canada grew up having to come to grips with different languages and different cultures, and that meant we had to learn to understand other people and their preoccupations. It made us more sensitive to the underdog. Empathy bred respect; respect bred accommodation; and accommodation bred compromise. Even when the goal is to get what we want for ourselves, we can't just bully everybody into submission – with the tragic exception, of course, of our shameful treatment of Aboriginal peoples. We have to work our way toward a practical solution, and that has become our international trademark. As His Highness the Aga Khan once put it, "The history of Canada has a great deal to teach us in this regard, including the long, incremental processes through which quality civil societies and committed cultures of pluralism are built." It's why Canadians have been particularly successful on the world stage in peace missions and multilateral organizations. As I like to say to those of my American friends who see a black-and-white world in which principle is monolithic and compromise a sign of weakness, "Don't worry, one day you'll be as lucky as we are and be a bilingual country too." They laugh, but it's a fact that the United States is becoming a bilingual society, like it or not. Just spend an hour in the Miami or San Diego airport. And I think it will make the United States a better, even greater nation as a result.

My belief in the importance of bilingualism for Canada led me to get involved in a number of organizations such as the Union Internationale des Avocats, the French-language equivalent to the International Bar Association. It turned out to be a wonderful way to expand my understanding of civil law, to broaden my international network in La Francophonie, and to meet lawyers from all over Quebec, not just Montreal. We went to international meetings together, I visited them in their hometowns, and they paid me the compliment of supporting my election as vice-president for Canada – a rare endorsement for an Anglo from Toronto.

At the same time I became active in the Toronto branch of the Alliance Française, one of more than a thousand centres that France supports around the world for the advancement of French language and culture. Founded in 1883 by a group of prominent intellectuals, including Louis Pasteur and Jules Verne, the Alliance had started in Toronto as early as 1902, and I joined its board soon after my return from Paris as a way to keep up my French, meet some interesting people, and help the organization grow. It's basically a non-profit language school whose surplus funds go into subsidizing various cultural programs. For years it had been run almost like a social club by a wonderful Swiss woman who taught at Victoria College, Laure Rièse, and in 1977 André Petit, an energetic and activist Frenchman, took over as its executive director.

One day in 1978, André phoned me at the office to make sure I would be attending the Alliance's annual general meeting that evening. We chatted for a few minutes about the agenda, though I was distracted by my work and barely paid any attention to what he was saying. So I went to the AGM ready to hold up my hand automatically as André went through the minutes, the finances, and the election of officers when I suddenly heard him nominate me to be the new president. "Me?" I said. "No, no, there's been some mistake." It turned out I had inadvertently agreed to take on the job during our phone call. As if I weren't busy enough.

The next ten years turned out to be an exceptionally rewarding experience. One of André's first ambitions was for the Alliance to acquire its own property, instead of paying rent for the inadequate facilities in an old house on Charles Street in central Toronto. We heard of one good prospect, but when André went to check it out, he found it was located near a popular pick-up spot for prostitutes. "Our students will think they're entering a bordello," he groaned. Eventually we bought a four-story building at 895 Yonge Street, large enough for eight classrooms and a gallery but still too small. Because it was more than the Alliance could afford, even with a $200,000 grant from the French government, I ended up having to guarantee the mortgage myself.

A couple of years later, a guy came round offering to sell us a grand Victorian home at 24 Spadina Road. Besides being just a block north of a subway stop on the Bloor line, it was more than twice the size of what we had. It was also substantially more expensive. We had no hope of getting another grant from Paris or another mortgage from the bank. In the end, however, we figured out a way in which the owner of the Spadina building could swap it for our more centrally located building on Yonge and still come out financially even. The Alliance has been happily settled there ever since, and in 2013 it initiated a major expansion to add more classrooms and a performance space. By that point the Toronto centre had become the largest French-language school in Canada, with over six thousand students and more than one hundred events a year, operating in four different locations around the city. Interestingly, one of the most active centres for the Alliance is in Hong Kong, because of the large number of Chinese who want to get extra points on their Canadian immigration forms by having a knowledge of French as well as of English.

In 1983 I went to Paris as part of a Canadian delegation to attend the grand ceremonies marking the Alliance's hundredth anniversary, with President François Mitterrand in attendance, and there I had the delight of being presented with the Silver Medal of the City of Paris by its mayor, Jacques Chirac. Two years later I became one of the few Canadians at that time, along with René Lévesque, to be given France's highest accolade, the Legion of Honour, in recognition for my work with the Alliance Française. Nowadays Canadian citizens receive foreign decorations more routinely, and though they still require a special Order-in-Council, the process is largely a formality. My case actually came before the Mulroney Cabinet. I learned later that a few objections had been raised on the grounds that I had been a Liberal candidate in 1984, but I had enough friends at the Cabinet table to speak up for me, and it passed. "If I had known how difficult the procedure was, I'm not sure I ever would have started it," the French ambassador said to me during the presentation in Toronto. And though I was extremely grateful for his efforts and for the honour bestowed upon me, I reminded him in my remarks that everything I had done to promote the French language and French culture had been done not for France but for Canada.

The Alliance Française was linked to the Centre francophone de Toronto, an umbrella organization of local health, educational, cultural, and social services in French. Unlike in northern Ontario, eastern Ontario, and the Ottawa Valley, the French-speaking population in Toronto wasn't made up almost exclusively of the descendants of the original settlers of New France. It comprised a growing number of immigrants from the former French colonies, especially in Africa. Though they shared the aspirations of Franco-Ontarians for services that would foster the French language, they were less preoccupied with the historic battle for religious and linguistic rights than with building new social and cultural institutions. Our work didn't really have a political dimension. By chance, however, many of those French-speaking immigrants were concentrated in the downtown Toronto riding of Rosedale, and they proved key to my winning my first nomination battle. I already knew their communities, I had worked with their organizations, and they appreciated my contributions enough to offer their support, even if they sometimes criticized me for not putting enough French in my leaflets. The reality was, however much I believed in bilingualism in Canada, there were so few francophones in the riding, and so many other linguistic groups, that I couldn't cover every issue in both official languages.

At one point, I was asked by Roy McMurtry, the attorney general of Ontario, to sit on a small committee of lawyers to advise on the use of

French in the province's courts, and I became active as one of the few anglophone members of the Association des juristes d'expression française de l'Ontario when it was set up in 1980. Through this connection, I made new French-speaking friends in Manitoba and New Brunswick as well as across Ontario whom I would never have met otherwise. I was even interviewed to become the dean of the francophone law school in Moncton, New Brunswick, but neither Cathy nor I were eager to leave Toronto.

A lot of our work for McMurtry's advisory committee was journeyman stuff – correct terminology, comparative law, whether a mortgage has the same implications as *un hypothèque* – but every problem led to another problem that had to be solved before we could deal with the previous one. We said that Ontarians should be able to write a will in French, for example, and then we realized that there was no way of getting a will probated in French in Ontario. Given the nationalist climate in Quebec, the work was politically important and of great personal interest to the minister, who, I suspected, wanted to point to it as one of his crowning achievements if he decided to run to replace Bill Davis as leader of the Progressive Conservative Party of Ontario.

One day he invited me to go to Montreal with him for a meeting with Robert Bourassa, the former premier of Quebec who had been defeated by René Lévesque in 1976. Bourassa had just returned from studying the European Community in Brussels, and he was still deciding whether to re-enter politics. Over lunch he said to McMurtry, "Roy, you have to make Ontario officially bilingual. It's of absolute importance for national unity. Lévesque is about to hold his referendum on independence, and such a gesture from Ontario will have a huge impact in the minds of ordinary Quebecers."

"We can't do that," Roy countered, "because we can't deliver on it."

"Quebecers care less about the delivery than they do about the principle," said Bourassa. There, I thought to myself, is the perfect example of the divide between civil law and common law, between the Cartesian grand plan and the everyday practice, between the French and the English. As I used to explain to my students, civil law is concerned with the overall design of a building, whereas common law is about placing one brick after another and seeing how the design turns out later.

"Listen, Robert," Roy replied with all sincerity, "Bill's here with me, and we can promise you that we're working hard so that Franco-Ontarian lawyers will be able to argue their cases in French in our courts. We will also have at least one judge on the Court of Appeal who will be able to hear cases in French." But Bourassa didn't really care about the details: he wanted the dream.

Considering my education, my experience, my bilingualism, and my attachment to Canada, it was probably inevitable that I would be drawn somehow into the Quebec referendum battle in the spring of 1980, even though I was neither a voter nor a politician. The link came through my knowledge of the European Economic Community. With every poll showing that the Yes side would lose (and lose badly) if Quebecers were asked if they wanted to separate from Canada, the Parti Québécois government came up with a long and complicated question that wasn't about independence per se. It merely asked for permission to begin negotiating with the rest of Canada to achieve something called "sovereignty-association" – basically two equal countries bound in a common market with a common currency and one passport. As a result, there was a sudden new interest in the EEC. What was its constitution? What were its structures? How did it work? Who made its laws? Was the power within it equal or asymmetric? What happened in the case of conflicts? Who appointed the courts? One day, to my surprise, I found three civil servants from the Ontario government sitting in on a small and relatively obscure course on European law that I had been invited to teach at my old law school a year after my return from Paris in 1968. That led Yves Fortier to suggest to the Comité du Non that I be invited to spend some time in Quebec City as an adviser to the No team led by Claude Ryan, the Liberal leader of the Opposition.

Basically, my job was to draft statements whenever the Yes side said something misleading about Europe or international law as part of its propaganda war. The separatists were fostering an assumption that if Quebec signed on to a type of EEC, the province would become an independent country in a fifty-fifty partnership with what remained of Canada. In other words, there would be no risk of losing any of the economic and social advantages of being Canadian. For starters, however, the rest of Canada would never accept a deal in which a quarter of the population shared equal power over common institutions with everyone else. Second, even if an independent Quebec were to achieve the impossible by negotiating an association with the rest of Canada, it would end up with no more sovereignty (and in some circumstances less) than it had in the Canadian federation. The separatists failed to recognize that the European Community was itself an embryonic federal system in which its members had agreed to surrender sovereignty in exchange for the benefits of an economic union, what many called "pooled sovereignty."

Signing any international agreement means sacrificing some degree of sovereignty, because everybody is required to give up something. The only question is how much. On a scale of one to ten, you can have an integration that's a three or a five or an eight, but to suggest that you can have total sovereignty and total integration at the same time is irrational. In some respects, in fact, Europe was more fully integrated than Canada. Canadians were disadvantaged by all sorts of interprovincial trade barriers that the Europeans had to knock down decades ago to make their union work. To use the freedom of movement as one example, even a bricklayer from Ottawa had trouble crossing the bridge to work on a job in Hull because of interprovincial rules.

If my hope was to help carry the day by providing a few facts as background information and a host of fairly technical legal arguments so that Quebecers could actually have an intelligent discussion, I was naive. The referendum campaign was emotional and visceral, with wild distortions on both sides. I remember running into Jean Chrétien one night at the Montreal studios of Radio-Canada. As Trudeau's minister of justice in charge of the federal response to the campaign, he was taking the brunt of the heat from the separatists, and it left him shaken to the core. The TV journalists had treated him despicably, as though he were a sellout to his people – a *vendu*.

On May 14, 1980, six days before the vote, I joined thousands of No supporters at the Paul Sauvé Arena in Montreal's East End for the final rally. Standing near the front, I was unexpectedly grabbed by a friend and pulled onto the stage. "Come on, Bill," he said, "you've been a member of the committee, you should be up here." And so I found myself standing right behind Prime Minister Trudeau when he delivered his most famous and passionate speech in defence of Canada. I had never experienced anything like it. That's when I first learned what politics could be like at its finest, when you are in the centre of a massive, supercharged crowd and making history. It was dramatic, thrilling, and unforgettable as Trudeau launched into his famous defence of his English-speaking ancestors in Quebec, for it gave emotional force to his intellectual critique of the destructive, xenophobic dimensions of ethnic nationalism. Ironically, amid the noise level in the arena, I could barely hear what he was saying.

On referendum day Yves Fortier and I went to watch the vote in a school in a heavily immigrant district of Montreal – in all probability a No stronghold. A polling station in a general election normally has a half-dozen or more voting booths. You register at a desk, get your ballot, go to a booth, vote, and then you're on your way. At this station, however, the organizers were allowing just one person at a time into the hall, even though ten booths had been prepared. The line stretched away for blocks and blocks, and it was obvious that about a thousand people would never get a chance to vote before the polling ended. Just as obvious was the reason.

Yves became a tiger. He went up to the organizer and said, "You are a separatist. You are trying to undermine the will of the people to vote. I am going downtown right now to file a complaint about you with the Election Commission."

The guy was furious. "Well, if you're so smart, you run it."

"Okay," said Yves, "I will." So he grabbed me and we went outside. We organized everybody into different lines, steered them toward the various desks and booths, and had the whole mess cleared up in about two and a half hours. I never would have had the ability or the boldness to take the initiative he did.

That night we went back to his house to watch the results on TV: sixty-forty for the No side. Yves turned to me and said, "For the first time in a long time, I can now proudly say I am a Canadian." It certainly made me appreciate the emotional toll the debate had taken on Quebecers.

I WISH I COULD SAY I had a life strategy when I set off to learn French and study international law as a young man. In truth, I had no idea how important bilingualism was about to become in Canada; nor did I foresee the rapid pace with which globalization would blur the distinction between national laws and international norms, such that international law became much more important than ever before. I simply followed my interests and worked hard. Good fortune did the rest. My French took me from ordinary litigation to international commerce, and together they opened the door to Africa, to the Union Internationale des Avocats, and ultimately to a rewarding academic career at my alma mater.

In 1980, during a stop in Toronto between the contract negotiations in Niger and a land-claims case I was arguing in the Northwest Territories, I got a call at the office from Frank Iacobucci, the dean of the University of Toronto law school and later a justice of the Supreme Court of Canada, asking if I would be interested in teaching international law as a full professor. International law had leapt in importance during the two decades since Dean Wright had scolded me for wasting my time with it, and the faculty was now keen to deepen its international dimension at a time of increased globalization. In 1970, for example, with the *Internationale Handelsgesellschaft* case, the European Court of Justice declared that a properly constructed European law could have an impact on the Constitution of Germany itself. And in 1981 the European Court of Human Rights prompted the British Parliament to recognize that the criminalization of homosexual acts between consenting adults in Northern Ireland was a violation of the European Convention for the Protection of Human Rights and Fundamental Freedoms. "Now," said Professor Goldman on one of my visits to Paris in the 1980s, "we have to teach the rules laid down by the European Court of Justice."

I went home and discussed the idea with Cathy. Clearly, I couldn't work all over the world and teach in Toronto at the same time. My schedule was crazy, but I loved the challenges, the experiences, and the people who came with the job of practising international law. Still, the offer from the university came at a good time in my life. I felt scattered all over the place, both physically and intellectually. I was looking for an opportunity to try something different. And I had no interest in being a judge, which is how most litigation lawyers get off the fast-moving train of their careers. And so, in the fall of 1980, I left Fasken's and became a full professor in the same rooms where I had been a student. "You're pretty smart, Bill," said one of my former colleagues. "You saw another train going by that nobody else saw and you grabbed it."

The change marked a shift in the pace and focus of my life. Though I still worked hard and travelled frequently, Cathy and I had more time to enjoy ourselves and pursue our many interests together. Katy and Patrick finished their schooling at St. Clement's and Upper Canada College, respectively, and went off to university – she to McGill, he to King's College in Halifax. Cathy became heavily involved with the Celtic Studies program at St. Michael's College, the Parkinson Foundation, and the Ireland Fund of Canada. It had been founded by Hilary Weston to raise funds for programs designed to encourage peace and cultural connections between Northern Ireland and the southern Republic, and Cathy became chair from 1993 to 1995. We continued to spend a few weeks in Corsica during the summer and our weekends cross-country skiing at Glenariff in the winter. I indulged my love of horseback riding by joining the Eglinton and Caledon Hunt Club. Though I saw only one fox on the run in Ontario, I found it a beneficial form of sport and exercise. It even had a dangerous side, and not just for the fox; I broke my leg at least once and accrued more than a few scrapes and bruises over the years.

In addition to my old course on the law of the European Economic Community, I taught public international law (the law of war, for example, or the law of the sea), international trade law (which also involved private commercial law), and international commercial arbitration. I thought I knew the law quite well, but when I had to teach it I quickly realized how little I actually knew. Sometimes I was just a day ahead of the students, reading the cases and trying to figure out what they meant. The workload was heavier than I ever imagined, especially in public international law – an area in which I had practised very little. I vaguely remembered what I had been taught fifteen years earlier, but that wasn't much help because the field had changed so much in the interim. In the face of unprecedented global investment, global commerce, and global communications, the international legal systems that had been constructed amid the ashes of the Second World War were being reinvented or replaced altogether. The abandonment of the gold standard in 1972, the two dramatic price increases of the Organization of the Petroleum Exporting Countries (OPEC) cartel, and the rise of Asia had all had a revolutionary impact on the fundamental structure and regulation of my so-called area of expertise – international trade.

Human beings have traded since the dawn of civilization and probably even éarlier. One of my father's favourite books was *The Merchant of Prato* by Iris Origo, which showed how bills of exchange made their way through fourteenth-century Europe. A merchant in Siena would write out a bill of exchange and give it to a trader, who gave it to another, who passed it on to another, until it eventually reached London, where it could be redeemed for gold coin or some such currency. Raw materials and finished products moved back and forth, often without taxation. Tariffs and other barriers to the free movement of goods and people became more common with the rise of nationalism in the nineteenth century, when states sought to control their own economies and their imperial trade through taxation and pricing.

With experience, however, there arose a general recognition that these mercantilist policies were often a hindrance to economic prosperity as well as a cause of war. The abolition of the protectionist corn laws in Britain, which had ignited such a political uproar in the 1840s, was all about the benefits of free trade. As transportation and communications grew faster and the world grew smaller, multinational corporations became larger and more powerful, and they wanted freer access to markets everywhere as well as greater protection for their investments. New schools of economic theory supplied the intellectual arguments in support of looser trade rules and tighter investment guarantees. The Great Depression of the 1930s proved that "beggar your neighbours" policies such as the Smoot-Hawley Tariff Act had merely prolonged the economic suffering in the United States and elsewhere. As a result, a widely shared belief developed after the Second World War that an orderly, fair, and effective network of markets was the best route to global prosperity and world peace.

However, as I used to remind my students, "an international legal system can't possibly be like the domestic system, or no state would voluntarily enter into it." What country would agree to be bound by certain trade rules, knowing that, if it were found in violation of them, it would be compelled to pay billions of dollars in damages? It's one thing to conduct tariff negotiations on a reciprocal basis; it's another to pass sovereignty to a multilateral body that can smack you down at any moment. That's why the United

States backed away from the post-war push to establish an International Trade Organization (ITO) as a UN agency with an extensive jurisdiction and a court to enforce it.

Instead, the same forces that created the World Bank and the International Monetary Fund (IMF) at Bretton Woods settled for the establishment in 1948 of the General Agreement on Tariffs and Trade (GATT), a complicated, quasi-institutional trade system that evolved around a series of accommodations that were originally intended only as stop-gap measures before the creation of the ITO. The founders said in effect, until we can set up an international regulatory body, let's conduct negotiating "rounds" to establish a few rules around tariffs, obtain some tariff reductions, and penalize the cheaters. In the 1960s there was the Kennedy Round, and in the 1970s, the Nixon Round, which morphed into the Tokyo Round when Richard Nixon fell into disfavour. Out of these negotiations came various dispute-resolution mechanisms that referred complaints to the GATT council, to ad hoc working groups, or to arbitration panels.

The early negotiations were all about reducing tariffs on various goods. But as the water level dropped, new rocks appeared. The more the tariffs were reduced, the more important the non-tariff barriers became. What about banking? What about communications? What about common standards so that businesses could compete on a level playing field? Wasn't there a trade in services as well as goods? What about lawyers, architects, or engineers? What about the movement of labour and capital? Answering these questions was obviously more complicated than determining the size of a tariff reduction: there are millions of standards around the world, countless vested interests, and a multitude of national policies.

"Over time the GATT became like a multi-layered pagoda," said Jake Warren, a senior Ottawa mandarin who was one of Canada's most highly regarded trade negotiators. "Beautiful to look at but impossible to operate in."

As global trade became even larger and more integrated, pressure continued to mount for broader rules and better dispute mechanisms. Even the United States had come to recognize that if the GATT were to work, the rules needed more bite. There had to be better regulation of non-tariff barriers and some applicability mechanisms. Out of the Uruguay Round, which took place between 1986 and 1994, there emerged the World

Trade Organization (WTO), and with it came a permanent secretary, a permanent meeting of members, a court-like system whose judgments were more binding than GATT's, and a tremendous increase in legal staff. The WTO embodied more than an advance in scope and content. It represented a basic shift from a set of obligations not to do certain things to a set of positive obligations, as in the harmonization of standards and professional qualifications. It also represented a complete departure from the GATT's loose system of consultation and consensus to a more juridical system for the settlement of disputes.

Though this evolution had substantial consequences for national sovereignty, the penalties were still highly political in practice. One country couldn't solve a dispute with another by going to court and saying, "They cheated on the trade rules and it has cost our economy $5 billion, so they should write us a cheque for $5 billion." Instead, if a country could demonstrate that its rights had been violated and its economy had suffered, it was allowed to nick the hide of the other country by taking some retaliatory action that would earn back what it had lost. In other words, it conferred the right of reprisal, not a right of compensation. In practice, however, can any middle or small country inflict a retaliatory action on an economic powerhouse such as the United States or China without shooting itself in the foot? I was sometimes consulted by aggrieved parties about the best way to retaliate, but there was never an easy answer in a world of integrated economies. If they went after someone else's imports, they often risked hurting their own exports. During one trade dispute with the United States over computer parts, the only response Canada could think of that wouldn't backfire was to put a high tariff on Christmas trees coming north from New England – hardly a tough penalty. Another time, when some European clients of mine were angry with Canada over an issue involving the Liquor Control Board of Ontario, they wanted Europe to hit back by threatening to put a tariff on wine from British Columbia or strawberries from the Maritimes. "That makes no sense," I told them. "Why would the liquor control board care if some exporter in another part of the country is hurt?"

MY FIRST YEAR AS A professor wasn't an unmitigated disaster, but neither was it a great success. Besides having to bone up on the material, I simply didn't know how to teach well. As a practising lawyer I had prepared for

cases and attended lectures at professional meetings with only one purpose: to cram as much information as possible into my head in the shortest
time. In the words of Sergeant Friday, "The facts, ma'am, just give me
the facts." The brighter students loved all this information, but most were
frustrated and confused. When one complained that I talked too fast, my
only comeback was to suggest he listen faster. Needless to say, their comments were as bad as my ranking in the end-of-the-year student reviews.

I got quite wound up about it and went to Dean Iacobucci and said,
"Listen, Frank, it looks like you've made a mistake here. Why don't we just
admit it, and I'll go back to my practice?"

"No," he replied, "I think you've got the potential to be a good teacher.
But you've got a problem: you haven't a clue how to teach."

"Obviously. But how can I learn to teach without doing it? And I hate
having to make the students the victims while I learn."

"Well," he said, "I'm going to make a recommendation that will sound
silly. There's a summer course at the University of Victoria that trains
law professors how to teach law. Almost everyone in it will be recent
graduates in their twenties, so you'll be like their father, but———."

And so, in the summer of 1981, at the age of forty-two, I went back to
school. The course, run that year by Neil Gold, a gifted teacher who was
subsequently dean of the law school at the University of Windsor, Ontario, was a tremendous help. Without it, I probably would have quit
teaching. I had to conduct mock classes in front of the others and be severely
critiqued by them. I watched out for who was good and who was bad, and
I tried to analyze the differences. I listened to countless debates about the
potential impact of the new Charter of Rights and Freedoms on the law
and the teaching of law in Canada. Thanks to the course, I came to realize
that good teaching meant more than putting a load of facts into a wheel-
barrow, taking it into the classroom, and dumping it on the heads of young
people. It wasn't about studying the details of one case or another. It was
about their significance.

When I returned to Toronto for the fall semester, I stripped about half
the content out of my previous lectures and started focusing on the relevance of the remaining information – why it was important, what principles lay behind it, how it had an impact on society. As a result, I'm very

proud to say, my reputation and popularity climbed among the students, though in truth they had nowhere to go but up.

In 1980 I got a call from André Tremblay, a former senior civil servant, who was in charge of the law school at the Université de Montréal. Would I be interested in giving a course in international trade law to a graduate class there? And, a few years later, when Jean Castel and I were in the middle of co-authoring a book on the Canadian application of international trade law along with Armand de Mestral, a professor in the Faculty of Law at McGill University, Armand said, "Well, since you're coming to Montreal, why don't you teach at McGill as well?"

My fall schedule was a killer. I taught three days at the University of Toronto, flew to Montreal on Thursday to give an evening class at the Université de Montréal, taught at McGill on Friday morning, and returned home in the afternoon. Then, as if that weren't enough, the Université de Montréal asked me if I would teach international commercial law to its law students. That was another learning curve for me, because I now had more than a hundred students, almost all of them young francophones, who didn't know how the Constitution of Canada functioned, let alone the conceptually more difficult and technically more complicated workings of the GATT or the WTO.

It was fascinating to observe the differences between the students at McGill and at the Université de Montréal, just a few miles apart in the same city yet living as though on separate continents. At the superficial level, McGill was harder to get into, most of its law students already had an undergraduate degree, and there was more of a mix of anglophones and francophones. At a deeper level, I found that the McGill students accepted the bilingual framework of Quebec, Canada, and international commerce as a given. The Université de Montréal students, especially the younger and more aggressive ones, pushed back whenever I assigned reading materials in English. I understood that the first language of the course was French, and because of the United Nations and the GATT, I was usually able to find most of the best material in French. Nevertheless, I knew that anybody who wanted to be effective in international trade law had better have at least some grasp of English. "That's how the modern world out there works," I said, "and I'm only being helpful by suggesting you have to look at it."

The more intense debates took place with some of my faculty colleagues at the Université de Montréal, including Jacques-Yvan Morin and Daniel Turp. They were sophisticated intellectuals with a deep understanding of international law. I never became close to Morin, but Daniel Turp and I became genuine friends. He had a subtle approach to issues, and when he was elected to the House of Commons as a Bloc Québécois MP in 1997, his knowledge of international law made him a very useful member of the parliamentary foreign affairs committee. But as separatists with serious ambitions for Quebec's presence in the world, Turp and Morin were in the process of formulating the position that Quebec's international legal personality followed from its domestic personality as a province. Therefore, they argued, Quebec should have an international presence equal to Canada's on every issue over which it had constitutional jurisdiction. The most obvious example was Quebec's push to gain full status at the United Nations Educational, Scientific and Cultural Organization (UNESCO) on the basis that education and culture are provincial responsibilities. As a sort of extension of their doctrine, Morin and Turp advocated the idea of creating a Quebec association of international lawyers – a francophone counterpart to the Canadian Council on International Law, of which I had been a founding member in 1972.

The Canadian Council on International Law was an interesting organization. Before it existed, there was no place in Canada where the practitioners of international law could meet with academics and government officials to network and exchange information. The Canadian Bar Association had a constitutional law section that included some international law, and later it created a section on international law, but that wasn't sufficient to meet the growing importance of the field. The Canadian Council held an annual conference to which it invited leading experts from across Canada and around the world to discuss a particular theme, whether the laws of war or the law of the sea. It also brought together a host of key scholars and civil servants, such as Ronald St. John Macdonald, Marcel Cadieux, Alan Beesley, and Mark Jewett – Canada's representative at the United Nations Commission on International Trade Law (UNCITRAL) in Vienna at the time.

In 1985 Jewett invited me to join his team in negotiating an international agreement to harmonize the rules governing commercial arbitration. For several years, we worked with delegations from a number of nations to create a model law that would enable arbitration to be done by arbiters with a knowledge of different legal systems, but according to rules based on general principles of law that were satisfactory to all the signatories. All participants had to dilute the purity of their own national systems, and much of our work was rooted in the concept of *lex mercatoria,* shared principles of commercial law that had been applied ever since medieval traders had travelled from fair to fair throughout Europe.

Once the Model Law on International Commercial Arbitration was drafted, it needed to be incorporated into the laws of the various countries, including Canada's, so it could be used and referred to by Canadian lawyers with international clients. However, Ottawa could adopt it only within areas of federal jurisdiction. To make it truly effective, we had to have it adopted by the ten provinces as well – an almost insurmountable task. By a stroke of great luck, Brian Smith, the attorney general of British Columbia, wanted to run for premier, and part of his platform was to make Vancouver a centre of commercial arbitration. I flew out to meet with him. "If you want to do this," I said, "you're going to have to adopt the Model Law in BC." After that success, we got somebody working on it in Quebec, and then everywhere else.

On the private-law side as well as on the public-law side, extraordinary strides were being made in evolving transnational trade and commerce in an integrated legal system. One result of the increasing network of treaties and arrangements governing states was that the blurring of the lines between international law and domestic law, already under way, simply intensified. Shortly after my appointment at the University of Toronto, for example, I attended a faculty meeting during which I was asked why international law was relevant. I went around the table and pointed out that no one was teaching exclusively the law of Ontario or of Canada anymore. Other laws applied too. Even the specialists in land law, which dealt with real property in the province, had to know the laws of other countries because more and more of their clients had time-shares in the United States, family properties in Europe, or investments in Asia. In the early 2000s a political controversy flared up over the issue of whether

Sharia law should be recognized in Ontario because of the increasing number of Muslim immigrants to the province. "We're a common law society," shouted the opponents. "We shouldn't import the laws of other places." But when Ontario adopted the Model Law on International Commercial Arbitration, I pointed out, it in fact adopted concepts from the French system, the Soviet system, the Arab system, the Chinese system, and so forth. In our interdependent world, there's not a lot of legal "purity" left.

The same applied to Quebec, but the separatists continued to believe that they could stand apart from reality. That's basically what I told Daniel Turp when he talked about establishing La Société québécoise de droit international in 1982. "We've got the Canadian Council on International Law," I argued. "Why on earth do we need another organization?" But he and Morin saw it as another assertion of Quebec's international presence, so in the end I was one of its early members and almost alone as a non-Quebecer. Better to be in the tent than out, I reasoned, and it was actually quite instructive. Though I didn't attend a lot of its meetings, because of my commitments in Toronto and elsewhere, it did give me another insight into the thinking of Quebecers on various issues, both legal and political. Once again, to understand where someone is coming from is to empathize with another point of view, even when you don't agree with it.

I always remember a Quebec colleague of mine, a judge, saying to me during a Canadian Council dinner, "You know, Bill, you anglophones are more separatist than we are. We read your judgments in English, because we have to, but very few of you read our judgments in French or deal with the French fact in Canada."

It was a pertinent comment. As a francophone lawyer, he had been obliged to become integrated into the English language and the English common law system because he couldn't afford not to. If he argued a case before the Supreme Court, he would be expected to know the jurisprudence on which he would be questioned. Most anglophone lawyers, however, never gave a damn whether they had read the French law, even in translation. That is unwise. Cases have been won by referring to the French version of the statute to reinforce a disputed interpretation of the English version.

Some years before, I'd gone to the Supreme Court with Walter Williston on a case involving the bribing of a municipal politician. The argument came down to the phrase *"on t'offre."* Walter, being an anglophone, used a straight translation. "This is just a speculative statement," he told the judges, "that maybe, someday, somehow, there's a possibility you could be offering something. That's not the same as, here, take this." The francophone judges laughed, because in Quebec that's the colloquial way of offering someone something.

"Walter," I said, "this isn't going to get us anywhere, I promise you."

"Shut up, Bill," he whispered. "It's all we've got."

My experiences during the 1980 referendum, at the Université de Montréal, and with La Société québécoise de droit international were incredibly helpful in my understanding of Quebec issues and the point of view of informed Quebecers. I may not have had much contact with workers in La Mauricie or farmers in the Beauce, but there were scores of people I could call up in Montreal, Trois-Rivières, or Quebec City if I wanted to find out what was going on. By the time I got into politics and government, I had over twenty years of learning about Quebec and building friendships there. As I tried to warn Michael Ignatieff, another professor and UCC Old Boy, when he was about to enter Canadian politics in 2006, "You know, Michael, it's tough to walk into this business without having lived and breathed the issues of Quebec for a while. You're going to fall into pits full of snakes you don't even know exist."

4

NEVER TWICE
WITHOUT A THIRD

As a student of history I have always been interested in politics and international relations, but that was a long way from seriously thinking of running for public office myself. When I bounced the idea off my father one day as a kind of romantic possibility, he said, "Politics is a dirty game, Bill. I'm not sure you want to get involved in that."

Like many successful capitalists, Dad was a fiscal conservative intellectually and a Progressive Conservative politically. He associated with wealthy Republicans in New York and California, considered Roosevelt's New Deal bad economics, and once told me how proud he was to have been introduced to an American audience as the Alexander Hamilton of Canada. Nevertheless, it wasn't in his nature to be doctrinaire about anything, except perhaps in his contempt for the socialist views of the CCF/NDP. He gave money to the Liberals as well as to the Conservatives. He became close to C.D. Howe, Louis St. Laurent's "Minister of Everything," after they had taken a business trip to Argentina together in 1934. And in 1960 he had an epiphany moment that turned him against John Diefenbaker for the remainder of his life.

Dad and Max Bell owned FP Publications, which in turn owned the *Edmonton Bulletin* and the *Victoria Times Colonist*. One evening in London, Dad and I had dinner with Roy Thomson, the Canadian-born media tycoon, who talked about his purchase of the Edinburgh-based *Scotsman*, which had come with a television licence as well. "Forget about the bloody newspapers, Ronnie," he said to my father. "It's TV that makes all the money." So Dad put together a consortium of leading Vancouver business figures and applied for a television licence from the Board of Broadcast Governors, the federal regulatory agency that was later transformed into the Canadian Radio-Television Commission. But Ottawa turned him down on the grounds that, because he already owned the newspaper in Victoria, having the TV station would be an unacceptable level of media concentration. Okay, said Dad, I may not like it, but that's the public policy for the national good. Shortly afterward, who should apply for a TV licence in the Toronto area but the Eatons and the Bassetts? Who owned the *Toronto Telegram*? The Eatons and the Bassetts. Who were prominent backers of the Diefenbaker Tories? The Eatons and the Bassetts. And they got it.

I remember the morning Dad came down to breakfast with the news. "That's the last time I'll ever give any money to the goddamn Conservative Party," he fumed. "Typical of the East," he continued, like so many other Easterners-turned-Westerners before and after him. "They've betrayed us again."

Dad was no Colonel Blimp type of Tory, and though he was honoured to have Prince Philip as a houseguest, he wasn't a fervent monarchist. Rumour said that he'd been asked to serve as lieutenant-governor of British Columbia, but he didn't want to live in Victoria. He was proud to be an honorary colonel of the Fifteenth Field Artillery Regiment, but he hadn't a military bone in his body. Indeed, I think he would have been horrified to know that I became defence minister. Finance: bravo. Foreign affairs: okay. But defence rated a much lower level of significance.

As it happened, however, my younger brother David grew into something of a caricature of a nineteenth-century British gentleman. He played polo, became a master of the foxhounds in Dorset, England, and for a time sat on the executive of the BC wing of the Progressive Conservative Party. Indeed, thanks to David, who had been singing my praises as a young lawyer with a French doctorate, I received a call not long after Cathy and I returned from Paris inviting me to Ottawa to meet with Robert Stanfield, the Tory leader of the Opposition. Over a pleasant lunch in the Parliamentary Dining Room, the first time I had ever been there, Stanfield offered me the newly established position of research director for the party's caucus.

I was both flattered and tempted. The job would have been interesting, and I wasn't particularly attached to any political party at the time. When

I thought about it, however, I realized that I had gone through all these studies so I could practise law, not do something else. I also realized how impressed I had been by Pierre Trudeau during our brief encounter in Paris. Though Stanfield was certainly an improvement over Diefenbaker, the Tories were still too close to the anti-French, anti-Catholic Loyalists of British Canada. They didn't understand Quebec, they resisted official bilingualism, and it seemed evident to me that the Liberals were the only party capable of solving the national unity issues that were threatening to tear Canada apart.

I got to watch Trudeau at work through a funny set of circumstances. A friend of mine from law school, Ed Roberts, had returned to his native province and become a member of the Newfoundland Legislative Assembly in 1966 under the colourful Liberal premier, Joey Smallwood. Ed sent me a booklet that Smallwood had written, and in my thank-you note I said I thought it contained some good ideas. When Ed showed my letter to Smallwood, the premier said, "Your friend sounds like a very bright guy. Let's get him down here." And that's how I was invited to join the small Newfoundland delegation to a federal-provincial constitutional conference held in Ottawa, with Trudeau only a few feet away. It was intriguing to watch from a second-row seat as these politicians made history.

"Prime Minister," Smallwood said at one point, "you look at that Ontario over there. The amount of money we're discussing doesn't mean anything to them, but to us in Newfoundland that's a big amount of money. When I was a young man, I worked in New York in the basement stock-room of one of those tall skyscrapers. Whenever a big wind came up, the top of the building swayed, but we felt nothing down below. Well, Canada is like that building. Ontario is the ground floor, Newfoundland is the top floor, and something that doesn't make any difference to them will make a huge difference to us. So just send something our way."

When we went back to the premier's hotel room for lunch, Smallwood offered me a glass of sherry. I wasn't used to sherry at noon and asked if I could have white wine instead. No, it was sherry or nothing. In came Alex Hickman, Smallwood's attorney general, who later became chief justice of the Newfoundland Supreme Court. "Alex," said the premier by way of introducing me, "I want you to meet this young man. He's going to be the dean of our law school." Life's moving along quite nicely, I thought: just finished my doctorate, attending a first ministers' conference, and about to be named the dean of a law school.

The fantasy was quickly punctured when Hickman replied, "But, Premier, we don't have a law school."

"Well, we should have a law school," Smallwood countered. Forty-five years later, Newfoundland still didn't have its own law school.

I didn't get a chance to speak with Pierre Trudeau beyond saying a brief hello. He was preoccupied with chairing the meeting, and there was no reason why he should remember me from Paris. In later years I saw him at various events and exchanged a few words, most notably at a Liberal Party convention in Winnipeg when he and I got into an animated conversation about the merits of proportional representation. I argued that it would be a good thing for the country if the Liberals had a few seats in Alberta and the Conservatives had a few seats in Quebec. "But the prime minister of Canada is powerful enough in a parliamentary system," Trudeau countered. "If you also gave him the right as leader of the party to select a list of candidates, as they do in many proportional representation systems, it wouldn't be good for democracy."

Perhaps the most intimate insight I had into his character took place by chance. On one occasion in the 1970s when I went with a private delegation to Ottawa, we were invited to have supper with Jeanne Sauvé in the dining room of the Speaker's chambers. She led us on a tour into the House of Commons. I decided, just for fun, to go and sit at Mr. Trudeau's desk. Curious to see what was in it, I lifted the lid and peered inside. There I saw an official pad on which was typed a note: "Prime Minister, call home – the kids need to speak to you." No matter how great a leader or how burdensome the affairs of state, he was above all a father.

THOUGH I CAN'T remember precisely when I joined the Liberal Party of Canada, I certainly worked in the 1968 campaign to help elect Donald Macdonald in my downtown Toronto riding of Rosedale; I helped John Evans, the president of the University of Toronto, secure the nomination in 1978; and I was a fairly active member of the party in the four federal elections between 1972 and 1980. Nevertheless, I was surprised to receive a call out of the blue one day in 1983 from the president of the Rosedale Liberal Association, inviting me to consider running in the next federal election. I was open enough to the idea to agree to have lunch with him and a few other members of the executive. "You'd make a great candidate for us, Bill," he said when we met. "You're a law professor, you're bilingual, you know business – you'd be perfect."

"Thanks, I replied, "I'm flattered to be asked. Is there anybody else running for the nomination?"

"Yeah, as a matter of fact there is," came the response. "Gerry Doucet. He works up in Ottawa but is interested in running in Rosedale."

Because they were asking me to run, I presumed they intended to support me. But, going around the table, each and every one of them declared for Gerry Doucet. "Call me naive, call me stupid, but there's something I'm not getting here," I said. "Are you asking me to run because a horse race would create some buzz and be good for Gerry?"

"Yes, that's sort of it. If Gerry just comes in and gets the nomination because we give it to him, it's not going to look very good. A big nomination battle between two good candidates would revitalize the party."

"Well, I don't go into auctions," I said rather haughtily, my vanity wounded.

Later in the day I vented my indignation to my friend John Campion, a young lawyer at Fasken's and an ardent Liberal. John was even more annoyed. "That's ridiculous. It's worse than ridiculous, it's insulting. We can't let them get away with it." By this point he was practically bouncing off the walls. "One thing's for sure, Bill. You've got no choice but to run and beat them."

I wouldn't say that politics requires a great deal more sacrifice of time and effort than many other busy professions. Nevertheless, it does take a toll on family life because you usually lose your free weekends and a certain amount of your personal privacy. If you're worried that the sacrifices will be too much, I used to tell people, you shouldn't get into politics at all. In fact, Cathy and I decided that I wouldn't get into the game until after our children had gone through high school, in part because that was the advice given to me by the three judges on the air-traffic commission, all of whom had previously run for public office. And though Cathy personally was more drawn to organizing the annual Trinity College book sale than to the world of party politics, she was supportive because she understood the importance of government. She also understood me well enough to know that I wasn't cut out to spend my days reading dusty tomes in the library and writing scholarly articles that hardly anyone would read. I was too energetic and gregarious to be happy in the ivory tower; I needed to get out of my privileged cocoon for my own growth as a human being; and I wanted to make a mark in public life and engage in its issues.

Before I got serious about pursuing the nomination, I had to find out whether community activist Anne Cools, who had run for the Liberals in 1979 and 1980, intended to contest another election. So I decided to pay a courtesy call on her, accompanied by John Campion. At the time Anne was managing a women's shelter on Spadina Avenue, and after a long delay while an assistant tried to figure out why two men were standing at the door, John and I were escorted down to an office in the basement. "Yes, yes," we overheard her saying. "I'd be very honoured." When the call was over, to our utter astonishment she did a little jig. It turned out that Pierre Trudeau had just invited her to become the first black Canadian in the Senate. The timing of her appointment led a few people to believe that I had somehow persuaded Trudeau to clear the way for my nomination run, which was nonsense, but if they wanted to believe I had so much influence, who was I to disillusion them?

To test the waters for a campaign, Cathy and I threw a party at our house and invited about a hundred people we knew. I gave a speech, Campion gave a speech, everybody cheered. It was, I thought, a great success and very encouraging. The next morning I received a phone call from Tom Wilson, my old friend from Trinity days, who was now a lawyer and very active in Toronto municipal politics and community organizing. After a bit of praise for how well the event had gone, he asked, "By the way, Bill, how many people do you think you will need to sign up to win a contested nomination in Rosedale?"

"About a thousand, or so I've been told."

"And how many did you sign up last night?"

"Let's see, we had a hundred people here, and they were all enthusiastic. So I'd guess we got most of them."

"There was a table in the front hall with sign-up forms," Tom said. "Why don't you go downstairs and see how many forms were filled out?"

I went downstairs and counted the forms: one, two, three. I was crestfallen.

"You're hopeless," Tom said. "You think making speeches is how you're going to get the nomination. You're completely unorganized. You haven't a clue what you're doing. Come down and have breakfast with me. If you're going to put your name forward, you've got to do it right."

Tom and his wife, Elizabeth, an academic administrator at the University of Toronto, set about launching my campaign off the ground. The first item of business was for me to put together a committee consisting of themselves, John Campion, and Rosemary McCarney, a corporate lawyer with deep knowledge of international law and development. Then, because many of us were rank amateurs, we decided to hire a political organizer. Politics wasn't as professionalized as it is now, and few people organized campaigns for a living, but we eventually found Scott Cavalier, an experienced campaigner who later became a city councillor. We set up an organization and proceeded to hold dozens upon dozens of coffee meetings, cocktail parties, and social events to expand our range of supporters and elicit financial contributions.

I hated fundraising. I particularly hated harassing the same small group of friends, time and time again. It was more a psychological problem than a practical one because it wasn't all that difficult to find the $75,000 I needed in a well-to-do riding like Rosedale. Moreover, raising money was easier in those days because the limits on election financing were much higher, which meant that candidates didn't have to rely on getting small amounts from thousands of donors. In my early nomination battles and election campaigns I had no trouble getting what I needed from a few generous supporters or lending the campaign a bit of my own money to get the ball rolling. Indeed, the Liberal association usually had a small surplus left over. I even made a point of leaving some money in the kitty for my successor, which wasn't apparently a common thing for MPs to do.

Not every fundraising experience was unpleasant. Once, years later, I was invited to have lunch with Frank Stronach, the founder of the auto-parts giant Magna. After exchanging a few pleasantries, he talked non-stop for an hour and a half about his management theories and his views on capitalism while I just nodded and told him how interesting it all was. Two days later one of Stronach's assistants showed up at my house with a cheque for $5,000. "Frank thinks you're one of the brightest politicians he's ever talked to," he said.

One day a sweet woman of Eastern European origin came into my campaign office. I had got to know her from a rather seedy bar on the corner of Wellesley and Parliament Streets where I often took my team for a beer and something to eat. She washed the dishes there. "Bill," she said, putting a brown bag on my desk, "I have something for you." Opening the bag, I found it contained $1,000 in cash.

"But I can't take $1,000 from you," I protested.

"Why not? I gave Ian Scott $1,000, and he didn't refuse it." In other words, if the provincial Liberal candidate had taken it, why shouldn't the federal Liberal candidate?

It turned out that she was one of those people who never spend a dime. She lived in a one-room walk-up and literally stuffed her savings into her mattress. Remembering all the tedious cocktail parties and business lunches I had endured to raise much less, I thought her gesture was one of the most touching moments of my entire political career.

If I had to get used to asking people for their money, I also had to get used to asking them to help me secure the Liberal nomination in Rosedale. The first thing was to encourage all my friends and relatives to join the party – and then, in turn, to sign up all their friends and relatives. I shamelessly reached out to my network of connections in the Toronto francophone community. Greg Wong and Adrienne Clarkson's father, Bill Poy, introduced me to the Chinese Canadian community. I hit one really big piece of luck I hadn't foreseen when two Korean Canadian students in my law class got me invited to the large Korean church in the riding. As a result, a substantial number of their community got organized and came to vote for me at the nomination meeting.

My opponents and some of the media accused us of creating "instant Liberals," which was true in that the membership jumped from 300 to 2,500 in just three months. But bringing new people into the party was one of the purposes of the nomination process, and all of them were legitimate voters. In the end, on May 10, 1984, the Rosedale nomination became one of the most hotly contested fights in the country. More than a thousand people packed into a convention room at the Hilton Harbour Castle, a large turnout for downtown Toronto, though hardly comparable to the many thousands who were brought in for the fierce showdowns in the populous suburban ridings. When the dust settled, I was the Liberal candidate.

A month later, as the newly minted Liberal candidate for Rosedale, I went to the national convention in Ottawa to bid farewell to Pierre Trudeau and help elect a new leader. I remember being impressed by the strong list of candidates. I admired what Jean Chrétien had accomplished as Trudeau's minister of justice in fighting the 1980 Quebec referendum and enshrining the Charter of Rights and Freedoms. I liked John Roberts, not least for throwing the best parties with the liveliest band at the convention. I knew Don Johnston as a tax lawyer in Montreal to whom I was remotely connected by marriage through a cousin of mine. Though Mark MacGuigan had taught me jurisprudence at law school, I had a very awkward moment when he sat me down on the bed in the inner sanctum of his hospitality suite to ask for my support. "Sorry," I said, "I think that John Turner is the right choice this time."

I had known John for a long time as a smart, gregarious, highly accomplished person, a devoted Canadian and one of the brightest lights of his generation. His stepfather, Frank Ross, a Vancouver businessman and lieutenant-governor of British Columbia, had been a good friend of Dad's. As a student at UBC, John had dated my sister Jane. When we were both practising law in Toronto, I saw him fairly regularly, having lunch at the York Club or at social events around town, and I always found him easy to talk with despite his somewhat intimidating reputation. I didn't know him well, however, and never had any professional contact with him. Nor was he involved in any way with my decision to enter politics or my run for the nomination in Rosedale. Yet I trusted that the party was in good hands when he was elected our leader and when, only ten days after being sworn in as prime minister, he called an early election for September 4, 1984.

THE ROSEDALE RIDING, later renamed Toronto Centre, was among the most diverse constituencies in Canada, almost unmatched except for a couple in downtown Vancouver and Montreal. It was divided in every way imaginable by Bloor Street, a major east-west artery that runs through the city centre. North of Bloor, you had the solid, middle-class houses of Moore

Park and the tree-lined, undulating streets of Rosedale proper, one of Toronto's wealthiest neighbourhoods and home to some of the most successful people in Canada. South of Bloor, you had the high-rise apartments of St. James Town, one of the most densely populated places in North America, with twelve thousand residents from around the globe, including the Philippines, South Korea, China, Sri Lanka, and the Republic of the Congo. We calculated that fifty-five languages were spoken in St. James Town when I first ran, and sixty-seven by the time of my last election in 2006. Farther south was Regent Park and Moss Park – 1950s experiments in subsidized housing, heavily immigrant, and poor. Then, in the far south, the demographics went upscale again, with the first of the many massive condominium towers going up near the business core and along the shore of Lake Ontario.

To the east was Cabbagetown, a gentrified neighbourhood of single-family homes, popular with university types who tended to vote NDP, and an Aboriginal population, located around the Toronto Council Fire Native Cultural Centre at the corner of Dundas and Parliament Streets. In the middle were Ryerson students, new condo dwellers, and the burgeoning gay village around Church and Wellesley Streets that was – and still is – an important component of the riding. To the west were several large student residences belonging to the University of Toronto, next to the Ontario Legislature on Queen's Park. The riding included Canada's most important financial district, six major hospitals, Ryerson, George Brown College, and two University of Toronto colleges. With so many students among the voters, the question of whether an election was held during the school year or during the summer break could be of critical importance. I always found that St. Michael's College tended to vote Liberal, whereas just around the corner Victoria College often went Conservative. The students at Trinity College, my alma mater, lived in an adjacent riding, so they were never put to the test.

Of equal significance, I came to appreciate, were the eighteen housing co-operatives, the largest concentration anywhere in Canada. They were scattered all over the riding and had a variety of types, mixtures, and complicated funding arrangements – some federally financed, some provincially financed, some municipally financed, some for persons with disabilities or AIDS, some subsidized for lower-income families, some not subsidized at all. Though the co-operative movement is a powerful, well-organized political force in Canada, I was told not to waste my time canvassing in the co-ops because, historically, they had always been NDP strongholds. In time, however, I established a credible connection through a common involvement with international issues, particularly South Africa, and a host of humanitarian organizations. "We should work together on federal funding," I said, and we eventually did.

In my first election the riding extended along Queen Street East to the Leslie Street Spit, where only a few hundred people lived. When I first saw this strip on the map in the campaign office, it looked like a forgotten outpost, and I couldn't figure out what it had to do with Rosedale. When I went there and started knocking on doors, however, I discovered that almost every resident was a fervent Liberal supporter from Portugal. "Mr. Trudeau brought us to Canada," they said. "We're for you 100 percent." I never did find out how that little enclave got attached to my riding, and it was gone by the next election, but it turned out to be one of my very few good polls in 1984.

FROM THE VERY START of that first campaign, as it had been for me as a lawyer, I was particularly interested in international affairs. One of the reasons I ran for office was that I was aware of the increasing impact of Canada's international obligations on our domestic laws and, in turn, on our whole society. How many MPs understood that, how many journalists, how many voters? By treaty and association, we were being integrated into a new global system without any real debate in the House of Commons or in the media. My contribution, as I saw it, was to call attention to the new reality.

"I'm interested in politics from an international dimension," I told my campaign committee at our first meeting. But the general reaction was that nobody cared, except perhaps for a few CEOs in Rosedale or professors in Cabbagetown. I was constantly told by all the experts that no one in St. James Town or Regent Park really gave a damn about world affairs as an issue. Yet that wasn't my experience. South of Bloor, in fact, many immigrants saw almost every issue from an international dimension. I could hardly walk into an apartment or get into a taxi without being drawn into a debate about Serbia, North Korea, Eritrea, Pakistan, or Sri Lanka. And whenever I mentioned to a constituent from Turkey or Afghanistan that I had driven through their country in 1960, they wanted to engage in long conversations about what I had seen or how things had changed.

Just as international norms were finding their way into domestic legislation, so international issues were making an impact on domestic politics. Tamil Canadians were worried about what was going on in Sri Lanka. Jewish constituents were concerned about Canada's policy toward Israel. The Eritrean and the Ethiopian communities imported the debates that were current in their homelands. Many Sikhs in Canada dreamed of an independent Khalistan. One day the Armenian genocide sprang up as a Canadian political issue, leading to a resolution in the House of Commons. Why? What jurisdictional concern did Canada have about something that had happened in present-day Turkey in 1915? None, but a large group of Armenians who had migrated to Canada were now voting citizens, and they wanted their MPs to acknowledge this tragedy from their past. Nor were diaspora politics confined to Canada. The Cuban exile community in Florida had an inordinate influence in Washington, DC, for example, and the Indo-Pakistani conflict played out in constituencies across England.

I remember talking with a French politician shortly after the 2001 terrorist attack on the World Trade Center in New York City. There was already speculation that the United States might retaliate by invading Iraq. "I don't think France will participate in that," he said. "There are 5 million Muslims living in France. We are not about to get involved in a war in the Middle East – it's that simple." It wasn't that simple, of course, and there came a time when France could not avoid becoming embroiled in the affairs of Islamic countries.

It might not have been the case in every Canadian riding, but in Rosedale there was a serendipitous alignment of international issues, both as an academic concept and in the real lives of ordinary voters. Because so many constituents had come from nastier, more oppressive societies, they were concerned about human rights, valued international codes of standards and conduct, appreciated free trade and free markets, and wanted to make Canada even better. Later, whenever I attended international gatherings either as chair of the Standing Committee on Foreign Affairs (SCFAIT) or as foreign minister and found myself seated beside representatives from Europe, Asia, Africa, or the Americas, I tried to make a connection through someone in my riding who had a difficult personal history or relatives left behind. "They expect us to work together to make a better world," I often said.

In other words, far from having to reinvent myself from being a professor of international law, I found that my knowledge and experience were major selling points as a local politician. In turn, the voters' own knowledge and experience helped me to see how the issues I had been teaching affected individuals I never would have met otherwise. That made me a better lawyer and a better human being – relevant in ways that surprised everybody, including myself. What I had been teaching the students – how to create an international legal regime to make a safer and more prosperous world – turned out to have genuine appeal.

Of course, lecturing to a class of captive students wasn't exactly the skill set I needed to win votes in Regent Park; nor did my only previous political experience – running to be head of arts at Trinity – serve me all that well in campaigning to become a member of Parliament. Unlike many of the MPs I later met who were happier on the hustings than sitting in the House of Commons, I never really got to love election campaigns. I felt comfortable enough giving speeches and conveying ideas, but I found it awkward to go up to strangers and ask for their vote. Though my campaign manager instructed me to ask point-blank, I resisted making that kind of abrupt appeal. The best I could do was to say, "I hope you'll consider voting for me."

I also had trouble adjusting to the instruction not to waste too much time talking policy. In the early days I naively assumed that was the whole purpose of a campaign. But the tried-and-true technique was to meet as many people as possible in the shortest amount of time – introduce myself, distribute my material, ask for their vote, and move on. Whenever I got absorbed in a conversation for more than two minutes, someone on my team would start yanking at my sleeve, saying, "Come on, you've got fifty other apartments to do in the next twenty minutes." For most voters the two minutes may have been enough, and maybe even more than they wanted, but I often felt caught in a tug-of-war between making contact in a meaningful way and pressing on efficiently. Once, when asked about my position on abortion, I'd launched into a long, involved answer about court decisions and trimester frameworks when my daughter, Katy, said, "Stop being so dense, Dad, you're pro-choice."

I reconciled myself to the process as I came to realize that you can make a psychic connection in a few seconds. It's uncanny – a handshake, a look in the eye, a word or two, that's usually all that was needed to let people gauge if they could trust me, and for me to gauge if I had their vote or not. At one door a guy threatened to sic his dog on me. "I've got a pit bull with AIDS," he said, "and he's going to bite you 'cause you're a Liberal." Another time a big dog bit my hand in Regent Park, without any prompting at all. Most times, however, I found dogs a good way to make contact with their owners. I'd ask about their breed, pat them on the head, comment on how nice they were, and then ask the person holding the leash to vote Liberal. I had a personal theory that, if you like a dog, its owner will like you. My son, Patrick, used to joke that I knew the dogs in the riding better than I knew my human constituents.

Going into the campaign, I was told that people north of Bloor would be more polite than those to the south. The reverse was true. North of Bloor tended to be Conservative territory, and I came to see some streets in Moore Park and Rosedale as what Cathy called the Heart of Darkness, where I never got a single vote. Well-to-do householders who looked like perfect gentlemen on the surface shouted at me irascibly to "get off the porch, you goddamn Liberal." "You'll have better luck if you go around to the back door," Don Macdonald advised me. "You'll usually get a more sympathetic reception there." Eventually even Cathy refused to canvass north of Bloor – it simply wasn't as rewarding or as much fun as south of Bloor. She and Adrienne Clarkson preferred to campaign in Moss Park or South Regent. "What are you two doing walking around here?" they were often asked. "It's not safe, you know, even during the day." But nobody ever bothered them; in fact, they were welcomed.

One day Anne Cools took me down to the strip bars along Dundas Street East. "You have to go and talk to these people, Bill," she said. "They vote too." But when she saw a young girl working the streets, she created a loud scene. "How old are you, young lady? You shouldn't be here. This is disgraceful." Within minutes we were surrounded by a bunch of pimps who threatened to beat us up if we didn't take our pamphlets and vanish. Another time, out canvassing with Patrick, we dutifully made our way into a derelict building that turned out to be a house of ill repute. "What the hell," I said, "let's check it out. You never know where you might get a vote." But it soon became clear that these constituents were more interested in something other than voting.

Sometimes I campaigned with Iris Owen, a peppy little Englishwoman who went out for hours on end knocking on doors. It was as hot as hell in Regent Park and Moss Park, where there was no air conditioning in the old buildings. If I heard Iris say from down the corridor, "This one's for you, Bill," I knew I was likely to encounter a semi-dressed or even stark naked man who had left his door open, trying to get a breeze circulating through his apartment. Another time, out with Patrick, the door was opened by a young woman wearing a riding cap and holding a crop. "Oh, do you ride?" I asked naively. Over her shoulder I saw three men in her bed. She invited us to join them, but Patrick moved us along quite quickly.

Campaigning was always full of surprises. I was handing out pamphlets along a stretch of Wellesley near Parliament Street, now increasingly gentrified but in those days mostly rundown rooming houses, when I was approached by a resident of a hostel for reformed alcoholics and the destitute. "Your cousin is one of the nuns in charge of my place," he said. My cousin? A nun! That's impossible, I thought: Dad had been raised a Protestant, and Mother was a virulent anti-Catholic. But, sure enough, as I discovered the next day, Dad's brother Fred had a daughter Leona, a wonderful woman who had converted to Rome and joined the Sisters of St. Joseph. I had never heard of her, let alone met her, until then. I was delighted personally, but my organizers were even more thrilled politically. With a Catholic nun as a cousin in the riding, they imagined my making inroads into a whole new community.

If north of Bloor Street was historically a fight between the Liberals and the Conservatives, south of Bloor was always a fight between the Liberals and the NDP. This time, however, the Conservatives had a star candidate, David Crombie. Formerly the "tiny perfect mayor" of Toronto, he had already won the riding three times. Personally charming, politically popular, a Red Tory, an excellent Cabinet minister in Joe Clark's government, David had the ability to reach across traditional party lines. And he had all the advantages of incumbency. I must have been crazy to imagine I could beat him, but what did I know in those days? No matter how tough you believe a boxing match is going to be, you enter the ring full of energy and hope – until you get slugged in the nose.

The city loved David Crombie, and he worked hard to earn its love. At one point my campaign manager said to me, "You have to get to know Regent Park and, more important, get known there. I'm putting you in Regent Park for three weeks, and don't come back until you've knocked on every door in every building." I did as I was told, and I still remember traipsing down those corridors with the smells of exotic foods adding to the tropical effect of that summer campaign. But what drove me really crazy was when people said, "Oh, the mayor was just here," or "Nice of you to come by, but Crombie was here a week ago," or "Who the hell are you, Mr. Johnny Come Lately? Crombie's already been and gone." He was like the Scarlet Pimpernel, here, there, everywhere. Eventually I realized that, while I was spending day after day knocking on doors, he just had to walk into the courtyard, blow a few kisses, and have everyone voting Tory. My first run at public office was game-over before it even started.

I might have had a fighting chance if the Liberals' national campaign had been going better. In any election, the literature tells us, the results are about 60 percent the party, 30 percent the leader, and only 10 percent the candidate. If the candidate stays a while, and builds a good reputation, he or she might be able to have a greater impact. In my case, as a neophyte, I probably had less than 10 percent. I was a cog in a machine, and the machine was severely broken.

As a newcomer, I followed the national campaign without ever feeling a part of it. It was like some large, threatening monster let loose across the country, and my only goal was to figure out a way of not getting trampled by it. I watched the news and learned along with everyone else that the Liberal organization was in a total shambles. It started off with the decision to replace Trudeau's key strategists with Turner's new team. Things got so bad that the veterans had to be brought back from exile in mid-course, but by then it was too late. Turner had emerged rusty after nearly a decade out of politics. He had been wounded in the bitter leadership campaign against Jean Chrétien, and during the TV debates he stumbled over the issue of Trudeau's last-minute patronage appointments. The Liberals had been in power for twenty of the previous twenty-one years, and the economy was hurting, with interest rates above 20 percent and unemployment at 12 percent. Brian Mulroney, whom I had known socially through Yves Fortier when we were all young lawyers hanging around the bar in Place Ville Marie, was about to make a historic breakthrough for the Tories in Quebec as a fluently bilingual native son. Frankly, however, David Crombie would have won Rosedale no matter what happened at the national level. Mine was considered such a lost cause that, near the end, the party decided to dispatch a bunch of my best volunteers – "my tigers," as I called them – to help John Turner win his seat in the neck-and-neck contest in Vancouver Quadra.

On election day, September 4, 1984, I dashed around the riding offering words of encouragement and thanks to the hundreds of volunteers who were working hard to get out our vote and scrutinize the ballots. I got home around eight o'clock, just as the polls were closing in Ontario. I was about to pour myself a stiff Scotch when the phone rang. It was our friend Linda L'Aventure, calling from her house in Grand Manan, New Brunswick. "Oh, Bill, I'm so sorry," she said.

"Sorry about what?"

"About losing the election."

"Don't be ridiculous," I said. "They've hardly even begun to count the votes." But she was right. With only three polls reporting, the CBC had projected Crombie as the winner in Rosedale. In the end, I got exactly the same percentage of the vote in my riding as the Liberals got nationally – a mere 27 percent. After months of hard effort, I hadn't influenced the result one way or the other.

IN HINDSIGHT, LOSING the 1984 election made me better prepared for a life in politics than I would have been otherwise. I made a win-win deal with Rob Prichard, the new dean of the University of Toronto's Faculty of Law, whereby, in return for half salary, he cut my course load in half and compressed it into one term. Though I ended up doing a lot more for the law school than was now expected of me, I was freed for eight months of the year to do other things. I taught at the Université de Montréal and at McGill, worked on the UN trade-law negotiations, and took on some interesting jobs in international arbitration from Alabama to Mexico.

One time I was sent to New York City to work on a contract dispute between Giorgio Armani and its US distributor, during which the Italian aristocrat representing the design label took offence when the American lawyer referred to the "clothes" in question. "We are not talking about clothes; we are talking about fashion," he declared haughtily. "Clothes are only to protect you from the environment. Fashion is about power, desire, sex."

In truth, despite my family background, a few directorships, and my legal career at Fasken's, I didn't really fit in as a Bay Street lawyer. I knew many business leaders and establishment figures, and I had access to them if needed. But neither Cathy nor I were socially ambitious, and our weekends at the farm and summers in Corsica put us at a distance as well. Given a choice, we invariably preferred to read a book, see a play, or prepare a simple meal with the children and old friends.

At this point, however, I wanted to become more knowledgeable about the practice of trade and commerce, not just the theory. I got more involved with Graymont, the family investment company that my father had founded in 1948, which deepened my grasp of finance and management at the same time that it tightened the bonds to my large, loud, opinionated, witty, and remarkably close-knit clan of brothers and sisters. I certainly wouldn't have come to know them as well, particularly the ones in Vancouver and Montreal, if not for our regular board meetings, which were serious, sometimes argumentative affairs followed by hours of funny stories and tall tales over dinner and drinks. I served as a director of Scott's Hospitality, which owned restaurants, hotels, and a bus company, where I learned from such successful entrepreneurs as George Gardiner, Jim Gillies, David Beatty, and Tony Arrell. As the only independent director on Crédit Lyonnais Canada and chair of its audit committee, I gained an insight into the world of banking regulation and loan-to-capital ratios. That helped me later, when, as an MP, I walked into meetings with the superintendent of financial institutions, the president of Export Development Canada, and other government officials.

From time to time, as well, I gave public speeches and media interviews on international issues. One high-profile event occurred when I agreed to participate in a debate with Glenn Babb, South Africa's outspoken ambassador to Canada, on January 31, 1986. Babb had created a firestorm by criss-crossing Canada and saying that our Aboriginal policies were no better than apartheid. Despite the myriad problems with those policies, however, no rational person could equate them with the overtly racist laws and gross violations of basic human rights then in effect in South Africa. As a result of protests that had prevented him from speaking at Hart House, university policy required that he be provided with another opportunity to speak. I was asked by the Hart House Debates Committee there and a group of law students led by Tony Clement, later a provincial and federal Conservative Cabinet minister, if I would take on the ambassador publicly at the Faculty of Law.

We actually had two debates. The first, which Patrick dubbed "The Babb and Blab Show," was hosted by a local radio station. It ended with Babb's quoting, for no obvious reason other than his flair for the dramatic, the famous line from Shelley's poem "Ozymandias," "Look on my works, ye Mighty, and despair!" Not to be outdone, I responded just as irrelevantly, "The lone and level sands stretch far away."

"Oh," said Babb, piling stupidity upon arrogance, "I've never met a Canadian who ever knew any poetry before."

The next day was more serious. In fact, the ambassador was escorted into the law school's Moot Court Room by two Mounties, who had instructed him to wear a bulletproof vest. I hadn't been told to wear anything special, so I was surprised and alarmed when I found this out. We went at each other like two gladiators, though toward the end it was often hard for us to hear each other over the shouting of the hundreds of protesters that had gathered outside and had begun pounding on the doors. No one could have predicted then the dramatic speed with which South African apartheid would be dismantled or that, as an MP twelve years later, I would be invited to join Nelson Mandela as he opened a school in Regent Park that had been renamed in his honour.

Meanwhile, I kept working the riding. For all its frustrations, I decided I liked politics, and I particularly liked Rosedale south of Bloor. The people and the problems were interesting, and I believed more than ever that I had a contribution to make if I had a second run. Whether I could win was another question. However, nobody blamed me for losing to David

Crombie, especially given the Liberal Party's national campaign, and I went unchallenged for the nomination for the next election.

"Okay," I said to my riding association, "we're going to be active from the start, we're going to reach out to the various communities right away, and we're going to begin organizing now. People north of Bloor tend to vote Conservative because that's the way they and most of the people they know have always voted. Their minds are made up. People south of Bloor can be swayed by personal contact and by our presence in the community. That's where we can make a difference as individuals, so that's where we're going to focus our energies."

The idea was to build a brand by doing things. Because the riding was so complex and diversified, we had to examine each community individually to see how we could earn credibility in it. The riding association raised money to buy hockey equipment for kids in Regent Park. We supported school events and multicultural groups. We got heavily involved with the gay community, which was then in the throes of the AIDS epidemic, the bathhouse raids by the Toronto police, and a host of legal issues. We worked with leaders in the Filipino, Tamil, and Somali communities on refugee and citizenship matters. In some cases these activities even transcended their origins in competitive partisanship when the cause was important. We worked with Michael Meighen, a Conservative senator, to launch a program in which privileged students from Upper Canada College shared homework, life experiences, and hockey equipment with inner-city children at Winchester School – a meaningful interaction for everyone involved. We joined with John McFadden, a prominent Tory in the riding, to actively support Spiros Papathanasakis in operating the Cabbagetown Youth Centre, off Parliament Street. Like-minded souls from every party used to drop into the Cabbagetown Community Arts Centre, run by David Blackmore with the enthusiastic participation of Dave and Diane Broadfoot, and we raised money to help Ken Bhagan organize a steel band at the St. Jamestown Youth Centre.

The election was called for November 21, 1988. Though I knew it would be a tough battle, I had more reason for hope than in 1984. For starters, and perhaps most important, David Crombie had decided to leave politics. He was replaced as the Conservative candidate by David MacDonald, a genial Red Tory and former MP who was in many ways a perfect fit for the riding – except that he was from Prince Edward Island. As I knew from my nomination battle against Gerry Doucet, voters usually don't like candidates parachuting in from on high. Second, after four years in office, Brian Mulroney and his government were unpopular and scandal-ridden. Finally, John Turner had improved his leadership skills and mounted a vigorous campaign.

The wild card was the Free Trade Agreement (FTA) with the United States that Mulroney had signed the previous January, though it had yet to be implemented by Parliament. On the surface, it was just another of the many bilateral or multilateral deals by which countries were building highly sophisticated integrated models to liberalize the movement of their goods, their services, and sometimes even their people. After Europe led the way in creating a bigger, more secure market with binding rules and effective courts, North America, South America, and Asia followed, though none went as far as the European Union. To some extent, these free-trade blocs were seen as a temporary measure until the slow, cumbersome rounds of the GATT finally produced a global regime with teeth.

The FTA revealed for all to see the degree to which economic globalization and foreign obligations were cutting into Canada's national sovereignty and domestic policies. The intensity of the debate offered dramatic evidence of the relevance of international issues and even international law to our local politics. It ignited more passion and analysis than almost any election issue since 1911, when Laurier lost amid fears that Canada would be sucked into the United States. Mulroney barely contained the backlash by those who feared the loss of Canadian jobs and Canadian culture. "Don't tell me the average voter isn't interested in the world beyond local politics," I said afterward. "Canadians fought a whole election over an international trade agreement – and I've got the scars to prove it."

I have always been on the side of free trade, whether with the Americans or anybody else. Everything I had taught, every case I had fought, convinced me that the lowering of tariff and non-tariff barriers was good for the world economy in general and for the Canadian economy in particular. The Royal Commission on the Economic Union and Development Prospects for Canada, headed by Donald Macdonald, Trudeau's former finance minister and the one-time MP for Rosedale, came to the same persuasive conclusion. In fact, my good friend Gerry Godsoe, a UCC Old Boy, Halifax lawyer, and executive director of the commission, had invited me in 1982 to be its counsel, and I was initially very interested. But Frank Iacobucci talked me out of it. "Bill," he said, "nobody's going to take you seriously as a law professor around here if you keep running off. You've only been here a couple of years, and now you want to take a leave of absence." So I didn't pursue the offer, which was no doubt for the best because the commission didn't report until 1985 – by which time the Conservatives were in office.

I was in an awkward position, accordingly, when John Turner announced that the cornerstone of the 1988 Liberal election campaign would be our party's opposition to the Free Trade Agreement. Though it fell within my area of expertise, I was too far down on the totem pole to have any impact on the development of the party platform; nor do I recall any major discussions about it at our policy conferences. Furthermore, once a campaign begins, there's always a disconnect between the election headquarters and the candidates. Campaigns create their own issues, their own momentum. The people on the ground wake up to discover that the leader made an important policy announcement on TV the night before, and they spend the rest of the day defending the party position on doorsteps and in the media. If you're not in Ottawa or on the national tour, you have no influence. In the middle of the fray, no one would have the time or the interest to phone Bill Graham and ask for his opinion.

There was, however, a significant flaw in Mulroney's deal that enabled me to reconcile my own intellectual position with my party's political position quite comfortably. Though I had no quarrel with the principles embedded in the FTA, the devil was in its details, especially with regard to the protection of Canadian culture and the lack of adequate dispute mechanisms. If the Americans were to subsidize some of their industries or penalize some of ours unfairly, what recourse would we have under the agreement? We could take the United States to the GATT, or we could use the FTA arbitration panels set up to deal with such issues. Neither was going to work, in my opinion, because I didn't think that the Americans would accept any really genuine, binding arbitral decision process.

My reservations were based on two decades of study, practice, and teaching in the field of international trade law. If you're going to have economic integration, you'll need an institutional framework to oversee it. The tighter the integration, the more sophisticated that institutional framework has to be. The Europeans understood that when they established a customs union, common institutions, and a real court to make their free trade work. But the Americans would never agree to a similar framework in North America: they were not willing to give up that much sovereignty. Nor were we, despite the fact that Canada needed those protections more than the United States did. As I said to my students, if you put the Canada-US relationship on a graph of one to ten, it would score about seven in terms of economic integration, but only about three in terms of political integration. The result was a North American model with inadequate institutional mechanisms to protect our interests. Given the asymmetry, the most powerful guy usually rules.

During the election campaign, I made one relatively minor mistake that would have been hilarious if it hadn't been so embarrassing. In an attempt to be hip in the pre-Facebook, pre-Twitter world of modern technology, my team decided to produce and distribute thousands of copies of a little plastic record – an idea we picked up from Ian Scott, who had successfully used it in his provincial campaign. The record looked cheap, but believe me, it wasn't. It came in a sleeve with my picture on the front and some campaign information on the back, and when voters put it on their turntables, they heard a piece of stirring introductory music followed by a message from me denouncing the Mulroney Tories, the government scandals, the Free Trade Agreement, and the condo towers going up along the waterfront. Much to my chagrin, however, the records had "Made in the USA" stamped clearly on them. Both the Tories and the New Democrats made much hay with that at the all-candidates' meetings. Although I don't think this promotion affected the election results one iota, it completely boomeranged as a crowd-pleasing gimmick. I went from feeling proud to feeling stupid in an instant.

Meanwhile, the Conservatives came up with a better idea. They sent out thousands of letters to households north of Bloor about the importance of the Free Trade Agreement, which were "personally signed" by a machine in Brian Mulroney's headquarters. All at once I was being stopped on the street by people telling me they had just received a personal letter from the prime minister, and what did I think of that? I couldn't believe they had fallen for it. "Yeah," I would say flippantly, "it's amazing how he found the time to write to you and several thousand other people around here while running the country and conducting an election campaign." But it was hopeless. North of Bloor was looking for a reason to vote Tory, and this "personal" letter was certainly effective.

In addition, I had one consequential factor working against me. In those days the sitting MP had the right to nominate the returning officer, and because the Conservatives held the riding, they had nominated a woman who was a well-known Conservative supporter. Part of her job was to get the voters' names on the enumeration list. Not a single person north of Bloor was left off the list, but I heard many complaints from south of Bloor. "You have to understand, Bill," she told me. "Our enumerators are having a lot of difficulty getting into those buildings in Regent Park and St. James Town."

I had a fierce argument about it with my own campaign manager, Tim Murphy, a bright young lawyer who subsequently became an Ontario MPP and Prime Minister Paul Martin's chief of staff. "We're not getting enumerated south of Bloor, Tim, and that is going to be a problem," I said. "I think we should send a couple of dozen of our campaign workers to help with the enumeration." But Tim thought it was more important for us to get out our campaign literature, and ultimately we decided that we would do our job and let the returning officer do hers. It was a crucial mistake. More than a thousand people reported that they hadn't been able to vote when they showed up at the polls, and three-quarters of these voters were probably ours. Partly as a result of similar situations in ridings across the country, the rules were subsequently changed to allow people to be added to the voters list on election day.

The New Democrats made a strong showing in the riding. They ran a successful national campaign under the leadership of Ed Broadbent and had a dynamic local candidate, Doug Wilson. Doug was an impressive advocate for same-sex rights and for people suffering from AIDS, then a relatively new and terrifying disease. Tragically, the disease would claim Doug himself in 1992, at the age of forty-one.

I was particularly sensitized to the issue of the AIDS crisis by James Thatcher, a smart, energetic young man from Bermuda, who showed up one day and said, "I want to help you get elected, though I'm dying of AIDS and don't have a long time to live." At the time, the nature of the disease and its transmission were not well understood, but Cathy and I trusted James when he told us that it couldn't be passed on by drinking from the same coffee cup or anything like that. He became my principal assistant on the road and was by my side almost every day, driving me to events, fetching me coffee, and charming one and all. Everybody became very fond of him. Before his death in 1993 at the age of thirty-six, he videotaped a dramatic plea for more public and private money for AIDS research and patient care. It made him famous in his last days, and at his request his funeral was a joyous celebration of life. His name, along with the names of too many other friends, appears on the memorial to AIDS victims at the 519 Community Centre on Church Street.

At the start of the campaign, I encountered a mixed message when I knocked on doors: "You're okay, Bill, but I don't think much of your leader." After the televised debate in which Turner launched a vigorous and effective attack on the trade deal and its threat to Canadian sovereignty, the message became "You're okay, Bill, and your leader is terrific." Our team could feel the buzz as we worked the riding, and it felt fantastic. Then, just as quickly, we could feel it fizzle. Two nights before the election, I was out campaigning with Ian Scott in the large apartment buildings on Davisville Avenue. "It's a totally different atmosphere," he observed. "We're not getting the reception we got after the television debate." I felt the same shift of mood at the bus stops in Cabbagetown and the subway entrance at Wellesley and Yonge. A subsequent analysis revealed that we had been losing 1 percent per day in the last week of the campaign. At that rate, if the election had been one day earlier, I would have won by 500 votes. One week later I would have lost by 3,000 votes, and the national party might have been wiped out.

The polls were open until nine o'clock. At about eight Katy, who had returned from Paris with her fiancé, Matthieu Debost, to help in the campaign, said to me, "Dad, we can't do any more. We're exhausted."

"No, come on," I said, "we have to keep going. You never know, one vote could make all the difference." But a half-hour later, completely worn out, Katy and I headed home.

The early returns indicated that I was going to win by a narrow margin. The mood was euphoric at the post-campaign party we held at the Pickle

Barrel restaurant, and I could hardly contain my excitement at the thought of heading for Ottawa. However, the large number of absentee ballots, most of which were cast by Conservative voters, turned the tide against me. I was slightly behind by the time I went to bed but so close that the results had to go to an official judicial recount. After an agonizing and suspenseful wait, it confirmed that I had lost by eighty votes, out of almost fifty-five thousand cast. It was a crushing blow. "Oh, Dad," Katy said, "if we had just kept going." Everyone on the team felt the same way – if only we had done one more poll, if only we had pushed a little harder.

"Guess what, kids?" I told my students the next day. "Eighty votes and you've got me back. If you had campaigned for the Liberals, you would have been rid of me."

Shortly afterward, Cathy and I went to Grand Manan, an island in the Bay of Fundy, to recover. We were staying with our friend Linda L'Aventure, who owned an inn there. One day she said, "There's a large delegation from the People's Republic of China here. They're looking at buying a herring factory or something. Anyway, I've got to serve them lunch, and I'm going crazy." So Cathy and I offered to help.

"What can I do to be useful?" I asked.

"You could clean the fish, that would be great."

I actually knew quite a lot about cleaning fish from my trout-fishing days in British Columbia, so I happily set about gutting some large, smelly halibut out on the lawn. Just then the Chinese delegation arrived, escorted by a Chinese Canadian woman. "Excuse me," she said, "aren't you Bill Graham? I live in Rosedale, and I just voted for you. What are you doing here?"

"Cleaning fish," I replied.

When she told the group that I was a distinguished law professor who had run for the Liberals and lost, they became firmly convinced that this punishment is what happens in a democratic society: run for the wrong party, lose the election, and you're banished to a remote island to work in a kitchen cleaning fish as part of your re-education.

THE CLOSENESS OF THE defeat, coming after so much arduous work with all its highs and lows, left me exhausted, bruised, and unhappy. The campaign and the four years leading up to it took a toll on Cathy and our

children as well. Politics had become a kind of family business, with everyone pitching in from dawn to dark to achieve success, and failure left us
feeling raw and fragile. I remember a woman grabbing me on the street
and saying, by way of encouragement, "There's an old expression, Bill –
'jamais deux sans trois,' never twice without a third." Though I didn't say,
"Never again," it was way too early to think about another run. I needed a
break and some breathing space. Brian Mulroney was secure with a second
majority for another term in office, and nobody in the riding was rushing
to reassess the situation. Or almost nobody.

Not long after the election, Cathy and I were invited to have dinner at
the home of Tom Vegh, an active member of the riding association who
ran an employment bureau that helped people in St. James Town find a
job. In the midst of a pleasant social evening, Tom suddenly said, "Bill,
I've got something to show you." And he pulled out a stack of papers con-
taining a poll-by-poll analysis he had done of the election. The results, he
concluded, proved that I couldn't win Rosedale, because I was a north-of-
Bloor person who would never manage to get enough votes south of Bloor.
Someone who had credibility south of Bloor – someone very much like
him, it seemed – could get voters to flock to the Liberals by the tens of
thousands. Perhaps, he suggested, I might step aside and let him take the
nomination.

"Well, I did reduce the Tories' margin of victory from more than ten
thousand down to eighty," was all I could think to respond.

Cathy left the dinner steaming. "That guy just sandbagged us. He invites
us for a casual dinner and then tries to drive you into saying you're not
going to run again so he can run. Now you'll just have to run again."

"Maybe I don't want to."

"Oh, you will, you must."

I was astonished. Cathy had been incredibly loyal. She had put up with
a lot of garbage and proved an excellent campaigner, not least because of
all her experience in dealing with people as a volunteer with the Junior
League and the Ireland Fund. She was strong, she was good with people,
and she was an astute adviser. But she was also a relatively private, low-
key person who had never been all that keen about my running for public
office in the first place. She thought it was actually quite loopy. Yet here she
was, practically ordering me to run again. So did a lot of other people –

close friends, riding activists, community leaders, and party workers who had been forged into a tight corps by the hardships and friendships of the 1988 campaign. "Come on, Bill," they said, "why throw away the magnificent team you built? You don't want to be a professor all your life. You came so close. Once more into the breach!"

And so I decided I would run once more. "Okay," I said, "but if I'm going to do this again, I've got to improve my chances of winning."

Nobody wants a nomination race if it can be avoided. It's expensive, time consuming, and often divisive. On the other hand, it did have the benefits of mobilizing my troops, testing the depth of my support, and reigniting my competitive spirit. Only Tom opposed me. After waffling for a bit, then manoeuvring behind the scenes, he showed his hand at the annual meeting of the Rosedale riding association when he put forward a slate of candidates to be the executive. I put forward my own slate and won, but we had to work hard to get out the votes. It was like a mini-nomination, because if I had lost control of the executive, I would have lost control of the riding. By the time the actual nomination took place, I was able to trounce him.

If I'd had my druthers, I would have laid back a while and bought time before committing myself. But once forced to commit, I became more active. By now I had some confidence that I knew what I was doing. I understood the importance of polling results as well as of policy speeches. I found a tough, crafty, nuts-and-bolts organizer, Jim Cooper, to be my campaign manager. I sat down with my team and looked at the riding from every angle and with an eye to the gritty details to which I had previously been somewhat indifferent. We figured we had at least two years to get ready. We assumed there would be a change of leadership in the Liberal Party, and we decided there were grounds for real, as opposed to naive, hope if we got out the vote and resolved to win. I was determined to prove to everybody, not least the hundreds of volunteers who were working so hard for my victory, that I wasn't some kind of dilettante playing at politics as if it were a game of polo.

By this point I had also become more active in the national party. As a veteran candidate, I attended all the Liberal conferences and conventions, sat on policy committees, and had the opportunity to build friendships with MPs and executive members in Ontario and Quebec. The party became a new factor in my life, along with my teaching and my business. Consequently, when John Turner announced his resignation in May 1989 and the leadership race began, I was asked if I would chair the all-candidates' debates leading up to the convention in Calgary in June 1990. It was an important role that came with a national profile in the party and the media, higher than I had ever had before. Moreover, the debates were a fascinating process, particularly when watched up close. The best one, in my opinion, was in Yellowknife, partly because it was the first debate but mostly because it was the only one not televised. There was a camaraderie among the contenders, a genuine give-and-take. Afterward, in Vancouver, Toronto, Montreal, and Halifax, there was more heat and less light in the discussion, more open warfare, more playing to the cameras, and more caution, due to the knowledge that any slip-up would be forever recorded.

As the impartial chair, I had to take an oath not to support any candidate. At the time that struck me as a gift from heaven because it meant I didn't have to support any candidate. I had gone to law school with Paul Martin Jr., and we were personal friends in a way I wasn't with the other leading contenders, Jean Chrétien and Sheila Copps. The direction of the race was set fairly early, however, as I noticed the Chrétien forces moving rapidly through the riding associations in Quebec and sewing up their delegates.

If I didn't make any enemies being chair, I didn't make any friends either. I was the arbitrator whom everyone tears to pieces when the negotiations are over. I was neutral Belgium, getting stomped by the boots of clashing armies. At several moments during the debates, I had to smack down all the candidates in turn or tell them their time was up. During the Halifax debate, I interrupted Chrétien in full flight, and when he walked past my table in the restaurant where Cathy and I were having dinner that evening, he gave me a look that caused her to say, "Why do I get the impression that you'll never be in Mr. Chrétien's Cabinet if he wins this thing?"

On another occasion, this time in Montreal, I came to his defence when some of Martin's youth organizers began shouting abuse at him. The party was torn apart over the issue of whether to support the Meech Lake Accord, the package of five constitutional amendments that Mulroney and the ten premiers had initialled on June 3, 1987, but which required ratification by every legislature within three years. Pierre Trudeau had led a fierce battle against the clause that would recognize Quebec as a "distinct society" within the Constitution, arguing that it was a step toward the disintegration of Canada. Martin and Copps defended it as a reasonable and politically necessary concession to Quebecers. Chrétien was caught in the middle, for which he was vilified as a *vendu* by the nationalists and the press in Quebec. At the debate, bizarrely, one young English-speaking Martinite began yelling "Fondue! Fondue!" The noise level was so great that the only way I thought I could restore order was to smack my hand against the microphone. I almost blew out the ears of the poor woman who was doing the simultaneous translation, and she stormed out of her booth, threatening to kill me if I ever did that again.

From an intellectual point of view, I was drawn to Trudeau's stance: a door to separation was being partly opened by the distinct-society clause, and that would present a danger unless it were closed. From the political point of view, however, weren't we better to grab an imperfect thing and try to make it work? Yves Fortier and most of my Quebec university colleagues – or at least the federalist ones – were strong proponents of Meech Lake as the only possible solution to a constitutional war that they had been fighting for decades. They hoped it would mean peace and were bitter when the opportunity was lost. Later, when I was seatmates in the Commons with Elijah Harper, who had single-handedly impeded the accord from passing in the Manitoba Legislature, I told him, "You have no idea how much some of my friends in Quebec resent what you did."

Weighing the pros against the cons, I think that being chair of the debates worked to my advantage. It was like being involved in a national election campaign for the first time: I had never crossed the country so quickly or been on the inside of the hothouse atmosphere of media scrutiny. If it didn't raise my stature in the eye of the general public, it certainly brought me to the attention of senior Liberals. Everywhere we went, I met the most experienced powerbrokers in each region and got known by them. In retrospect I can see that it was the first step in the long transition process of moving up the ranks within the party, from being a failed Toronto candidate to being a national player with potential. As well, it gave me a tremendous education to watch the pros Jean Chrétien, Paul Martin Jr., and Sheila Copps at close hand, how they handled questions, how they dealt with criticism, how people reacted to them – all the little tricks and techniques of being a politician – and I saw how tough these campaigns could be on the families and friends of the candidates. Once the ballots had been counted at the Calgary convention and Chrétien declared the winner, I happened to come upon Paul Martin Sr. sitting by himself in the lobby of the Palliser Hotel and looking forlorn. He knew me as an old friend of Paul's and had been kind enough to invite me to drop by when he was Canada's high commissioner in London. Now I got the sense, talking with him over a drink, of how hurt he felt by his son's defeat, more than by his own three failed attempts to become leader of the Liberal Party.

After Chrétien won the convention and became leader of the Opposition, I paid him a courtesy call in his Wellington Street office, across from the Parliament Buildings. He himself didn't have a seat yet, and I wanted to talk to him about my prospects in Rosedale after losing two elections. This was our first real conversation – amiable, for sure, but with no pleasantries or jokes. I found him intimidating and rather formal in those days – not cold, but workmanlike, tough in a game when you obviously had to be tough. What stood out was how well he knew the system. First elected in 1963 and familiar with every major ministry in Ottawa, he came across as a highly pragmatic doer not given to philosophical musings or agonizing decisions. He intuited by experience what would or wouldn't work.

"You'll have to decide for yourself whether you want to run again," he told me, "and you'll have to deal with the nomination on your own. I'm not going to interfere in nominations. But you'd make a good member of Parliament, so good for you."

I next saw him at the policy conference held in Aylmer, Quebec, in November 1991. Attendance was by invitation only, and a lot of us had waited on pins and needles because receiving an invitation was a sign that the party brass saw you as a player. I found the conference a sincere collective effort to come up with good policy ideas for the really complex issues facing modern society. The discussions were open, the work serious, the exercise useful. It never struck me as stage-managed, though its tilt back toward free trade and its middle-of-the-road economic slant clearly reflected Chrétien's own views. Out of it came the so-called Red Book, the election platform that Chrétien waved proudly at every campaign stop.

In February 1993 Brian Mulroney announced his retirement, and on June 13 the Conservatives elected Kim Campbell as their new leader and, accordingly, the first female prime minister of Canada. I had met her a year earlier at my brother David's fiftieth birthday party in Dorset, England. It was held at the grand country estate of the Hon. Charlotte Townshend, co-master with David of the Cattistock Hunt – a post, he liked to remind me, much more important in the county than that of a mere member of Parliament. Kim, who was Mulroney's minister of justice at the time, knew David from his days on the executive of the BC Progressive Conservative Party, and she flew over for the celebrations.

"Bill," she asked as we danced, "what are your plans for the next election?"

"I'm going to run again for the Liberals in Rosedale."

"You can't be serious?" she said. "Dave MacDonald has it in the bag. Don't waste your time."

She certainly started strong in the polls. Young, bright, and feisty, she attracted a lot of interest and support. But her inexperience soon tripped her up: she made a couple of careless statements, and her team let her down with an attack ad on Chrétien that he was able to turn to his advantage. To my good fortune he came twice to campaign at my side in Rosedale. Campaign managers seem to spend half their lives on the phone, trying to persuade the national organizers to send the leader into their riding, and the fact that we got him twice attested to how key downtown Toronto was seen to the party's prospects for victory. Of course, he stayed for only an hour before being whisked away to half a dozen other ridings, but he brought with him a pack of media and his legendary energy.

Like everyone else, I couldn't help but be impressed by Chrétien's incredible stamina and by his popularity. Whereas I could stand in front of a subway station for hours without being recognized by more than one out of ten passersby, he was instantly recognized everywhere by everyone. Focused on making an impact in the south end of the riding for obvious strategic reasons, we were walking through a throng around St. James Town when a bus pulled up at a nearby stop. "Come on, Bill," he shouted, "let's get on and see who's there." It was total pandemonium. The media scrambled to jump on the bus with us, the driver lost track of who had paid, and Chrétien worked his way to the back shaking hands and making jokes. A few stops later we hopped off. It was chaos but very effective politicking. I wish I had the guts to do that, but only Jean Chrétien could get away with it.

The campaign attracted more press attention than usual because of two of my opponents. One was Doug Henning, a celebrated magician who was running for the Natural Law Party on a platform of world peace through transcendental meditation and yogic flying. He brought out people to our all-candidates' meetings that usually didn't frequent such events. I once ran into my son, Patrick, who had recently completed his master's degree in classics at Dalhousie, and thanked him for coming to show his support. "I didn't come to hear you, Dad," he said. "I came to see Doug Henning." The other high-profile candidate was the NDP's Jack Layton, a municipal councillor at that time. I don't know what made Jack think he could win. The press always called Rosedale a tight three-way race in order to create a story, but in those days the riding swung between the Liberals and the Conservatives. The NDP never came close to victory. A strong Tory could sweep north of Bloor and carry some polls south of Bloor if the NDP and Liberals split the vote, but even a strong New Democrat couldn't win enough north of Bloor to place better than second.

Even if he couldn't muster the votes, Jack got a lot of new support and press attention. The New Democrats even brought in campaign workers from other ridings to help him, and they won the co-ops handily. I got to know him fairly well and liked him. If you rarely come out of an election thinking of your opponents as friends, you certainly get to know their good qualities as well as their flaws. We agreed on many issues and had some good debates, after which he and I would often go for a beer with David MacDonald. I used to tell Jack about my two losses and assure him that he would be elected someday, though never in my riding. In fact, Jack was to come in fourth, behind the Reform Party candidate.

As election day approached, I had a new and very pleasant feeling: I could tell from the reaction at the doorsteps and the subway stations that I was likely to win. The atmosphere was totally different from my previous runs. The national election team worked well, the Red Book of policy promises resonated with the voters, and Jean Chrétien proved a flawless campaigner. On October 25, 1993, the Liberals won a majority government, including all but one seat in Ontario. More startling was what happened to the Opposition. The mighty Progressive Conservative Party was reduced to just two MPs. Out of its ruin emerged two regional protest parties of almost equal weight – the neo-conservative Reform, with its base in Western Canada, and the pro-separatist Bloc Québécois in Quebec (winning almost three-quarters of the seats in the province). The NDP tumbled from forty-four MPs to a mere nine. My own victory was declared early in the evening, though it didn't sink in until David MacDonald came over to our election-night party at a pub on Carlton Street and graciously conceded defeat. Having lost twice myself, I had some sense of how he must have felt.

Many people came up to me and said, "Bill, it's great you won, you've certainly paid your dues." But I never perceived the process as paying dues. It was more like mountain climbing: you start off full of hope and energy, take one step after another as the slope gets steeper, reach one ledge, and see the next ledge even higher. There was no ten-year plan for success, no expectation that I deserved to win just because this election was my third attempt. People saw me working hard – and they like to reward hard work – but in all honesty I rarely found it disagreeable. It was often fun and always interesting, especially south of Bloor. Frankly, if the riding had consisted only of north of Bloor, it certainly wouldn't have had the same appeal. It wouldn't have been any more exciting than going to the law school every day or working for a downtown firm.

Getting elected to the House of Commons was a hugely important event in my life. I was honoured and thrilled to be given an opportunity to participate in the political life of my country. And, on a personal level, it felt like the first major achievement I had ever earned on my own. Of course, I had earned the gold medal at law school and a place with Fasken's on my own efforts, but I had been given so many advantages in life – education, money, connections – that I usually felt I was getting a free ride. This achievement was different. Nobody handed me a seat in the Commons; nobody smoothed the way. I did it by myself, with the help of my wife and the team I had put together, and that made victory all the sweeter. Even if I had never become a Cabinet minister, the fourteen years I spent as a member of Parliament turned out to be an incredibly satisfying experience – and for that I feel truly fortunate.

PART 2:
FOREIGN MATTERS

5

HOUSE DUTY

The day after the election I felt like the dog that has finally caught the bus: Now what? The phone was ringing off the hook, with the old pros telling me to get to Ottawa as quickly as possible to grab a good office and butter up the whip. But what was a good office? Who was the whip? I was entering a completely new world, which felt something like my first days as an eleven-year-old new boy at Upper Canada College. And it quickly became clear that, as a freshly elected backbencher, I was at the bottom of a very complicated food chain with an awful lot to learn.

Take the apparently simple question of the office. As a lawyer or a professor, I never cared much about the size or location of where I worked. Big, small, next to the boss, on a corner – it didn't really matter as long as I had a desk, a chair, some shelves, and a place to hang my hat and coat. In Ottawa, however, it became a very big deal, and there were sharp elbows in the race to secure the biggest and best. The closer you are to the House of Commons, the faster you can get to a vote when the bell rings. Very near, you can dally ten minutes and saunter downstairs. Very far, you have to drop everything and run to catch the small green shuttle bus. But a backbencher isn't likely to bag an office near the Commons in the Centre Block unless it's a cubbyhole. To get one of a decent size, you have to accept being put at a distance – unless you're able to persuade the party whip to give you an office in the West Block. The insiders know what a neophyte does not: the West Block has a tunnel under Parliament Hill, which means no raincoat, no snow boots, no waiting for the shuttle, just a brisk three-minute sprint.

Too naive to campaign hard for the best location, I was sent along Wellington Street to the seventh floor of the Confederation Building – the very top except for a kind of roof-top attic to which my friend John Godfrey was exiled. It was fine for a while, but as I rose in the ranks and was given more responsibilities, I needed more space for meetings, staff, visitors, documentation, and so forth. My own elbows sharpened with each passing year, and over the course of a decade I was able to assemble quite a sizable suite of offices in the West Block to accommodate what one government whip joked was my "mini-foreign ministry."

It was a thrill, of course, to walk into the House of Commons as an elected member of Parliament for the first time. In this chamber, every prime minister since 1922 has risen to speak, governments have fallen in dramatic votes of non-confidence, and Winston Churchill delivered one of his most famous wartime speeches. It is where the business of the country gets done and where the representatives of the people ultimately cast their ayes or nays. Less certain, however, is whether the debates that take place within its walls have much influence over those votes. MPs rarely change their minds because of something said on the floor of the Commons.

In fact, the chamber is virtually empty for much of the day. A certain number of MPs from all parties have House duty, which required them to be there for a quorum call or a vote, but even then they were more often on the phone or doing business in the lobby than sitting in their seats. Whenever I made a speech as a backbencher, it was usually before 8 or 10 of the 295 MPs, and those who did show up to serve as cheerleaders for a minister or because of an issue of particular concern to their constituents rarely lingered once the debate was over. I never became an expert in the arcane parliamentary rules, so I was generally mystified by all the complex procedures. In fact, because my seat was at the back corner of the last row, I could often sneak out behind the curtain to get some real work done.

What made the House such a waste of time was the lack of any real discussion. In previous times, nobody was allowed to read a speech or even a comment. I soon discovered, however, that MPs generally arrived with prepared copy and often played shamelessly to the TV cameras, as if the real audience weren't in the chamber but back in their ridings. The primary purpose of these debates wasn't to convince or elucidate but to fill the time allotted for the passage of the bill, and we frequently spoke at length on subjects we knew nothing about. Though there was nothing procedurally illegitimate or intellectually dishonest about this practice, it was in no way conducive to a lively, enlightened debate. Worse, the government MPs on House Duty sometimes just read speeches that had been prepared by officials in the department overseeing the legislation before the House. This, obviously, was helpful if you didn't know much about the subject of the bill. The first time I delivered such a speech, I got a note from David Kilgour, the deputy Speaker whom I had known at law school, which chided me severely: "Bill, I never thought that you, of all people, would stoop to such a disgusting practice." When I became a minister, however, I had no choice but to read speeches and statements that had been researched and polished by my staff. The files were so varied and complex that there was barely time to absorb the material and rarely time to craft something that was really mine.

One of the best debates in the Commons I ever participated in took place by accident when a small group of us were stuck on House duty one Friday afternoon and assigned to consider the protection of Canadian culture through budgetary measures and subsidies. Instead of the usual political posturing, we slid into a genuine conversation about the issue, back and forth, for about three hours. Afterward, one of the Reform members, Herb Grubel, said to me, "I've been here for three years, and this is the first day I've ever enjoyed myself in the House of Commons. Normally it's just somebody shouting at somebody else. This time we actually had a genuine interchange about whether this is a good idea or a bad idea."

In sharp contrast to the routine business, the House came alive during Question Period, which had a dynamic all its own. Despite the gratuitous yelling and juvenile silliness in the background, a certain amount of key information penetrated through the din. Everyone wanted to be there, partly to support the team, partly for the sheer thrill of it. Similarly, all of us were drawn into the House whenever there was the promise of a major historical moment. A Speech from the Throne, a statement by the prime minister, a budget presentation by the minister of finance, and the national unity debates were obvious occasions, but I also went to listen to Lucien

Bouchard, Lloyd Axworthy, Charles Caccia, and a few others on both sides of the floor who had either a commanding presence or something meaningful to say. On those occasions I felt reassured that I was participating in a serious exercise vital to the fate of the nation, not some vain delusion of importance. Jean Chrétien stood far above everybody else as a presence in the House. His skill wasn't classical oratory, but he always expressed himself with such plain sense, sharp wit, deep experience, and force of character that he was a unique and powerful speaker. You always knew that he spoke for himself, not as a mouthpiece for some official, and you always knew where he stood. Paul Martin's style as a parliamentary debater was different from Chrétien's but effective in its own way. He put an enormous amount of effort into polishing his speeches, and it showed.

For all the talk of his benevolent dictatorship, most Canadians – including most journalists – never understood the deference that Chrétien showed toward the traditions of the House and the MPs and senators of the Liberal caucus. In fact, he insisted that his ministers show up at caucus meetings as a key part of their job, and he even kept a list of their attendance. Backbenchers could skip caucus without consequence or chat at the rear of the room, but ministers did so at their peril. The prime minister wanted them to listen to every opinion, to hear the complaints about their department, and to endure a scolding if an MP was having trouble getting help to deal with a problem. There was no avoiding anyone here, no staffer keeping charge of the gate, not even a note-taker from the Prime Minister's Office (PMO). The MPs jealously guarded their private time with the prime minister, and they wanted to make their views known to him without any filters.

After a few weeks of wandering around Ottawa in a state of complete bewilderment, I settled into the caucus routine. On Tuesday evening there was a meeting of the Greater Toronto Area caucus at which we MPs discussed the issues we had in common, such as transportation or immigration. Often, like Toronto City Council, we were divided by the tensions between the inner-city ridings and the outer-ring ridings. When the downtown MPs came to defend the co-ops against budget cuts, for example, our suburban colleagues couldn't see why we had made it our number-one priority to bring to the attention of the Cabinet and the prime minister. Subsidized housing and homelessness weren't big issues in their ridings, after all, but that's because, as we often saw it, the suburbs were dumping a lot of their social problems on us. Our constituency offices often had to operate as social agencies because of the number of teenaged kids who were thrown out of their homes for using drugs or were beaten by their fathers for being gay, and who ended up living in the inner city.

At 8:30 on Wednesday mornings, the Ontario, Quebec, Atlantic, and Western caucuses met separately. Again, although the Ontario MPs shared a number of common concerns, it was obvious that the views of Thunder Bay or Cornwall MPs differed from those of Toronto MPs. These diversities were in no way a bad thing. They allowed us to understand differing perspectives, interests, opinions, and solutions. A rural MP had reasons to oppose gun control that an urban MP did not, for example; and whereas I could bike around my riding in a matter of hours, some of my northern colleagues couldn't cover theirs by car in several days. In that way we all gradually learned about the complexities of governing a country as large and varied as Canada. Interestingly enough, the Quebec caucus generally spoke with one voice. It would get together and ask, "What are the two things we want to bring up this week that are important to our province?" The chair focused on them, everyone else reiterated them, and the discipline was remarkable. (That was true with the Quebec ministers in the Cabinet as well, I later discovered.) Meanwhile, the rest of us tended to be scattered in our opinions. If the chair of the Ontario caucus said that black was black, one of our colleagues was sure to stand up and say, "No, black is white – our chair is crazy."

At ten o'clock on Wednesdays we all came together for the national caucus, where the chairs of the four caucuses gave their reports, as did the chairs of the women's caucus and the various caucus committees that had been set up to examine an ever-changing array of priorities – from housing to childcare to the environment. This segment of caucus usually took about an hour, though the backbenchers kept pushing to speed things up so they would have enough time to raise their own particular matters. Some MPs had regular issues, others had expertise in certain areas, and quite a few were obsessed with the politics of the day. Even before the meeting began, they scurried around to gather allies for their arguments, to build coalitions of like-minded individuals, or to horse-trade their questions week by week.

The whole game of advancing your agenda in caucus became a political mini-campaign in its own right that had to be figured out by experience alone. MPs often gathered into informal, self-selected groups, sometimes across party lines, to discuss and push forward issues or interests of importance to their constituents, whether steel production or chicken quotas. Rosedale had more restaurants, co-ops, and universities within its boundaries than perhaps any other riding in Canada, so I was active in those "caucuses" too. The lobbying wasn't confined to office hours but carried on over countless drinks and late dinners, though I drew a line at staying up for the regular all-night bridge games. If you inadvertently stood in someone's way, you had to watch out. Early on, when I made an innocuous intervention in caucus about trade policy, Roy MacLaren, the minister of international trade, came over, steaming. I received a verbal thrashing for somehow obstructing him from getting what he wanted.

A good deal of Mr. Chrétien's effectiveness came from his decades as a member of Parliament and Cabinet minister. He understood the perils of isolation at the top. He appreciated the need to keep even the lowliest backbencher satisfied and in the loop. He felt that every member, including Opposition members, deserved his respect. As a result, he made a point of saying that his door was always open to any MP who wanted to speak to him. It might take a few days or even a few weeks to get an appointment, but he kept his word. I didn't take much advantage of that standing offer. If I wanted something done or needed some advice about a particular problem, I usually went to see the prime minister's chief of staff, Jean Pelletier – a patrician gentleman, polite, receptive, and tough as nails. If he couldn't handle it, he would suggest that I talk to "the boss," but that was rarely necessary. Less frequently, but now and then, I consulted Chaviva Hošek on policy issues and Eddie Goldenberg about politics. When I got more comfortable with the system, I sometimes sent them ideas or speaking notes for the prime minister's consideration.

Another channel that Chrétien kept open was to invite individual MPs to have lunch with him at 24 Sussex on a rotation basis. Unlike Pierre Trudeau, who occasionally used the Parliamentary Dining Room as a way of remaining accessible, Chrétien preferred to eat at home, generally alone with his wife but sometimes with guests. He seldom included his ministers, because he saw them more regularly; rather, he treated these occasions as an opportunity to relax with his backbenchers and get to know them better. A gifted raconteur, he broke the ice by telling countless stories about Quebec under Duplessis or his early days as a politician, and once he re-enacted for us the famous incident when he almost clobbered a would-be assassin, who had broken into the house in the middle of the night, with a heavy stone Inuit carving.

The prime minister remained much the same man who had won the election, though the aura around him changed markedly. The office, the staff, the advisers, the raw power separated him from the rest of us and increased his own innate sense of formality. Already reserved, he became more reserved; already intimidating, he became more intimidating. Now he could make or break your career, advance or hinder your pet projects. Yet there were complicated dimensions to his character. He could be extremely engaging and personal when he was in the mood, and though he worked hard in public to remain the *petit gars* from Shawinigan, in private he had a highly sophisticated taste in reading and classical music. One day, when he invited me to his office for a chat, we got talking about Europe in 1919 because we had both just been reading Margaret MacMillan's book on the subject. At night he much preferred to read a good biography or history than watch the television news. "It would just make me lose sleep over something I can't really do anything about," he once explained.

Buttonholing him in the House or the caucus never worked. He was usually preoccupied with bigger issues. His hearing wasn't good, especially in a noisy room. He liked order and politeness. But you could always slip him a note in the lobby or on his way out the door, and he was extremely patient if you put on his desk a photograph to be signed for a constituent or a copy of the Charter of Rights to be autographed for a fundraiser. It was all part of getting you re-elected, he well understood, and if you weren't re-elected, he might not be prime minister any longer. Like all of us, of course, his mood could swing from week to week – sometimes gruff, sometimes inspirational, sometimes emotional, sometimes analytical, and sometimes very funny. In the last week of the 1995 referendum campaign, when the polls were turning against the federal side, he wept, not from despair or fatigue but at the thought of the breakup of Canada.

When the Martin forces mounted their drive to push him out of office, he was cranky. When he explained his reasons for keeping Canada out of the Iraq war, he was brilliant.

At ten minutes to noon, as regular as clockwork, Mr. Chrétien concluded the caucus meeting by summing up what he had heard, what was important, and what we were going to do. He invariably mentioned how interesting he had found the meeting, even when it had been low-key and banal. Caucus was a sounding board about political and party issues that drained out the venom by letting people talk about them. It was a place where people could discuss everything from the problems in their ridings to the direction of the country. Later, when a group of us was assigned to look into the role of parliamentarians, we concluded that the best way for a prime minister to stay on top of the current political situation was caucus. Not the sophisticated pollsters, the high-priced political consultants, or the PMO advisers, but ordinary MPs standing up and speaking frankly about what was happening in their jurisdictions and why.

"I may be just an ordinary backbencher in your eyes," I used to tell my constituents, "but I happen to be one of about two hundred people in the entire country who gets two hours every Wednesday morning with the prime minister and his Cabinet to ask them or tell them whatever I want."

THAT WAS OBVIOUSLY a bit of bravado because it recognized, within itself, that the real power lay with Chrétien and his ministers. As a newly elected backbencher, I had no expectation of being elevated immediately into the Cabinet. By the time the prime minister found places for his main leadership rivals, his long-time loyalists, a few experienced veterans, and the regional representatives, there obviously wasn't room for a neophyte from the Toronto area who had supported John Turner in 1984 and was an old friend of Paul Martin. The notable exception was Allan Rock, a star candidate who had been treasurer of the Law Society of Upper Canada and therefore an excellent choice for minister of justice. The most I hoped for was a job that made use of my interest and experience in international affairs.

I was therefore pleased to be appointed vice-chair of the Standing Committee on Foreign Affairs and International Trade (SCFAIT), particularly since this was something of a coup for a first-time backbencher. Being vice-chair of a committee was lower in the pecking order than being a parliamentary secretary to a minister, but I wasn't going to be made a parliamentary secretary right off the bat either. That was fine with me, not least because it didn't require me to put my personal holdings into a blind trust. And, as I quickly discovered, there are a lot of non-job jobs on Parliament Hill. They come with a perk or fancy title but carry no weight at all. Nevertheless, people push and shove to get them to show their constituents how important they are in Ottawa. When I asked one young MP from Quebec how he liked being parliamentary secretary to the solicitor general, Herb Gray, he replied rather despondently, "I've never met with Mr. Gray. He doesn't have time to see me." If I had been asked years later to serve as the foreign minister's parliamentary secretary, with this or that task to perform, I might have accepted, but I made it clear to everybody that I preferred to be left on SCFAIT. I developed quite a good working relationship with the chair, Jean-Robert Gauthier, a courtly Franco-Ontarian who had first been elected to the Commons in 1972. He gave me a lot of independence to pursue my interests, respected my bilingualism, and occasionally asked me to speak to francophone groups – a role that quickly gave me a better understanding of their political issues.

Parliamentary committees come in various forms for various purposes: standing committees, ad hoc committees, Senate committees, joint committees. The standing committees normally have a dozen or so MPs, divided according to the parties' representation in the Commons, who meet regularly to review legislation, monitor departmental spending, or produce reports on important subjects commissioned by the government or of their own choosing. In my view, the substantive discussions in the committee rooms are at the core of Parliament's work – much more so than the formal debates in the House of Commons and apart from the actual adoption of legislation. Having MPs engaged in the study and evolution of public policy, bringing different perspectives to the concerns of the day, building an all-party consensus around the solutions, and coming up with considered recommendations are all useful. But this system is meaningful only when it gives MPs a sense of influence and independence, not when they feel pushed around, ignored, or even silenced by their leadership. No parliamentary committee in Ottawa, however, ever comes close to replicating the power of the Congressional committees in Washington, DC, which control the purse strings in ways that the Canadian system doesn't permit.

To my great good fortune, no sooner had I been made vice-chair of SCFAIT than I was named to the special joint committee of MPs and senators that was set up by the government as preparation for the major review of Canadian foreign policy that came out in 1995, similar to the ones Trudeau had done in 1970 and Mulroney in 1985. Though joint committees are rare and awkward creatures, with two chairs, two sets of advisers, and two ways of doing business, in this case the government really wanted to make use of the wealth of expertise within both chambers. One of the side-benefits I received was the opportunity to learn from political veterans of the calibre of the committee's co-chairs, Senator Allan MacEachen and Jean-Robert Gauthier. MacEachen was a special character whose institutional memory dated back to his first election in 1953. Sometimes I had lunch with him on committee business in the Parliamentary Dining Room; on other evenings he came to my apartment and, over a couple of glasses of Scotch, told wonderful tales of Cape Breton campaigns or the Pearson years. He hadn't been nicknamed the Old Fox for nothing. He could skate rings around any argument that stood in the way of the result he wanted, as my colleague John English and I once discovered when we tried to persuade him of a particular course of action but, by the end of the meeting, found ourselves converted to the opposing view.

Over the course of seven months the special committee received 561 briefs from academics, businesses, and non-government organizations (NGOs). We held hearings in ten cities from coast to coast to coast; we organized a series of round-table discussions with specialists on everything from security to trade, the environment to education, development to northern affairs; we pored over more than ten thousand pages of evidence and a number of specially commissioned studies; we travelled to Europe and the United States; and we met with officials from the United Nations, the European Union, the World Bank, the International Monetary Fund, the Organization of American States, and the North Atlantic Treaty Organization (NATO), among many others. This was a privileged way for a newcomer to see the whole picture of where Canada had come from as a nation and where we should go.

My most significant contribution, together with John English, was to insist that the final report include a chapter on the role of Canadian culture. At the local level, my riding was home to many eminent writers, artists, actors, dancers, filmmakers, and others who work in the cultural sector, as well as to scores of theatres, recording studios, and broadcasters. At the national level, preserving our cultural institutions under any free-trade agreements was hugely important. If we were ever penalized for invoking our protectionist cultural exemptions under the agreement, we would lose our identity as a people.

There were also important international dimensions to safeguarding our culture. As the American political scientist Joseph Nye once postulated, the integrated world is a three-level chessboard. The top level is military power, which is the exercise of "hard" sovereign might. On the second level are economic relations between states, including international agreements on trade and financial regulation. The third level represents transnational relations that exist outside of state control. Here, according to Nye, is where the importance of "soft power" comes into play. Soft power is the ability to persuade without recourse to military, economic, or diplomatic muscle. A nation's soft power can be developed by asserting its culture and values abroad, often through books, film, music, and other cultural expressions.

Whenever a piece is moved on one level of the chessboard, the pieces on every other level are also affected, and the United States obviously shapes the international environment at all three levels. For a less powerful nation such as Canada, as John Ralston Saul argued in the paper he wrote for the committee, without the military and economic clout of the superpowers, culture plays a particularly key role in achieving an effective foreign policy. It projects our image around the world. It gains us respect abroad. It makes us more competitive in the global knowledge-based economy. It disseminates our values of freedom, diversity, and education. And its effect is felt directly by the citizens of the world, not just by their governments.

"Never before has a Parliamentary Committee reviewing Canadian foreign policy received such a simple message from so many witnesses," the report noted. "Canadian foreign policy should celebrate and promote Canadian culture and learning as an important way of advancing our interests in international affairs."

Though Senator MacEachen in particular liked the idea, the final report mostly dealt with the traditional two levels – military power and economic power – because of their fundamental importance. In doing so, it anticipated many of the major issues that the Chrétien and Martin governments would have to face going into the new millennium. With the rise of globalization, Canada would have to expand free trade, increase domestic productivity, create sustainable jobs, participate in the construction of a new rules-based international trading order, and become a more competitive, innovative player in the world market. With the collapse of the Soviet Union, we needed to reconsider the role of NATO, reassess the efficacy of UN peacekeeping, advance the cause of nuclear non-proliferation, and re-examine the elements of continental defence. A report written in 1994 couldn't have prepared us for the attack on the World Trade Center, the fight against global terrorism, the invasion of Iraq, the occupation of Afghanistan, the civil wars in Libya and Syria, or the Russian bear in Ukraine, but it did seek to define the institutional framework necessary to respond to such events.

6

PARLIAMENTARY DIPLOMACY

Sometime in 1994, while I was still vice-chair of SCFAIT and a member of the special joint committee on foreign policy, Mr. Chrétien called me into his office. Would I, he asked, represent the Liberal Party of Canada at Liberal International? An association of more than a hundred parties and affiliated groups from around the world, it had been founded in Oxford in 1947 as a vehicle by which liberal democracies could foster their values and institutions in the post-war environment. Smaller than the Socialist International on the left and the International Democrat Union on the right, Liberal International concerns itself with issues such as human rights, social justice, and free trade, and it helps fledgling centrist parties in Africa, Asia, and Latin America.

"Of course," I said, both chuffed and honoured, "but I'm not sure I'll be able to get the expenses out of my parliamentary budget."

"You won't be expected to. You see, it's party business, not parliamentary business, so you can't claim it." Here he gave me a sly wink. "But maybe you could afford it." Years later he admitted privately that the choice of representative had been either me or Barry Campbell, another Liberal MP from Toronto, because he couldn't think of any other caucus backbenchers who could spend their own money doing it. I admit to feeling a bit deflated when I realized I had been chosen more for my financial means than my mind, but this was part of a long tradition. Senator Al Graham (no relation) had represented the party at his own expense for years.

"Liberal International was really important to me when we were in Opposition," Chrétien said. "I made many of my personal contacts in Europe at its meetings. Now, if I need something in Holland or Germany, I can pick up the phone and connect to the right person on a first-name basis."

That was to be my own experience too. My participation in Liberal International initiated me into a truth that turned out to be of profound importance: personal connections are essential to the successful conduct of foreign affairs. As with politics, business, and perhaps every human endeavour, getting different people to work together is the grease that lubricates the machine. To borrow an idea from Margaret MacMillan, the prominent historian, international relations are not simply the sum of interactions between states but are also the continual interactions that come from the movement and meeting of people. In fact, the relationship between states is often highly dependent on the extent to which individuals know and understand one another. Diplomatic relations "at the top" are shaped and driven by the friendships, professional associations, and shared engagements developed by people "on the ground" in every field, not just the political. In other words, networking isn't about name dropping or cocktail parties: it's about getting good things accomplished.

At the biennial congresses of Liberal International, I got to know such interesting people as Amnon Rubinstein from Israel, John Alderdice from Northern Ireland, Viktor Orbán from Hungary, and Otto Graf Lambsdorff from Germany. Though the Democrats in the United States should have been members, they shared the general American aversion to becoming entangled in international organizations. The US-based National Democratic Institute was there as a co-operating organization, however, and I had many occasions to meet informally with senior party officials, such as Governor Howard Dean of Vermont (who stood as a presidential candidate in 2004), to gain insights into what was happening in Washington and the United States.

From 1996 to 2000, I served on Liberal International's London-based executive "bureau" as co-treasurer, along with liberals from Austria, Hungary, and Switzerland, wrestling with the perennial question of who would pay for the operations and travel costs. The bigger the political party, the bigger the fees, the more votes at a convention. As a result, Liberal International tends to be dominated by the Europeans, especially the Germans, whose parties get millions of dollars of funding from their parliament for this type of activity. By contrast, the cash-strapped Liberal Party of Canada paid its dues by passing the hat among its financial supporters and asking delegates to pay their own way.

Control mattered, not just for the running of the organization but for its policies as well. Indeed, the very definition of liberalism was at stake. The Dutch, for example, had two parties that were members of Liberal International, one on the left and another on the right. Italian and German liberals tended to be free-trade, free-enterprise, low-tax conservatives. The Liberal Democratic Party in Japan never joined, because it was far to the right of us, whereas even the conservatives in our crowd were to the left of John Howard's so-called Liberal government in Australia. There were nominal liberals in Latin America who supported dictatorships, making some of our human rights discussions rather awkward. When I went looking for liberals in France, I was told by its former president Valéry Giscard d'Estaing, "Oh, they're around, but you'll find them under different labels." In fact, we never did have any luck recruiting the French to Liberal International.

"As far as we Germans are concerned," Lambsdorff used to tease me, "you guys in Canada are communists. And if not communists, certainly socialists. You really should be in Socialist International instead of Liberal International."

At first Viktor Orbán, the powerful leader of the Fidesz Party in Hungary, was an active vice-chair of Liberal International for many years, even though he veered increasingly to the right after becoming prime minister in 1998. Suddenly, in 2000, he and his party quit and joined the centre-right European People's Party. When I asked him what he was doing, after working side-by-side for many years, he replied, "Well, I've analyzed it, and politics today are becoming more and more polarized. There's no room remaining for the middle, so I'm joining the right."

This fundamental debate came to the fore in November 1997, when Liberal International observed its fiftieth anniversary by gathering in Oxford to update its founding manifesto. The discussions vividly exposed the difficulty of trying to accommodate both the laissez-faire liberals and the social democrats or, as in Canada's case, the pragmatic centrists. Certainly the type of free-market, low-tax, small-government rhetoric that the Germans and Dutch were pushing sounded a lot like the Reform Party policies from which Mr. Chrétien was trying to distance our party. So we and similar-minded members pushed back just as hard, and the final document struck a reasonable compromise among the different positions.

Perhaps if you stay in the middle of the road, as my brother Philip liked to say, you're more likely to get hit by trucks coming from both directions. But it's been the belief of the Liberal Party of Canada – and the reason, I would suggest, for its enduring strength – that it can spread itself wide enough to send the oncoming traffic into the ditches on the far left and the far right. And in the integrated world in which we live, it's in Canada's interests to encourage similar-minded political movements in other countries as well.

LATE IN 1994, Jean-Robert Gauthier decided he wasn't going to seek another term as a member of Parliament. Rather than wait for the next general election, the prime minister appointed him to the Senate and called a by-election in his riding. I was then asked to step in as chair of the SCFAIT. I was very pleased, and at the next caucus meeting I went up to Mr. Chrétien and thanked him. "I really appreciate the confidence you've shown in me," I said.

Distracted by the demands of the MPs pressing around him, he gave me the verbal equivalent of a smack in the face. "Well, don't expect to stay there long – it's just a temporary thing."

When I ran into Eddie Goldenberg in the hall, I told him what had happened. Was the PM angry with me for some reason? Did he hold a grudge against me for not supporting him in the two leadership campaigns? Did he see me as an inexperienced intellectual, a political dilettante, without the skills necessary to be effective? "He's just in a bad mood today," Eddie said. "Don't pay it any attention. It'll go away." Sure enough, it did, and Chrétien even apologized several years later after I had proved myself in the job. With hindsight, I can see that he was probably being pushed to appoint someone with more seniority for such a highly sought-after position. In the meantime, however, I felt under intense pressure to perform well.

An opportunity presented itself almost immediately. In 1992 the Mulroney government had followed up its Free Trade Agreement (FTA) with the United States with a North American Free Trade Agreement (NAFTA) involving Canada, the United States, and Mexico. Parliament was dissolved before the agreement could be ratified, however, and the Liberals campaigned in the 1993 election on the promise that we wouldn't sign unless we could get improvements to the deal.

The core problem as I saw it was that NAFTA, like the bilateral Canada-US Free Trade Agreement, was strong on economic integration but weak on the institutions to manage that integration. Free trade with the United States, though generally beneficial, simply wasn't as reliable as Mulroney had promised it would be. No matter what international treaty an American president signs, the US Congress often finds ways around the obligations, and there's little even the president can do about it. In the most egregious case, the Americans put countervailing duties on Canadian softwood lumber without just cause. Even more unjust, though lumber falls under provincial jurisdiction, the US duties were applied nationally, which meant that every province was penalized for something that British Columbia might or might not have done. We appealed to the dispute-resolution panels and the WTO, spent millions of taxpayer dollars in legal fees and lobbying expenses, and won decision after decision, but the United States always found a way to circumvent the rulings. Whenever we protested, the White House blamed Congress, and Congress blamed the White House. In the end we negotiated a settlement that changed how lumber was harvested in various provinces, somewhat proving the argument made by some Canadians opposed to free trade that the Americans would be satisfied only when our industrial practices mirrored theirs.

Similarly, the Mexicans, having secured a guarantee that their trucking industry would have access into the United States or across the United States into Canada, discovered all sorts of arbitrary excuses by which the Americans reneged on their obligation for years. As the less powerful parties, Canada and Mexico needed tough international rules to prevent the United States from using its size to bully them into submission. The looser the rules and the looser the dispute-resolution mechanisms to enforce those rules, the more the Americans could get away with. Later, in fact, after I became foreign minister, I spent a lot of time discussing the problem with Jorge Castañeda, Mexico's secretary of foreign affairs from 2000 to 2003. Like me, Jorge had done his doctorate in Paris and studied the European Union, and we shared the view that NAFTA needed to replace its bilateral, ad hoc dispute-settlement panels with a tripartite and permanent court. If we could get something similar to the European Court of Justice, it would develop a coherent set of judgments that focused on the general good rather than on specific disputes, while at the same time building up precedents that would constrain the exercise of raw power. Unfortunately, our discussions never led to anything. It was clear that the Americans preferred the existing system because it worked to their advantage. Some Canadians, too, didn't like the restraints that a more binding arrangement would have created.

Within days of taking office, Chrétien succeeded in getting President Clinton to accept enough changes to allow both Canada and the United States to ratify NAFTA without a loss of face. Though they didn't alter the balance of power as much as we might have wished, unscrambling an omelette is very hard once it's been made, and a deal was certainly better than no deal. When the United States decided it wanted a free-trade pact with Mexico, Canada couldn't afford to be left out. We had to be a party to it, or we would find ourselves in a hub-and-spoke situation in which the United States controlled everybody one-on-one. Moreover, though every free-trade agreement contains within itself the problem that jobs and money will tend to flow to the lower-wage economies if companies want to stay competitive, NAFTA significantly increased trade and investment between Canada and Mexico, especially in the automotive and aerospace sectors. It integrated into the supply chain of many Canadian manufacturers. And the formal relationships among the federal governments were supplemented by new working relationships among certain Canadian provinces and Mexican states.

NAFTA also proved a perfect example of the domestic impact of Canada's engagement in the global economy. Much of international law is "conventional" international law, meaning that it is contained in treaties and conventions. When Canada enters into a treaty, international law requires it to comply with the obligations it has assumed, but the treaty's rules aren't binding within Canada until they are incorporated into Canadian law by way of legislation. On one level, that's obvious. If you sign an agreement abroad, you must ensure that the laws at home permit it to be implemented (though no province is compelled to implement any rules that concern matters under provincial jurisdiction). Less obvious is that the obligation to create the appropriate legislation results in a significant change in the nature of the legislative process. The content of international law used to be fairly distinct from domestic law. Today, because of globalization, some regulations that were once exclusively a matter for a national legislature or agency are now imposed on us by an international agreement. The integration of our international and domestic obligations has been accelerating at such a pace that most of us are not aware of it happening. We talk about having to do something without realizing that the reason we have to do it is because of a decision made overseas. When I was on the board of Crédit Lyonnais Canada, the French bank's Canadian subsidiary, for example, we went through an arduous process of adjusting to capitalization rules laid down by the Bank for International Settlements in Geneva.

Though I had been teaching for years about the impact of our international obligations on domestic legislation, I was astonished to discover as an MP how great that impact was in practice. I once calculated that about a quarter of all the laws adopted by the House of Commons involved the application of our international obligations. In fact, for NAFTA to take effect, the Parliament of Canada had to adopt or amend twenty-seven different pieces of legislation pertaining to its details, from the Crow Rate transportation subsidy to pharmaceutical patents.

This very complexity helped me prove my mettle. Soon after my appointment as chair of SCFAIT, Don Boudria, the government's House leader, came to me and said, "We think your committee would be the best one to get these laws through since they deal with so many different subjects. The problem is, we're in a hurry. I need them back in the House next week."

That was indeed a problem. Some of the legislation was highly controversial; some was the size of a book. "All I can do is my best," I said.

"Well," he replied, "if you can steer this through, there's no question you'll remain chairman of the foreign affairs committee for as long as you like."

I felt confident that I could manage the task because I had already laid the ground for what had to be done. First I went to see Charlie Penson, the leading Reform MP on the committee. "Charlie," I said, "you guys are in favour of the free-trade agreement, aren't you?"

"Absolutely," he said.

"Well, so are we, and we need to get committee approval of the legislation, which is a bit of a brick, for next week." He didn't see a problem.

Then I went to Stéphane Bergeron of the Bloc Québécois and said, "In Quebec you guys have been talking in favour of NAFTA, maybe because of its economic benefits, maybe because you think it will give you more independence from Canada."

"Right," he said. So I had his co-operation.

The NDP had campaigned against NAFTA but hadn't won enough seats to get official party status. As a result, there were no New Democrats on the committee at the time, so I was spared having to go through weeks of wrangling to win their approval. Thus, with everyone else onside, I had a deal. The committee met one morning. We went through the legislation bang, bang, bang. I made a report in the Commons a couple of days later. Everything went for a vote the following week – and I remained chair of SCFAIT for the next seven years.

THE FOREIGN MINISTER in those days was André Ouellet. Because he was much more interested in Quebec politics than in world issues, I got a higher profile than a SCFAIT chair normally does. When the press needed a quote, they often came to me. When the minister wasn't available, I did the talk shows on radio and television, and gave scrums to the journalists outside the Commons. Besides allowing me to hone my media skills, this exposure boosted my political credentials in Ottawa to some extent and gave me an unexpected profile in the riding and elsewhere in Canada. But my moment in the limelight came to an abrupt end on January 25, 1996, when Ouellet was replaced by Lloyd Axworthy, an extremely bright, powerful, and dynamic minister. Once the reporters could get to him, they no longer needed me. Overnight he was everywhere I had been. I ceased to be an important person, and nobody in the press gallery gave a damn what I was doing, when all the time I thought they had liked me for myself. It was a rude awakening to the fickleness of politics. But at least I got to keep my chairmanship.

Not that I had any issue with Lloyd's appointment. On the contrary, I had nothing but respect for his intellect, his idealism, and the job he did for Canada as foreign minister. As chair of SCFAIT, I had many collaborative dealings with him at committee hearings and in caucus, and I admired the way he used his influence in the Cabinet to advance the proactive humanitarian agenda I was later to inherit. He was a consummate politician, whether in his Winnipeg riding or in the halls of the United Nations; he knew from years of experience how to work the system; and he assembled a formidable team of very smart people in his office to help him. As a result, through his blend of toughness and charm, with strong opinions firmly expressed, he succeeded in getting Canada to punch above its weight in the world – a goal enthusiastically endorsed by Prime Minister Chrétien.

On a personal level, had it not been for SCFAIT, I think my relationship with many of my House of Commons colleagues from the Opposition parties would have been less close. Perhaps only the gay rights legislation, which cut so deeply across party lines because of its human and moral dimensions, was as valuable in this respect. By sharing their interest in international trade, I earned enough credibility with Charlie Penson and Bob Mills, two Reform MPs, to convince them to give me a few concessions on human rights, which they considered a somewhat loopy issue. I spent a lot of time with the Bloc Québécois members to get them involved in shaping Canada's foreign policy in positive ways. Because I was as horrified as Stéphane Bergeron or Francine Lalonde by the poor quality of the French documents we initially received from the translation bureau, we used to sit down together after committee meetings to untangle the mess. As a result, if I needed something from the Bloc, they would steer me in the right direction as to who in their caucus was worth approaching and who was a waste of my time. After the 1997 election, when the NDP won enough seats to get a voting member on SCFAIT, I also developed a good working relationship with Bill Blaikie and Svend Robinson.

Whenever possible, I wanted every MP on the committee to be on board with every single one of our recommendations: a unanimous report that reflects the wishes of all the parties in the House, no matter what their ideological orientation, is taken more seriously than a partisan report that merely echoes the will of the governing party. I took each draft to the committee, one recommendation at a time. The members then had a chance to tinker with the wording or hone the idea before it went to a vote, yea or nay. Sometimes that required weeks of arduous political horse trading, and unanimity wasn't always possible. However, as the result of all the efforts to engage the Opposition and obtain multi-party input, our reports and recommendations were mostly unanimous, with only an occasional supplementary or dissenting opinion.

When the Reform Party first turned up in Ottawa, it brought with it a mindset that all MPs live high off the hog at the taxpayers' expense, corrupted by the outrageous perks of office. It took the Reform MPs about two years to realize that these so-called perks are tools that enable members to do a better job for the country and for their constituents. At first they saw even the Parliamentary Dining Room as an unessential boondoggle until they discovered how useful it is as a vehicle for meeting other MPs, understanding problems, and finding solutions. In fact, quite a lot of the business takes place during lunchtime in the collegial atmosphere of that room. Because many MPs, senators, and even some ministers regularly eat there at the same tables, there are plenty of opportunities to lobby them if need be or simply to engage in casual banter about a particular piece of legislation and the political crisis of the day. It's also an easy way to catch up on the news and make friends – or acquaintances at least.

Similarly, convincing the Reformers to appreciate the value of committee travel took experience and persuasion. I once bumped into Jason Kenney looking absolutely amazed as he wandered around Peter the Great's spectacular palace on the outskirts of St. Petersburg. "This is quite the pad the guy had here," he said, and that's when I realized how little he had seen of the world. But the process of meeting people, listening, and understanding other perspectives is more than just basic education: it's the stuff of world peace and national unity.

Although some committees need to travel farther and more often than others, and therefore require the bulk of the money divvied out by the liaison committee over which I presided for a while, everyone has a legitimate claim to doing business away from Parliament Hill. How can MPs vote on international issues or even the domestic legislation influenced by Canada's international obligations if they don't go to other places? Similarly, in a country as vast and diverse as ours, how can parliamentarians grasp the circumstances and views of the various regions if they don't get out of the Ottawa bubble? That's especially true when it comes to the preparation of committee reports. Although MPs can imbibe a certain amount by commissioning research and calling in witnesses, at some point they have to experience what's happening across Canada and around the world if they really want to come to grips with the complexities of global politics and the international economy.

Thus, when SCFAIT decided to do a major report on the Canadian Arctic in 1996, committee MPs visited think-tanks such as the Arctic Institute of North America in Calgary and the Boreal Institute in Edmonton. Some of us went to the Yukon and the Northwest Territories to experience a personal immersion in the circumpolar North. Some of us travelled to Russia, Norway, Finland, Sweden, and Denmark. In this case, the Reform Party was less hasty to dismiss our work as a boondoggle, in part because its own MPs on the committee were supportive, and most of the travel was inside Canada. But the very fact that SCFAIT was studying the Arctic signalled that the economic, environmental, and security issues of the Canadian North weren't domestic issues alone. They were also matters of international regulation and global politics, as evidenced by the creation of the Arctic Council, which held its inaugural meeting in Ottawa in September 1996, and the Conference of Parliamentarians of the Arctic Region.

The alienation felt by many Canadians in the outlying regions is particularly acute in the Arctic. Not only has it long been run from Ottawa like a colonial fiefdom but its small population also means that the North has only three members of Parliament, severely limiting its ability to influence government policy. When we visited Kuujjuaq, Iqaluit, Cape Dorset, and Resolute Bay in the western Arctic, a noteworthy number of the community leaders said that they had never met an MP before, not even their own, let alone so many in one room. In Yellowknife one night, we went to one of the famous local bars near Ragged Ass Road. Predictably we had been warned not to go in. Just as predictably we found that even the roughest of roughnecks were happy to meet some new people, and even more than interested when they found out we were federal politicians. Every one of them expressed frustration or anger that the decisions influencing their lives were being made by people who didn't have much direct knowledge of northern conditions.

Perhaps more than any other SCFAIT report in my time, *Canada and the Circumpolar World* demonstrated the value of ambitious committee work. Key to its success was the excellence of our clerk Janice Hilchie, our indefatigable research director Gerry Schmitz, and his assistant Jim Lee. It flagged the importance of the Arctic. It offered new ideas for its governance, including a role for the northern peoples in northern governance. It was an early call for official attention to the environmental degradation that was taking place in the North, stressing the impact of climate change on traditional Aboriginal ways of life, the implications for the geopolitical realities in the region, and the increased access to mineral and other resources. In fact, for many years after its release in April 1997, the report was used in some universities as a helpful template for Arctic studies.

If the committee's trips helped give the Reform MPs the picture of a bigger world, they also helped give the Bloc MPs the picture of a bigger Canada. In Inuvik, for example, Nellie Cournoyea, the former premier of the Northwest Territories who was then head of the Inuvialuit Regional Corporation, had talked about how "small is beautiful" when it comes to responsive local government. That prompted Philippe Paré, a Bloc MP, to start putting words into her mouth, essentially his own arguments in favour of Quebec independence. "But we can't live by ourselves up here," Nellie responded. "We understand we're part of a wider, more interconnected world, whether we like it or not, and as a result we're better off in Canada. What we want is a voice in how that power is exercised in dealing with global problems that require global solutions."

At one point Colleen Beaumier, my lively colleague from Brampton West, decided she was going to dance to the rock band with Philippe. When I pointed out that dancing barefoot on a wooden floor might not be such a great idea, she told me to mind my own business. "Philippe and I are having a serious conversation," she said, "and I don't think that he'll still be a separatist afterward." The next morning Colleen could barely walk into the dining room. Her feet were so full of big black slivers that she appeared to have stepped on a porcupine. There was nothing for it but to have her feet soaked and then try to remove as many of the splinters as possible with tweezers. To her credit, Colleen sat through the day of meetings without a complaint, proving once again the strength of her character. Camaraderie like that helped unify the committee members, despite our partisan differences, as did the moment we shared in Tuktoyaktuk when several of us rolled up our trousers, took our shoes off, and stood in the Arctic Ocean, just to be able to say we had done it.

For the most part, the Bloc's separatist agenda didn't obstruct our business. Obviously it was a factor if we were discussing the separation of Slovakia from the Czech Republic, but there wasn't a substantial difference of opinion when we were studying human rights or most other international issues. It did occasionally surface, sometimes dramatically. In May 2001, for example, two groups of SCFAIT members travelled to the South Caucasus and Central Asia at the request of Lloyd Axworthy, who foresaw a greater Canadian engagement in the region. Given its long-term importance to NATO, Iraq, and Afghanistan, he felt – and I agreed – that the Canadian government and Canadian parliamentarians should have an informed understanding of its intricate geopolitics.

Among my group of five was Francine Lalonde, the Bloc's foreign affairs critic. I had come to know her quite well through the committee's work; we understood each other's point of view even when we didn't agree; and I earned a few extra brownie points from her when we arrived in Tbilisi, Georgia. As chair, I was given a suite with a private bathroom and tub, whereas she got a poky room with a shower down the hall. "You take my suite, Francine," I said when I realized how much she was craving a bath after the exhausting eighteen-hour bus ride across Azerbaijan, "and I'll switch to your room."

She was grateful, but her gratitude stretched only so far. That night we had dinner with the Canadian ambassador and Nino Burjanadze, a bright, high-spirited Georgian parliamentarian who had been a professor of international law and would subsequently serve on two occasions as her country's acting president. Dinners in Georgia aren't for the faint of heart. There was course after course of delicious but rather heavy food, and the wine flowed copiously. At some point in the midst of all this celebration, Francine decided that she needed to get up and deliver a lecture to our Georgian friends about Quebec's grievances with Canada, its oppression by *les maudits anglais,* and its aspiration to be an independent country. She produced a classic nationalist rant, no worse perhaps than we heard day after day in the House of Commons, but the Canadian ambassador was pretty upset.

"What are you going to do about this?" he whispered to me as Francine went on and on.

"Me?" I asked. "What am I supposed to do?"

"Well, you're the chair of this committee, you've got to shut this woman up. This is outrageous. We're in a foreign country, and the people here will be left with a terrible impression of us."

"Maybe," I said, "but, as a member of Parliament, she's entitled to say whatever she wants, for good or ill. I have no right to tell her to shut up." Still, it was unusual for a parliamentary delegation to get into this type of domestic debate abroad, and tempers were getting rather hot.

I turned to Nino for help to calm things down. "Don't worry, Bill, I know exactly what to say." When Francine finished her lecture, Nino immediately stood up. "Thank you, Francine, that was a very interesting exposition on your part about Quebec and its issues. But it seems to me, as a Georgian, that you're very fortunate to live in a country like Canada. I can tell you, our fields are knee-deep in blood as a result of speeches like yours. We're trying to tone down this type of rhetoric."

That was all she said, but it was enough. In fact, it was one of the most dramatic international putdowns I have ever witnessed. I thought how Pierre Trudeau would have applauded such a succinct and devastating repudiation of ethnic nationalism.

I HAD COME TO KNOW Nino Burjanadze through our involvement with the Organization for Security and Co-operation in Europe (OSCE), which had been set up as a permanent offshoot of the East-West détente conferences of the early-to-mid 1970s. Its purpose was to help deal with security in a broad sense, including issues such as human rights, arms control, and the rule of law in Central and Eastern Europe. Initially, it was created to help stabilize and reduce conflict in Europe during the Cold War and to ensure the observance of some basic human rights behind the Iron Curtain. Later, it took on a new role in assisting Europe in the transition to a post-Soviet era. Given our close interests in a peaceful and secure Europe, Canada has always been a member. When Lloyd Axworthy was our foreign minister, he often relied on it to provide us with an entrée to the countries of the former Soviet Union. Through it I developed a remarkable network of serious players from disparate countries, just as I was doing with Liberal International. I knew that building personal links meant building peace and prosperity.

The OSCE has done some very important work in the areas of arms reduction, conflict prevention, and crisis management. It created the Treaty on Conventional Armed Forces in Europe and the Kosovo Verification Mission and has provided hundreds of observers to monitor democratic elections from Albania to Uzbekistan. It provided human rights missions to Serbia and Tajikistan. It also played an especially useful role in the mid-1990s when Turkey was going through a critical evolution from the military dictatorship into a modern democracy, and more recently it worked at great risk to its staff to establish peace on the Russian-Ukrainian border.

In addition to its governing ministerial council, its Vienna-based secretariat, and its executive chairperson-in-office, the OSCE established a consultative assembly of several hundred parliamentarians from the signatory nations, with its own secretariat based in Copenhagen, its own secretary general, and its own annual plenary session. One of a dozen or so Canadian MPs and senators who joined the OSCE Parliamentary Assembly, I spent four years on its executive, first as a vice-president, then as treasurer. Though it had a fairly substantial budget, trying to make its books balance was no easier than it was at Liberal International. Many people were reluctant to pay fees to be part of a debating society that adopted resolutions but had no legislative power. Even Canada's own Finance Department never really understood the usefulness of the OSCE: it's neither a military pact like NATO nor a cultural agency like UNESCO, and the number-crunchers were always trying to get us to withdraw from it. "It costs $27 million a year to belong, and what's the return?" went the common complaint. "It accomplishes nothing. It just talks."

"Well, it may just talk," I argued, "but as Churchill said, 'To jaw-jaw is always better than to war-war.'" In other words, the OSCE and its Parliamentary Assembly were designed to be places where a large number of influential people could come together, if not to solve old problems, at least to prevent new ones. They are forums for dialogue between East and West on the development of democratic rights, fundamental freedoms, and economic and environmental co-operation, all of which are as much a part of peace and security as military alliances and trade deals.

Moreover, the OSCE Parliamentary Assembly was part of a worldwide trend to give legislators a role in international affairs, which had usually been seen as the exclusive preserve of governments. As global trade and regulation became more integrated, they required more international rules, which in turn penetrated deeper into domestic political territory. Thus, parliaments became more inextricably involved in international issues and law, and MPs were increasingly engaged in the crafting of international systems. The resulting rise of "parliamentary diplomacy" has been one of the most significant but least noted developments in modern foreign relations.

In June 1998, for example, I happened to be in St. Petersburg for a gathering of the OSCE Parliamentary Assembly's executive at the same time that the Commonwealth of Independent States (CIS) Inter-parliamentary Assembly was meeting. The CIS had been created in 1991 by members of the former Soviet Union to try to accomplish by compromise what Moscow used to dictate by fiat. In March 1993 it set up a consultative body to bring parliamentarians together to deliberate on the issues. Gennadiy Seleznyov, the powerful Speaker of the Russian Duma, invited me to sit in as an observer. "Bill, I have a real problem," he said at one point, pulling me aside. "Because we sit alphabetically, Azerbaijan and Armenia are cheek by jowl, and they've been at each other's throats over Nagorno-Karabakh for years. If you don't mind, I'm going to put you between the two of them."

It was fascinating to listen to these delegates dealing with each other over issues such as the harmonization of standards for telecommunication devices and electrical appliances in their countries. "You guys are no different from the European Union," I said afterward. "You're just a bunch of capitalists like the rest of us, trying to figure out how to make the legislative system work among various countries, and you have to deal with the same rather boring, technical, but important issues."

This kind of window into what was happening in Russia, the Caucasus, and the so-called Stans was the reason I decided to devote so much time to the OSCE Parliamentary Assembly in the first place. A Canadian MP wouldn't normally have an opportunity to get to know a parliamentarian from Turkmenistan or Kazakhstan, and I kept in touch with many of them on a regular basis through a host of other institutions and occasions down through the years.

In December 1998, while on a visit to Casey House, an AIDS hospice in my constituency, I learned about a new initiative, the Canada AIDS Russia Project (CARP), to develop training and education programs to deal with the high incidence of HIV/AIDS in Russia. Though CARP had succeeded in establishing a working relationship with a medical research institute in St. Petersburg, it couldn't get any official co-operation at the municipal or state level. Bill Flanagan, a former student of mine, later dean of the law school at Queen's University and an active promoter of the program, came to me to see what I might do. So I agreed to raise the matter with Seleznyov when I met him a few weeks later in Vienna.

"What's it about?" he asked me.

"AIDS," I replied.

"AIDS?" he said. "Oh, no, we don't talk about AIDS in Russia."

"But this is a really important issue for some of my constituents. They want you to be seen forming this link between Toronto and St. Petersburg because it would make an important statement coming from somebody as powerful as you. I would like you to consider it."

It took persistent convincing. In May I wrote to invite him to accompany me on a visit to CARP's field office when I was in St. Petersburg in July for the annual session of the OSCE Parliamentary Assembly, and he agreed as a personal favour. When we arrived, we found TV cameras and press reporters waiting, which only made Seleznyov even more nervous. However, the next day's headlines were full of praise for him: "Finally somebody gets it. At last we have a politician with the courage to recognize that AIDS is a problem that Russia has to come to grips with." From then on, he used to tell people that I was his political counsellor.

On the same visit to St. Petersburg, I dealt with another tangential matter that again illustrates the direct links between my constituency responsibilities and my international work. Alexander Nikitin was a Russian naval officer who had been accused of espionage for exposing the alarming degree of nuclear pollution from aging and poorly designed submarines. The charge was really a trumped-up excuse to stifle environmental activism in Russia. His wife happened to be living in Toronto, and she was trying to get him a visa to join her in Canada. Because I was a player with the OSCE and not just some ordinary Canadian MP, I was able to talk to Nikitin when I was in St. Petersburg for a meeting of the OSCE Parliamentary Assembly, which also adopted a resolution in his defence. The Russian government wasn't happy, but the concerted efforts on Nikitin's behalf by governments, legislators, and NGOs had an effect on his eventual acquittal.

I witnessed the same importance of interpersonal relationships at a higher level when my position on the Parliamentary Assembly executive earned me an invitation to attend the two-day summit of the OSCE's heads of state in Istanbul in November 1999. At one point Boris Yeltsin, seemingly drunk though it was only eleven o'clock in the morning, got up and launched a tirade against the West's "intervention" in Russia's internal affairs with regard to the crisis in Chechnya. President Bill Clinton responded brilliantly. "What would have happened if the Boris Yeltsin whom I admired standing on that tank in Moscow defending democracy had been arrested?" he said. "Wouldn't we have protested? And, if we had, would that have been an intervention in the internal affairs of Russia?" Soon after, Yeltsin cut short his visit to the conference and returned home.

During part of the debate, much to Mr. Chrétien's surprise, I was seated at the head table along with the OSCE chairperson-in-office, the president of the OSCE Parliamentary Assembly, and President Clinton. Chrétien hadn't been told that I would be present or why I was better placed than he or his foreign minister, and I caught him giving Lloyd Axworthy a quizzical look as though asking, "What the hell is one of my backbenchers doing up there?" But I was put in my proper place a short while later when Lloyd asked me to accompany him to a meeting with the president of Montenegro. As we waited outside for a car to pick us up, the heavens suddenly opened and the two of us were caught in a torrential downpour. Though Lloyd had a coat and a hat, and I had neither, a young foreign-service officer came rushing up and offered the minister the use of the only available umbrella. I was left to get soaked to the skin. I used to tell the umbrella story whenever I railed about the scant resources that ordinary MPs were given to do their jobs. We needed umbrellas too!

THE OSCE PARLIAMENTARY Assembly is just one of many multilateral or bilateral organizations in which Canadian members of Parliament are able to engage in parliamentary diplomacy. The others include the Inter-Parliamentary Union, associated with the United Nations; the NATO Parliamentary Assembly, an active group founded as early as 1955; the Canada-Europe Parliamentary Association; the Assemblée parlementaire de la Francophonie; the Conference of Parliamentarians of the Arctic Region; bilateral parliamentary associations with Britain, France, Mexico, China, and Japan; interparliamentary groups with Germany, Ireland, Israel, and Italy; and friendship groups with more than five dozen other countries. Obviously the joint associations funded out of the Commons and the Senate budgets are considered the more important ones, whether bilateral or multilateral, and the people appointed to them can afford to travel more and engage in more activities.

None of these parliamentary assemblies or friendship associations have any direct power. They are largely about sharing information, fostering discussion, forging networks, and building bridges. But they can have influence, and their resolutions or recommendations have on occasion swayed the decisions of national governments. The Taiwanese government, for example, as part of its campaign to gain international recognition, has always been active in recruiting MPs to go to Taiwan. Though I never went myself, MPs were constantly being invited to fly first class, spouses included, all expenses paid, and I think some of the problems the Harper government had with mainland China when first elected could be attributed to the fact that so many Reform MPs had gone to Taiwan on a regular basis. Whether because of their anti-communist bias or their pro-democracy principles, they simply didn't have the same knowledge of or contacts with the People's Republic of China.

When I was first elected to the House of Commons, David MacDonald graciously invited me to have lunch with him, even though I'd just destroyed his chance to regain a seat in Parliament. "Come, Bill," he said, "I'll tell you what goes on up there." After giving me some helpful tips on how to find an office and put together a staff, he added, "If you're really interested in international issues, whatever you do as an MP, join the Canada-US Inter-Parliamentary Group. It was the most rewarding thing I did in the whole time I was on the Hill. It gave me great insights to what's going on in the United States." And so, following his advice, I became a member right away.

The Canada-US Inter-Parliamentary Group, which was set up in 1959, has kept abreast with the integration of our economies, the closeness of our military ties, and the importance of Congress as an originator of legislation that may have an impact on Canadians. It gets substantial funding to do its work and is generally well run. In my day its members prepared seriously for the annual meeting, which alternated between Canada and the United States, and they took personal responsibility for studying the topics under discussion in the subcommittees, which dealt respectively with trade, cross-border, and international issues. For a while I co-chaired the international-issues subcommittee with Lee Hamilton, the extremely influential Democratic representative from Indiana who had first been elected in 1964, and we dealt with everything from immigration rules to trade with Cuba to NATO to cigarette smuggling.

Many MPs and senators want to join this group, creating a tricky problem because there's rarely room for more than a dozen of them at the meetings. Marlene Catterall, the Liberal whip whose power included control over which MPs got to go on what trips, once complained, "Every time I try to find a place for our people to go on one of these US trips, you're always already there. Why the hell do you have to be there? You do lots of travel anyway." But I was one of the few, along with my fellow MP Joe Comuzzi and Senator Jerry Grafstein, who had built the personal relations with Lee Hamilton or Ben Gilman, the Republican representative from New York who chaired the House Committee on Foreign Affairs after 1999, as well as with senators and congressmen I had met through my work with SCFAIT and various other organizations. For instance, I got to know Steny Hoyer, the Democratic congressman from Maryland who served as minority whip in the House of Representatives and later House majority leader, through his good friend Spencer Oliver, the long-serving secretary general of the OSCE Parliamentary Assembly.

People have no idea about the time constraints on US congressmen. In the past they arrived in Washington on Monday, stayed until Friday, and were free most evenings, but now they fly in on Tuesday, leave on Thursday, and dash all day and long into the night from meetings to votes to receptions to fundraisers. It's like a circus, with bells ringing incessantly and everyone hurrying hither and yon. Ben Gilman had a staff of thirty people working for him and over a hundred others working for his committee, compared with my staff of three and SCFAIT's staff of three. I had to develop my own technique to manage to see him. I would never phone Ben directly. Instead, I called his chief of staff, whom I had gotten to know over drinks after meetings and other social occasions, and he was usually able to fit me in for a few minutes while Ben was having a coffee in his office between meetings.

One day, in fact, the chair of the German foreign affairs committee said to me, "Bill, can you get me in to see your friend Gilman? I can't get an appointment."

"You might try taking his chief of staff out for a drink," I replied. "It's the only way I know."

When the Republicans gained control of the House and the Senate in 1994, the Canada-US Inter-Parliamentary Group could hardly convince any of them to come to our meetings. They sounded like the American version of our Reform Party: "Oh, no, we can't travel, that's a perk. Besides, foreign affairs is a bad thing. We don't even have passports." Though we retained many good contacts among the Democrats, getting the Republicans to pay any attention to Canada was difficult for a couple of years. Gradually they started to come back after they realized they had a host of problems that required our help, whether softwood lumber exports or the Detroit-Windsor bridge. Senator Frank Murkowski from Alaska and Representative Amo Houghton from New York were particularly useful in encouraging some of their colleagues to join.

Because the legislative branch controls the purse strings in the American system, building relationships with members of Congress has to be a key consideration in Canada's foreign relations. But though Canadian MPs from across the country push and shove to get into what they consider an exclusive club whose decisions make an impact on every riding in a major way, few American congressmen and senators are as interested in knowing us. The main exceptions are those from the northern border states, for obvious reasons. The many links between southern Ontario and upper New York State forged the lifelong friendship that Cathy and I have with Amo Houghton and his wife, Priscilla. The other exceptions are those from parts of California or Florida, where there are a large number of expatriate Canadians, or "snowbirds." In my day, for example, David Dreier, the congressman from California, represented an estimated 500,000 Canadians in Los Angeles, and Senator Bob Graham, a former governor of Florida, used to say to me, "Bill, you've only got a hundred thousand voters in your riding. That's nothing. I've got millions of Canadians in my state."

I got to know Bob Graham through the Inter-American Dialogue, a Washington think-tank that works at establishing better relations between North and South America. Peter Hakim, its president, asked me to become involved in its various activities as a way to bring a Canadian perspective into an organization that was predominantly focused on US relations with

Latin America. I attended some of its interesting meetings on the strengthening of democratic institutions and a conference in Miami on party finance and the relationship between political parties and the press. In January 2000 I went on a trip sponsored by the organization to Brazil and Bolivia with Bob Graham, then the powerful chairman of the Senate's Intelligence Committee. Bob took to introducing me as his cousin, as did his sister-in-law Katherine Graham, the legendary publisher of the *Washington Post,* when I got to know her on the Trilateral Commission.

Once, when I visited him in his Washington office, he said, "Bill, I think I found my family's cemetery up on an island off Scotland. Do you think your branch came from there too?" Our ambassador, who was with me, was amazed by the banter. "Is that what always goes on when you two get together?" he asked afterward. But, again, it all went back to the importance of personal relations and a sense of fun.

Given his influence in Washington, his Florida constituency, and the fact that Miami is the de facto financial capital of South America, Bob was met with open arms wherever we went on our trip. "How are we going to fit all this in?" I complained. "Everybody wants to talk to us." But it quickly became obvious that he was the one they wanted to talk to. I certainly had greater access to more powerful people in Brazil with Bob at my side than I had during a previous visit on my own, though I was able to one-up him by speaking French with President Cardoso. We met with the Foreign Affairs Committee, the Finance Committee, and various Congressional committees. After the formal business was completed, it turned out that virtually every senior Brazilian politician had family or investments in Florida and needed Bob Graham's help. All the great affairs of state, all the complicated issues of international law, were immediately tossed aside for an aunt who had a visa problem in Miami or a cousin who wanted financial assistance for his orange grove, thereby confirming the old adage that all politics is local politics.

In Bolivia we were introduced to the head of the navy. "Oh," I said, "I wasn't aware that Bolivia had a coastline."

"We don't," he replied, "but we're going to get it back from Chile one of these days." This was the first I heard of the century-old border dispute in which Bolivia had lost its access to the Pacific in 1904. Ever hopeful, it still kept an admiral and a few ships on Lake Titicaca.

As we prepared to leave for home, Bob and I were presented with a pair of beautiful silver pots used for drinking a tea made from mashed coca leaves as well as two large bags of the leaves, which are said to be very good for your health. "Bob," I said as we walked through the airport, "what are you going to say to the customs in Miami when they ask, Senator, what's in your bag, and the answer is a bunch of coca leaves? We'll both end up in the slammer for sure."

"You're right, Cousin," he said. "We've got to find somewhere to leave these bags without insulting our hosts." So we skulked around the airport until we found a bin in which to deposit them, then away we dashed.

Canada's ambassadors and their officials didn't always appreciate having MPs show up in Washington. They never knew what we intended to say or do, particularly the New Democrats and Bloquistes, and they couldn't control us even if they did know. Mostly, however, they recognized that lobbyists were being paid a fortune to have the kind of access we were getting for free. We spent whole weekends with high-powered congressmen and US senators, fishing at a lodge in Muskoka or cruising down the Mississippi in a riverboat. Our wives, who were always invited to come along, made their own friendships too. It got to the point where our ambassador asked me to bring him along whenever I saw Ben Gilman or Bob Graham or to invite them on his behalf to an embassy dinner.

As political power shifted in the United States to the south and southwest, Canada's ability to manage the American legislative process through our network of inter-parliamentary contacts became more limited. Increasingly, border issues came to mean the US-Mexico border, and Canada got sideswiped by Washington's preoccupation with Mexican migrants and Mexican drugs. The northern senators and representatives were often as horrified as we were by the low level of attention paid to Canadian interests and issues, but they no longer had the controlling voices. Whatever progress we had managed to make, however, changed with 9/11, and much for the worse.

7

DEMOCRATIC DEFICIT

During the 1990s most of SCFAIT's attention was focused on economic rather than military power. My first report as chair was about reforming the post-war Bretton Woods financial institutions, the International Monetary Fund (IMF) and the World Bank. The second report was on the role of small and medium-sized enterprises in Canadian international commerce; the third was a call for action to end the exploitation of child labour; the fourth concerned circumpolar cooperation; and the fifth looked into the OECD's proposed Multilateral Agreement on Investment. Others examined the future of the World Trade Organization (WTO), the Export Development Act, a free-trade area of the Americas, Canadian interests in Central Asia, and our relations with Mexico and the United States. The sole exception before 2000 was a study on nuclear weapons, which we undertook at the specific request of Lloyd Axworthy in 1998.

Our emphasis on commerce rather than defence was due to several factors: the collapse of the Soviet Union, the ending of the Cold War, the liberalization of world markets under Reaganomics and Thatcherism, the rapid expansion of the Internet and its impact on international finance, and the growing authority of the global financial and trade regime since the Second World War. The turmoil in Russia gave the world some breathing room, as it were, in which the threat of war took second place to the pursuit of growth. Reductions in military expenditures in many countries, leaving space for expanded social programs, were referred to as the "peace dividend." Domestically, as well, Prime Minister Chrétien's first two terms were fixated on reducing the deficit, creating jobs, and defeating separatism in Quebec.

Globalization kept increasing the need for a closer co-ordination of governmental policies to manage the system, and that, in turn, required a greater transfer of domestic jurisdiction to a variety of international arrangements. The tighter the integration, the tighter the regulations and the international obligations on nation-states had to be. As the clamps on national sovereignty became tighter, individual citizens began to feel a greater pinch and voiced their reactions. Yet they were also able to turn the system against their own governments. Within the European Union, for example, a Frenchman could now argue in a French court that a piece of French legislation violated the Treaty of Rome. If an Englishman wanted an injunction against the Crown to restrain his government from implementing a measure he didn't like, he could claim in court that Britain's European Union responsibilities trumped a thousand years of British common law. At the same time, however, both the Frenchman and the Englishman might feel that their lives were being affected for better or for worse by faceless people in a foreign institution over which they had no control. They might see their jobs moving somewhere else or fear for the survival of their customs and culture.

To some extent, national governments didn't mind that shift in focus. Instead of having to take responsibility for more flexible labour laws or less generous social benefits, they could blame somebody else for their own unpopular political decisions – "Europe made me do it" – just as the American administration blames the WTO, and the Canadian government blames the United States. When Cathy and I bought our house in Corsica in 1973, the village of Pigna was in a remote *département* of France, yet very much under the control of Paris. Now our Corsican neighbours tell us that Paris is far less relevant to their daily lives than the European Union. Brussels directs the noise level for their tractors and the quality of their sheep's milk. Brussels subsidizes the village theatre and the mountain roads. Some distant European bureaucrat has taken charge of what can and cannot be put in a sausage.

In Europe much of the initial protest was directed at the Council of Europe and the European Commission – in effect the executive – which were accused of being undemocratic because they weren't directly elected by the people (even though they represented the democratically elected governments of the day). As a result, the European Parliament, whose members were voted into office, developed over the course of thirty years from being little more than a talk-shop to being a legislative body with more power, more credibility, and more legitimacy in the eyes of the people. Even so, tensions remain that are all too familiar to Canadian federalism. When the Greeks rioted against the painful currency adjustments and structural reforms imposed on them by the European Union in 2011, I was reminded of going to Newfoundland in the early 1980s when interest rates were pushing toward 20 percent in the Bank of Canada's war against inflation. The Newfoundlanders were full of anger at what they saw as a policy designed to help the economies of Ontario and Quebec. Their own economic growth had been sideswiped, yet they could take no independent monetary action to ameliorate the provincial situation within the federal system. But at least Newfoundland can avail itself of the benefits of full integration with the rest of Canada and a system of transfer payments, whereas members of the Eurozone have a common currency without the political and economic underpinnings necessary to make the union work equitably for everybody.

Many Canadians feel a similar sense of impotence vis-à-vis the United States. Even if NAFTA and the GATT were designed to reduce the imbalance of power inherent in a bilateral agreement, there was concern that we were surrendering our ability to protect our cultural identity, social programs, labour standards, human rights, and environment. A constituent of mine, a well-known campaigner against the spread of pornography in any of its forms, once told me that the whole purpose of NAFTA had been to allow Canadian trees to be turned into paper, shipped to the United States, and returned to us in the form of American pornography. Although that might be a consequence, I argued with her, it could hardly be considered a purpose. But if your primary focus as a citizen is stopping the spread of pornography, you will see all these agreements through the prism of that concern.

The disproportionate power of the United States and Europe became more and more apparent in every part of the world as Western multinational corporations shifted ever more capital into Africa, Asia, and Latin America. They wanted the rule of law, trade regulations, protection for their investments, and the free movement of goods and services, which meant a more sophisticated WTO. But when the Africans, the Asians, and the Latin Americans began asking for something in return, they hit a wall. I remember talking to political leaders in India who said, "Okay, we'll give your companies the right to come in here, but we want free trade in people too. We want Indians to be able to go and work in North America because our biggest problem is population."

As long as the pie kept growing, nations were willing to sacrifice some of their sovereignty for a bigger slice. But when growth either stagnated or benefitted the few over the many, there was a blow-back against the World Bank, the IMF, the WTO, and every other multilateral institution. Trade liberalization became a hot political potato everywhere, and the heat was greatest during really hard times when voters were much less forgiving of foreign competition. In the 1997 financial crisis that hit Asia, there was a strong and understandable reaction among Asian governments against the impositions of the IMF. "We're not going to accept having Western medicine forced down our throats," was the mood, "and we damn well want to be in the room when you're writing out the prescriptions." If you're weak, you have to put up with it. If you're strong, you don't. In the United States itself, there has been a loss of popular support for the very system that the Americans had pressed into existence and continue to dominate. If at first they saw the improved, more judicial institutions as allies in the promotion of legitimate trade policies, they increasingly counted themselves among the losers, even though they and the Europeans were still the predominant winners. Now every candidate for the US presidency has to run on a solemn promise to protect the American economy from Japan or China.

Once, when my colleague Barry Campbell and I flew to New York to meet with George Soros, James Wolfensohn, Paul Volcker, and a whole host of experts as part of SCFAIT's study of the Bretton Woods institutions, I asked Soros if he thought they needed reform. "Yes, there are problems with them," said the legendary investor and philanthropist, who impressed me with his magnetic personality and his encyclopedic knowledge of global finance. "They're fallible, like all human constructs."

"So your business is finding where the fallible bits are, is it?" I asked.

"Yes," he said. "That's where the money is – in the fallible bits."

But not everyone could find advantage in the flawed system as Soros did.

AS HAPPENED WITH THE European Union, the anti-globalization protesters and NGOs zeroed in on the "democratic deficit" of these multilateral institutions, particularly the IMF and the WTO. They served only the elites, went the argument; they were removed from popular accountability. I wasn't convinced. In fact, I thought that the NGOs and the protesters, particularly those who engaged in violent rioting during the WTO ministerial conference I attended in Geneva in May 1998, were often themselves less than representative. Whether they are social-justice and environmental advocates or lobbyists for powerful economic and financial interests, most NGOs tended to be self-appointed groups with particular axes to grind, responsible to no one but their own small, special-interest bands. I remember returning to my hotel amid the police barricades, with helicopters buzzing overhead, and seeing the overturned, burnt-out car belonging to the ambassador from Jamaica – hardly the source of the New World Order so hated by the anti-capitalist left. Not all the protesters were rioters, of course; the majority had come to demonstrate peacefully. For me, though, the sight of that smoking car underscored the extent to which many activists were out of touch with the needs of developing countries for a fairer and more inclusive free-trade system.

Many of us who believed that the democratic deficit was a problem also believed that elected representatives were a better solution. "MPs are the best representatives of the civil society," I argued, "because they are actually elected to represent their constituents."

Nevertheless, something had to be done to bolster democratic participation in the WTO. So, while in Geneva, I joined a small group of parliamentarians who were interested in creating a WTO parliamentary assembly, not unlike those of NATO or the OSCE. Because that sort of institution would include members of the Opposition as well as members of the government, it would give a broader range of representatives more of a voice in the decision-making process. Over the next three and a half years I worked to get the idea off the ground with a diverse and dynamic network of interested people, both parliamentarians and NGO activists from across the political spectrum. We encountered quite a bit of resistance from the WTO's director general and those of its member states who worried about the time, money, and headaches involved in creating yet another standing body. Some preferred to let the Inter-Parliamentary Union, founded in 1889 and closely aligned with the United Nations, host the WTO's parliamentary dimension. Dictatorial regimes and the weaker democracies were adamantly against us because the last thing they wanted was to have their Opposition going to international trade meetings and making trouble. I could understand their position to some extent, because the Government of Canada always had problems when it sent Opposition members and provincial representatives, as well as industry and agricultural representatives, along with the negotiators, who were federal ministers and trade department officials. At one meeting I almost throttled Svend Robinson, the NDP member of SCFAIT, when he antagonized the Chinese by asking whether Taiwan should be included in a WTO parliamentary assembly.

Nevertheless, I firmly believed that inclusiveness was the best way to increase the WTO's legitimacy, even if it came at the expense of efficiency. For the same reason, when SCFAIT was asked to prepare a report on the future of the WTO in advance of the ministerial trade negotiations scheduled for November 1999 in Seattle, we held extensive hearings across Canada, included a cross-section of opinion in the final report, and even produced a "Citizen's Guide to the WTO" as an educational resource. Janice Hilchie and Gerry Schmitz hardly slept for a couple of days as they rushed to complete it for Pierre Pettigrew, our international trade minister, before the Commons recessed in June.

In November 1999 I attended the WTO negotiations in Seattle. Though not a member of the official Canadian delegation, I was invited in my role as chair of SCFAIT and chair of its trade subcommittee to go to various sessions at which the Canadian ministers and their senior officials briefed us on the progress of the negotiations. Pettigrew was especially effective at these international meetings. Fluent in English, French, and Spanish, he was a highly respected go-between for many people in the "Green Room," where all the secret deals took place. The rest of us then got a chance to express our opinions and ideas. Being in Seattle also gave me another opportunity to pursue the idea of a WTO parliamentary association at the discussions organized by US senator William V. Roth, chairman of the Senate Finance Committee.

As it happened, the massive demonstrations and violent protests that were taking place in the streets of Seattle gave urgency to our argument that some kind of democratic reform had become necessary. At one point Pierre Pettigrew had to climb over a fence to get to a meeting that the rioters were trying to interrupt. Another time we couldn't leave one of the conference hotels because of the tear gas in the air. My own hotel was across town, so I resigned myself to being trapped for the night without a room. "You can always sleep on the floor of our room," volunteered the wife of Chuck Grassley, the Republican senator from Iowa whom I had come to know through the meetings of the Canada-US Inter-Parliamentary Group. Senator Grassley looked less enthusiastic, indeed horrified, and understandably so. "Now, Chuck," Mrs. Grassley said, "you're not being very gentlemanly to our Canadian neighbour." Around two in the morning, however, the tear gas cleared and a group of us were taken back to our hotel by bus. Apart from the damage done to businesses and buildings in the city itself, the riots also crippled the ability of the negotiators to do their work. If the demonstrators didn't actually prevent an agreement from being reached, they certainly made it more difficult, and the vehemence of their protests was in essence an illustration of the unease over the changes provoked by globalization.

The next round I attended was held in November 2001 in Doha, Qatar, chosen presumably because it was less subject to interruption. The Doha Round was different, and not just because it was held in such an unusual place. To some extent it was an attempt by the WTO to recognize the angst that had been produced in Seattle. If the previous rounds had been a case of the Americans and the Europeans getting together with a few of their friends to figure out what they wanted and then getting everyone else to fall in line, Doha was where the Chinese, the Brazilians, the Indians, and the less developed economies had the strength to insist on their own interests.

The Canadian delegation included officials from the provinces as well as representatives of the federal government. I noted then, as I have noted before and since, that Alberta and Quebec were highly active participants, whereas Ontario was virtually absent. That never ceased to surprise me, given how dependent its economy is on international trade. Canada's agricultural marketing boards were also there in droves to protect their own interests. I hadn't really appreciated until then how thorny those issues were in terms of domestic politics or how hugely consequential to their regional economies. The marketing board reps were interesting as a group, and after I got to know them better, I liked to joke that I too represented a rural constituency because I had Riverdale Farm in my riding. "It's seven acres in a park in Cabbagetown," I said, "with a pig barn and a bunch of chickens." They laughed, but trade was a serious, complicated matter on which many livelihoods and ways of life depended. In fact, agricultural protection seemed to be on everybody's agenda, whether France or India, and it often pushed the free-trade forces into full retreat. "You're our most powerful minister here, not Pettigrew," I teased Lyle Vanclief, the federal minister of agriculture.

In the end, all the work on behalf of a WTO parliamentary assembly came to little. It simply morphed into a parliamentary conference on the WTO, created in 2003 by the European Parliament and the Inter-Parliamentary Union, which meets at least once a year but without the kind of power I had hoped such an institution would have. But the value of parliamentary diplomacy as a means of fighting the democratic deficit was so high that I was already engaged in trying to make it a success on a totally different front: Latin America.

DESPITE DECADES OF Canadian investment and a huge potential market for our goods and services, Canada came rather late to Latin America. In part, that had to do with our reluctance to join the Organization of American States (OAS), yet another institution that had been founded in the aftermath of the Second World War to settle disputes, encourage trade, and promote human rights. It had grown out of a series of hemispheric conferences beginning in 1889 and, headquartered in Washington, DC, is run by a permanent council, a general secretariat, and an assembly of delegates from each member state.

Our principal reason for staying out was a suspicion, not unfounded, that the OAS was basically an instrument by which the United States sought to protect and advance its own interests in the region. Thus, when Fidel

Castro turned communist, the Americans managed to have Cuba's membership suspended in 1962 over the objections of those Latin American nations who, like Canada, felt that it was better to dialogue with the Cubans rather than isolate them. Joining the OAS looked like a no-win scenario: either the Latin Americans would criticize us if we sided with the Americans or the Americans would criticize us for not voting with them. Despite the risks, Prime Minister Brian Mulroney decided in 1989 that it was time for Canada to sign up as a full member, and I thought it was the right thing to do. Refusing to take the seat that had been reserved for us no longer made sense. The OAS is an important organization in our hemisphere; it is key to the development of our trade relations with Latin America; and it is a vehicle to foster democracy. And US hegemony in the Americas is no longer what it was, as evidenced by the rise of Brazil.

I became more fully aware of how complex Latin America was when I represented Canada as a guest at the meeting of the Non-Aligned Movement in Cartagena, Colombia, in October 1995. Though Canada wasn't among the more than one hundred participating members, we were invited to send observers, and the government asked me to attend as Canada's representative. My role as chair of SCFAIT lent me enough weight from a protocol perspective to talk to officials from a number of countries with which we were trying to do business. Our embassy in Bogota arranged a long list of bilateral meetings and informal "pull-asides" to discuss free trade with the Chileans, for example, and Canadian mining activities in Colombia. It was my first exposure to an international summit, which was attended by a host of world leaders, including the presidents of Indonesia, the Philippines, and Zimbabwe, the prime ministers of India, Pakistan, and Malaysia, and Yasser Arafat representing Palestine.

I was struck by the fact that everybody spoke the language of globalism no matter how far their governments were to the left. Though Cheddi Jagan, the president of Guyana, kept the largely sympathetic audience spellbound with his attack on capitalism in general and the United States in particular, Fidel Castro showed up wearing a business suit. I didn't have to know much Spanish to be captivated by Castro's presence and the drama of his oratory. When I next heard him speak at the WTO meeting in Geneva, he overran his allotted few minutes by an hour, yet no one either wanted or dared to cut him off. On that occasion he concluded by declaring his support for Europe's efforts to develop its own currency, the Euro, which he saw as a way to lift the world from the "oppressive imperialism" of the Yankee dollar. "Vive the Euro!" he shouted, and the entire audience – except for the Americans, of course – rose up and cheered. It showed how one speech can turn a debate on a dime.

As was happening everywhere in the world, the liberalization of international trade and the integration of global finance gave rise to a number of multilateral pacts in Latin America such as ALCA and MERCOSUR, equivalent to NAFTA in North America or AFTA in Asia. Underlying every one of these deals were the same questions about democratic legitimacy that haunted the WTO. One response, the brainchild of Brazil, was the creation in 1997 of the Parliamentary Confederation of the Americas (COPA), a non-legislative forum in which parliamentarians from North, Central, and South America could come together to discuss issues of mutual concern.

However, Canada and a few other primarily federal countries had a problem with COPA because it had been designed to include subnational as well as national states. That wasn't wrong in theory. Given the blurring of domestic and international affairs, parliamentarians from states in Brazil or Mexico, just like the Canadian provinces, were involved in global issues that had a profound impact on the lives of their citizens. Why then shouldn't they be involved in the discussions of those issues? There was even a time when I argued that Ottawa should set up a special foreign affairs committee that would include members of the provincial legislatures. Though it would probably have been cumbersome to operate, it was certainly justifiable as an idea. But it went wrong in practice when it was used to work against the national interest. Lucien Bouchard's Parti Québécois government was especially proactive in using COPA as a vehicle for promoting Quebec separatism in international circles. Quebec City even spent millions of dollars to host the organization's first conference in September 1997.

Don Boudria, Canada's minister for international co-operation at the time, returned from the conference appalled by Bouchard's grandstanding on the world stage. "Would it be possible," he asked me, "to create a parallel organization under the aegis of the OAS that can be confined to the national level?" As a result, I was given a mandate by the Government of Canada to try to establish an OAS parliamentary assembly, along with additional funds to pay the administrative costs and hire a Spanish-speaking person to help me and a group of officials launch the idea.

"Why are you doing that?" the Bloc Québécois MPs asked in the House. "You're doing it just to thwart Quebec."

"No," was our answer. "It's not to thwart Quebec but to serve Canada." That was a legitimate response – the idea had taken on a value of its own.

For the next three years I travelled throughout the hemisphere to press the case for an interparliamentary organization that would be a kind of unofficial democratic arm of the OAS. I worked hard with Peter Boehm, our ambassador to the OAS, to overcome the OAS's own hesitations by meeting frequently with its secretary general, César Gaviria, a former president of Colombia, and by lobbying the ambassadors of the various member states. In the process, I came to know the chairman of the Foreign Affairs Committee of the Parliament of Argentina, whose government shared Canada's concerns about COPA's threat to national unity. Nicaragua, Costa Rica, and Barbados came onside without much trouble. Through my involvement with the Canada-Mexico Parliamentary Association, I lobbied prominent Mexican colleagues including Beatriz Paredes Rangel, then president of the House, and Gustavo Carvajal Moreno, a former president of the powerful Institutional Revolutionary Party, who were at first skeptical but also concerned about the anti-centralist agitation in Chiapas.

Oswaldo Sandoval, the energetic chair of the Peruvian Foreign Relations Committee, who had a warm regard for Canada because of his close contacts with Canadian senators through the Asia Pacific Parliamentary Forum, was another great ally in rallying South American support. The Brazilians were initially resistant because they didn't appreciate other people muscling in on what they saw as their hegemony. In fact, President Fernando Henrique Cardoso agreed to see me only because of his respect for Prime Minister Chrétien. Their close friendship was partly based on the fact that Cardoso had had an academic career in France at one point, so he and Chrétien could speak French together at international summits, as did I during all my conversations with him. It was another small but telling example of the benefits of Canada's bilingualism. Once the Brazilians began to see how COPA was seeding some separatist problems for themselves as well, they became more open to our initiative.

The United States proved the hardest nut to crack, especially the US Congress. With each passing decade following the Second World War, the Americans had become increasingly resistant to setting up new international structures, for fear that their country would be pulled into a quagmire or badly outnumbered. Instead, they preferred to play everybody off individually, one-on-one and one against the other. Years later, when Jorge Castañeda and I tried to interest Colin Powell in establishing an annual meeting of the three NAFTA foreign ministers to help work out a few issues, he adamantly refused. "God, no," he said, "I won't do it. I just can't go to any more meetings. I see you guys all over the place, I'm happy to talk to you on the margins, but I'm not going to formalize yet more meetings."

But without the Americans, creating an effective parliamentary assembly of the Americas would have been impossible. I enlisted the help of Peter Boehm and the Canadian embassy in Washington, and we eventually managed to persuade one congressman, Cass Ballenger, because of his personal interest in Latin America. He knew Hugo Chávez quite well and later liked to entertain us with his tales about hosting Chávez at his home in Hickory, North Carolina, in 2001. When Cass agreed to join, that was enough to break the logjam, though the strains remained between those Americans who feared that the assembly would lead to a loss of US sovereignty and those in Latin America who feared it would become a tool of US imperialism.

The final obstacle was, predictably, the expense: Who was going to pay for the administration and travel costs? No country ever wants to be burdened with a perennial financial commitment. In this case, however, Canada agreed to pick up the tab to at least get it going. And so, on March 7, 2001, representatives from twenty-six countries gathered in Ottawa for the inaugural meeting of the Inter-Parliamentary Forum of the Americas (FIPA), which was rebranded ParlAmericas ten years later. I was honoured to be elected chair of the meeting and the organization's first president. However, I wasn't able to complete the two-year term because, the following January, I was appointed to the Cabinet.

"I was proud of the role that Canada played in establishing this new institution, which will serve to link parliaments and peoples throughout our hemisphere," I said when I stepped down at the second meeting in Mexico in March 2002. "I am firmly convinced that its role will increase in significance as the forces of integration continue to bring us closer and closer together from the north to the south poles."

A MONTH AFTER FIPA's formation, it presented its first recommendations at the Third Summit of the Americas, hosted by Canada in Quebec City in April 2001. Thirty-four leaders attended, including President George W. Bush on his first visit to Canada since his inauguration, the anti-American Venezuelan president Hugo Chávez, and Brazil's president Cardoso, who was asked to sit close to Chávez and keep him under control. Also present were an estimated fifty thousand demonstrators, who filled the streets with their chants and placards as they had in Geneva and Seattle, whether in opposition to free trade and global finance or in defence of the environment, women's rights, Aboriginal affairs, and democracy.

As it happened, in preparing the summit's agenda, the Canadian government had already undertaken extensive consultations on most of those very issues, including the development of an OAS charter designed to make the governments of the Americas more democratic and accountable. The process was a good example of the more inclusive approach that Jean Chrétien wanted to bring to international forums. If the summit had been held in Brazil, for instance, I doubt whether President Cardoso and his people would have gone out and consulted widely about what they should be doing. In fact, the collaborative approach was unprecedented. Some countries even resented it. They didn't want outsiders coming in and asking, "What do the Opposition members in your parliament think about this business?"

As chair of both SCFAIT and FIPA, I was nominated as the parliamentarian responsible for carrying out the consultations, along with Marc Lortie, a smart, popular Foreign Affairs officer who had been Canada's ambassador to Chile and who would go on to serve as our ambassador to Spain and France. We reported directly to the prime minister on our findings and recommendations. That involved months and months of extra work, but it was exciting and interesting. I chaired several committees and spent a lot of time talking with Latin American politicians, NGOs, and activists. Because the Aboriginal section would be an important part of the Inter-American Democratic Charter, we met with Indigenous groups throughout the Americas and organized an assembly for their leaders to come together, building on what SCFAIT had learned from its report on the Arctic and our hearings into the plight of Colombia's Embera Katio peoples, whose lands were endangered by the Urra dam project that was financed with bonds guaranteed by Canada's Export Development Corporation.

The cynics said we were only paying lip-service to democracy as a kind of public-relations exercise. "You're just papering over the problems," I sometimes heard. But once you start a process that allows people to make a contribution, it's difficult to bring it to a halt. If you open the doors, you have to pay attention to the people who enter the room. If you want to be credible, you have to respect their right to be heard. In the end, however, all Marc and I could do was deliver our report to the prime minister for consideration. It was then fed into the government's background papers, out of which emerged a draft declaration that was shared with the other member states who were coming to Quebec City. During the course of the summit itself, I kept reporting to Mr. Chrétien on a regular basis. For the first time, I felt I had a genuine professional working relationship with him, one-on-one, face to face, day after day. "What do you think about this?" he would ask. "What are these guys doing? What can we do about it?" Except for maybe a couple of times in caucus, he had never asked me what I thought about anything. We had real exchanges, real discussions. I liked being at the centre of the action, even if it sometimes meant I had Eddie Goldenberg barking at me for opening the wrong doors, and I learned a great deal about the decision-making process on the inside.

Outside, meanwhile, all hell broke loose around us. Although most of the protesters were peaceful, a few turned violent. When some threw rocks, the police responded with tear gas. Daniel Turp and I got caught in a cloud of it while walking over to a meeting near the Quebec Legislature. During the formal dinner I had my first conversation with Colin Powell. Shortly afterward, my cell phone rang. It was Martha Butterfield, one of our closest friends. She was in a protest march with many other people we knew, including Elizabeth May, Maude Barlow, and Judy Rebick. "Bill, where are you?" Martha shouted above the noise, and then I heard her say, "Judy, come over here and listen to this. Bill's in there talking to Colin Powell while we're out here being attacked by the police." For years afterward she used to counter my arguments by saying, "Oh, aren't you the guy who was inside there having a party while we were outside on the barricades trying to save society from the evils of globalization?"

As I saw it, however, we were on the same side. In fact, the leaders of dozens of NGOs were outside on the streets one moment and, the next, inside at meetings with Cabinet ministers and the heads of the multilateral institutions. No sane person wanted to put an end to international trade. Some 40 percent of Canada's GDP related to exports, and it was impossible to imagine us depending on our internal economy alone. At the same time, no one could deny that the globalized economy challenged national governments and their individual citizens in every area of life. The Quebec City summit was just another in a series of holistic efforts to promote good governance and social justice, combat poverty and corruption, bolster health and education, and reform the conditions under which trade itself is conducted. And though the media chose to focus on the demonstrations, the summit's substantial six-page declaration and its comprehensive eighteen-point plan of action were indications of remarkable progress.

AT THE HEART OF the conflict, whether in Seattle or Quebec City, was a basic disagreement over whether free trade and global finance strengthen or weaken the spread of democracy and human rights. Like Prime Minister Chrétien and his government, I believed and still believe that the reduction of trade barriers between countries, accompanied by appropriate institutional safeguards, will ultimately prove more beneficial than harmful to most people. Why? Because, over time, trade will draw more and more countries into a nexus of international laws, regulations, and institutions that will create a safer and better-governed world. Despite the ups and downs of current events, I point to Canada's experience with the People's Republic of China as but one example.

After adopting the Open Door Policy in 1978, China realized it needed to improve its understanding of the rules of international trade law and trade practices, particularly as it was keen to become part of the GATT. For two years in the 1980s, through a program funded by the Canadian International Development Agency, I had helped to teach trade law and international law to young Chinese officials from the Ministry of Foreign

Economic Relations and Trade who were attending a special course organized by my friend Rosemary McCarney. In 1990 Cathy and I joined Rosemary and her husband, Barry Fisher, on a reciprocal program in China. We lived in rather rudimentary accommodations in a village outside Beijing, which gave us some sense of the real life of the Chinese people, and I felt I was learning a lot more than I taught.

China's strong commitment to preparing the country for full integration into the nexus of international law was evident by the time I returned in September 1999 as chair of SCFAIT at the invitation of my Chinese counterpart Zeng Jianhui. I was accompanied by several parliamentarians, including the first Chinese Canadian woman MP, Sophia Leung, who was born in the southern province of Wuxi, where her father was a general under Chiang Kai-shek before fleeing to Taiwan in 1948. With Cathy joining us at her own expense, we toured the Forbidden City and climbed the Great Wall, saw the magnificent terracotta soldiers in Xian, took a river cruise to see the famous Li Mountains, and admired the magnificent reclining Buddha outside Chongqing, which was twinned as a Sister City with Toronto in 1986. There I met the father of a constituent of mine, then in his nineties, an extraordinary gentleman who had been a personal secretary to Zhou Enlai and subsequently governor of Sichuan province. When we parted, he presented me with a piece of calligraphy he had done, which read in Chinese, "To Bill Graham, chairman of the foreign affairs committee, from his friend." It hangs above my desk to this day.

Wherever we went, we had high-level meetings with prominent officials and local authorities, from Beijing politicians to provincial governors to the mayor of Shanghai. As a result, we came away with a better understanding of where the Chinese were coming from, not just at the national level but at the regional and municipal levels as well, and many of us made long-lasting connections throughout China. Of course, belting down a large number of toasts in rapid succession might have created a false bonhomie. At one dinner I had what I believed was a very interesting and profound conversation with a governor, though he spoke no English, I spoke no Chinese, and the interpreter had disappeared!

Normally I love Sichuan cooking, but I admit to being challenged at one of the fabulous meals the Chinese love to host. In the middle of the meal two large vats were wheeled out in front of us, one of steaming oil and one of steaming broth. While we looked on, the waiter held up a frog, eviscerated and skinned it with a knife, dropped the body into the broth and the skin into the oil, and served up the results on our plates. As in Niger, we knew that diplomacy sometimes required eating the inedible for the sake of your country.

When I taught trade law, I used to have on my wall a cover photograph of the *Economist* showing Margaret Thatcher with the premier of China. "What do you think they're doing?" I asked my students. "Talking about war and peace? No, she's trying to sell him British airplanes. She's a saleswoman. That's the nature of the modern world."

Prime Minister Chrétien understood very clearly how international trade is often a matter of human relations. That was the idea behind his seven Team Canada missions, in which he led hundreds of business executives, university presidents, cultural representatives, and the provincial premiers on what were essentially sales trips to nine different countries, including China in February 2001. In many ways the Team Canada trips were characteristic of Chrétien – well organized, professional, effective, yet totally unorthodox, relatively informal, and very pragmatic. They succeeded because they were based on people networking and socializing. Indeed, they were sometimes as effective in connecting the Canadian delegates with each other as with the foreigners. On the road, lasting friendships were forged between politicians and business leaders, between federal and provincial officials, and across party lines and competing interests, as we all came together in one united effort to secure contracts, recruit students, or foster investments.

In January 1997, for example, I went with Team Canada to South Korea, the Philippines, and Thailand, which was of great interest to me because of the large Asian community in my riding. One of my purposes was to help a constituent who had a specific business proposal in the Philippines. I found some interest and made some contacts that led to further contacts. At the same time I was able to have long talks with the premier of Ontario and others in the delegation about business opportunities, trade regulations, and politics.

In China, in particular, if you want to do business, you don't just walk in and start dealing. You have to approach the right people at the right level, and that means taking the time – often a lot of time – to lay the groundwork, learn the protocol, and develop trust. Achieving success is like feeling your way through a minefield, and few things are accomplished without official government contacts. Moreover, trading with China did not mean ignoring the darker side of Chinese society. Canadians have obvious interests in developing cordial relations with an extraordinarily powerful nation and an increasingly important trading partner, but we also have clear values regarding democracy and rights. So, do we throw over our interests for the sake of our values, or do we throw over our values for the sake of our interests? Good foreign policy is often about finding that the two may become mutually reinforcing.

I think the Chrétien government did a good job in striking the right balance. When Lloyd Axworthy was foreign minister, he was constantly under attack for being too values-oriented at the cost of our economic or security interests. On the other hand, Mr. Chrétien once got into trouble with the media for joking that he couldn't tell the premier of a province what to do, so how was he expected to tell the premier of China what to do? "If you want me to try to run the whole world, fine," he said, "but don't criticize me if I don't get very far." That was typical of him: a serious point made inside a light remark. It was also common sense, and he was right to recognize the reality. Canada could no more force China to change its political system than it could prevent the United States from invading Iraq, if that's what the Americans were determined to do.

That said, on every visit I made to China, I always raised the issue of political and human rights with our interlocutors. At first, because I was fairly low on the totem pole, they brushed aside my questions as a matter for the government leaders. The discussions grew more intense after I became foreign minister, for my brief included explaining Canada's values and interests to the Chinese. The trick was to deliver the human rights message in a way that was instructive without being insulting or patronizing, to explain how listening to what I had to say was to their advantage, just as I myself would benefit from hearing what they had to say. And what was the alternative? Suspend trade? Declare war?

When my counterpart Tang Jiaxuan, one of the few cold and imperious officials I met in China, treated me to an hour-and-a-half rant about the evils of Falun Gong, I replied, "You may not want me to talk about these things, but I'm a politician, I have voters in my constituency who came from your country. Some are members of Falun Gong, and they're decent, hard-working people. They come to me with their concerns about what they perceive as abuses or injustices in your system. I want to be able to tell them that I met with you and that you also want to make the system better. Better for them, better for you, better for everybody. Wanting to make things better is our duty as politicians. So what can we do to help?"

Slow, respectful help may not be dramatic, and for some people it will never be enough, but in my view our values will enhance our interests in the long term, because a democratic, law-abiding China is more likely to be a peaceful, prosperous China. As elsewhere, becoming a party to hundreds of international treaties and conventions has had a profound impact on the law in China, and even though China has rejected the authority of many multilateral institutions, it has become more involved in ensuring that its own interests and values are reflected in the formulation of those international treaties and conventions.

"If you're going to be an effective participant in the WTO," I used to argue, "you have to understand that there are things that other people will expect, among which are commercial courts that can render real justice. No foreigners are going to invest in China if they think they're going to be subject to the whims of some Communist judge left over from the old system. You have to overhaul your judicial system to make it more responsive, more transparent, more just." Indeed, the estimate is that the Chinese government, as part of its accession to the WTO, has had to repeal or alter almost three thousand pieces of domestic legislation and regulations.

At times, in a quiet, low-level way, Canada was able to do some good. In 1997 we established a joint committee on human rights with China to address such issues as political and civil rights, religious freedoms, and women's rights. I once visited an institute where Chinese judges were being trained in commercial matters in preparation for China's coming into the WTO through a program financed by the Canadian International Development Agency. The agency also helped fund an important program that allowed Chinese judges to study in other countries, including Canada, to enhance their legal training, and it later initiated courses taught in China for Canadian lawyers to help build a new rapport and familiarity with Chinese society, law, and legal culture. That initiative eventually contributed to the establishment of Canadian law offices in China, particularly Shanghai.

Because of the rich matrix of personal and professional relationships that binds our two countries together, Canada proved particularly well placed to engage with China in a world that would be increasingly Pacific-centric. Almost 1.5 million Canadian citizens come from a Chinese background, and Chinese is the country's third-largest mother tongue after English and French. Tens of thousands of Chinese students have studied here, and tens of thousands of Canadians have worked in China. When I attended the Association of Southeast Asian Nations (ASEAN) forum in Jakarta in 2004, Chinese foreign minister Li Zhaoxing teased me about the fact that I spoke only English and French, not Chinese.

"So many people speak Chinese in Vancouver," piped up Chris Patten, the former British governor of Hong Kong, who was standing beside us, "that it's sometimes referred to as Hongcouver."

Li laughed and said, "Bill, you should make Chris the governor of Hongcouver."

It was a joke, of course, but with a sharp point: How would the people of Canada feel if a foreign power governed one of our major cities as an imperial outpost? Once again, I saw the importance of empathy in understanding other views, and I recognized how the empathy we had developed as a nation to deal with our internal diversity could be directed to our dealings with international issues. Nor is international law a one-way street. The norms, conventions, treaties, and customs that make up the body of international law are but a reflection of the interests and values of the states that agree to define and, in turn, obey the law.

International law has always been informed by global politics. To date, it's fair to say, its gradual development has been largely influenced by the perspectives and interests of the West, due to the political, economic, and military realities of the nineteenth and twentieth centuries. However, as we enter an increasingly multipolar world, the question will be whether China is going to accept the multilateral legal rules that others have evolved (such as the GATT and the International Criminal Court), insist on bringing a whole new set of international norms to the table (vide the Asian Infrastructure Investment Bank), or (as in the case of its unconventional claims in the South China Sea) argue that it is acting in accordance with its own particular interpretation of international law.

"Right is only in question between equals in power," the historian Thucydides observed almost 2,500 years ago, "while the strong do what they can and the weak suffer what they must."

8

HUMAN SECURITY

While the accelerated integration of the global economy was forcing a reassessment of the international institutions, laws, and regulations built to deal with it, the sudden disintegration of the Soviet Union initiated a similar reassessment of the multilateral institutions, laws, and regulations built to deal with the Cold War. Nothing was spared: the role of the United Nations and its peacekeeping missions, the purpose of the North Atlantic Treaty Organization (NATO) and its possible expansion, the defence of North America, the notion of the sovereignty of nations, the place of nuclear weapons – everything was on the table.

It was telling that SCFAIT's single report on military issues in the 1990s had less to do with preparing for war than with expanding the peace. In 1996, at the request of Lloyd Axworthy, we undertook a review of Canada's nuclear-weapons policy. Ours was the first such study conducted by national legislators, well in advance of the formation in 2000 of Parliamentarians for Nuclear Non-proliferation and Disarmament, which was made up of five hundred representatives from seventy countries. We held hearings across the country, interviewed numerous experts and NGOs, and examined hundreds of submissions from individuals and organizations. I was particularly struck by how many of those who had been most intimately involved with nuclear weapons were among the most skeptical about their usefulness. One of our witnesses, Robert McNamara, who had been secretary of defense under Presidents Kennedy and Johnson, was convinced that nuclear weapons served no military purpose except to deter one's opponent from using them, and several former US generals, now out of uniform, decried the role of the nuclear arsenal for which they had recently been responsible.

Our report came out in December 1998, with fifteen recommendations for the progressive reduction and eventual elimination of nuclear weapons, including what was then a highly controversial proposal that NATO should consider reducing the role of nuclear weapons in its strategic plan. Both the United States and the United Kingdom let it be known that they were unhappy with SCFAIT's work, though we hadn't gone so far as to endorse a "no-first-use" policy. The attention our report received within the Canadian government and other NATO member states again demonstrated the important and relatively new role that parliamentarians were playing in the shaping of policy on international issues.

The 1990s were not a decade of universal peace, but the exceptions tended to be civil wars rather than conflicts between nations: Rwanda, Sierra Leone, Somalia, Haiti, and the former Yugoslavia. Though each of them involved the Western powers to some extent, none was of more concern to Europe than the barbaric fighting that broke out in 1992 in the newly independent country of Bosnia and Herzegovina, generally referred to as Bosnia. When Yugoslavia disintegrated in the early 1990s, the former socialist republics of Slovenia, Croatia, Macedonia, and Bosnia broke away, leaving Serbia and Montenegro to reconstitute themselves as the Federal Republic of Yugoslavia under the leadership of the Serbian ultra-nationalist Slobodan Milošević. Shortly after declaring its independence, Bosnia descended into a vicious civil war between the Eastern Orthodox Serbs and Muslim Bosnians, with the Roman Catholic Croats pursuing their own agenda, sometimes seeking more autonomy for their own people and other times fighting with the Muslim Bosnians against the Serbs. The Serbian rebels, backed by Milošević's government, began a three-and-a-half-year siege of Sarajevo and launched a campaign of "ethnic cleansing" against Muslims and Catholics alike. To complicate matters even more, the Serbs inside Bosnia founded their own breakaway republic, the Republic of Srpska, where non-Serbs were also ruthlessly "cleansed."

Shocked by the resurgence of armed ethnic conflict on the doorstep of the European Community itself, the UN Security Council responded in February 1992 by dispatching a peacekeeping force, to which the Mulroney government agreed to contribute troops. Two years later, when the mission produced only limited success, NATO decided to engage in the first use of military power since its formation in 1949 by launching airstrikes against Serbian positions. But even NATO's involvement didn't curb the heavy fighting that took place all through 1995, including the massacre in a single week of an estimated seven thousand Muslim men and boys in Srebrenica, supposedly a UN "safe area." After Srebrenica, NATO stepped up its aerial war, which eventually helped drive the Serbs to the bargaining table. In December 1995 the Dayton Peace Accords were signed, and NATO took on the responsibility of fielding a new peacekeeping force of 60,000 troops, including 1,200 Canadians, on a mission that would last nearly a decade. In 2004 I would visit Bosnia-Herzegovina as defence minister to oversee the handover from NATO's peacekeeping forces to an EU-led mission.

Our long-standing involvement in the Balkans was yet another example of how an international obligation determined a domestic decision. Canada was in Bosnia because the UN and our NATO allies had chosen to be there. If we were going to support multilateralism and enjoy the benefits of belonging to the club, we had to pay our dues.

In November 1997 I visited Bosnia with members of SCFAIT and the national defence committee to study whether Canada should continue to participate in NATO's peacekeeping mission. I vividly recall witnessing the damage done by the siege of Sarajevo. Our group visited one hospital that had been under constant sniper fire and taken a couple of hundred hits from shells. My notes described the building as looking like "Swiss cheese." A doctor showed me the bullet holes in the wall behind his desk, one of which had narrowly missed him.

A drive through the countryside revealed a startling contrast between the stunning mountainous beauty (which reminded me of Corsica) and the ruins of countless homes and villages. I was told that many of the recent mass graves had been dug beside mass graves from the Second World War and earlier, all the way back to the time of the Ottoman Empire. "Layers on layers of death," I wrote. In Banja Luka, the largest city of the Republic of Srpska, which by this point had been reintegrated into Bosnia, we met with its leader, President Biljana Plavšić, a biologist and former Fulbright scholar. Perhaps hoping to impress a group of visiting Canadians, she represented herself as a moderate Serb nationalist who was interested solely in getting the Dayton Accords off the ground. She never gave even a hint of the deeply racist views that emerged when she was indicted as a war criminal by the International Criminal Tribunal for the former Yugoslavia a few years later.

As always in my travels to regions where Canadian Forces were deployed, I was impressed by the professionalism and enthusiasm of our troops stationed there, and my conversations with them and other members of the NATO mission increased my understanding of the complex nature of contemporary armed conflict. As one colonel put it, Bosnia was a long way from being a traditional military operation because every soldier had "to understand all the political ramifications, election monitoring, etc., in order to understand what the military mandate is to guarantee safety." Major-General Angus Ramsay, a British division commander in the Republic of Srpska, pressed upon me the distinction between "peace enforcement" and "peacekeeping." NATO had chosen a peace enforcement approach, he explained, because the earlier attempts by the United Nations at peace-keeping in Bosnia hadn't worked. Without proper rules of engagement that would allow multinational peacekeepers to defend themselves and prevent atrocities, they would – and did – find themselves in intolerable situations. Beginning with Bosnia, NATO was playing an entirely new role in the post–Cold War world, and in the years to come it would find itself operating farther and farther afield from Europe.

NATO's twelve original signatories had first envisaged it as a vehicle to deter Soviet expansion westward and to prevent a revival of nationalistic militarism in Central Europe. Or, as Lord Ismay, its first secretary general, wryly put it, the purpose of NATO was "to keep the Americans in, the Russians out, and the Germans down." In effect, the partners agreed to sacrifice a degree of independence for the sake of their mutual security – another step toward the political integration of Europe whether intended or not. Even today, despite the existence of the Common Security and Defence Policy under the authority of the European Council, Europe still relies primarily on NATO for its security and defence.

For Canada, as well, NATO remains a key part of our security architec-ture, and despite some episodic efforts to reassess our membership or reduce our expenditures, we have maintained a good reputation within the organization. As NATO secretary general Lord Robertson once put it, "Canada may be low on its defence inputs, but it's large on its outputs." That remained true even when we grew frustrated with the NATO command structure, particularly during the later conflict in Afghanistan.

With the end of the Cold War, Canada became a particularly strong proponent of NATO expansion into the former Soviet satellites. I got involved in the issue through my work with the OSCE Parliamentary Assembly. Expansion wasn't only – or even mostly – about security and defence. NATO saw itself as a means of advancing the values of democracy and freedom among the peoples of Eastern Europe. And because it perceived itself as an association of like-minded countries that didn't accept dictatorships, entry required a demonstration of civilian control over the military and a respect for human rights. Aspirant countries such as Hungary and Romania viewed getting into NATO as the first step to achieving their real ambition – joining the European Union for economic reasons. If that meant more democracy, so be it.

However, being accepted into NATO is a long, difficult process. One of the advantages of this delay is that it gives the allies time to compare the country's actual progress against the promised goals. When Georgia applied, for example, we thought it was a good candidate under NATO's Membership Action Plan. After its war with Russia in 2008, however, few NATO members were keen on the prospect of finding that NATO's principle of collective defence obliged us to intervene because some belligerent Georgian had decided to poke the Russian bear in the eye. One of the disadvantages of this lengthy process is that it can jeopardize ever reaching the goal. As the Finnish foreign minister once explained to me over dinner, the three-year process to join Partnership for Peace – a condition for any eventual membership in NATO – had created numerous political problems in his country. Having been invaded by Russia in the past, Finland obviously wanted to use NATO as a shield, but the long waiting period enabled Moscow to exert intolerable pressure to prevent that from happening. Instead, the Finns joined the European Union. Unlike those countries that saw NATO as a stepping stone into the European Union, Finland saw the EU as an alternative to NATO. Once the Finns were in, they figured, they would be under the Europeans' security umbrella anyway.

The Russians I met always expressed serious concerns about what NATO was doing. Whenever I talked with Vladimir Lukin, my Russian counterpart as the chairman of the foreign affairs committee of the Russian Duma, we got into fierce arguments about it. "We're not expanding against anybody," I said. "These are small countries that feel they need protection from you. If you were Hungarian, wouldn't you want to be a member of NATO?"

"Nonsense, of course it's against Russia," he replied. "If you're expanding, you must be expanding against us."

In hindsight, given what happened in Ukraine in 2014, these sentiments might have been better heeded as a warning. Indeed, the joint committee's foreign-review report in 1994 had cautioned that NATO enlargement, by humiliating Russia and stoking its nationalistic tendencies, "would make it far more difficult to bring Russia into the process of building a new collective security regime to cover the whole of Europe, and could set the stage for a new confrontation with Russia." Despite concerns around the NATO table about the wisdom of arousing Russian antagonism, we seemed to think that establishing confidence-building measures with Russia through joint exercises would suffice. Subsequently, in May 2002, we created the NATO-Russia Council in Rome as a high-level institution to ensure consultation and collaboration.

In 1998 and 1999 NATO and Russia had found themselves at odds when militants of Albanian heritage in the Serbian province of Kosovo sought to separate from Slobodan Milošević's Federal Republic of Yugoslavia. The Milošević government countered with a concerted and premeditated military operation against them. Over a million Kosovar Albanians were terrorized by the systematic use of rape, torture, murder, and expulsion by the very police and military who were charged with their protection. Hundreds of thousands of refugees began flooding into Germany and Macedonia, with nothing but the belongings they could carry out, as I saw when I travelled at Lloyd Axworthy's request as part of a parliamentary delegation to Skopje in May 1999 to assess the situation. I visited several camps, met with international and local political authorities and NGOs, and witnessed the humanitarian tragedy that was engulfing the region – all so different from the happy memories I had of driving through it almost forty years before.

As it happened, my son, Patrick, was also in Macedonia as a correspondent for the *National Post,* and when we met for dinner he gave me an excellent briefing on what was happening on the ground. It wouldn't be the last occasion when my life as a politician and his as a journalist intersected in the middle of an international conflict. I also ran into the New Democrat MP Svend Robinson, who had journeyed to Belgrade in the middle of the NATO bombing campaign and was touring the refugee camps. His trip to the war zone was typical Svend – brash, theatrical, and a little crazy – but I had to admire his courage. In the end I came away deeply affected by scenes that had evoked "the horrors of World War Two," as I later described it. I briefed the Liberal caucus on what I had seen, and I think our report contributed to the feeling that Canada had to do something to help alleviate the terrible suffering.

Initially, Russia had supported UN efforts to broker peace in Kosovo, but it subsequently threatened to veto any Security Council resolution that would allow for an armed intervention by the international community. NATO decided to act on its own, and Canada backed that decision. Our support was more than simply a treaty obligation: in our view the global community had a duty to act forcefully to limit a state's right to murder and pillage its own citizens. In March 1999 NATO launched a prolonged series of airstrikes to compel Serbian forces to get out of Kosovo and allow for the deployment of a multinational peacekeeping force. After seventy-eight days and approximately thirty-eight thousand strikes, Milošević agreed to withdraw his army, and Canada contributed some 1,400 troops to a UN-authorized, NATO-led peace mission.

Canadians followed the war and its aftermath intently: Canada's role in Kosovo represented our largest single overseas deployment of troops since the Korean War. There were a series of debates in the House, and SCFAIT and the defence committee held joint hearings on the Kosovo crisis. During the period of the NATO bombing campaign, our members frequently came together to learn what was going on and what the prospects were for a successful resolution. We had regular briefings by Jim Wright, a senior expert in the Foreign Affairs Department, and General Ray Henault, then deputy chief of the defence staff. Furthermore, as a way to engage other MPs and the Canadian public, we decided to broadcast our hearings live from the Television Room on Parliament Hill. With a substantive issue like the bombings in Kosovo, TV can be a very effective tool in public education. It's also a way to give people a better understanding of what their MPs were thinking and what the committees did.

Indeed, because TV was such a useful platform to become better known, plenty of people were soon competing to get on camera. Just as when live cameras were introduced into the House of Commons, television affected the dynamic of debates in the committee. MPs can't help but play to their constituents, and that translated into more partisan politics than collegial debate. No government member wants to look anything less than fully supportive; no Opposition member wants to look anything less than earnestly critical. I had to take care that televising our hearings didn't threaten the working relationship among the parties and their willingness to collaborate, so I avoided the cameras whenever I thought a meaningless procedural spat would make us look like fools wrangling over an inconsequential technicality.

At one point we decided to question Robert Fowler, Canada's ambassador to the United Nations. Bob Mills, the Reform MP, intended to go after him on a lunatic corruption charge because of some personal grievance left over from when Fowler had been the deputy minister of national defence. Don Boudria, the party whip at the time, got nervous and, without telling me, arranged the night before to have our meeting moved from the Television Room to an obscure corner of the third floor.

"This is ridiculous," I told him. "Now the news will be that the government has grown afraid of this inquiry and is seeking to hide it in a broom closet. The reporters are already calling me. If I were you, I'd get us back on TV right now. And there's nothing to be afraid of – we can handle this one." In fact, there was no problem in the end.

The Kosovo debate was especially heated because it brought to the fore the legal, political, and philosophical tension between national sovereignty and international law. According to the United Nations Charter, the only justification for using force against another country is as a last resort to maintain or restore international peace and security, with the authorization of a chapter 7 resolution of the Security Council or, in individual or collective self-defence, under article 51, until the Security Council has taken measures. In a strict interpretation of the UN Charter, therefore, bombing

17 Campaigning with Cathy, Katy, and Patrick, 1984.

18 Campaigning near Wellesley Station.

19 The gimmick that backfired during the 1988 election.

20   With Tom Wilson and Jack Layton on election night, 1993.

21 With Prime Minister Jean Chrétien, 1995.

22 Relaxing with Cathy and Jean and Aline Chrétien at 24 Sussex Drive, 1995.

23 With King Hussein of Jordan, Ottawa, 1995.

24 Discussing the case of William Sampson with Crown Prince
Abdullah in Jeddah, Saudi Arabia, September 2001.

25 With John Ralston Saul, Cathy, and Governor General
Adrienne Clarkson.

Serbia was "illegal" because NATO couldn't get permission from the Security Council after the Russians effectively vetoed any authorizing resolution. But NATO responded that international law did permit authoritative regional organizations to intervene in matters affecting their security, even without Security Council approval. In this case, because the mass atrocities in Kosovo were interpreted as a threat to the peace of Europe, the NATO allies had unanimously declared their legal right to prevent chaos from engulfing themselves and their European partners.

Few legal scholars accepted that argument, but international law seldom stops a state – especially a superpower – from protecting its basic interests. I would go so far as to say that when President John Kennedy stopped the Russian ships on their way to Cuba during the 1962 missile crisis, the United States was acting totally contrary to the international law of the day. What kind of a world would we live in if any and every power could arbitrarily order another nation's ships on the high seas not to proceed to a foreign country? That wouldn't just be a violation of international law but a virtual declaration of war, which is why the hotlines were burning between Washington and Moscow during the crisis, and schoolchildren were hiding under their desks in anticipation of a nuclear attack. Illegal or not, when a country feels threatened, the reality is full steam ahead.

At one point I wrote to the Department of Foreign Affairs on behalf of SCFAIT requesting its opinion on the legality of the Kosovo campaign in the absence of a Security Council authorization. That opinion was never furnished, presumably because its conclusion would have been negative. But the committee chose not to make a public fuss about it, because the debate over the Kosovo campaign had shifted from being a legal issue to a moral one. Then NATO bombings gained legitimacy because they were seen as preventing a mass atrocity that the world community could not allow to happen. Even the Opposition wasn't interested in embarrassing the government on this point. We all believed that it was necessary and the right thing to do. If so, however, would this set a precedent for outside intervention that could be used to justify the United States' invading Iraq without UN approval or Russia from taking over Crimea?

SCFAIT eventually published a report on Canada's involvement in the Kosovo conflict and its consequences. Despite the legal quandaries of the Kosovo intervention, and concerns over civilian casualties during the

NATO bombing campaign, most of us on the committee agreed "that Canada's actions were a legitimate response to the need to prevent a humanitarian tragedy of the most terrible nature." We couldn't have predicted that our argument about legitimacy, as opposed to legality, would have important ramifications when it came to the invasion of Iraq in 2003, the intervention in Libya in 2011, the atrocities in Syria in 2013, and the crisis in Crimea in 2014. Nor could we foresee that it would serve as an early articulation of the "Responsibility to Protect" doctrine, subsequently developed in an attempt to resolve the conflict between traditional notions of sovereignty in international law and a crying need for humanitarian assistance. Peace was maintained, atrocities were prevented, but the ghost of Kosovo haunted world geopolitics from then on.

CANADA'S DECISION TO intervene in Kosovo had been deeply influenced by the world's failure to stop the horrible genocide in Rwanda in 1994, when a million or more people were slaughtered in the civil war between the Hutus and the Tutsis. In our blindness, most of us became conscious of what had happened there only after it was over. General Roméo Dallaire's subsequent account of how he and the Rwandans had been let down by the United Nations and the Western allies undoubtedly strengthened our resolve to act in humanitarian crises, even in violation of the concept of state sovereignty, which had been considered sacrosanct since the Peace of Westphalia in 1648.

Rwanda, Bosnia, and Kosovo also prompted the Chrétien government to spearhead the creation of the International Commission on Intervention and State Sovereignty in September 2000. Its mandate was to define the circumstances in which the world community would be entitled under international law to intervene in the internal affairs of a sovereign state. With the strong support of UN secretary general Kofi Annan, Lloyd Axworthy played a central role in persuading the American-based MacArthur Foundation to put up the money that funded the commission, under the leadership of Gareth Evans from Australia and Mohamed Sahnoun from Algeria. Among its twelve highly distinguished members from politics and academe were Lee Hamilton, Vladimir Lukin, and a Harvard professor named Michael Ignatieff. Its recommendations came out in December 2001 and were in large measure approved by most UN members in 2005.

At the core of the commission's report was the Responsibility to Protect (R2P) doctrine. It effectively turned the notion of sovereignty on its head by positing that a state's sovereignty included the responsibility to protect its own people from mass atrocities. Without such protection, the principle of non-intervention gives way to the responsibility of outside powers to intervene on humanitarian grounds. That can include military intervention, but only as a last resort and preferably only when sanctioned by the UN Security Council. Thus, the right to intervene and the nature of the intervention vary, depending on the nature of the offence, and it's always diplomacy first, as was the case when Kofi Annan intervened to stop the ethnic violence in Kenya in 2008. In other words, though states have sovereignty, their sovereignty does not protect them under international law when they no longer act as responsible sovereigns.

Though interventions had been carried out in the name of humanitarian principles during the nineteenth century, not least the enforcement of anti-slavery laws, they were often discredited as a form of power diplomacy whose true intent was to impose an imperial vision on the world. That was particularly the case, for example, with the European powers in the Middle East and with the gunboat diplomacy of the United States in Latin America. Now, too, Russia, China, and some smaller states weren't prepared to endorse a doctrine that would open the door to an unfettered right of intervention, fearing that Western powers would use R2P as an excuse to act unilaterally for their own purposes. But when the role of the Security Council was reaffirmed to appease these concerns, the whole question of legality was reopened. After all, the problem with Kosovo had been the lack of Security Council support, but because the doctrine's authors seemed to make some allowances for exceptions, we were two steps forward, one step back.

Some legal scholars have argued that R2P is just another form of politics. But, to some extent, all international law is just another form of politics. Despite all the problems of trying to put it into effective operation, R2P has managed to achieve a remarkable level of international acceptance in a relatively short time. When the United States, the United Kingdom, Canada, and more than a dozen other countries decided on a military intervention to end the civil war in Libya, they made sure to obtain the legal imprimatur of a Security Council resolution first, using the language of R2P.

"INTERNATIONAL LAW IS to law what Swiss cheese is to cheese," I used to joke with my students. "It's full of holes." The Russians argue that it says one thing, the Brazilians another, the Americans something else. And even if you can get everyone to agree on what the law is, how do you enforce it? Unlike domestic law, which has both a court that can decide if somebody has violated it and a police force that can uphold the court's decision, international law has no court with mandatory jurisdiction over everybody in the world, and no police force with the authority to uphold even binding rulings.

Yet in the twentieth century there have been landmark prosecutions, starting with the Nuremberg trials, mounted by the Allied Powers in the wake of the Second World War and the horrendous experience of the Holocaust. Beyond prosecuting troops for war crimes committed in the course of combat, these trials made civilian leaders personally accountable for crimes against humanity or waging an aggressive war. In other words, individuals, not just states, were held to be responsible, and an international verdict could trump the law of the nation itself. The defence of "just obeying orders" was no longer valid. This attitude had no precedent. What had been an inchoate duty to greater principles was put into legal practice. Individuals were hanged or jailed for crimes that resulted because they had obeyed orders from a state to which they owed their primary loyalty.

However fair and impartial the Nuremberg trials tried to be, with real judges, real witnesses, and real evidence, they lacked the legitimacy of a truly universal, objective process because they were viewed as the victor imposing authority over the vanquished. In the aftermath of the Second World War, therefore, the Geneva Conventions (1949) built on previous humanitarian treaties to establish a stronger international law for war crimes and crimes against humanity. But rules contained in treaties and conventions bind only those states that are parties to them.

The deeper the lawyers got into the question of crimes against humanity, the more problematic it became. Take the case of genocide. No one will seriously debate that it isn't a crime under international law. The UN Genocide Convention affirms that there is a duty not only to punish but also to prevent genocide. Sometimes, however, this has had perverse effects, as in the case of Rwanda, where the Clinton administration wouldn't allow the horrors taking place to be described as genocide in the UN Security Council because the moment the word was used, there would be an obligation under the Genocide Convention to act. Still, arising out of the Barcelona Traction case and other developments in international law, the concepts of *erga omnes* and *jus cogens* have developed – *jus cogens* meaning supreme legal principles that bind all countries, whether they have signed a particular convention, and that cannot be overridden.

The need for an international body to hold states and individuals accountable for such acts was obvious and increasingly pressing. First came institutions such as the Permanent Court of International Justice and its successor, the International Court of Justice. Then came a number of ad hoc international criminal tribunals, such as the one set up in 1993 to prosecute war crimes committed in the former Yugoslavia, or another established in 1994 in the aftermath of the Rwandan genocide. Finally, on July 17, 1998, delegates from 120 countries gathered at a conference in Rome to create an independent court and prosecutor by which previously codified rules could be given the credibility that comes from enforceability. Canada was a lead participant in the negotiations and one of the first countries to sign the Rome Statute, which brought the International Criminal Court (ICC) into existence. And we lobbied hard over the next four years to get the support of the sixty countries whose ratification of the Rome Statute was necessary for the ICC to come into being. The Rome Statute became effective on July 1, 2002, and the ICC's first president was Belgian-born, Quebec-based Canadian lawyer Philippe Kirsch, whom I knew from the Canadian Council on International Law and later as our ambassador to Sweden. Thereafter international criminal law wasn't just a concept: it was a much tighter system that could actually be applied.

In the end we were unable to convince Russia, China, and Israel to join. Equally disappointing, though President Clinton signed the treaty, his successor withdrew from it. The George W. Bush administration was adamantly against the idea, even though one of the principles of the Rome Statute – that the prosecutor in The Hague would have jurisdiction over a crime only if the country that had jurisdiction was unwilling or unable to prosecute – was put in primarily to satisfy the Americans. Once again, American exceptionalism trumped even the best efforts to bring the United States into the fold.

Nor had the United States shown up in Ottawa in December 1997 to sign the Convention on the Prohibition of the Use, Stockpiling, Production and Transfer of Anti-Personnel Mines and on their Destruction, even though Lloyd Axworthy was probably denied the Nobel Peace Prize because the purists were angry with him for trying to cut a deal with the United States. (Ironically, the prize went to an American anti-mines activist, Jody Williams, instead.) You would think that a people as good-hearted as the Americans, particularly with a Democrat as president, would have rushed to embrace a ban on one of the most devastating weapons ever devised, not least because landmines continue to kill and maim innocent people long after the conflicts have ended, whether farmers working in their fields, children playing in a meadow, or herders trekking across a desert. But the Americans insisted on the need to keep landmines between North and South Korea, or they would have to send another 200,000 troops to defend the border, they claimed. Lloyd was willing to consider an exemption if that's what it took to get the Clinton administration to sign, but in the end others prevailed in having a pure – even if less effective – convention.

Like the R2P doctrine and the landmines convention, the International Criminal Court fits into Canada's vision for a "Human Security Agenda," which was about protecting individual human beings through a system of international law. If international law had once been about the business of nations, it now embraced the concept of individuals with enforceable rights. In 1998, under the leadership of Lloyd Axworthy and the foreign minister of Norway, a group of thirteen like-minded countries began meeting together as the Human Security Network to advance the agenda in proactive, innovative ways. The goal, as with the ICC, was to establish legal refuges within the international legal and political structure where the poor and the vulnerable were made safer in a cruel world of human slaughter, whether by strengthening human rights and refugee laws, curbing the proliferation of small arms, or stopping the recruitment of child soldiers.

I had many arguments with Colin Powell about Washington's refusal to support the Rome Statute. "Come on, Colin, there's nothing in your war manuals that's any different from what's in the ICC rules. You've prosecuted war crimes, from Nuremberg to the My Lai massacre."

"Our troops are out there around the world," he said. "We're going to be harassed by all kinds of unreasonable prosecutions."

"No, because there's got to be evidence of a genuine crime for someone to be taken to The Hague, and then only if you refuse to prosecute. I mean, do you really foresee a war crime that your guys are going to commit that you aren't going to prosecute?"

"Well, you never know," was his only reply.

The big worry for the Americans, in my opinion, wasn't that their troops would be indicted for crimes committed in battle, but that the state and its leaders might be prosecuted. What would happen if a third party declared that high American officials should be arrested for crimes against humanity, no less than General Pinochet had been? This became a real problem for the Americans when activists began using a Belgian "universal jurisdiction" law to charge US officials with war crimes. "Fine," said Donald Rumsfeld, "so I guess we're going to have to move NATO out of Brussels." It didn't take long for the Belgian government to get the message, and the law was repealed.

I thought it rather hypocritical of the Americans to complain about extraterritorial jurisdiction whenever it might apply to them, while at the same time claiming jurisdiction over matters involving foreign governments and foreign companies whenever it suits their interests. That's the nature of American exceptionalism, I suppose, and we would probably do it too if we were powerful enough to get away with it. But they pushed it to the extent of bullying others not to support the ICC. When Canada went to get the support of the Caribbean nations, the Americans threatened to cut off their aid if they signed. Most of them had the guts to sign anyway. "You guys are crazy," I told my American friends. "Are you really going to refuse to give them money to fix up their airports for the fight against terrorism and drugs on the grounds that they're going to sign the Rome Statute? Isn't that rather counterproductive?"

The ICC has already served as an effective check on the bad behaviour of certain states and their leaders, but it has also put restrictions on what Canada can do. Though parliamentary approval is not required for Canada to ratify a treaty, Parliament did have to incorporate the Rome Statute into the law of Canada. Normally amendments to the Criminal Code would have gone to the justice committee, but in this case they were sent to SCFAIT because of our knowledge of international law. Besides myself, there were two other international law professors on the committee, Daniel

Turp and Ted McWhinney, and we recruited Irwin Cotler specifically for his expertise in the field. This work was no academic exercise – it had practical consequences. From that point on, if a Canadian soldier commits a war crime somewhere in the world, that soldier has committed a crime under the Criminal Code of Canada as well. Canada even places legal advisers with our troops to ensure that the lives of innocent civilians will not be risked without justification. In other words, we were assuming new legal responsibilities, but we did so willingly in the belief that they were an expression of both our humanitarian values and our interest in living in a safer, more just world.

9

ALL GEOPOLITICS IS LOCAL

I never failed to be struck by how directly connected the interests of my constituents were with my international work. It wasn't always easy to explain in a speech how jobs in Toronto flowed from an orderly framework of peace, law, trade, and good relations around the globe, but I often tried to make the link. The fact is, though a lot of foreign policy has to do with institutions and ideas at the highest levels, much also has to do with individuals and communities at the grassroots, and I was in constant motion between the two. Even when I couldn't be as devoted to my constituents as many of my colleagues were to theirs, because of my international activities, foreign issues often helped me to assist people in other ways that were relevant to their lives. If all politics is indeed local, local and international were often one and the same thing in my riding.

I became friends with a doctor from Nigeria, for example, who lived in Regent Park and needed help in getting his credentials to practise medicine in Ontario. The frustrating process took six long years, while Dr. Egbo-Egbo and his wife took on a variety of menial jobs to make ends meet. We watched their son Thompson grow up playing the piano and developing his musical talent at the Dixon Hall music program, which we also supported, and we felt as proud as his parents when he emerged as a very successful jazz performer and composer. One day Dr. Egbo-Egbo invited me to meet Ken Saro-Wiwa Jr., the son of the famous Nigerian activist who had been hanged in 1995. In that way, through a constituent who became a friend, I learned about the dreadful human rights situation under the military dictatorship in Nigeria.

Similarly, I became familiar with the war in Somalia from knowing a group of extraordinary Somali women refugees who lived in Regent Park. They came to me for help because they had no papers, and without the proper documents they couldn't enrol their children in school, had problems obtaining health cards, and faced barriers bringing their husbands in to join them. Getting them their papers was a huge struggle in Ottawa. In the course of solving it, I came to have a huge respect for those women and the strict way in which they raised their children to get through school and into university. In fact, the only time I introduced a private member's bill in the House occurred during 2000, when I sought to gain equal access to student loans for children of refugees. The bill had the government's agreement and would have passed if not for the presence of a few mean-spirited Reform MPs who prevented the unanimous consent needed in the House to take it through third reading. This failure was a big disappointment for me – and, even more, for many industrious young people who wanted to get ahead and make a contribution to the country.

Similarly, through my friendship with Filipino immigrants, I found that the politics of the Philippines was replicated in Regent Park and St. James Town. In those days the community was deeply divided between the supporters of Ferdinand Marcos and those of Cory Aquino. That division subsided over time, but it left its mark on those Filipino Canadians who tended to vote Conservative or to vote Liberal. As a candidate and then as an MP, I attended a constant round of Filipino dinners, parties, and festivals, and eventually had the honour of being made an honorary commander of the Knights of Rizal, one of their major social agencies. It was party politics mixed with government business, to be sure, but it was also a part of my social life – meeting people, working together, and having fun. I saw many of them often on many different occasions, official or unofficial, and they became almost like family.

In January 1997 I invited one of my key organizers, Luong Tran, to join me on a visit to Vietnam. As a young man, he had fled the country at the end of the American war. Now a successful businessman, he was interested in rebuilding a Canada-Vietnam relationship, unlike many of his fellow refugees who remained bitter about what the communists had done to the land of their birth and wanted no contact. We were warmly received in Hanoi by Vice-President Madame Nguyen Thi Binh (the president himself being ill); the vice-chair of the National Assembly, Dang Quan Thuy; the minister of the committee on children's care and protection; and other senior officials. The most dramatic moment came when we had dinner with my counterpart, the chairman of the foreign affairs committee. He had been a colonel in the Viet Cong when it invaded Saigon. "Just think," said Luong Tran to him, "you were probably shooting at me as I tried to escape" – and they toasted each other with another glass of mai tai. It was a vivid and moving reminder to me of how important are efforts to make peace and how much they rely on warm human connections.

Tamil Canadians were another community I got to know well: not only were there many of them in the riding but they were active in defending the rights of their people in Sri Lanka. Cathy and I used to have dinners in their Regent Park apartments, and we were invited to their weddings and family celebrations. My office helped them with their immigration problems.

However, I had to tread carefully. Tamil refugees to Canada were overwhelmingly sympathetic to the idea of an independent state or at least a large degree of autonomy in the northern part of the island, though not necessarily supportive of the tactics of the Tamil Tiger rebels, the LTTE. Most of the ones I knew supported the reasonable middle, and I was sensitive to their plight. But the Chrétien government was understandably hesitant to support a separatist movement, however different the minority situations of the Tamils and the Quebecers happened to be, and the Tamil Tigers were themselves guilty of terrorist acts. Personally I opposed their use of violence and thought that the Tamils in Sri Lanka would be better off if their leaders tried to work within the constitutional structure. Though raising money for the LTTE was illegal, I knew that it was happening in the riding. One day I was even duped into marching in a Tamil Tigers' parade, and when I realized what was going on, I beat a hasty retreat.

My connections to the Tamil community in my riding soon led to my developing a deep interest in the Sri Lankan conflict, and, ahead of many other politicians, I became involved in its issues. As chair of SCFAIT, I supported Bob Rae's efforts with the Forum of Federations in advocating federalism as a possible solution. Later, as foreign minister, I accepted an invitation by my Norwegian counterpart, Jan Petersen, to become involved in the peace process in Sri Lanka. In October 2003 I met with the president, the prime minister, the foreign minister, and other senior officials in Colombo and Jaffna to discuss the virtues of federalism, not just for the Tamils but also for the Buddhist majority and the substantial Muslim population in the southwest. I also got to know Joseph Pararajasingham, the Tamil Christian politician who was tragically assassinated just after receiving Communion at Midnight Mass on Christmas Eve, 2005.

When I wasn't away from my riding, I was visiting every community in it. I was luckier than most MPs because Toronto was fairly close to Ottawa, so I didn't have to spend countless hours flying there and back every weekend. Though I was used to working long into the night as a lawyer and a professor, one of the most difficult aspects of an MP's life is juggling all the invitations you receive and deciding which events to attend. When I was teaching law, Cathy and I went to the farm every weekend and sometimes spent an extra day there, but that was impossible during the thirteen years I was in politics. The best we could do was go up late Saturday night or early Sunday morning. There was always something to do in the riding – including all the celebrations for the various nationalities I represented. I enjoyed these events – meeting people from around the world and learning about their countries and traditions. It was endlessly interesting, usually fun, and rarely felt like work. If I weren't being myself, if I didn't like socializing, if I wished I were reading a book instead of being kissed on TV while handing out the Female Impersonator of the Year Award, I would have been cranky and exhausted the whole time. But the requirements of the job didn't feel oppressive, and I never felt that I'd rather be doing something else.

I was honoured to be selected half a dozen times as the Most Popular MP in Toronto by the readers of *NOW* – the hip, left-of-centre weekly. Though I probably earned some extra points just for being a downtown MP who did a lot of work with immigrants and the gay community, I certainly tried to be responsive to the needs of my constituents. And if at first the personal connections I forged had mostly to do with getting elected, many of them evolved into genuine, long-lasting personal relationships.

One of my early political advisers once said to me, "Don't spend a lot of time doing immigration stuff. Even if you help people with visa problems, they may or may not vote for you anyway. It depends on a host of factors."

But I made a point of working hard on the immigration files, either personally or through my staff. We examined the cases, decided which ones had merit, and proceeded in a rational way, based on the principle that though everybody has rights, some claims are more pressing than others. Many constituents never understood why an MP, especially a minister, couldn't just pick up the phone and get a visa for their nephew or a grant for their business right away. We had to educate immigrants who had arrived from more despotic countries that power wasn't arbitrary power in the Canadian system. We also knew that the Immigration Department saw no point in dealing with MPs who yelled abuse all the time. Instead, we established a good rapport with key officials, and whenever I intervened directly, they understood it was an important matter that I took seriously.

One day a local lawyer, who was well known as a Tory organizer, called my office. A client of his had a passport problem and needed urgent help. My staff solved it in four hours. "I almost became a Liberal on the spot," he told me. "I didn't know that MPs actually could make things happen." Over time, in fact, I was able to earn the respect – and even the votes – of a number of traditional Conservatives north of Bloor. Some of them liked my prominence as chair of SCFAIT; others appreciated that I was a fiscal conservative even if a social progressive; and still others drifted toward the Liberals when the Conservative Party was absorbed into Reform. "You got three votes in my house last election," a diehard Tory admitted, "and you'll probably get four in the next one."

All MPs had the same basic budget to spread as they chose between Ottawa and the riding. I had two full-time and one part-time staff in both places, though I was able to get some additional help once I became the committee chair, and I went to great lengths to run a professional office by hiring bright young people who liked dealing with tough issues. That freed me up, and the files were handled by someone who was invariably more competent than I would have been.

One time a young woman came to me. She wanted to work in the riding office but was worried that her only experience was as a waitress. "Perfect," I said. "You've had to cope with demanding, sometimes irascible customers. A lot of this job revolves around tough federal responsibilities like immigration cases and tax files. You'll be dealing with people who are unhappy because they've been waiting for years to get a visa for their spouse who's in a refugee camp in Somalia, or they have no passport and need to get to the Philippines right away for a wedding or a funeral, or they can't get any action from a department about a grant or a rebate. Often these are difficult, heart-wrenching issues. Many of them can never be solved. But even if you can't always succeed, you have to listen carefully and make a serious effort to respond."

After a couple of years, many of my staff were burned out by all the demands. Sometimes I gave them a break by switching their duties for a while; sometimes they quit to do something else; but I never encouraged anyone to stay on, even the really good ones. These jobs in constituency ridings and on Parliament Hill are short-term opportunities to provide young people with an introduction to government and some experience at the start of their careers, but they are not lifetime occupations. My role as mentor was to give them a start, then help them move on when they were ready. Some, like Mora Johnson and Warren Mucci, went to law school and later joined the public service; Chris Drew became active in provincial politics before pursuing a career as an urban planner; Jeremy Broadhurst, a key adviser who had worked for me from the very beginning, became national director of the Liberal Party. My first chief of staff was Bill Charnetski, a bright former student of mine who hired and fired and made the place hum. He moved on to become a special adviser to Justice Minister Allan Rock and eventually head of global government affairs and public policy for one of the fastest-growing drug companies in the world. Suh Kim, who took Bill's place in 1996, would go on to practise at Torys, the prestigious law firm, and later became in-house counsel at a private equity firm. Brian O'Neil, a management consultant in his thirties, showed up one day and said, "I'm making good money, but I'm bored. I want to learn something." He followed me from the constituency office to Foreign Affairs to Defence, where he played a pivotal role in the minister's office. To my great benefit, Brian is still working with me as a highly effective investment adviser and manager.

Staying in touch with constituents was a constant challenge. The loyal and dedicated Frank Clarke made this job easier at my constituency office in Toronto, and Philip Pietersma proved similarly invaluable at my office on Parliament Hill. They and their colleagues helped ensure that I remained

attuned to the concerns of my riding and kept me on track with the voluminous correspondence and calls I received. Many MPs are really good at
phoning, but I have always preferred to write letters or meet face to face.
Though I made enormous efforts to reply to all the correspondence I received, I was rarely satisfied with sending out a form letter that looked as
though it had been generated by a machine. "If you're writing back to
constituents," I told my staff, "you have to pick up on the specifics of the
issues they are addressing, so they know it's an actual, considered response."
As a result, I earned a reputation as somebody who was slow to reply. One
day a woman came into my office and said, "It took six months to get a
response back from you, Mr. Graham, but at least it's clear you wrote it
yourself and you understand what the problem is."

WHEREAS MY JOB as chair of SCFAIT kept me focused primarily on international issues and frequently abroad, the Chrétien government was fixated
on two extremely important agendas at home: the unity of the country and
the reduction of the federal deficit.

I wasn't nearly as active in the second Quebec referendum in 1995 as I
had been in the first. Though I kept abreast of developments through Yves
Fortier and other friends in the province, my responsibilities as an MP
in Ottawa and my riding kept me from the kind of deep involvement I
had accepted in 1980. I remember campaigning for a couple of days,
however, with Senator Céline Hervieux-Payette in Montreal. Céline proved
a tireless campaigner. When we came to one house that was draped with
Quebec flags, she insisted on banging at the door, even though I suggested
we were wasting our time. A diminutive but very feisty lady came out and
launched a tirade in support of the Yes side. Céline introduced me as a
bilingual anglophone MP from Toronto, and I attempted to lighten the
tone by apologizing for speaking French, as the old expression went, "like
a Spanish cow."

"Now, Bill," Céline said graciously, "don't insult the Spanish."

"Or the cows!" said the little lady, slamming the door in our faces.

At the start of the campaign everyone assumed we would have another
straightforward sixty-forty victory, just like the vote in 1980. However,
when Lucien Bouchard suddenly replaced Premier Jacques Parizeau as the

de facto leader of the Yes team after a few weeks, the dynamics changed completely. Bouchard's charisma and oratory, not to mention his apparently miraculous recovery from a life-threatening illness, lit a firecracker under the separatists. It confirmed the impression I had formed of him in the House as a brooding but extremely powerful force, and when he needed to turn it on, by God he could. His impact on the campaign was an amazing phenomenon that showed once again how one person can change the course of history. Overnight the mood in Ottawa became tense. The polls were saying we might even lose the vote. The caucus was concerned and incredibly nervous. Mr. Chrétien was as emotional as I had ever seen him.

On October 27, just three days before the vote, I joined an estimated 100,000 other Canadians from inside and outside Quebec in a massive show of goodwill in the streets of Montreal, and my constituency staff organized a group of about thirty people from Toronto Rosedale to attend the unity rally. Though we all felt better for waving the flag to show our support for the federalist side, subsequent polls suggested that our good intentions could have cost us half a point in the final outcome. Many Quebecers resented the interference of outsiders in their affairs. As it was, the result was a nail-biter as the returns swung back and forth between the Yes and the No all through the evening. We won, but with only 50.6 percent of the vote.

In the aftermath, Chrétien recruited a smart, courageous federalist, Stéphane Dion, to join his Cabinet. Like most of the caucus, I knew nothing about him other than his reputation as a gutsy political science professor, and when he popped up in Ottawa out of nowhere, I shared the first impression that many people had of him as a bit of a geek with a backpack instead of a briefcase. There was no question he was very much his own person, tough to work for, with high standards for both himself and others. Chrétien used to tease me by calling me "Professor," but Stéphane was far more professorial, both in appearance and manner.

However, I soon came to admire the series of public letters he wrote to refute the myths of the Parti Québécois, now led by Lucien Bouchard, who had left Ottawa to succeed Parizeau as premier of Quebec. Many of us had been trying to make the same arguments for years, and I was impressed by the way he framed their essence. "It's clear that you've written them yourself," I said to him in caucus during our first personal conversation.

"I've seen so many ministerial documents that are just bureaucratic bumph. But these letters are the work of somebody who has thought about the content and taken a principled position in expressing it."

Subsequently, as minister of intergovernmental affairs, Dion was instrumental in pushing through the Chrétien government's so-called Clarity Act, designed to prevent the separatists from using another convoluted and tricky question in their attempts to hoodwink the majority into voting for independence. Henceforth a clear question and a clear majority would be required before any separation was legal. First, however, there was much debate in caucus. Many of our Quebec MPs worried that the Clarity Act would be seen as a provocation, stirring up the nationalists after their defeat. Others felt just as strongly that it was time to take a stand. I thought the risk was worth taking: you shouldn't break up a country with ambiguity. As it turned out, the federal Liberals gained ten more seats and went up eight percentage points in Quebec in the next general election – prompting a very discouraged Lucien Bouchard to quit public life in 2001.

The other important national issue of the time bore more directly on the lives of my constituents and demanded more of my attention. On entering office in 1993, the Chrétien government discovered it had inherited from the Tories a national debt above $500 billion, an annual deficit of $42 billion, and interest payments that were consuming 37 cents of every tax dollar every year. It was an unsustainable fiscal legacy. The Liberals had vowed in the Red Book to halve the deficit from 6 percent to 3 percent of GDP by the end of our third year in office, and the prime minister was determined to keep that promise.

Economics was neither my passion nor my strength, but if my father had taught me one lesson about business and finance, it's that debt will kill you. That lesson was reinforced by the summer course in economics I took in Florida in 1981 as a way to fill this important gap in my education, especially since I had begun teaching anti-trust law. The course was intended to give judges, lawyers, and professors such as myself a grounding in basic economics and its impact on the law. Though the location was very pleasant, the work was hard: we had to cram about two years of study into a few weeks. The basis was clearly conservative, much more Milton Friedman than John Maynard Keynes. One of my fellow students, a law professor from Belize who later became his country's representative to the United

Nations, was so disgusted by the right-wing slant that he dropped out. In general I found the course helpful, even if I didn't buy into the notion of economics as the essential driver of all human behaviour, including law and religion.

However skeptical I remained of the small-government, low-taxes school of politics, I have always believed in balancing the books. That had landed me in trouble when I was invited, as a newly minted Liberal candidate, to attend a party meeting in Ottawa shortly before the 1984 election. When I mentioned that a lot of people in my riding were concerned about the debt, a left-leaning Liberal senator gave me a public scolding. "That's Tory talk," he said in a denigrating way. Liberals weren't even allowed to raise the issue, it seemed, without being attacked as traitors to the cause.

Ten years later there was still much angst in the caucus about the cuts to the social programs. MPs who were interested in the military were vocal in their opposition to the huge cuts to national defence. MPs from the Maritimes were concerned about the social, economic, and political costs of reforming unemployment insurance – with good reason, as it turned out, since many of them were to lose their seats. A group of us, mostly ex-professors or MPs with universities in their ridings, formed a caucus to make the case for preserving funds for higher education. All the various interest groups fought to defend their pet projects, and I suspect that the fights were even more intense at the Cabinet table than they were in the Liberal caucus.

But Mr. Chrétien took a hard line in private as well as in public. "I'm supporting my minister of finance," he said countless times in our meetings. "We have to meet our target. It will be tough, but we're going to do the cuts in the most socially progressive way."

Given the amount of poverty in my riding, I was one of those who actively fought for the preservation of the social security net as much as possible. Walking through Regent Park and St. James Town on the weekends, I was besieged by questions from worried, sometimes angry constituents. I was concerned about the plight of the many Aboriginal people who lived in downtown Toronto. I feared for the kids who were hanging out in the parks and dealing drugs. I tried to make sure that the money every MP received from Human Resources Development Canada (HRDC) to fund enterprises in the riding went to projects relating to the poorest neighbourhoods, such as Dixon Hall's multilingual computer training programs, the Fred Victor Mission's job training for the homeless and the disadvantaged, and the youth training at the Cabbagetown Youth Centre. The demand was overwhelming. If I had $300,000 to distribute, I had requests for $1.5 million. Knowing that some MPs didn't use all their allocations, I was in close communication with the officials at HRDC to pick up an extra $50,000 or $100,000. And, unlike those MPs who gave their allocation to industry or small business, I tended to give mine to programs that helped people in need.

Over time I came to appreciate the key role the churches play from a social-policy point of view in working for the down-and-out. The United Church developed the Christian Resource Centre into an important social service agency in Upper Regent Park. My local Anglican church, St. Simon the Apostle, started a homeless shelter that could take in twenty-five people on winter nights – Cathy and I joined others to cook breakfast on Wednesday mornings. Other churches did the same all over the riding and the city. A group called the Christian Leadership Council of Downtown Toronto, under the auspices of Our Lady of Lourdes Church, brought together the Catholics, the Anglicans, the Lutherans, and the United Church to work on social issues.

Once or twice a year I used to sit down with this group over a sandwich lunch at the church to talk about what we should all be doing. It was profoundly humbling to hear what these people were doing with their lives, how they were working on the streets and dealing with the problems they encountered. Most of them were highly educated people with a big picture of the world, and they often pressed me on Canada's foreign policy, from Third World development to nuclear war. At times a representative of the company that managed some of the St. James Town buildings came to our meetings and offered assistance on all sorts of practical issues. At other times the police would come with their input and advice.

It was a tremendous advantage to me, as an extremely busy MP, to have such intelligent, compassionate people serving in effect as eyes and ears in the community. I could pick up the phone and call half the priests and ministers in my riding to ask for their advice, or they could call (as they often did) to ask for my help. It was a genuine interaction. Though they were often critical, they were rarely hostile, and no one ever refused to help solve problems in a logical, sensible way just to spite the Liberal Party. It was all part of building a network of personal connections, no different from what I was doing as chair of SCFAIT in South America or Eastern Europe.

In a similar way I got involved with the socially engaged co-ops in the riding, many of which were sideswiped by the budget cuts to the federally funded Canada Mortgage and Housing Corporation (CMHC). There was some legitimacy to the criticism of their opponents that co-ops can be an expensive way to provide social housing. When I asked the CMHC for a list of every subsidized unit in the riding, I got an absolutely incomprehensible answer. Over the decades, with different policies under different governments of different persuasion, the system had grown topsy-turvy, and no one could really make sense of it. The total cost to the public treasury looked hefty. The cost-per-unit seemed high. The value of the social services they provided wasn't clear. Some buildings had only two units. And the whole question of who was really benefitting from the subsidies blew into a political issue when Jack Layton and his wife, Olivia Chow, were found to be living in a co-op apartment while earning substantial incomes as a municipal councillor and school board trustee, respectively.

In terms of partisan politics, as my hard-nosed campaign managers continued to remind me, you didn't gain much by going to the wall for people who were diehard New Democrats. Certainly the all-candidates' debates held in the co-ops during each election were usually where I got the toughest grilling. But I honestly believed that I was the MP for the entire riding. It was my duty to deal with whatever problem came across my desk, and for the most part I found that all but a few New Democrats and Tories were open to setting aside their political manoeuvrings for the sake of a workable solution. As well, part of the pleasure of being an MP is to learn about all kinds of new and different areas of life. You could go from knowing absolutely nothing to understanding the complex dimensions that make any and every subject endlessly interesting.

The more I looked into the concerns about the cutbacks, the more I came to understand how key a piece the co-ops are in the social fabric of an urban riding. More than a roof, they are a way of life. By presenting members young and old with an opportunity to participate in a community, by providing help for the disadvantaged, by preventing the poor and the abused from falling through the cracks, they are part of the glue that keeps a complex urban situation stable. I remember one woman telling me how she had led a life of prostitution and drugs until she moved into a co-op and got the support necessary to break out of her destructive trap. Children told me of the support they received from neighbours and friends when their parents were at work or their single parent was absent. One co-op specialized in assisting women who were victims of domestic violence. Others set aside space for people with disabilities and encouraged them to develop their potential to the maximum. I went from knowing nothing about the co-operative movement to being a fairly strong proponent of its social value, and the more I learned, the more the co-ops went from being the enemy to being allies in a common endeavour, even if they never voted for me. That didn't mean I was naive about the cost, but I did understand the important role they play in a city like Toronto.

I started attending meetings at various co-ops and at the Toronto East Downtown Residents Association to try to find solutions to troubling social issues such as street prostitution and drug trafficking. I began to forge good links with the leaders of the co-operative movement. I joined with several other inner-city MPs from across the country to form a kind of co-op caucus to protect the co-op movement inside the Liberal government. Together we made aggressive representations to Alfonso Gagliano, the minister responsible for the CMHC from 1997 to 2002, to prevent the downloading of jurisdiction over the co-ops to the provinces – a move that would have had disastrous consequences under Ontario's Conservative government. We met with the management of the CMHC to discuss operating costs and the interest rates on their mortgages. With Gagliano's endorsement, we worked to create an agency that would largely be run by the co-op movement itself and would co-ordinate funding and other issues with the provinces. If a co-op was helping people with AIDS, we asked for a subsidy from the minister of health. If a co-op was helping people with disabilities, we approached the minister of human resources. Though we weren't always successful, we were able to attenuate some of the cuts. One of my proudest moments as an MP occurred in April 1999, when I received an award for my "hard work and dedication" from the Co-operative Housing Federation of Canada.

The federal cuts did not have as much impact on the daily lives of my constituents as the provincial cuts made by the Mike Harris Conservatives. Federal social spending tended to be more on the periphery because the provinces were responsible for the big-ticket items of education, health, and housing support. Nevertheless, Ottawa's cuts undermined what the provinces could do, and I had to deal with the fallout. Solutions weren't easy to find. If Ottawa increased its income supplements to people living in Regent Park, for example, Queen's Park perversely clawed it back, so all we were doing was moving money from one level of government to another. The people who came through my door as MP, however, were asking for help with real problems. Even when those problems weren't of Ottawa's making, I couldn't tell them, "Sorry, I do nuclear war, immigration, and visas. I don't do classrooms or potholes. For those, you have to talk to your provincial representative or city councillor." Fortunately, I had a strong working relationship with my provincial colleague George Smitherman, and though city councillor Kyle Rae was of a different political stripe, we got along well.

When I think back on those years, I mostly remember the intense human anguish and the frustration. There were simply never enough resources, human or financial, to go around, and political partisanship sometimes got in the way of any rational compromise. I walked into many rooms where people were upset about something – and even more upset with me for not doing anything about it. I'm a non-adversarial person by nature, and that aspect of the job often took a personal toll on me. "You're wasting your time," some of my staff would say. "You're never going to solve these problems, and even if you do, you'll never get any gratitude."

Sometimes they were right. Once we had a major problem with a derailment on the track that runs across north Rosedale. The train contained chemicals and overturned near a school. For months I had to go to meetings at which my constituents in the area were understandably furious. But when I went to the rail companies and government regulators on their behalf, I discovered that the track transported most of Oshawa's automobile production to the United States. "Sorry, this is the only track," I was told. "If you shut it down, you'll shut down the economy of Canada."

In many cases, however, spending time with people and getting to know them better taught me that most human beings are receptive to working together. A lot of politics is about trying to turn negative energy into positive accomplishment. That means listening to the drama of people's lives, empathizing with the issues beneath it, and channelling it into a productive action. That's what I tried to do, sometimes successfully, sometimes not.

THE 1997 ELECTION campaign, which was launched on April 26, was more fun than any of my previous ones because I was more or less guaranteed to win Toronto Centre–Rosedale, as my riding was now called. By then I had become accustomed to the rhythm of campaigning – where to go, what to do, how to speak. In fact, the whole process became rather formulaic in terms of what the candidate did. The goal was for my canvassers and me to cover every poll by election day. Every evening I came back to our headquarters on Gerrard Street East and marked my progress on the wall map of the riding with a coloured pencil. In practice it was impossible to knock on every door or visit every high-rise apartment, so the campaign manager figured out which polls were sure for us, which were sure for the Tories, and which always went for the NDP. After that, I spent most of my limited time in the swing polls during the five-week campaign.

I often spent half a day in just one of the apartment buildings in St. James Town, starting at the top floor and walking down the stairs floor after floor. A team of three or four canvassers went ahead of me, knocked on the doors, and invited the residents to speak with me or dropped off some brochures. The problem with canvassing in the daytime was that most people were out working. Many immigrants weren't able to vote or pretended not to be home – an unexpected knock on the door had often meant trouble in their native countries. On many days I spent a huge amount of time and energy for very little return.

One time I knocked on the door of an apartment and a young boy answered. I saw a large television in the living room and another through the open door to a bedroom. To put him at ease, I asked him how many TV sets his family had.

"Four," he answered. "How many do you have?"

"One," I said.

"Oh," he asked, "do you live in a one-room house?"

The best hours were in the early morning or from four in the afternoon till about eight at night. But we were always running into problems. The doormen at the more expensive condos often wouldn't let us into their buildings to knock on doors or drop off literature, even though they were required to by the Canada Elections Act. "I'll check with my board of directors," they said, but by the time the directors had considered it, the election was over. In fact, the huge and impersonal apartment condos going up in every major Canadian city were changing the nature of doing politics because they made it harder for a downtown politician to establish a face-to-face relationship with voters. Given the increasing difficulties of connecting with people at their doors, whether in dense downtown ridings or vast rural ridings, the day of the traditional campaign may be coming to an end.

Talking with my American friends, I understood the difference between being an MP in a riding of 100,000 constituents versus being a congress-man with half a million constituents and very few opportunities to meet even a fraction of them in the flesh. Even so, I noticed the change in my own campaigning between 1984 and 2006, with the increased reliance on computer-generated calls and media advertising in place of handshakes and conversations at the door. Knowing where your supporters are and getting them out to vote remained the basis of the campaign team's work, but more and more organizations began looking at new ways in which to reach large numbers of people, especially through the Internet and other forms of communication. Today's social media have obviously replaced face to face.

At one point I started a telephone campaign, though when an automatic call went out by mistake at four in the morning, it wasn't very helpful. I sought out groups of people and went to their meetings. Instead of going into a building, I waited outside and talked to people as they went to work or returned. I held coffee parties in apartments or in the lobbies. I stood at subway stations or bus stops every rush hour, even though that, too, became a challenge as more people started listening to music through ear-phones and in a space all their own. Regardless, I always felt that you can create a certain psychic energy with somebody if you're genuine about meeting them, even if it's a very brief encounter.

"These people are on their way to work," I explained to my canvassers. "They're busy. Suddenly we're intruding in their lives. So don't just hand them a piece of literature. Say 'Bill's here, he really wants to meet you.' You've got to somehow make a personal contact with that individual in less than five seconds. If you don't, they're gone forever like a fish that got away."

I also made a point of attending every one of the all-candidates' debates. Though many ridings had only two or three in the course of the campaign, Toronto Centre often had four times as many. At the beginning of the election, all the campaign managers met to bring some order to them: one in north Rosedale, one in Regent Park, one in St. James Town, another in the always lively and unpredictable gay and lesbian community centre at 519 Church Street, and so on, but when various other groups insisted that we come to them too, the system quickly broke down. Sometimes disruptively rowdy, sometimes poorly attended, the meetings were for the most part a great opportunity to talk with large numbers of people, even if there were probably few independents among the hundreds of vocal partisans who packed the halls. I particularly liked the line from the Communist candidate, who always began his remarks by stating, "We all know who's going to win this riding, but listen to me anyway."

One thing I did not like was being grabbed and abused by irate constituents. Once, during the bombing of Kosovo, I was threatened by a group of angry Serbs who showed up at my annual MP's picnic in a Cabbagetown park. Instead of the back-and-forth of a gentlemanly debate, I had to get used to being called a Communist stooge, a capitalist pig, a fascist, or a total idiot without responding in the same tone. I also had to recognize that arguments can be very powerful, even when they're not factual. Politics can make people say anything, no matter how inaccurate or stupid, if they think it will help their climb up the greasy pole of success. And because I'm not confrontational by nature, I found some aspects of the public meetings hard to take. I survived, but unlike some politicians, I can't say I ever saw the sport in being jeered by a crowd.

One of the NDP candidates who ran against me liked to get up and say, "I'm not a limousine Liberal like Bill here. I don't drive around in a big Cadillac the way he does." Pigeonholing me that way was mere grandstanding and completely untrue. "Bill rides a bicycle!" my supporters used to shout. "Bill rides a bicycle!" A while later, in fact, I happened to ride past the candidate while he was sitting outside a coffee shop. After I gave him a wave, I heard him say to a friend, "Holy shit, he really does ride a bicycle." Not that I did it to create an impression. Bicycling was a genuine pleasure as well as the fastest means of getting through traffic, excellent exercise, and an efficient way to meet people, though I was notorious among my staff for leaving my bikes unlocked or forgetting where I had chained them. They used to say that I had my very own Give a Kid a Bike charity.

I didn't even own a car in Ottawa, and many a morning I would bike from my apartment near the Hill along the beautiful trails that followed the Ottawa River, sometimes all the way out to Aylmer, Quebec. One day I was invited to give a talk at a training session for diplomats in a Hull school across the Ottawa River. It was a beautiful day, and I rode my bike across the bridge. As I was wrapping up my remarks, I got a note that the Reform MP who was to follow me was running ten minutes behind schedule, so I kept going until she arrived. She rushed in, flustered and a bit embarrassed, and opened with, "I'm sorry to be late, but I don't have a limousine to travel around in as my Liberal friends do." I was astonished and slightly peeved. I mean, I had never met her before that moment, I had just done her a favour, and yet I had to put up with that kind of gratuitous insult.

Of course, there are always mean-spirited and ad hominem attacks in politics; it goes with the territory. And the fixation on irrelevant personal issues sometimes threatens to push aside serious considerations of public policy and may keep some talented people from entering public life. In the course of my own public career, I was no exception in undergoing a fair bit of scrutiny and criticism for all sorts of reasons, but overall we live in a country where people are more focused on your job performance than on your private life.

I have a vivid memory of the day during the 1997 campaign when I was visited by the editor of *Xtra!*, Toronto's gay magazine, who informed me that its board was considering "outing" me in the next issue. This had been a concern of mine since deciding to enter politics in 1984, but my family and I had always endorsed the idea that the state has no place in the bedrooms of the nation. Cathy and I loved each other deeply; we had raised a wonderful family; we enjoyed a happy and fulfilling life together;

and our private life, we felt, was precisely that: private. That said, now that the matter was likely to become a public issue, I raised it with my campaign team and gave my blessing to anyone who might want to depart at that point. Not only did no one leave, they all suggested that I get back to campaigning. It was, for me, a liberating moment.

Though *Xtra!* decided not to run its story, I was grateful that I had had the opportunity to confront the rumours openly with those who had worked so hard to get me elected. And whenever the question was raised again in the media, especially after I was appointed to the Cabinet, my answer remained the same: all aspects of my personal life are known to my family and friends and to the prime ministers who put their confidence in me. I never lost their wholehearted support; nor did I ever take a position in public life that was inconsistent with my private life. In the end, I am proud to say, I also never lost the support of a majority of my constituents.

In fact, among my campaign staff there was more discussion about my decision to allow a film crew from CPAC to follow me around for an entire day, as a way to get my party's message across and show people how the system works. "You're crazy," Jim Cooper, my campaign manager, said. "Anything can happen in one day. You can slip on a banana peel, and there it's going to be, on tape, for the rest of your life." It was a risk, because you never know when somebody's going to attack you or expose you as an idiot on TV for all to see, but it was also a way to build up my name recognition among the constituents. In fact, one guy did scream at me, and on another occasion, I was attacked by a dog. But mostly it turned out well. CPAC ran it over and over again, and years later people would stop me on the street to say how interesting they had found the business of campaigning. Just as well, I thought, that the producers had cut the episode with the woman in Regent Park who had expressed her opinion about Bob Rae's provincial government in a graphic way not usually heard on CPAC. "I voted NDP last time," she said, "and then they took me in the shower and told me to bend over and pick up the soap."

On June 2, 1997, the Chrétien Liberals were re-elected with a second majority. Though we lost a number of seats, particularly in the Maritimes, where the effects of the deficit cuts were most adversely felt, we won all but two ridings in Ontario. In Toronto Centre the split between the Progressive Conservatives and Reform allowed the NDP candidate to place a distant second – none other than the same David MacDonald who had beaten me in 1988, and whom I had beaten in 1993 when he was still a Tory.

IN THE AFTERMATH of the 1997 election, the old tensions that had existed between Jean Chrétien and Paul Martin began to resurface. Though I wasn't privy to any behind-the-scenes intrigues, everyone in Ottawa knew that certain Martin supporters were desperate for him to become prime minister before he was too old for the job. Some of the Martinites undoubtedly believed they would get into the Cabinet or the PMO with Paul. But my whole life has been about arbitrating differences, finding solutions, bringing people together, and I couldn't imagine that two intelligent men who belonged to the same party and shared most of the same goals would jeopardize everything just for the sake of fighting each other. Obviously, Chrétien didn't confide in me about his feelings toward Martin; nor did Paul ever unleash on me his frustrations with the prime minister. On one of my birthdays, I remember, he invited me to have dinner with him at a little restaurant in Hull, and though we talked for about four hours over two bottles of wine, he never once mentioned any plot to depose Chrétien. If those conversations were happening, they weren't happening around me. I wasn't an intimate. I wasn't trying to build my career around belonging to one faction or another. I simply wanted to get elected in Toronto Centre and keep doing my job as chair of SCFAIT.

It's true that I had known Paul ever since law school, a lot longer and much better than I had known Jean Chrétien. Some people dwelt on Paul's volatile temper and demanding standards, but I always thought of him as an amiable, self-deprecating guy with a keen sense of humour who would rather play hockey than study law texts and never put on any airs because of his famous father. I hadn't kept in touch with him after he moved to Montreal to work for Power Corporation, took over Canada Steamship Lines, and developed a business that made him a wealthy, successful corporate executive. Even after I was elected to Parliament in 1993, we moved in different circles and rarely saw each other outside official meetings. He was an extremely busy, highly powerful finance minister while I was still learning the ropes as a backbencher. Soon after I arrived in the Cabinet, he left.

If anybody had asked my opinion, I would have said that Jean Chrétien deserved to make his own decision about when to step down. Turning on him would have been highly counterproductive, I assumed, and that assumption proved correct. But nobody ever asked my opinion. Following the 1997 election, the Martin organizers made sure that, in the next leadership campaign, they wouldn't repeat the mistake they'd made in the previous one: they worked at taking over as many riding associations as they could in order to control the convention delegates. Fair enough, if and when Mr. Chrétien decided to step down after two majority victories. But when there were rumours that he might run a third time, they started manoeuvring to hasten his retirement.

On March 10, 2000, they invited a couple of dozen Liberal MPs, including me, to a meeting at a hotel near the Toronto airport to survey the political scene in advance of the Liberal Party's biennial convention. I couldn't go because of a previous commitment, which turned out to be just as well because the media interpreted this get-together as part of a plot to oust the prime minister. That's one of the problems with internal strife: you innocently have lunch with someone, and you get tagged by association as a co-conspirator. And if that were the intention of the Martin supporters, it backfired badly. The news reports goaded the Chrétien loyalists into action, and whenever the prime minister appeared at the convention a few days later, some delegates started shouting, "Four more years! Four more years!" With the encouragement of his wife, Aline, Chrétien made up his mind to run for a third term. A couple of months later, on my return from a trip during which I met with Süleyman Demirel, the president of Turkey, I mentioned to the prime minister that Demirel would be leaving office because the parliament wouldn't extend his two-term mandate. "That's the advantage of fixed terms. You don't have to anguish over staying," Chrétien said. "But of course he's much older than I am!"

It was clear that he relished the idea of another fight. "You guys don't like elections," he used to tease the caucus. "You don't want elections." And though I was no longer nervous about losing, I preferred governing. So I wasn't thrilled when Chrétien picked up a reckless challenge to call an election from the new leader of the Opposition, Stockwell Day, and dissolved the House on October 22, 2000. Though many of his MPs and advisers feared that, coming only three years into the second mandate, an election would spark a backlash, the prime minister was more worried that the economic picture might worsen. Besides, he always opposed the notion of fixed election dates on the grounds that one of the most important levers a leader has in a parliamentary democracy is the ability to time the vote.

As for me, not only did I dislike the thought of having to run again so soon but it threw a wrench into all the plans I had been making for over a year with Liberal International to hold its congress in Canada that October. The two events coincided, and I had to be in Ottawa as one of our representatives. My campaign team predicted doom if I wasn't knocking on doors in my riding during those vital four days, and a number of important world leaders thought twice about travelling to Ottawa if Chrétien himself were going to be out on the campaign trail. The prime minister did his best, delivering a speech and shaking hands with as many people as possible, but it was evident that several government leaders and Liberal International officials were disappointed not to have had more of his time and attention.

Chrétien's political instincts proved right once again. The huge outpouring of grief and reflection on the passing of Pierre Trudeau on September 28, followed by the dramatic state funeral in Montreal's Notre-Dame Church that I attended with a delegation of parliamentarians, seemed to ignite party stalwarts across the country to fight the good fight for liberal values. In seven years we had transformed the deficit of $42 billion into a surplus of over $10 billion. We had reduced unemployment from 11 percent to 6 percent. Interest rates had fallen from 13 percent to 6 percent, representing enormous savings for every household with debt. We had retired billions of dollars of the national debt, provided substantial tax relief for middle- and lower-income Canadians, cut corporate taxes to encourage entrepreneurship and investment, increased spending on higher education and low-income children, and concluded an agreement with the provinces to preserve and strengthen public health care in Canada. Moreover, we had done it in a Liberal "third way," balancing fiscal discipline with social programs.

Indeed, Mr. Chrétien saw the campaign as a battle between opposing values rather than between specific policies or issues, with the Liberal legacy in sharp contrast to the neo-conservative, evangelical Christian bent of the Canadian Alliance Party – the old Reform Party now under Stockwell

Day, who had been elected leader in June 2000. Despite an initial honeymoon with the press, as a young, energetic, and attractive new face, Day was harmed by his inexperience, beset by gaffes, crippled by comments from some of his more extremist candidates, and ultimately brought down by reports that his party was planning to privatize our health-care system. No matter how hard he tried to deny it, even resorting to holding up a piece of paper reading "No two-tier health care" during the televised leaders' debate, he couldn't shake off the suspicion that Alliance harboured a secret right-wing agenda. Worse for any politician, his party's promise to hold citizen-initiated referenda on such sensitive matters as abortion and capital punishment turned to ridicule when the comedian Rick Mercer organized a mass petition calling on Day to change his first name to Doris.

In the end, on November 27, 2000, the Liberals won a third majority, increasing our number of MPs from 155 to 172, winning 100 of Ontario's 103 ridings and an additional 10 in Quebec, and regaining 7 seats in the Maritimes. In Toronto Centre I won by more than 55 percent of the vote, with the Progressive Conservatives, the NDP, and the Canadian Alliance far behind.

10

MARCHING AS TO WAR

One day in November 1999, a year before the election, the prime minister and I were driving to the airport after an event in Toronto when, uncharacteristically, he began to speak warmly of my work as chair of SCFAIT. "You're now the caucus expert in international affairs," he said. "You never come to my office and complain about anything."

"I'm very happy doing what I'm doing, Prime Minister."

"Then you're the only one. All the other guys are always in my office wanting to be Cabinet ministers. I know you'd rather be the foreign minister, but there's only room for one."

"Don't worry about me, sir. I love my job. My only regret is the lack of resources the committee chairs are given."

It's easy to fall into a false nostalgia about the past, but Canada at the dawn of the second millennium does indeed look like an easier, more innocent time. Certainly nobody foresaw the dark storm approaching, the speed with which it would be upon us, how prolonged its duration, or even the direction from which it came. I certainly didn't, and like most Canadians, I was mainly concerned about my job, which was going pretty well. The economy was strong, the federal deficit gone, and employment up. The Parti Québécois and the Bloc Québécois were in disarray following the smooth passage of the Clarity Act. We had a liberal, sympathetic friend in the White House with Bill Clinton, and billions of dollars of goods were flowing more or less freely across our borders. We were playing a highly respected, proactive role in the world, whether at the UN, in NATO, or through a host of multilateral organizations. And though there were any number of really serious issues at home and overseas, they seemed the usual sorts of problems, persistent but familiar, tough but containable.

No one could have predicted that the entire world was about to enter a period of new conflicts, new dangers, and even new kinds of conflict and danger, and would lose much of its progress in international law and human security as a result. Suddenly the spectre of terror following 9/11 threatened more than our lives. It threatened the principle of legal conflict, the doctrine of the responsibility to protect, and the sanctity of democratic rights. At the same time it jolted us into trying to grasp the complex political and sectarian power plays of the Middle East and the widespread influence of radical forms of Islam.

I felt the tremors of the coming seismic shift, without fully understanding what they implied, when I was sent on a mission to Iran in January 1999 to discuss human rights and arms control. The country had certainly changed since Patrick Wootten and I had travelled through it more than thirty-five years earlier. The shah had been overthrown in 1979, and the government had fallen into the hands of a group of Shia clerics whose religious fervour, similar to what I had seen in Mashhad in 1960, led them to turn Iran away from the West and Western values. They fed the flames of anti-Americanism, as dramatized by the infamous hostage crisis of 1979, and the United States came to see Iran as an evil enemy. Meanwhile, having fought a war against Saddam Hussein's Iraq during the 1980s, Iran was also engaged in a competition for ascendancy with the Sunni-dominated states in the region. In fact, the American overthrow of Saddam in 2003 served to advance Iran's geopolitical ambitions.

I arrived in a transition period during which more moderate voices were starting to be heard, and there was some hope of progress toward more openness. Our ambassador at the time, Michel de Salaberry, was a Quebecer of exquisite refinement, broad culture, and great sophistication, and he seemed to know everybody and everything worth knowing. I sometimes felt like a nuisance dropping in on our embassies, as though a mere committee chair didn't deserve the fuss that the staff had to make on my behalf. But Michel saw my visit as a good excuse to arrange government meetings and host social events with people he would otherwise have had difficulty seeing. Far from making me feel like a burden, he turned me into an opportunity. He hosted a lunch for me to meet some Canadians who were trying to do business in Iran. He introduced me to political dissidents and artists, and took me to see the marvellous sights in Shiraz and Persepolis, which I hadn't been able to visit in 1960. One of our hosts, who had been a secretary to the shah, greeted us when we arrived at his vast estate with the delightful words, "Would you like a martini?"

Through Michel, I met two very different types of Iranian officials. The first group reminded me of Gertrude Bell's description of the "subtle charm" of the Persians, whom she found "all philosophers of nature, whether prince or muleteer." Some were essentially Westernized but in positions where they had to defend Iran's national interests above all else; others, such as Ali Larijani, the vice-chair of their foreign relations committee, successfully camouflaged their doctrinaire conservatism by their brilliance, liveliness, and courtesy. An astonishing number had received their postgraduate education in the United States, including Mohammad Javad Zarif, the deputy minister of foreign affairs, who was an international law professor with a degree from the University of Denver. The thrust of Zarif's defence, whether talking about nuclear weapons, chemical weapons, or human rights, was that Iran was no worse than many other states, including Saudi Arabia and Israel, and therefore it was unjustly singled out by the West. "No matter what we do," he said without rancour, "you will never give us the benefit of the doubt and treat us fairly."

A second group, however, struck me as deeply religious, highly orthodox, and still very suspicious of the West. They included Hassan Rouhani, the powerful chairman of the foreign affairs committee of the Iranian parliament. Though a moderate by reputation, he hid his pragmatism behind a gruff, clerical manner. I certainly never could have guessed that he had done his postgraduate studies in Scotland or spoke fluent English, for we had a stilted, uncomfortable conversation through translators about the landmines treaty and the human rights of the Baha'i minority. When Rouhani became president in 2013, I was somewhat surprised to see the *New York Times* describe him as "charming," and even more surprised when he championed weapons negotiations with the Americans.

Early in September 2001 I saw the other side of the Shia-Sunni divide when I visited Saudi Arabia for the first time at the request of Prime Minister

Chrétien. He asked me to be his personal envoy to take a letter of concern to Crown Prince Abdullah on behalf of William Sampson, a Canadian citizen who had been arrested the previous December on charges connected to a car bombing in Riyadh. Sampson pleaded guilty and was sentenced to death, but when reports emerged that he had been tortured into confessing, his plight became a political and diplomatic *cause célèbre*. It was complicated by the fact that Sampson was also a British citizen. At one point, feeling let down by the Canadian government, he said that he preferred his case to be handled by London. Nevertheless, we were determined to do whatever we could to secure his release, and our ambassador made extraordinary efforts to protect him.

I flew out of Rome on Friday, September 7, had a six-hour layover in Cairo, and arrived in Jeddah at four o'clock on Saturday morning. A few hours later guards escorted our ambassador, Melvyn MacDonald, and me into King Fahd's personal palace, where scores of finely garbed sheiks were attending on the royal family. "Salaam Aleikom Malik Fahd," I managed to say when I was introduced to the frail monarch. Because of his stroke, mine was purely a courtesy visit in which we shared a cup of coffee and expressed mutual respect. Also present was Saud Al Faisal, who had been foreign minister since 1975, his long tenure no doubt helped by his membership in the royal family as much as his unquestionable personal skills.

The ambassador and I were then passed along to the heir apparent, Crown Prince Abdullah, who kept us cooling our heels for an hour while he finished up with the president of Gambia and concluded his prayers. In the meantime, I spoke with Prince Nayef, the minister of the interior, a tough character whose intelligence system reached into every corner of the kingdom. Indeed, Melvyn MacDonald told me that we couldn't talk in my hotel room, which was a first for me. We had to go into the garden to carry on the conversation because the bugging system was as bad as in Russia. I was astonished at how anti-American Nayef was and how violently he opposed what he saw as my interfering in his country's internal affairs. Instead of mutual respect, I encountered raw contempt, and beneath it I sensed a massive inferiority complex, as though he felt pushed around by the Western powers. "If you want to succeed in Saudi Arabia," he lectured me in a snooty fashion, "you must respect Islam and our way of doing things."

"Look," I replied firmly, "most of the world, including Saudi Arabia, has signed on to the Vienna Convention on Consular Relations. Because Mr. Sampson is a Canadian national, we are entitled to be here. If you want to get into the WTO, you'll have to learn to play by the rules of the world community." At that point our conversation disintegrated into something of a shouting match.

By contrast, Crown Prince Abdullah welcomed us politely and listened intently when I delivered Chrétien's letter, with its strong message that any torture or mistreatment of Sampson, a Canadian citizen, was important to the Government of Canada and to the prime minister himself. "Torturing people is contrary to Islam," the prince responded, "so we can't possibly be torturing anybody."

"I'm sure that's very true of yourself, Your Highness," I said, "but in many systems, even in our own system, there are bad apples. We have to recognize the possibility that rogue policemen may be doing things that are contrary to the precepts of Islam and Saudi Arabia's international obligations. I just want to be able to go and see Mr. Sampson to reassure the prime minister——."

"I'm sorry," he interrupted, "but that's not possible." However, he did accept that the case was a political issue and that it threatened to interfere with the good relations he sought between our two countries, especially given his high regard for Mr. Chrétien. Saudi Arabia had an incentive to solve this issue because it wanted to open its new embassy in Ottawa with an official visit.

Much like Iran, Saudi Arabia presented conflicting facets to the world. On the one hand, like the urbane Abdullah, were those eager to maintain good relations with the West and to position Saudi Arabia as an important ally in the region. On the other, like Prince Nayef, were the more conservative-minded Saudis who resented Western interference in the Middle East. Some of them even sought to export their own fundamentalist brand of Islam known as Wahhabism. I had first heard the term during SCFAIT's trip to Central Asia and the South Caucasus in May 2000, when a Turkish official in Ankara told us of the dangerous forms of Islam that were being disseminated in madrassas throughout the region and even as far as Russia and China. This sort of theology lay behind the Taliban in Afghanistan, he warned us, and much of it was being funded out of Saudi Arabia.

In the end it took another two years of effort to get Sampson released, while he had to endure solitary confinement and repeated torture. But I had done all I could for the moment. Having delivered Chrétien's message, I retraced my journey from Jeddah to Cairo, Cairo to Rome, and Rome to Toronto, arriving home just in time to watch the horrific events that struck New York City and Washington on the morning of September 11, 2001.

AT FIRST, LIKE MOST people who had turned on their television sets after the first plane flew into the World Trade Center, I assumed it had been an accident. When the broadcasters started screaming about a second plane only a few minutes later, we all realized to our shock and grief that we were witnessing a deliberately hatched and thoroughly horrendous act of terrorism, the worst attack on American soil since Pearl Harbor in 1941. Almost three thousand innocent people were murdered, including about a hundred Canadian citizens. I remember phoning a few friends and officials in Ottawa, but no one knew any more than I did. Nor was there any chance of jumping on a plane to Ottawa, because all flights across North America were grounded.

Like every Canadian, I felt a special pride in the Newfoundlanders and Nova Scotians who housed and fed more than thirty thousand stranded travellers. And, like many Canadians, I couldn't help but feel disappointed when President George W. Bush failed in his speech of thanks to the world to recognize Canada's extraordinary help during those terrible days. Worse, I was angry about the high-level suggestion, which persists to this day, that the terrorists had entered the United States from Canada due to our incompetent security services or lax immigration laws, when the evidence proved that almost all of them were Saudi citizens who had been living and training inside the United States. Even Janet Napolitano, the US secretary of homeland security, claimed a Canadian connection to the attacks, which absolutely was not true.

When I met Hillary Clinton, then a senator from New York, at an international security conference in Munich in February 2005, I took the opportunity to admonish her for repeating that canard. "I really wish you would stop spreading that rumour," I told her. "It's just not true. I can give you all the facts, and you really have to hear them." But she merely dismissed my complaint as though it were unimportant. "Yeah," she said, "I get told that a hundred times." To be fair, she was much more interested in meeting with me to discuss getting a Rochester-Toronto ferry service going as a way to boost her state's economy.

It took every tool in our toolbox to get through to the US administration, Congress, and the American people to tell them the facts and protect our interests. At the request of Michael Kergin, our ambassador to Washington at the time, every MP on the Canada-US Parliamentary Association went to see our friends and contacts in the capital to keep the border traffic flowing and the lines of communication open. Meanwhile, SCFAIT moved quickly to turn a study we had already been planning of North American relations into a high-priority examination of Canada-US security and border-related issues.

On September 14, just three days after the tragedy, a dramatic memorial service was held on Parliament Hill at which 100,000 people defied the threat of further attacks by gathering to show their solidarity with the American people. It was a moving event, with the governor general, the prime minister, and the US ambassador to Canada in attendance, designed as much to reassert our values of liberty, tolerance, and pluralism as to express our sympathy. As a child of the days when the Roman Catholic Church controlled every aspect of life in Quebec, Chrétien was especially determined to keep religion out of politics. As one of the authors of the Charter of Rights and Freedoms, he wanted to ensure that no anti-Muslim backlash would follow in the wake of 9/11. By visiting an Ottawa mosque at the height of the crisis, he reached out to the vast majority of Canadian Muslims and sent a message to all Canadians that terrorism was a criminal aberration of true Islam.

In fact, though there were some outbursts of anti-Muslim sentiment in parts of the country, I would say that the place of Islam in Canada has changed for the better on the whole. We began celebrating the festival of Eid on Parliament Hill, for example, and Toronto Centre went from having no mosques when I was first elected to having three when I retired. Many Muslim constituents felt comfortable coming to my office to talk about how they and their children could best make a contribution as citizens of Canada. Some imams in the riding even came to me with their concerns about a particular madrassa in Montreal where, they claimed, young people were in danger of becoming radicalized. In other words, these religious leaders wanted to combat the threat of extremism in Canada, not foster it, and it's important for us to keep it that way.

Nevertheless, there was a broad consensus that we had to do something to prevent further terrorist acts. The threat wasn't only to the United States of America. There was a real risk that something could happen in Canada as well, and failing to recognize that reality would have been irresponsible. Furthermore, from a foreign policy point of view, we had to assure the Americans that, though we were not involved in what had happened there, we were taking active steps to make certain that Canada would not become a safe haven for extremists on their northern frontier.

As the old adage says, "Act in haste, repent at leisure." The Anti-terrorism Act, which was introduced in October and passed in December 2001, was certainly done in haste. In the heat of the crisis, when fear and anger ran high, there wasn't enough time or will for reflection. The police argued that this legislation would give them the power they needed to confront terrorism – the machine gun, as it were, rather than a mere handgun. Even strong voices in the caucus who always spoke up for human rights supported the most draconian restrictions of civil liberties ever known in Canada up to that point, including preventive arrest and secret investigative hearings. We were told – and we believed – that the legislation would withstand a Charter challenge because of the nature of the threat. Even so, because we were nervous about where this legislation would lead, many in the caucus wanted to add a "sunset" clause by which Parliament would be forced to re-examine the most severe measures in five years. If the law proved to have gone too far, we would back away from it. In 2007 the Conservative minority government tried and failed to extend it, but in 2012 it was replaced and even toughened by the Combating Terrorism Act once the Conservatives had a majority.

There is no doubt that the state must take measures to protect its citizens and that there is a need to combat extremist groups such as al-Qaeda. However, I felt at the time that the legislation risked unfairly penalizing perfectly legitimate organizations that didn't support violence. The UN, after all, had issued a list of terrorist groups; fundraising for them was a criminal act; and the police had all the powers they needed to enforce the law. Going after innocent people would simply stir up the very problems that the legislation was designed to prevent. In a counterproductive way, it could marginalize the moderate, law-abiding people who wanted to combat extremism and participate in community policing. As but one example, a host of Tamil Canadian organizations that had nothing to do with violence were lumped in with the Tamil Tigers in Sri Lanka – the equivalent of saying that all the separatists in Quebec should be considered FLQ terrorists. In Toronto Centre a group of Tamil-speaking professors had spent a lot of time building a Tamil library on Parliament Street. It was a source of great pride to the community and a significant centre for the preservation of their language and culture in Canada. Now they feared that the library might be listed as a terrorist organization merely because some of its books advocated the independence of Tamil Eelam from Sri Lanka.

In fact, even labelling the Tamil Tigers as "terrorists" raised its own problems. Both the Norwegians and the Japanese urged Canada not to take this step. "We are trying to achieve a peace accord," Jan Petersen told me, "and this will just animate people to be more violent, more radical. We may need to talk to persons you have classified as 'terrorists.'" Similar strains appeared in the United States, where a Sri Lankan peace conference had to be moved to France because some of the participants would have been arrested the moment they arrived. The basic question is simple: How do you move people from terrorism to peace if you create a wall through which they can't penetrate? Yesterday the IRA was branded a terrorist organization in Northern Ireland; today former leaders of the IRA sit in the Northern Ireland Assembly. Yesterday Nelson Mandela and Menachem Begin were considered terrorists; today they are remembered as great leaders of their countries. The route from one situation to the other was through negotiation.

The tragic truth was that Canadians had been killed in the World Trade Center. September 11 was – and felt like – an attack on us, as well as on the United States. So, on October 4, 2001, Canada vigorously supported NATO's decision to invoke for the first time article 5 of the Washington Treaty, committing the organization to come to the defence of any member that is attacked. Article 5 bound Canada to lend a hand to American-led efforts to hunt down the al-Qaeda terrorists behind the 9/11 attacks, which led to the overthrow of the Taliban regime that allowed them to use Afghanistan as a base of operations. As quickly as October 8, 2001, our defence minister,

Art Eggleton, set in motion Operation Apollo, a Canadian mission allied to the United States' Operation Enduring Freedom. We deployed four naval vessels to the Persian Gulf, followed by surveillance and patrol aircraft. Some critics called it a token contribution, but our aircraft extended the coalition's surveillance capabilities inland to areas that ship-based radar could not cover, and our ships were the most heavily armed vessels in the coalition naval force, providing protection against suicide attacks like the one that had targeted the USS *Cole* in Aden a year earlier.

In November 2001 the Chrétien government announced that it was prepared to send in up to a thousand regular ground troops, but for no longer than six months, and we entered into negotiations on taking part in the International Security Assistance Force (ISAF), the European-led force based in the Afghan capital, Kabul. Established under the December 2001 Bonn Agreement, ISAF was a UN-mandated mission to provide security as the Afghans established a transitional government. It seemed, therefore, the type of modest, low-risk mission with which Canadians were familiar and comfortable, more like classical peacekeeping under multilateral auspices than open combat alongside the Americans.

At one time we took command of the allied task force in the Gulf, and in early December we deployed Joint Task Force 2 (JTF2) special-operations commandos to Kandahar in southern Afghanistan to work alongside US Navy SEALs. As usual with any special operations, only those with a "need to know" knew what their mission entailed. Secrecy is what makes them effective. Most Canadians weren't even aware that we had Special Forces in Afghanistan until their presence was revealed in a newspaper photograph in January, showing Afghani prisoners being held by Canadian soldiers. The defence minister took the heat about the presence of the JTF2, but I was to inherit from him the troubling issue of detainees.

ON JANUARY 9, 2002, during the Christmas break, I flew to Mexico for a gathering of the Council of Europe in Mexico City, a meeting with the governor of Oaxaca, and a lunch at the Canadian embassy to discuss the Inter-Parliamentary Forum of the Americas (FIPA). Then Cathy and I drove in a tropical downpour to Cuernavaca, where we were booked to take a one-week intensive Spanish course. As chairman of FIPA, I had decided I should learn Spanish. Cathy wanted to learn too, so we began with a teacher in Toronto and computer lessons, and now we had a chance to go a step farther.

We arrived at night in the rain and a cold, somewhat sinister, fog, but when we woke the next morning we found ourselves in a charming boutique hotel in a jungle setting with a beautiful vista overlooking a river. "This is going to be great," said Cathy. "A week in paradise, and nothing to do but learn Spanish." We were very happy and found the class full of really interesting people, including three municipal councillors from Texas who had realized they'd better learn Spanish if they wanted to get re-elected and do a decent job in their cities. When one of them asked me why I was there, I said, "Same reason – politics – but at the international level."

About eleven o'clock there was a knock on the door. A man came in and announced, in Spanish, that there was a call for me from the Prime Minister's Office in Ottawa. Cathy rolled her eyes and gave me a "what now?" look as I left the room. After a bit of trouble with the line, I got through to Percy Downe, who had succeeded Jean Pelletier as Chrétien's chief of staff. "You've got to come back," he said. "We thought of sending a plane for you, but it didn't work out."

"You don't usually send a plane for the chairman of the foreign affairs committee, Percy. What's going on up there? We just got here, the course only lasts a week. Why don't I come back on Friday?"

"No, Bill, you're short-listed for the Cabinet, and the prime minister wants you here now."

I went back to the classroom and broke the news to Cathy. "Every trip we've ever taken recently has been screwed up by politics," she sighed, "so why did I believe this one would be any different?" She was unhappy, and I didn't blame her. We were in an enchanting place, we were excited that we had already made some progress with Spanish because of our French, and now we had to leave. It was really disappointing. Later I used to laugh when Mr. Chrétien boasted that I was trilingual. Thank heavens we had no Spanish-speaking reporters on the Hill.

After lunch by the pool we reluctantly got in the car and were whisked back to the Airport Hilton in Mexico City by six, whereupon I was informed that we were booked on a commercial flight to Toronto early the next morning. At eight o'clock that night, when I reported back to Percy Downe, he put Mitchell Sharp and David Zussman on the line. Sharp, I knew, was a distinguished former senior civil servant and Cabinet minister who had been lured out of retirement to serve as the prime minister's dollar-a-year adviser. Zussman was a long-time consultant to Chrétien on governance issues.

"Would you mind telling me what's going on?" I asked.

"No, I can't tell you, but it's terrific. I'm very happy for you," Mitchell said, and then became more businesslike. "Bill, we have to put you through a bit of an 'examination.' Have you ever taken a bribe?"

"No."

"Any problems with your election financing?"

"No, no issues. There's no corruption in the riding association. We're completely open about everything."

"Any possibility of an embarrassment?"

I raised the fact that an aspect of my private life had been featured in *Frank,* the muckraking magazine, and that Cathy was perfectly aware of it and supportive. So, it turned out, were they, and it was never an issue for the prime minister.

After about twenty minutes of questions, Mitchell said, "Fine, fine, I just had to satisfy myself on these points. I want you to make sure that your record is clear. We'll get back to you shortly. Oh, hang on a minute, I see somebody coming down the hall. He wants to speak to you."

Then the unmistakable voice came on the line. "Bill, would you like to be my foreign minister?"

I still didn't understand what was happening because I really didn't expect it. Though I figured something important was up, I thought I might be offered the secretary of state for Latin America or some such job. To go straight from the backbench to foreign minister would be astonishing to everyone. Oddly enough, my mind skipped to the November 1999 conversation I'd had with Chrétien as we drove to the Toronto airport. "But two years ago you told me you had a foreign minister," I blurted idiotically.

"Bill, do you want the job or not?" he asked.

"Of course I want the job. I'm incredibly flattered, and I'd love to do it. Thank you very much."

"I'll explain it to you later, but we have a big problem here. Tobin has just resigned the Cabinet. I was planning to do a shuffle in June, but I've decided to do it now. Herb Gray is stepping down, Manley's going to be deputy prime minister, and you'll take his place. You've been highly recommended by many people. It will be announced tomorrow. So hurry up, we've got work to do. I can't talk any longer. Goodbye."

Meanwhile, Cathy had become so upset that she had gone into the bathroom and stuffed toilet paper in her ears so she wouldn't have to hear the bad news. "Darling, where are you?" I called. "Guess what? I'm the new foreign minister of Canada."

Thrilled by this incredible and totally unexpected development, we ordered a bottle of champagne, which we later discovered cost $500, and called our old friend Adrienne Clarkson, who in her capacity as governor general had already heard the news. We were so excited that we could hardly sleep, and anyway, we had to get up at 5:00 a.m. to catch the 6:30 plane. As we were about to board, I looked down the hall and saw Keith Christie, our ambassador to Mexico, rushing toward me. "What the hell are you doing here at this ungodly hour, Keith? I don't think you've come to wave goodbye to the chairman of the foreign affairs committee."

"A little bird told me that you might not be the chairman of the committee anymore," he said. "In fact, at three o'clock this morning, I got a wire from Ottawa saying that the foreign minister is here."

"Word gets around fast," I said. Then Cathy and I flew to Toronto and on to Ottawa, arriving late on January 15, 2002, having missed the swearing-in ceremony for new ministers held earlier that day.

"It gradually sinks in how much my life (our lives) will now change," I recorded in my journal.

PART 3:
FOREIGN AFFAIRS

11

FRIENDS IN HIGH PLACES

athy and I were up early on Wednesday, January 16, 2002, and arrived at Government House shortly before nine o'clock. There, with Prime Minister Jean Chrétien and Governor General Adrienne Clarkson in attendance, Mel Cappe, the clerk of the Privy Council, swore me in as a minister of the Crown in both official languages.

"We had to get to the age of sixty before getting anywhere," Adrienne said when she congratulated me. However dignified the occasion, it seemed almost a family affair, given our long friendship with Adrienne since our days at Trinity College. Her appointment had come as a complete surprise, though Cathy and I suspected something was in the air when we got a call in July 1999 inviting us to a wedding. After more than a decade together, Adrienne and John Ralston Saul were going to be married on the last day of the month by her old friend Michael Peers, the Anglican primate of Canada. "There's a reason," Adrienne said when I asked her, "but we're not prepared to tell you what it is." A few weeks later she became Canada's twenty-sixth governor general.

Adrienne proved a perfect choice for the job: conscientious, professional, stylish, eloquent in French and English, and a living symbol of the new Canada. Though the nitpickers at the *National Post* liked to fuss about her expenses, I saw first-hand how effective her official visits were to Argentina, Germany, Russia, and the Canadian North in terms of trade, diplomacy, and our international image. They had many beneficial consequences, some intended, some fortuitous, and they greatly enhanced the understanding of Canada's position in the world, both among the people who accompanied her in her delegation and the people they met abroad.

On a personal level, having Adrienne and John in Ottawa brought a happy change to our social life. The House of Commons is not a matrimonial-friendly institution. I saw a lot of marriages fall apart because one partner was at work in Ottawa, the other was back home with the kids, and the weekends were full of political obligations, allowing little time for family or friends. Nor is there much of a role for spouses in the capital. They get invited to the governor general's reception at Rideau Hall to mark the opening of Parliament; the Parliamentary Spouses Association makes an effort to organize events; and the political parties normally have a parliamentary spouses group. But after a period of staying in our Ottawa apartment, Cathy realized that she rarely saw me anyway. The working hours were long, the evening engagements were more often business than pleasure, and taking her on an official trip wasn't considered appropriate, even if there were a budget to do so, because the press would have called it a scam. (The one exception was the Canada-US Inter-Parliamentary Group, which encouraged spouses to attend its meetings. As a result, many political acquaintanceships developed into warm personal friendships, which in turn made for more effective working relationships.) Sometimes the only way that Cathy and I could get a chunk of time together was for her to pay all her own expenses on one of my many trips overseas. There's another point too: an MP's spouse can often feel useful back in the riding, where there's a role to play as a kind of surrogate representative. Cathy was good with people and always willing to participate; she worked hard at campaigning and was an asset at riding events. So long as I was an ordinary backbencher or committee chair, however, she had no formal duties, and living between two cities obliged her to resign from her volunteer activities.

Now, with Adrienne as governor general, Ottawa became an enriched experience for us. We were included in state dinners to which a mere chair of SCFAIT wouldn't normally be invited. Rideau Hall went from being a venue for official events to a place where we were warmly received, often as a family. We spent many informal evenings and several Christmas holidays with Adrienne and John, including one at the magnificent residence in Quebec City overlooking the St. Lawrence River, when we went for long winter walks on the Plains of Abraham and got to know a variety of other guests, both francophone and anglophone, from politics, journalism, and the arts. When Adrienne went to South America and Russia on state business, Cathy was able to go along, always paying her full share of expenses.

Her life changed again as soon as I assumed the portfolio of the Department of Foreign Affairs and International Trade (DFAIT). A spouse is considered a real asset in that portfolio and is often called upon to act in a quasi-official capacity. Cathy travelled with me to international meetings, she got to know the wives of other foreign ministers, and she hosted receptions at the Pearson Building for diplomats and their spouses. In fact, with her gracious presence, her ease with people, and her fluency in French, she proved the ideal foreign minister's wife, not only helping me do a better job but contributing a great deal to the country in her own right. It's unfortunate that, in the thirteen and a half years of my parliamentary career, we had a chance to work together as a team in that department for only two and a half years.

COMING OUT OF Rideau Hall after the swearing-in, with the press shouting questions, the prime minister said to me, "You'd better hurry and pick up your files. We're having a Cabinet meeting in half an hour."

I might have panicked if not for the fact that Gaëtan Lavertu, my new deputy minister, had briefed me the night before about what to expect on my first day. "Technically I'm violating Cabinet secrecy," he said, "but we have to show you these papers now so that you can familiarize yourself with the department's priorities. You're going to be responsible for some of the items on the Cabinet agenda."

Given the number and complexity of the issues for which a minister is responsible, I had to rely heavily on the information and advice that filtered up through the hierarchy – from the ambassadors to the regional desks, and then to the assistant or associate deputy ministers in charge of different areas, and onward to the deputy minister who oversaw the whole department. I had scheduled meetings at least twice a week with my deputy minister, first Gaëtan Lavertu and then Peter Harder, who also signed off on the memos that actually reached me. Otherwise I would have been overwhelmed by the plethora of documents the system produced for the "minister's eyes only." I frequently met with individual assistant deputy ministers to discuss a specific crisis in the news or to prepare for an overseas conference. Ron Hoffmann, a DFAIT officer seconded to my office, served as my liaison to what was happening in my department; I held monthly meetings to talk about policy matters with the associate deputy minister Jonathan Fried, and from time to time dealt directly with our legal officer, Colleen Swords. Sometimes I used to drop into the cafeteria for lunch to find out what the junior officers were doing or thinking.

In addition to the permanent civil servants I inherited at DFAIT, I quickly had to assemble a new political staff to complement the ones I already had in my offices on Parliament Hill and in the constituency. At the urging of the PMO, which no doubt wanted to position someone it could trust at the side of an untested minister, I recruited Dan Costello to be my chief of staff. Dan, who had extensive experience working for Chrétien and Elinor Caplan, the minister of citizenship and immigration, inspired tremendous confidence, and he guarded that most precious of assets – my time – which was programmed almost to the minute from seven in the morning to ten at night, by arranging my priorities, filtering the myriad demands and requests made of me, and monitoring access to my office. He quickly persuaded Robert Fry to come over from Herb Gray's office to be second-in-command, and they made a formidable team. Daniel Laprès was my liaison with Quebec, and he took advantage of my French-language skills as well as his own extensive contacts in academia to secure speaking engagements for me at universities throughout the province. The fourth of my key advisers was my invaluable communications director, Lillian Thomsen, a public servant seconded to the minister's office, and her successor, the equally invaluable Isabelle Savard. I probably saw more of them than anybody in the course of a week because they had to be constantly at my side to handle the media, whether at home or abroad.

But first I had to find my office. Striding proudly into the Pearson Building, I was stopped by the commissionaire at the door. "And where do you think you're going?" he asked.

"I'm the new minister," I replied with all the dignity I could muster. Fortunately at that moment a message appeared on the television set in the lobby, welcoming me to my new portfolio, and I was able to point to my picture on the screen. I barely had time to reach the tenth floor and hang up my coat before dashing over to Parliament Hill for the weekly ten o'clock meeting of the Cabinet in Room 323-S of the Centre Block.

No sooner had it begun than I was thrown head-first into the deep end, when Mr. Chrétien asked me to present my department's views on two complex defence matters: the implications for NORAD of changes to the US military command structure in the wake of 9/11, and the deployment of Canadian Forces in Afghanistan. I launched into the speaking points that my officials had given me and was just getting into the details when I saw the prime minister frowning at me and making a strange gesture with his hands. "Does that mean I should wind up?" I asked him.

"Yes, you should wind up," he said. "You're not a professor now. We're not here in the Cabinet to talk a lot. We're here to get things done." Lesson one: keep it brief and to the point.

Lesson two came when I tried to secure for myself the corner office my predecessors Lloyd Axworthy and John Manley had occupied in the Centre Block. Lloyd particularly liked it, he once explained, because of its location: he could get on the nearby freight elevator, go down to the basement, walk out an obscure back door, and jump into his car without being seen by the gaggle of reporters who were always lying in wait around the members' entrance to ambush him with their questions. However, though I may have been the foreign minister, I was at the very bottom of the protocol list as the newest member of the Cabinet, and plenty of other ministers were coveting that office as well. "We've never had a foreign minister with so little seniority," Marlene Catterall, the chief government whip, told me, "so there's no way you're going to get it. We'll find somewhere else for you."

Disappointed, I went to Manley for advice. "Well," said John, "I had that office equipped with a very sophisticated computer system to allow me to communicate directly and securely with the Foreign Affairs Department. It cost about a quarter of a million bucks."

I went back to Marlene. "I'm told there's a very sophisticated communication system set up in that office," I said. "If I can't get it, I assume you'll be the one to explain the waste and the extra $250,000 that'll have to be spent on my new office."

"Okay, I get it," she quickly responded. "I'll tell the others that we couldn't afford to move you."

Lesson three was the travel required for the job. Forty-eight hours after my appointment, I was en route to London for a meeting of the Commonwealth Ministerial Action Group, which had been set up to respond to serious infringements of the organization's fundamental values. There I met many of my fellow foreign ministers for the first time, including Jack Straw (United Kingdom), Alex Downer (Australia), Yashwant Singh (India), Billie Miller (Barbados), and Sule Lamido (Nigeria). The two main items on the agenda were Pakistan, which had been suspended from the Commonwealth following the military coup that brought Pervez Musharraf to power in 1999, and Zimbabwe, where Robert Mugabe's government had been cracking down on his political opponents in advance of the presidential election scheduled for 2002, threatening the independence of the judiciary, intimidating the media, and inciting violence.

Zimbabwe dominated the discussion at a dinner hosted by Don McKinnon, the affable New Zealander who was serving as secretary general. On one side, Billie Miller pushed for action, arguing that "we'll have no self-respect left if we don't do something," while Alex Downer declared that the Commonwealth's credibility and relevance were at stake. On the other side, Sule Lamido suggested that sending in election monitors would be a form of colonialism. "Sule's body language is really negative to any criticisms," I noted at the time. "Nigeria is in a very difficult position." Botswana's Mompati Merafhe countered that the situation had nothing to do with colonialism or blacks against whites, because black Zimbabweans were being killed by the regime. The era had passed, he argued, "when you can kill people in the name of sovereignty." In the end, Lamido promised to get his president, Olusegun Obasanjo, to call Mugabe and plead for a free and peaceful vote, though he suspected we wouldn't be satisfied until Mugabe was gone. "For you to think that there have been fair elections," he said, "he must lose."

The next day, in sharp contrast, Lamido wanted us to take a hard line on democracy in Pakistan. "I agree," I said, "provided that it will apply to a later file as well," obviously referring to Zimbabwe. Jack Straw gave me a wink and a thumbs-up, but Sule refused to see the contradiction in Nigeria's position. "African leaders are working hard to engage Mugabe," he insisted, "and this pressure is more effective than any European action." Nevertheless,

I worked hard with the others to help craft the recommendation that heavily criticized Mugabe's repression of human rights and warned of possible consequences. When the Commonwealth Heads of Government met the following March, they decided to suspend Zimbabwe from the councils of the Commonwealth for one year, and in 2003 Zimbabwe withdrew from the organization.

I found the meetings of the Commonwealth and La Francophonie, its French-speaking equivalent, invariably interesting and a useful way to develop a matrix of effective networks with other foreign ministers. On countless occasions Canada was able to benefit from connections made at Commonwealth and Francophonie meetings to solve a problem at the Security Council, a crisis in Haiti, or a trade issue with Vietnam. Similarly we used those connections to build political alliances to secure agreements on the International Criminal Court, the eradication of landmines, and a host of other initiatives. That said, I think these organizations play a less important role in the conduct of our global affairs than they once did or might yet do. By any objective measure, they aren't on the same level as NATO, the G8, the United Nations, or even the forum for Asia-Pacific Economic Cooperation. They aren't defence pacts, trade zones, or creators of international norms, even if some of their actions or codes contributed indirectly to the formation of customary international law.

In my experience, moreover, though the Commonwealth retains its historic, almost romantic association as the tie that binds Canada to the old British Empire, La Francophonie has emerged as the more vital international forum because of our domestic political situation and the fact that Quebec has its own say in it on matters of education and culture. Whenever the Parti Québécois is in power in Quebec, it pushes hard to use its seat in the organization as a window on the world, no matter what the Canadian government might want, and there have been times when its separatist aspirations have even been encouraged by the French government. As a result, La Francophonie tends to have a more direct impact on Canada's internal politics than the Commonwealth does, and therefore it gets more attention from the Canadian foreign minister. Though Don McKinnon was always urging me to become more engaged, not least because Canada is seen as a helpful player by a lot of the members, I learned fairly early

that I had too much else on my plate to take a really active role in Commonwealth issues. Traditionally, too, that role was played most effectively by
the Canadian prime minister.

WHEN PRIME MINISTER Chrétien asked me to take on DFAIT, we talked
about what I would like to achieve in the portfolio. I had my answer ready.
Through my work with the Inter-Parliamentary Forum of the Americas
(FIPA) and my trips as chair of SCFAIT, I had learned how important Latin
America was to our hemispheric interests and how vital to our trade and
commerce, yet it remained a neglected region in terms of Canada's foreign
policy. We still tended to see ourselves as a North Atlantic nation, midway
between Europe and the United States. We were beginning to see ourselves
as a Pacific nation as well. Now we needed to integrate Canada into the
Americas through trade pacts, such as NAFTA and the one-on-one agreements we signed with Chile and Costa Rica, and through cultural exchanges. The opportunity was there and the timing was right.

"Lloyd focused on human security," I said. "I'd like to make Canada more
relevant in Central and Latin America. We're not focused enough on the
Americas."

"Good for you, Professor," Chrétien said. "That sounds like a good project. And lucky you, to be able to do that."

Instead, I was drawn deeper and deeper into the politics of the Middle
East – first Israel, then Iraq, and eventually all the way east to Afghanistan
– where I found international law struggling to reassert itself amid the
chaos of regional conflicts and the war on terror. Perhaps 9/11, coming on
top of the unresolved animosities of this strategically important area, had
made that inevitable, but the speed and degree of my involvement took
me by surprise. In fact, it began with the very first speech I made as DFAIT
minister to a policy conference of the Canada-Israel Committee in Ottawa
on March 6, 2002.

A ministerial speech, I soon discovered, isn't intended to be a personal
statement. It's an articulation of an official position, delivered by the minister on behalf of the Government of Canada. Given this, I was often
frustrated by the bureaucratic tone of many of the speeches I delivered.
Even if I had it in myself to reach Churchillian heights in language or wit
(and, of course, I did not), I, like all ministers today, lacked the time to

write my own speeches. Churchill had the leisure to contemplate his words, hone them, test them, rehearse them, and memorize them. He could speak with his own voice about issues he knew intimately. Now a group of people in the department prepare a draft that percolates up through the bureaucracy to the top, where a civil servant in the minister's office rewrites it, and the political advisers fiddle with it. Few, if any, are professional speechwriters. They're usually academics or bureaucrats, and their texts tend to read better on the page than from a podium.

Preparation time is one problem; delivery time is another. Whether in the House of Commons or at an after-dinner engagement, no one wants to hear more than twenty minutes on anything. But you can't explore complicated issues in twenty minutes. As Pascal once wrote, "I made this longer only because I did not have the time to make it shorter." A short speech that catches the facts and ideas necessary for the full understanding of a public policy is much tougher to craft than a long one. And there's never enough time in this high-speed, attention-deficit world before people start looking at their watches and eyeing the exits. If you digress from the text to follow a thought or tell an anecdote, the next thing you know you're five minutes behind, you've got three more pages to go, the audience is flagging, you start skipping paragraphs and picking up your pace, and your rousing finale or brilliant summation is lost in a breathless dash across the finish line.

Almost every minister I knew complained about the quality of their speeches. Although there are some excellent speechwriters in Ottawa, the process of generating speeches made it difficult to get a punchy, interesting product. I used to beg for more human stories, more good lines, but I resigned myself to the fact that I would never be totally satisfied. The best that modern ministers can hope for is to keep the dry blather to a minimum and get a copy of the text a day in advance to familiarize themselves with the content. Even wresting a speech from all the people who wanted to keep revising it up to the last moment was usually a losing battle.

It wasn't abnormal, therefore, as I made my way to the venue to deliver my speech to the Canada-Israel Committee, to receive a call from Eddie Goldenberg in the Prime Minister's Office with suggestions for a few changes. In particular, he advised me to remove the references to Israel's demolition of civilian housing, its incursions into refugee camps, and its continuing settlement activity in the occupied territories. Though factually accurate, they seemed to him unnecessary for that particular occasion.

Because this was my first major speech, the department had drafted it with particular care to make sure it reflected Canada's traditional position. Our agenda since the founding of Israel in 1948, reflective of our general approach to world affairs, was to see what we could do to bring warring parties together for the sake of peace through international institutions that functioned well. We recognized Israel as a special place and acknowledged its extraordinary security challenges. At the same time we were working to foster a lasting peace in the region, based on security guarantees for Israel in exchange for its withdrawal from the territories it had occupied since the 1967 war. Nothing I intended to say deviated from that long-established policy, so nothing and no one forewarned me regarding what was about to happen.

I HAD BEEN FASCINATED by the Middle East even before Patrick Wootten and I made our extensive trip through the region as university students. I frequently returned to Lebanon on legal business for the Toronto Dominion Bank, which owned a bank there, and I'll never forget the chilling conversation I had in Beirut one evening with a very wealthy businessman who had been a great friend of my parents. During dinner at his palatial home, surrounded by servants and bodyguards, he told me that he gave $10 million a year to Yasser Arafat.

"But why would you do that?" I asked. "If Yasser Arafat were in charge, you'd be shot as a rich capitalist."

"My grandparents, you see, had an orange grove in Haifa," he replied, "and they were driven out by Israeli machine guns. If I go back someday, it can only be with a machine gun." The animosities run deep.

I got my first serious exposure to internal Israeli politics through my involvement with Liberal International, where I made friendships and contacts with members of Shinui – in particular with Amnon Rubinstein, who became a minister in Yitzhak Rabin's coalition government. I formed my own perspective on the two-state solution and other Palestinian issues in large measure from their ideas, and I adopted middle-of-the-road positions that were closer to the editorials in *Haaretz* than those of the *Jerusalem Post*. However, I didn't get to visit Israel until November 1995, when I went on a one-week fact-finding mission, organized by the Canada-Israel Committee, with a group of eight MPs from all parties and some of our spouses. "Hard to describe one's immediate reactions and emotions on arrival in Israel," I wrote in my notes, "the country has been so much thought about ... [and] the Middle East has been central to so many interests for so many years."

We travelled throughout the country, from the Golan Heights to holy sites around the Sea of Galilee. We dined with five members of the Knesset, including Moshe Dayan's daughter Yaël, a strong and impressive politician whose dramatic personality belied her balanced views. We lunched at a kibbutz; visited settlers on the West Bank; met in Jericho with Saeb Erekat, a prominent member of the Palestinian Authority; and took a dip in the Dead Sea. We paid an incredibly moving visit to the Yad Vashem Martyrs' and Heroes' Memorial of the Holocaust and went to Mount Herzl to offer prayers at the grave of Yitzhak Rabin, who had been assassinated less than two weeks before. We met with a wide range of wonderful, intelligent people, from politicians to businessmen to academics. At one dinner I remember asking Colonel Yosef Kuperwasser, the deputy chief of intelligence for the Israeli Defence Force, what he did for recreation. "I read Arab poetry," he replied, partly to develop his understanding, partly to develop his empathy.

Our hosts were open, generous, and accommodating, particularly Shimon Fogel, our astute, open-minded facilitator. They didn't object when our delegation paid an unofficial visit to Orient House in the Arab quarter of Jerusalem for a breakfast meeting with Faisal Husseini, an elegant and sophisticated Palestinian spokesman whom I had met in Canada when he testified at SCFAIT the previous month. Many of the MPs felt that it was one of the high points of the trip because of his articulate analysis of the problems and issues facing the Middle East. In the allegorical style so beloved by the Arabs, he said, "Jerusalem has the potential to become a warm sun or a black hole. It will be a warm sun if there is a shared jurisdiction of some kind." He clearly believed that some form of joint arrangement was possible.

The one impression we all took home was the liveliness of the debate within Israel itself. It was, in fact, a more vibrant and vigorous debate than I had ever been a party to in Canada – how best to advance peace and security, whether to use carrots or sticks, the role of religion, the future of democracy, the rights of the Palestinians, and so forth. I wished then, and still wish, that we could have that same level of informed debate in our country. When my son, Patrick, worked for the *National Post,* for example, he told me that an Israeli editor who worked with him at the newspaper used to joke that the *Post* was too pro-Israel to be published in Israel – no one would take it seriously. Since the newspaper's founding in 1998 by Conrad Black, whose media empire included the *Daily Telegraph* in London and the *Jerusalem Post,* the *National Post*'s vigorous, unapologetic defence of Israel, right or wrong, became part and parcel of his pro-American, neo-conservative ideology, and its editorial stance simply hardened after Black sold it to Izzy Asper, even though Asper had been a former leader of the Manitoba Liberal Party. Izzy once invited me to a breakfast where he introduced me to an Israeli friend of his who happened to be in town: Benjamin Netanyahu.

By seeking to remain an effective moderating influence, Canada risked being criticized by all sides. When your buses are being blown up or your homes razed, even-handedness can look like abetting the enemy. I was often reminded by Amanda Sussman, my adviser on the file and herself a descendant of Jews who had fled the pogroms of Russia and Poland, why Canada's Jewish community, the fourth largest in the world, justifiably cherishes Israel as the last lifeboat for the survival of their people in a sea of persecution.

Yet taking one side or another presents its own problems. In 1979, for example, when Prime Minister Joe Clark announced that the Canadian embassy would move from Tel Aviv to Jerusalem, all hell broke loose. Although it might have played well in terms of domestic politics, it caused a tremendous problem for Americans, the British, the French – almost everybody – because it implied a recognition of the Israeli occupation of the whole of Jerusalem, east and west, de facto *and* de jure, and thus pre-judged the outcome of where the ultimate border lines would be. Even the United States, Israel's most ardent supporter, was scrupulous in its respect for international law and the rules surrounding this issue. In the face of intense blow-back from our allies, not to mention from our trading partners in the Arab world, Clark quickly backed down.

It was a painful lesson in how cautious you have to be about the Middle East even in terms of domestic politics. Differing constituencies have very different perceptions as to what is right and wrong, what is just and not just, and all the protagonists want the Canadian government to take their side in whatever dispute is occurring at any particular moment. Worse is when the historical feuds and eternal grievances of their former homelands are imported to Canada by people who have no desire for reconciliation. (That's true not just in Canada but in most other countries, and it's true not just of the Middle East but of many other conflict zones, whether Northern Ireland, Armenia, Ukraine, or Punjab.) Their positions sometimes become more entrenched here than at home, and that entrenchment works against any and all government efforts to maintain a diplomatic balance if that is what is required in the circumstances. There are situations, of course, where diplomatic niceties are not appropriate, and one has to take a clear position.

What happened to Joe Clark also demonstrated the extent to which Canada's relationship with Israel is linked to our relationships with other capitals around the world. It affects our connection with Egypt, which is a strategic powerhouse in the region. Supporting moderate Jordan and its considered policies is crucial to the peace process. Lebanon remains constantly in focus because of Canada's large Lebanese diaspora, whether Sunnis, Shiites, Christians, or Druze. Syria has become a major international concern because of its terrible civil war. I learned how complicated those links can be when SCFAIT examined the Canada-Israel free-trade deal and discovered that many countries would not accept Israeli goods under the rules of origin if they were partly manufactured in the West Bank.

Circumstances are constantly in flux in the region, and everybody is forever dependent on what other people are doing at any given time. When George W. Bush replaced Bill Clinton, for instance, the US government's approach to Israel changed significantly, and 9/11 certainly eroded the Bush administration's willingness to expend the kind of time and effort on solving the Israeli-Palestinian issues that Presidents Carter and Clinton had shown. I remember talking at the time with one prominent European who had just come from discussing the Middle East at a high level in

Washington. "I wasn't sure," he said, "whether I was speaking to an American official or the Israeli foreign minister."

My tenure as foreign minister coincided with the Second Intifada – the Palestinian uprising that had broken out in 2000 and continued unabated for the next few years. Israel's response to this new wave of violence often drew international censure. The more Israel was criticized, the more the Canadian Jewish community came to its defence. In the eyes of many, there was no room for a middle way. It was a classic illustration of how foreign affairs works: Canada can have all the wonderful policies it likes, but other players will act in what they perceive as their best interest, with the result that we can't always advance our own agenda.

That same thread carries into multilateral forums, particularly the United Nations. What Canada stands for, how Canada is perceived abroad, is shaped to some extent by our statements and votes in the UN General Assembly on resolutions regarding Israel or the Palestinians. I'm not suggesting that our UN votes are largely motivated by this complex matrix of sometimes conflicting interests, but only that these interests must be taken into consideration if Canada is going to have a sophisticated, intelligent foreign policy. Complicating matters even further, many of the UN resolutions involving the Middle East are deliberately set traps. If we choose to vote to condemn the building of new settlements by Israel, for example, we have to disassociate ourselves from the outrageous anti-Israel sentiments that are often larded into the preamble. And if we seek to apply our values and the universal conventions on human rights to the Palestinian situation, we must ensure that Israel isn't being singled out unfairly by countries whose record of human rights abuses is no better or even worse. Quite often, therefore, the Chrétien government opted to abstain, only to be accused by all sides of not standing up for our principles.

Once I attended a UNESCO meeting at which a resolution critical of Israel was to be put to a vote. "We'll be abstaining on it," my officials told me.

"Why?" I asked. "UNESCO is about education and culture. This resolution isn't UNESCO business. It has no place here. It's just trying to politicize UNESCO for no good reason. That's crazy. We should vote against it."

"But we'll offend all the Arab countries if we do that," they replied. "The only people voting against it are Israel and the United States." Nevertheless, I insisted that we vote no.

I had some heated discussions in my office with leaders of the Jewish community who told me in no uncertain terms that Canada's position on many UN votes was cowardly. Some even argued that Canada should give up on the United Nations altogether and help form a new association of democracies. But, for one thing, the way the UN was designed, the US veto in the Security Council can always be used to protect Israel from the General Assembly. More importantly, as Shimon Peres once said to me, "You don't make peace by talking to your friends. You make peace by talking to your enemies." What's the good of talking only to people you agree with? It's like drinking your own bathwater.

In that regard, I was particularly impressed by the efforts of Arnold Noyek, a Toronto-based doctor who led projects throughout the Middle East to treat the hearing problems common to many in the region. Arnie was able to bring together Israeli, Palestinian, and Jordanian doctors to work toward common goals and foster mutual understanding, despite the extremely strained political climate. I met with Arnie many times and supported his work. To me, he represented the best of Canada, a great example of what many individual Canadians, NGOs, and religious organizations do to alleviate suffering and promote reconciliation around the world, even when state actors find themselves deadlocked.

Prime Minister Chrétien strongly believed that Canada could be of more use to everybody if we maintained an even hand, and though we can't pretend we're a big player, we can do our best to make small advances. While we adhered to the security of Israel as a core principle, therefore, we also worked to advance the human rights of the Palestinians, not least because we believed that the long-term stability and peace of the Middle East was key to Israel's security. In fact, when we chaired the Refugee Working Group dealing with the hugely important issue of defining a satisfactory outcome for Palestinians displaced by the conflict, an Israeli ambassador said to me, "Canada can be helpful to us at the United Nations because you're not like the United States – you can go and talk to the Arab states with credibility."

THAT WAS THE THRUST of my speech to the Canada-Israel Committee in March 2002. On the one hand, it denounced the Palestinians' use of violence and emphasized Israel's right to exist within secure boundaries and to take measures to defend itself. On the other, it supported the creation of a viable, independent, and democratic Palestinian state; suggested that Israel should give serious consideration to withdrawing from the lands it had occupied since 1967; and condemned the killing of innocent civilians as unjustifiable, detrimental to Israel's image, and prejudicial to the prospects for peace. "Too many Israeli and, I daresay, also Palestinian lives," I said, "have been lost or shattered and too many parents and children mourn."

As I worked my way through the text, the audience became unhappier and unhappier, feeling that I was more concerned with calling attention to Israel's faults than with recognizing its difficulties. The squirming turned to boos during the question-and-answer period when I denied that Canadian foreign aid was used to help distribute "vile and racist" educational material in Palestinian refugee camps and pleaded for Israel not to escalate the violence in response to Palestinian attacks. Interestingly, two members of the Israeli parliament who were present came up to me afterward and said, "We don't understand why everybody's so upset. We say this sort of thing every day in the Knesset."

If that weren't bad enough (and it was pretty bad), I then had to walk out of the room into a media frenzy. Copies of the speech had been distributed to the reporters before I had presented it, with the words "check against delivery" at the top, as was the norm, and they had noticed the cuts that Eddie Goldenberg had requested. "Why did you drop them?" they shouted. "Who told you to drop them?"

"It says 'check against delivery,'" I answered lamely. "I simply decided to shorten it. When I give a speech, I give the speech I give."

Occasionally, as chair of SCFAIT, I had been ambushed in the corridors by a small gang of journalists asking questions about the hot issue of the day, but nothing really prepares a new minister for the full assault of being scrummed. A scrum is purely adversarial. A tightly packed crowd of up to two dozen radio, TV, and print journalists scream at you from every different direction, some in English, some in French, with their camera lights blinding your eyes and their microphones pushed in your face. There's no time to compose a considered reply in your head. There's no opportunity for reflection or nuance. There's no option but to stand there and take whatever is thrown at you. All you can do is bat back a response as rapidly as possible and hope that it doesn't land you in trouble.

Most MPs have friends in the media. Parliamentarians and journalists work together on the Hill during the day; they socialize at parties and events in the evening; and once a year they come together to drink and throw buns at each other at the Press Gallery Dinner. I was on Don Newman's TV show so often that I got to know him fairly well and felt comfortable being interviewed by him. I was often invited to dine at the home of Susan Delacourt, the *Toronto Star*'s bright and gregarious bureau chief, along with Shaughnessy Cohen, Carolyn Bennett, and other colleagues. I had many off-the-record lunches with Jim Travers and my good friend from our university days, David Crane, both of the *Toronto Star*. I liked them as individuals and talked to them regularly, but anybody going through the media clippings would be hard pressed to find evidence that they had treated me more gently than any other politician. And I was never naive enough to suppose that they would cut me any slack if I made a mistake.

For the Press Gallery Dinner that took place a few weeks after the Canada-Israel Committee speech, I was talked into videotaping a mock speech while being pelted with chickens and bananas. The higher you climbed up the greasy pole, it seemed, the more savage the teasing became, especially after the dinners went from being private affairs to televised spectacles. Though the video was funny and done in good sport, no one in the room could miss its barb. I had just become minister; I hadn't mastered the media game; I had made a disastrous speech; and I was being attacked not for the intellectual content but over a political triviality. It reminded me of the immortal lines once delivered by President George H.W. Bush's budget director in defence of his boss: "He didn't say that. He was reading what was given to him in a speech."

Though Eddie Goldenberg and I had a good conversation about what had happened, I don't recall the prime minister ever mentioning it to me. I hadn't landed him in any trouble, and I was simply repeating what my department had been saying every day for decades. Some members of the Liberal caucus, who had much stronger opinions than I about what the Israeli government was or was not doing, congratulated me for articulating the real problems. Others criticized me to my face and behind my back. Several constituents patted me on the back, others called me a fascist, but I didn't get the impression it was a big issue in my riding. Nevertheless, a lot of people were mad at me. Old friends in the Toronto Jewish community gave me hell. I was branded by some as an anti-Zionist and an anti-Semite, which must have come as rather a surprise to my colleagues on the Inter-Parliamentary Council against Anti-Semitism.

IN THE MONTHS THAT followed, everything I did or said regarding the Middle East was seen through the lens of that speech. When I met Yasser Arafat in Ramallah a few months later, the *National Post* ran a large photograph of him greeting me with a warm smile, which was about as helpful to my public relations as a handshake from Hitler. It's true generally, but particularly true of the Middle East, that the media headlines often make it harder to come to grips with the depth and breadth of really serious issues. Every incident, every story, every picture tends to get distorted and blown out of proportion by both sides, which makes it all the more difficult to conduct a successful negotiation or to keep the lines of communication open.

In fact, the official trip I made as foreign minister to Jordan, Egypt, and Israel in May 2002 was not in any way controversial. I talked with young King Abdullah II at his palace one day and then flew the next day to Cairo to see President Hosni Mubarak. Mubarak, who was kept on a strict diet by his wife, told me he was appalled by Ariel Sharon's eating habits. "He calls for a roast of lamb at midnight," he said of the Israeli prime minister. "Lamb affects your brain. He's crazy from eating lamb." This notion was new to me: gastro-politics. In Jerusalem I had deep conversations with Shimon Peres, who was then the foreign minister and is a man I greatly respect, and with Aharon Barak, the president of the Israeli Supreme Court, who had a stack of Canadian jurisprudence on his desk because of his interest in our Charter of Rights and Freedoms and his admiration for Bora Laskin. Indeed, his court was one of the defenders of minority rights in Israel, and it often got itself into political trouble for its fearless judgments in complex areas of the law.

May 26 was a particularly hectic day. In the morning I went to Ramallah to see Chairman Arafat in his bunker. We had to pass through a labyrinth of sandbags and armed guards – even Arafat's communications adviser was wearing a machine gun on his shoulder – and descend to the basement. Arafat struck me as a rather pathetic figure, his uniform covered with an array of cheap friendship pins he had been given by various organizations and supporters from around the world. Though I had been warned that he could be incoherent on bad days, we had a good talk for half an hour. "I think you have to recognize," I said, "that the Israeli population is living in fear of their lives on a daily basis, and we must stop that condition so we can move on." I followed that visit with a round-table discussion with Palestinian academics over lunch and with Israeli academics in the afternoon. Then, at six o'clock, I met with Prime Minister Ariel Sharon in his office. I had never encountered so much security in my life. The Israeli Defence Force personnel who guarded the prime minister seemed surprised that we hadn't come armed ourselves. One of them even expected Isabelle Savard to have a gun in her purse, along with her notebook and tape recorder.

During the course of my frank, ninety-minute conversation with Sharon, I brought up Canada's concern that Israel's strict security precautions were impeding the ability of the Palestinians to live normal, economically productive lives and were seriously hampering the movement of people and goods in the region. "In our view," I told him, "these restrictions should be lifted immediately to enable better opportunities for peace discussions." Though he disagreed vehemently, I found him an immensely attractive personality, strong, vibrant, and even likeable. He knew what he wanted to do; he wasn't about to be diverted from it; and he had all the leadership capabilities of the successful general he had been to get his way. Talking with him was like talking into a gale or playing a salmon that ran your line for yards before allowing you to pull it back an inch.

Because Canada was such a strong believer in the two-state solution, we were also against any and all measures that might prejudice the possibility of that outcome, including the building of the wall – the West Bank separation barrier. As I said at the time, "Of course Israel is entitled to build a wall to protect itself but building a wall on somebody else's territory in a way that affects that person's livelihood is a totally different matter." When Amr Moussa came to Ottawa, I agreed with him that the wall was counterproductive to peace because it divided Palestinian communities in places and was being built without regard for international law. Yet I felt that seeking an advisory opinion from the International Court of Justice on this issue would be unwise. I feared – and rightly so, as it turned out – that the ICJ would hand down a judgment that wouldn't be respected. Though the court concluded that "Israel cannot rely on a right of self-defence or on a state of necessity in order to preclude the wrongfulness of the construction of the wall," nothing was done. Instead of advancing international law, the result was used by skeptics as another example of the ineffectualness of international law.

The Chrétien government was also opposed to the expansion of Israeli settlements in the West Bank and East Jerusalem. Ben-Gurion himself was in favour of getting out of most of the occupied territories, arguing that there would never be peace if Israel failed to do so. Indeed, visiting some of the settlements, talking to some of the settlers, I understood how difficult it would be to move them. They were prepared to fight to stay, leading to the real possibility of a civil war. At the same time, with the Israeli army becoming less secular in some respects and more friendly to the settlers, there was less and less likelihood within the politics of Israel of coming to a two-state solution.

Ultimately only an Israeli government elected by Israelis can determine what actions are best suited to defend itself in response to changing events. In 1967, seeing that they were going to be attacked, the Israelis decided that war was necessary, and they later responded to the intifadas with heightened security measures. Similarly, it seems to me, only Canada can determine from its own perspective what it can do to help ensure Israel's security within a context of encouraging behaviour on both sides to try to achieve a lasting peace. The responsibility of Canada's foreign policy is to advance Canada's interests and its values, even if that causes friction with one or another party in the region or with Canadian citizens who champion one or another side.

As Louis Michel, the Belgian foreign minister, once put it at a NATO meeting, "The War on Terror has to be more than just the use of force." It had to include alleviating the structural problems in the Middle East, whether the occupation of the West Bank, the new Israeli settlements, the unemployed youths with guns in their hands, or the indoctrination of kids

into terrorist cells. But when Mr. Chrétien and I attended the NATO summit in Rome on May 28, 2002, the focus of attention was on military and
security issues – with one very significant exception: the creation of the
NATO-Russia Council in the presence of Vladimir Putin. I couldn't help
but be struck at this meeting, coming as it did just one day after my trip to
Israel, when I heard President Bush and President Putin praise each other
and speak of the new era of collaboration. If this was possible, might Israeli
and Palestinian leaders one day do the same?

It never ceased to amaze me how different world leaders could be in
private from their public images. Heads of government who rattled their
sabres at each other in front of the press often sat down like old buddies
at a dinner table a few moments later, not least because they were all politicians at core, sharing the tricks of the trade with their fellow pros. In my
experience, for example, George W. Bush was a very cordial person, relaxed,
friendly, and polite with Mr. Chrétien even in the face of significant policy
differences. Though neither an intellectually curious person nor widely
read, he was clearly in charge of the meetings at which I saw him up close.
His advisers and staff deferred to him; he understood the background
papers; and if he never seemed to grasp the broader issues or articulate
them as thoroughly as Bill Clinton, whose in-depth comprehension was
truly impressive, he was his own man with his own political qualities.

Few things bind politicians more tightly than their shared complaints
about the media. One significant exception was Silvio Berlusconi. No doubt
because he was a media tycoon, he understood what the press needed and
played to the cameras shamelessly. At the NATO summit, after Chrétien
and I were escorted by cops waving machine guns out of their car windows
as they raced through the streets of Rome to get us to the air base where
the conference was being held, military jets flew overhead spewing thick
fumes in the three colours of the Italian flag, intending to impress the
delegates but actually leaving us feeling slightly nauseous – as did the red,
green, and white pasta we were served at lunch. The next day, Chrétien
and I had lunch with Berlusconi at the ornate Renaissance-era office of
the Italian prime minister. At one point, amid our discussions of important affairs of state, Berlusconi volunteered to give us an explanation
for the thick makeup and slightly bizarre-looking hair implants he was
wearing. "They're always taking my photograph," he said in French. As

we left, Chrétien turned with a shy little smile and said, "Bill, they take my picture all the time, too, but I don't think Aline would let me wear all that *maquillage.*"

This superficial, slightly surreal side of politics could not have contrasted more sharply with the gravity of the decisions these same mere mortals had gathered to make in the aftermath of 9/11. At that point Canada's focus was still fixed firmly on Afghanistan. That's where al-Qaeda was based; that's where NATO wanted us; that's where we had sent ground troops in the fall of 2001. When the Europeans dragged their heels on our offer to join the International Security Assistance Force to help in Kabul, we contributed in another way in February 2002 by sending a battle group from the Princess Patricia's Canadian Light Infantry to join the Americans in the southern province of Kandahar, where the Taliban were still strong.

This operation was obviously a combat mission, not a peacekeeping one, but because it was an obligation under NATO's article 5, with a low-key, limited commitment, it wasn't particularly controversial at home or abroad. By the time we arrived, the Taliban had been removed from power; most al-Qaeda and Taliban fighters had fled over the border to Pakistan with their spiritual leader, Mullah Omar; and the fighting was almost over. The only serious casualties of the six-month deployment came in the Tarnak Farms incident on April 17, 2002, when four Canadians were killed by friendly fire from an American F-16 pilot who mistook their live-fire exercise for a Taliban attack. That brought the reality of the conflict closer to home because the grandfather of one of the soldiers, Corporal Ainsworth Dyer of the Princess Patricia's, lived in my riding and asked me to attend his grandson's funeral with him. It was a heart-breaking ceremony that I got to know all too well when I subsequently became minister of national defence and received the remains of our brave dead at the Trenton air base.

AFGHANISTAN WAS MORE of a Defence issue than a Foreign Affairs issue, so I was less involved with it than was Art Eggleton or his successor, John McCallum. Both Afghanistan and Israel were on the agenda, however, when I hosted the Group of Eight (G8) foreign ministers in Whistler, British Columbia, in June 2002, two weeks before the leaders themselves were to meet in Kananaskis, Alberta.

The G8 was the natural heir of the international institutions that had been set up to handle the issues and problems of the world's post-war economic integration. In 1975, with the Security Council, the World Bank, and the IMF having become more bureaucratic and rigid, President Valéry Giscard d'Estaing of France and Chancellor Helmut Schmidt of West Germany felt the need for an organization where a few key heads of government could get together informally to discuss economic policy, exchange ideas, and shape the domestic policies of their countries in a co-ordinated way. In other words, the leaders had to be engaged on a personal level. They couldn't just leave the global economy to nameless, unaccountable technocrats. Given its players, the group quickly became the most exclusive economic club in the world. If it couldn't impose international law and order, it could certainly exert political suasion.

At first the group was restricted to just six free-market industrial powers: France, West Germany, the United States, the United Kingdom, Italy, and Japan. A year later US president Gerald Ford sought to counterbalance Europe with another North American, English-speaking member. "If Italy is there," he argued, "Canada should be there too, because it's of equal economic size." The G7 quickly became a central instrument of our foreign policy. It put us in the big league and gave us regular, privileged access to what was happening in Europe, the United States, and Japan. In 1998 Russia became a full member, and the G7 became known as the G8, though the European Union was also represented at the table by the president of the European Commission and its Council president in recognition of Europe's economic importance, so in fact the meetings usually involved as many as ten.

From time to time, as well, the host country is allowed to bring in special participants to help deal with a topical issue. In 1995 Mr. Chrétien had welcomed Boris Yeltsin as an observer to the summit in Halifax as a precursor to Russia's membership in the G7, and in 2002 he invited a number of African leaders to Kananaskis to give weight to his G8 initiative – the New Partnership for Africa's Development (NEPAD) – which hoped to establish a system of quantifiable accountability that could increase the effectiveness of foreign aid efforts. And, of course, because someone had to arrange the agendas and make sure that the leaders' agreements percolated down through everyone's political system, each head of government was allowed to be accompanied by one "Sherpa," named after the guides who escort climbers up the Himalayas.

Despite its original intentions, then, the Group grew in scale and scope as it grew in clout. An ongoing network of officials kept in constant communication between summits; a quasi-secretariat sprang up; and, because of the normal instinct of politicians everywhere, discussions of long-term economic strategies were pushed aside by the most pressing political crises of the day. In practice, any attempt to manage the international economy could not ignore the political realities. In this way the G8 foreign ministers began to get together regularly to supplement the work of their leaders. At our meeting in Whistler we discussed the situation in the Middle East, the conflict in Afghanistan, the crisis in the Balkans, the threat of a nuclear conflict between India and Pakistan, arms control, and the safe disposal of Soviet chemical, nuclear, and biological weapons in the wake of the end of the Cold War.

It was a fascinating initiation for me, as chair, into the heart of world affairs. As we spent a couple of days together in a relatively remote setting, I naturally developed a personal relationship with the individuals I would often encounter in the dramatic events of the year ahead. As the new boy in the room, I was amazed by how well these people knew each other and how comfortable they were to speak frankly, either around the table or over drinks at the end of the day. We were barely into the second hour of business when Joschka Fischer of Germany said something that irritated Jack Straw of Great Britain. "Oh, Joschka," Straw sighed somewhat jocularly, "you always were a Communist."

Joschka feigned outrage. "I never was a Communist. That's ridiculous."

"Well, if you weren't a Communist, what the hell were you?"

"I was an anarchist," Fischer said.

At which Igor Ivanov, Russia's foreign minister, weighed in by saying, "I think we're all Marxists now anyway."

"Chairman," said Colin Powell, the US secretary of state, "can we please get this meeting back to order?"

Whistler was where I developed a close working relationship with Colin Powell. "I wish you luck as the chair of this meeting, Bill," he said, "but I have to tell you, if it's as crazy as the one we had in Italy last year, where we wasted a colossal amount of time trying to draft a communiqué that nobody would agree to, it's the last one I'll ever attend."

As I subsequently discovered, Colin was quite obsessive about the wording of communiqués and reports. One day, during a meeting in Cambodia, I found him typing furiously on his computer and asked what he was doing. "I'm playing with a resolution of the Security Council," he said. "I like doing this kind of stuff." Wow, I thought to myself, that's pretty hands-on. My officials wanted only the broad picture from me; they would never have let me get into the wordsmithing of a UN resolution. Even more astonishing was the time that he gathered a bunch of us around him to show us how to buy handmade shirts online.

I was worried by Colin's threat not to come to any more meetings. If he didn't, no one else would bother either, and the foreign ministers' club would fall apart. Many of them came largely because the United States was there, particularly when we were discussing security issues. Even if the club survived, we would lose an extraordinary opportunity to spend quality time with the Americans and talk about their views on the world face to face.

"Instead of a communiqué, why not suggest that you have just a chair's statement at the end of the meeting as to what happened?" Jim Wright, my assistant deputy minister, suggested. "People can either agree or disagree because it's not binding on anybody, and you won't have to spend any time fighting over the words." Everyone thought it a great idea when I proposed it, and Colin was particularly pleased.

He was less pleased about a trade problem that had arisen between Canada and the United States. To get around a high protective tariff that the Americans had placed on sugar products, some Canadian companies had mixed sugar with butter, taken it across the border as "sugar butter," and then wrung the sugar out of the product for sale in the United States. "This is outrageous," Colin protested. "You're cheating on the rules."

"Maybe, but your sugar tariffs are insane," I said. "They're designed to protect a few wealthy guys in Florida. And considering how you've stretched the rules to shut out our softwood lumber imports, you can hardly complain if we use them to our advantage in this instance."

At the formal dinner that night, I got up and presented him with a wooden plank. "Now, Secretary, this may look to you like softwood lumber, but it has been soaked in maple syrup, so it's really maple syrup and we'll ship it to you as such. When we get it down to the States, we're going to wring out the maple syrup and sell the plank as softwood lumber." Everybody laughed and had another vodka. In diplomacy as in life, it's always important to have a sense of fun.

These sorts of hijinks sometimes threatened to get out of hand, especially at meetings of the Association of Southeast Asian Nations (ASEAN), where tradition required delegates to put on a skit after dinner. Colin became particularly leery of them after a performance in which he sang a version of the cowboy song "El Paso" and then pretended to fall dying at the feet of Makiko Tanaka, the foreign minister of Japan, who gave him a farewell kiss. It was captured on film and broadcast back to the States, where FOX News made much political hay out of the footage. "I'm never going to make a fool of myself again," Colin vowed, "and I don't care what the tradition is." Nevertheless, at an ASEAN ministerial conference in July 2004, he gave a show-stopping rendition of the Village People's hit song "YMCA," complete with hard hat and tool belt.

At another ASEAN meeting, in Brunei, I was pulled aside by Alex Downer, Australia's colourful foreign minister, with an idea for a skit. Though he was a very conservative member of John Howard's very conservative government, I couldn't help but enjoy his larger-than-life character, and we became good friends. Our Brunei hosts, being Muslim, didn't serve any alcohol with the meals, but Alex used to invite me over to his table to meet his "cousin" Johnnie. Cousin Johnnie turned out to be a case of Johnnie Walker whisky hiding at Alex's feet.

"Bill," he asked, "what are you Canadians planning for tonight's show?"

"I don't know yet, it's a real pain. Our ambassador and I have been scratching our heads all day about it. Worrying about it has taken up more time than the conference discussions. All we've come up with so far is doing a funny version of a Gilbert and Sullivan song."

"That sounds really stupid," Alex said. "I've got a better idea, something we can do together. We're going to walk out carrying a big brass gong. You're going to hold it, and I'm going to whack the shit out of it with a hammer. You'll let go, and it will fall to the ground. Then we're going to look at the Chinese foreign minister and say, 'Oh oh, fallen gong.' Falun Gong, get it? It's brilliant."

"Yeah," I said, "and the Chinese won't speak to us for six months. But let me run it past my ambassador." When I did, I was told in no uncertain terms that our delegation would tie me to a chair if I were crazy enough to agree.

In fact, we might have been too cautious about offending the Chinese. Many of their diplomats have a great sense of humour – as I know from my genuine rapport with one of their foreign ministers, Li Zhaoxing. One time he teasingly said to Cathy, much to the bewilderment of the nearby Colin Powell, "Oh, Madame, I have not danced with anyone since I danced with you in Phnom Penh."

If the intimacy of the G8 was a major asset, it did have a corresponding flaw. Having an international institution that excluded many of the most important economies, such as China, India, Brazil, and Saudi Arabia, became increasingly ineffective and unacceptable. This became particularly evident after the Asian financial crisis in 1997, when the IMF dictated measures that were highly resented by the countries most profoundly affected. So Canada's finance minister, Paul Martin, and his US counterpart, Larry Summers, got together and decided to make the G8 finance ministers' meetings much more inclusive. That eventually led to the establishment of the G20, one of Martin's singular achievements when he became prime minister. It was a major Canadian initiative and very much in keeping with our tradition of building multilateral structures of global governance. Of course, inclusion came at the price of the relative informality and efficiency that the smaller group of leaders continues to enjoy. There are fewer opportunities to get to know people over a drink or a walk in the garden, and the whole modus operandi had to adapt to the larger numbers. I had some sympathy for George W. Bush when he said over lunch one day in the White House, "I don't want to go to another one of those damn meetings where somebody's going to read a speech at me. I can go somewhere else for that."

ANOTHER NEGATIVE consequence of summit diplomacy was the need for heightened security. The more important the G8 and the G20 became, the more they attracted the same protests as the WTO, and for the same reasons: they were seen as too elitist, too capitalist, too undemocratic. Kananaskis had been chosen as the site for the 2002 summit because of its extraordinary natural beauty – and because the demonstrations could be kept far outside the security perimeter. There was, however, a large citizens' forum in Calgary that I attended on the government's behalf at which the NGOs and protesters had an opportunity to express their points of view. About four hundred people turned out for the ninety-minute event, and I was presented with a list of recommendations, which I conveyed personally to the prime minister. This was a typically Canadian affair, with none of the physical violence associated with protests at other international summits.

Cabinet ministers in Canada don't usually have a security detail. The governor general and the prime minister have serious constraints on where they can go and what they do, but the rest of us got security only on an as-needed basis, except for a few extra devices in our residences. Occasionally I would see a guy with an earphone around me, but if I asked what was up, he'd only say, "I can't tell you, but for the next couple of days we're going to be around." Most times it was nothing. One day I escorted Joschka Fischer to the St. Lawrence Market, where he ended up buying some gourmet mustard, which may seem a trivial thing for me to remember except that he never let me forget how good it was whenever we met afterward. When his bodyguard asked me where my guard was, he and his minister looked shocked to learn that I didn't have one.

I even continued to bike around Toronto and sometimes Ottawa. New Canadians sometimes stopped me to say, "In my old country a minister always goes around in a big car with machine guns and armed guards. He's totally inaccessible. Here I can stop you on the street. That's what makes Canada so great." And shortly after my appointment, a caller phoned a radio talk show to say, "I just saw the foreign minister riding a bicycle on Wellington Street. I like living in a country where the foreign minister rides a bicycle."

Travelling as a foreign minister in another country was different. The host is responsible for your safety, and the security can get quite heavy. In Russia once, even though I was still only a committee chair, my police escort turned on the sirens and sped like madmen down the wrong side of the street. They loved doing that sort of thing. Another time, in Paris for a conference of foreign ministers on drug trafficking in Afghanistan, I wanted to go to an exercise club to work out before the meeting started. As soon as I stepped out of the hotel in my sweat clothes, a policeman insisted I get into a car and be driven the few blocks with a full motorcycle escort. Later my daughter, Katy, who had married Matthieu Debost and was living in Paris by that time, phoned and said, "Dad, was that you going through Place de la Concorde this morning? I was in my car, and those guys almost drove me into the gutter."

It seemed crazy, but I soon had a reason to be grateful. On the way back from the gym, I decided to stop for a bite to eat in some fancy hotel dining room. The maître d' took one look at my workout clothes and refused to admit me. The police captain who was with me was totally mortified. He went up and explained that I was the Canadian foreign minister, and I was quickly escorted to a very good table in a discreet corner of the garden.

Another incidental benefit occurred when I was in Bangkok, for an Asia-Pacific Economic Cooperation meeting. I wanted to visit the Mercy Centre, a social agency of schools, orphanages, and health programs for slum families founded by Father Joe Maier, a remarkable American priest whom Cathy and I had got to know through Adrienne Clarkson and John Ralston Saul. Our son, Patrick, had spent a summer there and made a film about its work. "My wife has heard of it," said Surin Pitsuwan, the Harvard-educated former foreign minister of Thailand, "and she would probably like to go with you." Because the Mercy Centre was located in one of the roughest areas of the city, full of prostitutes and drug addicts, she came along with a huge entourage of armed bodyguards and motorcycle police-men. We sped through Bangkok at a tremendous speed, with sirens scream-ing and red lights flashing.

"Bill," said Father Joe afterward, "I cannot tell you what an enormous favour you have done for me. One of the biggest problems I have here is that I can't get police protection for the children. Last week I rescued a six-year-old girl for the price of a case of whisky. She had had all her front teeth knocked out so she could perform oral sex on male clients, and we were terrified her father was going to turn up to claim her back so he could pimp her out again. I was always having to go to the police station in the middle of the night to beg for help, but they wouldn't do anything. Having the wife of such an important person turn up here with all those policemen changed everything. Now it's 'What can we do for you, Father Joe?' and when I phone, they're swarming all over the place within minutes. You've given me a legitimacy in their eyes that I never had before."

The Foreign Affairs Department had a legendary protocol officer, Vaughan Johnstone, a kind of Mr. Fix-It who organized the ministerial trips and security. Vaughan seemed to know every airline schedule, every shortcut to the airport, every trick in the book on how to get his boss in and out of any place in the world. One of the first pieces of advice I received when I became minister was, "Don't go anywhere without Vaughan."

Vaughan had his own views about security. When I went to my first major international meeting, he said, "You'll have two RCMP officers with you."

"But I don't need security protection," I protested. "What would I need security protection against?"

"Against the Americans," Vaughan answered.

He was right, as I soon learned. When the US security men come down a hall ahead of their president or secretary of state, they don't give a damn who's in their way. They just push and shove everybody aside indiscriminately, with a breathtaking lack of tact or sensitivity. It turned out that I needed two beefy guys of my own, whose only job was to push back. Without them, I risked not getting to my car in time, and if I didn't get to my car in time, the cavalcade would take off without me and I would have no other way of getting to the meeting. It wasn't as though I could follow in a cab and be whisked through the security ring. The timing was choreographed precisely and without forgiveness, with Vaughan yelling, "This way, Minister! Hurry, Minister! Get in that car now, Minister!" He got me out of countless tight spots and near misses. Half the grumblings at a G8 or NATO meeting came from other foreign ministers or even leaders feeling pushed around by somebody else's security.

THE G8 FOREIGN MINISTERS don't usually attend the leaders' summits, so I had no official role at Kananaskis other than to escort President Putin from his plane to his car at Calgary airport, conduct bilaterals with a number of visiting dignitaries, and attend a dinner held in a relatively informal restaurant in a park-like setting for the four African leaders and Kofi Annan, who had been invited in conjunction with the NEPAD initiative. Kofi took the occasion to urge Canada to keep up its good work promoting the Responsibility to Protect (R2P) doctrine. I also happened to pass by President George W. Bush and have a brief chat with Prime Minister Tony Blair when I went to deliver my report on the Calgary forum to

Mr. Chrétien. It was enough to impress on me how respected a player he was on the global stage. I could see the degree to which the person who had been dismissed by the Tories in 1993 as a potential embarrassment had emerged as a major international statesman. His humour and humanity, amid all the pomp and importance of his office, coupled with an extraordinary rapport with people from all walks of life, served Canada at home and abroad.

But like every successful politician, he had both critics and rivals. One day in August 2002, much to my surprise, he called me up and invited me to join him for lunch at 24 Sussex Drive. It turned out that he wanted to talk domestic politics, not foreign affairs. And the question was whether he should run for a fourth mandate. Even in hindsight I can't be certain whether he was serious about running again or merely testing the waters, but it was almost a sure thing that he could win another term if he tried. The economy had turned upward, the Opposition was divided, the Liberals were riding high in the polls, and Chrétien was a healthy, vigorous sixty-eight-year-old who still preferred to run up a flight of stairs rather than take an elevator.

The only problem – and it was a big problem – lay within the party. Paul Martin and his tight, ambitious "board" of advisers had succeeded in securing the support of many in the caucus and taken over most of the riding associations across the country. Not only was Paul the obvious frontrunner to succeed Chrétien but he was probably in a position to try to oust him at the leadership review slated for February 2003. The feud between the prime minister and his finance minister came to a head on June 2, 2002, after Chrétien ordered his Cabinet ministers to stop jockeying for the leadership. One day Paul was in the Cabinet; the next day he was gone. As a result I had little experience working with him as a fellow minister. I was shocked, like the rest of my colleagues, and though I didn't speak to Paul about the details in the one conversation I ever had with him in which the subject of his dismissal arose, he was understandably bitter about how it had been handled. According to him, he was phoned and told he was out.

However, being out simply let him organize his leadership bid more openly, and all through the summer the pressure on Chrétien to retire mounted among the Martin forces in the Liberal caucus and the party headquarters. Clearly it was too late for the prime minister to regain full control. When Gordon Ashworth, the party's national campaign director, approached me to see what could be done to build back support for Chrétien, I had to tell him in all frankness that I thought it was too late. The majority of my riding association had become Martin supporters long before there was any idea of a race against Mr. Chrétien.

Although I tried to stay closely in touch with what was happening in my riding association, membership was obviously wide open, and if someone wanted to come in and pack it with good Liberals, I didn't think it was my role to intervene and stop it. Frankly, I was more concerned with ensuring that we had an executive with younger people and representatives from the diverse constituencies that made up the riding than with caring which camp they were in. I was paying less attention to the politics of the executive than to the resolutions the riding association wanted to advance on issues of particular interest or importance to us at the Ontario and national Liberal conventions. If Chrétien wasn't sure whether he wanted to run again, and if these constituents were working their hearts out every election to get me elected, why would I launch a battle against them on my own? In Toronto Centre, therefore, theirs was a quiet, gradual takeover. I had no doubt that this story repeated itself elsewhere.

At one meeting of Cabinet ministers from Ontario at which John Manley presided, he went around the table and asked each of us about the situation in our ridings. Lyle Vanclief, the minister of agriculture, said, "I have to tell you, my riding association executive are all probably Martin supporters, and there's nothing I can do about that."

Sheila Copps, the minister of Canadian heritage, exploded. "If you can't control your riding association, you have no right to be here. You should go home and start running it."

"Look, Sheila, I'm in the same position," I said. "I haven't been paying any attention to this issue, because there was no reason to pay any attention to it. If you want me to do something about it, okay, but it will take a couple of years of hard work to turn this thing around. I can't just walk into my riding association and fire everybody. That's not the way I do business in Toronto Centre."

"Well," she insisted, "you have no right even to be in the room if you don't control your own riding association." I remembered her words when she couldn't secure her own nomination as a Liberal candidate a couple of years later.

Copps wasn't the only one to suspect me of being part of an organized plot to oust the prime minister. I had known Paul since law school; some of my key organizers and staff members in Toronto Centre were prominent Martin supporters, not least my former campaign manager Tim Murphy and political adviser Earl Provost; and several of my closest colleagues in the caucus were active in promoting Paul's candidacy. Even the fact that Cathy and Paul's wife, Sheila, worked closely together on the annual Writers' Trust fundraising gala was cited as evidence of my true loyalties. On August 10 the *Toronto Star* made hay of the news that the Martin team had rented space in the same building as my constituency office. No wonder the prime minister wanted to know where I stood.

Personally, even though I believed that Paul Martin would make an excellent leader of the party and prime minister of Canada at the right time, I thought Mr. Chrétien should be given the dignity of making up his own mind as to when he would retire. He had been the winner – not the loser – of the last general election, with a mandate from the people that shouldn't be withdrawn by the party. He was in a good position to trigger a leadership race and the next general election when most helpful to his successor. And an internecine battle would only hurt the party and its chances for another victory. "My responsibility is bigger than my ego," he used to say. "I just want to do what's good for you MPs, the Liberal Party, and Canada." The reality was my chief of staff, Dan Costello, had the prime minister's trust; I had dismissed a proactive Martin organizer on my payroll at the PMO's request; and many of my friends supported other contenders besides Paul Martin.

"I know I'm perceived as an old friend of Paul's," I told Chrétien over lunch, "but you made me foreign minister. I've made it clear to Paul that I'm completely loyal to you, and he totally respects that."

"But people tell me that Martin's organizers are operating out of your office in Toronto. What's that all about if you're loyal to me?"

"Whoever fed you that information is being disloyal to both of us," I said. "It's true that the Martin campaign is in my building, but I'm on the eighteenth floor and they're on the tenth. I'm very annoyed about that, but there's nothing I can do about it. I didn't even know they were there until

I ran into one of them in the elevator. But I have to tell you in all honesty that my riding association, like most of the other riding associations that I'm aware of, was taken over by his team when everybody thought you were leaving, and that's a problem if you really intend to run again."

Satisfied with my response, Chrétien moved on to other matters. When I told him I had had a cancer scare and undergone an operation some years before to remove one of my kidneys, he expressed his relief at my recovery. "Maybe God wanted you to be my foreign minister," he added, completely out of the blue. It was an interesting insight into the complexity of his character.

Not long afterward, on August 21, there was a caucus retreat in Chicoutimi, Quebec. I happened to be in one of the meeting rooms when Eddie Goldenberg came along. "Where's your friend Martin?" he asked. Eddie, whose dedication to Chrétien was legendary, had always pegged me as too close to Paul.

"How would I know?"

"Well," he said, "please go and find him, because we want him in the room to hear an announcement."

I figured something portentous was up, though I didn't have a clue what it was, and I went off to search for Paul, whom I found chatting downstairs. Message conveyed, we both headed into the main salon in time to hear Chrétien announce his resignation – though it wouldn't take effect until February 2004. The sly fox had thereby dodged the leadership review scheduled for February 2003 and bought himself another year and a half in office. If the prime minister was handicapped in some ways by being a lame duck, he was freed in other ways from the need to fight another election. "I am so relieved with the decision I made," he told the caucus not long afterward. "My wife is happy, my family is happy. I've had to renew my driver's licence because I'm learning to drive again."

Those eighteen months turned out to be extremely active, historically momentous ones, marked by one of the most difficult foreign policy decisions in Canadian history: whether we should join our closest allies, the United States and Great Britain, in a "coalition of the willing" to invade Iraq and depose its dictator Saddam Hussein. The tensions around the buildup, the invasion itself, and the subsequent consequences spilled into every important area of Canada's foreign policy, including the United

Nations, NATO, our relations with the United States, and the Middle East. Iraq became totally preoccupying, and what issues it didn't drive from the table, it coloured and influenced. In the most dramatic way possible, it also highlighted many of the major issues of international law I had been studying for forty years.

12

THE UNWILLING

When the United Nations General Assembly reconvenes every autumn, a great many heads of government journey to New York City to make pronouncements about the state of the world, and in September 2002 Iraq was on everybody's lips. Rumours had been circulating ever since 9/11 that it would be the target of a unilateral military action by the United States, even though there was no proven connection between Saddam Hussein and al-Qaeda. Those speculations grew louder after President George W. Bush's bellicose State of the Union address on January 29, 2002, in which he placed Iraq in an "axis of evil" with Iran and North Korea. In fact, one of the very first questions I had to answer in the House as a freshly minted minister had been about whether Canada would be at the side of our American allies whatever they might do in Iraq. After I vigorously declared that "any future action will be determined in the interests of Canada," my Liberal colleagues responded with a standing ovation, mostly I suspect out of relief that the new kid on the block hadn't embarrassed them completely.

The question of what to do with Iraq was hardly a new one in the corridors of the United Nations. In the wake of its invasion of Kuwait in 1990, the UN Security Council had adopted a resolution demanding that the Iraqi government agree unconditionally to the elimination of all its weapons of mass destruction and ballistic missiles, subject to third-party inspections. Yet, in the subsequent years, Iraq didn't comply. It systematically tried to hide its arms programs from UN inspectors and eventually pre-vented them from completing their work. In December 1998, after a year of Iraqi provocation and American threats, the United States and Great Britain launched Operation Desert Fox, a bombing campaign designed to "degrade" Saddam's capacity to develop weapons of mass destruction. Though Canada didn't participate, we backed the US and UK decision to bomb. Ultimately the airstrikes did little to tame Iraq or satisfy those who feared that Saddam was continuing his weapons program. The fact that the Clinton administration – with Canada's support – had launched this military campaign without the explicit permission of the Security Council would become a key argument in favour of George W. Bush's subsequent unilateral action.

The failure of the first series of UN inspections led the Security Council to pass Resolution 1284 in December 1999, creating the UN Monitoring, Verification and Inspection Commission (UNMOVIC). Hans Blix, the for-mer Swedish foreign minister who had led the first international response to the Chernobyl disaster, was placed in charge of the commission.

Saddam's continued defiance brought international sanctions that resulted in tremendous hardship for the innocent people of Iraq, as SCFAIT learned when we held a series of hearings about them in 1999 and 2000. However noble the intentions might be, the sanctions were having the effect of mak-ing the thugs even wealthier and more entrenched at the expense of the health, education, and freedom of ordinary Iraqis. The key, our committee felt, was to "de-link" military and economic sanctions. Whereas an arms embargo of Iraq was obviously essential for international security, we wanted the Government of Canada to push for the lifting of economic sanctions for humanitarian reasons. In the end, however, though the international community could make sanctions "smarter" in their application, only Iraq could end them by complying with the Security Council resolutions.

As frustrated as everyone was by Saddam's lack of co-operation, no one was pressing the United States to take matters into its own hands. Such an action would not only weaken the authority of multilateral institutions but would be a flagrant breach of international law. Indeed, when Prime Minister Chrétien met with Prime Minister Tony Blair in Johannesburg at the end of August and with President Bush in Detroit at the start of

September, Canada delivered a clear message that the appropriate forum for any discussion and authorization of military action was the United Nations Security Council.

On Thursday, September 12, 2002, I was tasked with taking that message to the UN itself as official government policy. No one addresses the General Assembly without a certain degree of nervousness when going up to the podium and looking out at the grand hall, though, as is the norm for all such events, many of the seats were empty, delegates came and went chattering among themselves, and not everyone paid close attention to the text I had carefully prepared to deliver on behalf of the Government of Canada. (When Chrétien and I were there in 2003, a newspaper ran a photograph of me yawning, with a caption that read, "Our Foreign Minister, hard at work at the UN.")

"Let there be no doubt," I said, "that at the origin of today's tensions is the persistent refusal of the Iraqi government to comply with its obligations to us all under United Nations Security Council resolutions. For the past 11 years, Iraq has refused to demonstrate that it has abandoned its chemical, biological and nuclear weapon research and development programs, and even today it remains unwilling to do so. But let there also be no doubt: bringing Iraq into conformity with its international obligations must be the work of us all – together. We believe that our ability to find a solution to this challenge – one that is consistent with and, indeed, that reinforces the international framework that we have so painstakingly constructed since the last devastating world war – will define this generation and create precedents that may determine the future direction of our world."

Whether fighting terrorism or poverty, whether implementing the New Partnership for Africa's Development or the International Criminal Court, whether promoting the Afghanistan Support Group or the Responsibility to Protect doctrine, I put Canada's emphasis on the reality of global interdependence and the importance of the international rule of law. "Certainly there are problems with multilateralism and the institutions we have created," I concluded, "but that should not cause us to doubt the desirability of an effective rules-based system."

In a dramatic speech earlier that same day, President Bush declared that the UN had to take its obligations seriously or Iraq would be dealt with under other auspices. The threat was explicit but deliberately ambiguous. "If you live up to your UN obligations," he basically told Saddam, "all will be fine, but if you don't, we will deal with you." As it turned out, he didn't mean "we" the United Nations but "we" the United States and whatever coalition of allies it could put together. Six days later he asked Congress for authorization to use military force. Going back to the UN was, therefore, merely a half-hearted concession to global diplomacy to fulfill a commitment he had just made to Tony Blair in order to secure his support. At the time, however, Canada wanted to believe it was an honest effort, and we took Bush's speech seriously.

Meanwhile, Hans Blix and his UN inspection team were awaiting permission to return to Iraq to investigate the existence of Saddam's so-called weapons of mass destruction. I first met Blix at a cocktail reception in the UN at that time and had a brief chat with him. According to what he told me, though Saddam possessed the chemical weapons that the Americans and other Western powers had sold him during the Iran war and that he had used against the Kurds, there was no hard evidence that the Iraqis had nuclear weapons. When I said we were getting contrary information from the American intelligence sources, he warned me to treat it with great caution. "They're not reliable in this respect," were his words.

I was shocked by the thought that the United States might be contemplating military action in the absence of any definitive evidence of Iraq's nuclear capability. So when I had an opportunity to meet with Iraq's minister of foreign affairs, Naji Sabri, I told him that his government must accept the return of the UN weapons inspectors as early as possible and that it must work with them openly and unconditionally. Iraq's long history of obstruction and failure to comply with Security Council resolutions, I added, did not inspire great confidence in the world community. Sabri assured me that Iraq wanted the sanctions lifted so it could return to the family of nations.

Iraq wasn't the only item on the agenda during my week in New York. Because so many national representatives were present, they set up bilateral meetings with each other, usually in half-hour increments. If a Canadian mining company had a problem in Outer Mongolia, when else would I have a chance to chat to its foreign minister about it? If I needed to speak to the Indian foreign minister regarding Canadian investment issues, here was a rare occasion to establish a personal rapport that could be used later as a means to get through to him on the phone.

Virtually every minute was accounted for. I met with the foreign ministers of Austria and Norway to talk about the Human Security Network. I met with the foreign ministers of Iran, Sri Lanka, Turkey, Ukraine, New Zealand, Nigeria, Saudi Arabia, Angola, Colombia, Mexico, and the Netherlands. I attended a meeting of nations that had committed to providing development assistance to Afghanistan, and then I met with Abdullah Abdullah, Afghanistan's foreign minister, to talk about Canada's military presence in his country. There was a fifteen-minute "pull-aside" with Colin Powell about Iraq and Afghanistan, another with Jack Straw after the Commonwealth Foreign Ministers' meeting about Iraq and Zimbabwe, and a luncheon hosted by Joschka Fischer. I was briefed by the foreign ministers of Russia, Iraq, and Jordan as to what was happening in Baghdad. I spoke with the Brazilian foreign minister about his country's unfair subsidization of its aircraft industry and our then prevailing ban on Brazilian beef imports. And, whenever possible, I grabbed a few minutes with anybody I saw coming down a hallway or dining in the delegates' lounge. When I came across Amr Moussa, the secretary general of the Arab League, having lunch by himself, he invited me to join him. We spent an hour together that I wouldn't have had otherwise, and that serendipitous encounter proved useful a year later when I asked for his help in the case of Maher Arar, a Canadian citizen imprisoned in Syria.

As well, there were a couple of major social events, to which our spouses were also invited. One was the large Francophonie dinner that the French foreign minister hosted on the Monday evening at the University Club, a palatial nineteenth-century building with huge reception rooms and gilt walls – a perfect venue for the French to choose. The event was a classic example of the style with which France conducts its foreign policy as a way to put its stamp on the French-speaking world. As an indication of the role Canada plays in La Francophonie, I was placed at one of the head tables between Mrs. Kofi Annan and Mrs. Dominique de Villepin, while Cathy sat with their husbands. Afterward, she confessed to me with some embarrassment, "I had to ask Kofi Annan who the short, balding man across the table from me was, and it turned out to be Prince Albert of Monaco."

Two dramatically different events stand out in my memory. One was the moving interfaith service held on the morning of Wednesday, September 11 – the first anniversary of 9/11 – at St. Bartholomew's Church on Park Avenue at which Kofi Annan spoke and a wide variety of religious leaders offered prayers "dedicated to the victims of violence everywhere." The other was the reception to which Cathy and I were invited on September 12, hosted by President and Mrs. Bush at the Winter Garden, directly across the street from the ruins of the World Trade Center. I had paid my respects at Ground Zero the day before, and no one who looked into its deep crater could fail to understand its impact on the thinking of Americans and their government.

Still, Cathy and I were astonished by the security we encountered as we tried to get to the financial district. Limousine after limousine, protected by police cars and large black vans loaded down with heavily armed soldiers, raced through streets that had been totally closed to all other traffic between the United Nations and Lower Manhattan. If you didn't have a special tag on your windshield, or if you happened to be somewhere you shouldn't have been, you might well have found yourself confronted by a nervous nineteen-year-old guardsman with a gun in his hand. This was the first time that I'd seen an imperial motorcade from the inside – the armed escorts, the armoured vehicles, the cordoned streets, the snipers on the rooftops, the sirens, the rush – and it amazed me to think I was in the middle of New York City, the heart of American freedom and democracy.

Things got even stranger. When we arrived, we were instructed to line up to have our picture taken with the president and his wife. Ever the polite Canadians, we did as we were told, not unlike high-school graduates sheepishly queuing to shake hands with the principal. There were 191 members of the UN at the time, all represented by their foreign ministers and ambassadors, so the wait was a long one. Some of the dignitaries around us grumbled about the indignity and obsequiousness of the process, but being trapped together in a slightly humiliating situation turned out to be another chance to chat informally with people I never would have known otherwise. Suddenly the Chinese foreign minister showed up and went to the head of the queue. "I'm not standing in any lineup," he announced. "I'm getting my picture taken now or never." Afterward, to give George Bush his due, the poor guy signed and sent every one of those pictures, often with a personal note, as if applying a common domestic political custom to the world of international diplomacy.

When we finally got into the reception room, ravenous and thirsty, we were made to stand at attention and wait some more. Then coloured lights started to play on a grand staircase, a troop of Marines marched down the steps with scores of flags and a blare of martial music, and out came Bush to the tune of "Hail to the Chief." Most of the diplomats looked gobsmacked. It reminded quite a few of us of a Leni Riefenstahl production, both fabulous and sinister at the same time. We might have expected such a spectacle from an insecure Third World dictator, but not from the president of the United States. Deliberately orchestrated to awe and intimidate, it suggested a bellicose empire or an imperial presidency very much at odds with the mythology of the American common man. Nor, coming as it did after the president's speech to the UN and the visit to the devastation at Ground Zero, was its symbolism lost on anybody. It was setting the stage for an invasion of Iraq: "This is the power of the United States," it declared, "so don't mess with us." We were either extras in the play or the audience that was supposed to be impressed and applaud it. "This is insane," I overheard Igor Ivanov say, though watching President Putin's subsequent public spectacles would suggest that Russia took a leaf out of the same book.

Igor and I had a chance to talk the next day at the gathering of the G8 foreign ministers, which was held every year on the margins of the UN General Assembly. Canada was the chair, so we hosted an elaborate meal at the Pierre Hotel. Neither the food nor the setting, however, prevented the evening from degenerating into a bit of a donnybrook. Iraq was the *crise du jour* and it dominated our discussions, not least because it had become a major issue in the elections then taking place in Germany. Indeed, Gerhard Schroeder seemed to be running against Bush more than against his opposition parties, and Joschka Fischer was directly implicated as Germany's foreign affairs minister. In fact, Joschka had interrupted his campaigning to fly across the Atlantic for the meeting. He ate dinner, made a ferocious case against an invasion, which certainly intensified the tension around the table, and returned home soon after.

It amused me to observe how the various foreign ministers seemed to represent their national persona during the debate. If Colin Powell was the Yankee soldier, Javier Solana was the warm Spaniard whom everyone liked even when they disagreed with him; Joschka Fischer was the brutally frank German who thought what the Americans were doing was both crazy and immoral; and Dominique de Villepin was the Cartesian Frenchman. The exception that night was Silvio Berlusconi, the Italian prime minister who was present as his own foreign minister: he hardly said a word, which wasn't typical of him or his countrymen, and I managed to engage him in only a brief private conversation in French. The debate at dinner marked a very important moment because we all set out our positions, and, ultimately, none of them changed.

IRAQ WAS A MULTI-LAYERED problem. One level was Canada-US relations, another was multilateral relations, the third was domestic politics – and all three were interacting with each other all the time. When it became increasingly obvious that the Bush administration was gearing up for an invasion, the Canadian government's position was to play for time inside the United Nations. Insofar as possible, we wanted to use whatever influence we had to keep the unilateralist ideologues in Washington working within the constraints of the multilateral system that was so important for us.

"In these circumstances," I said in a speech to the House of Commons during a take-note debate on October 1, 2002, "unilateral action may have the benefit of clarity but it would lack international legal legitimacy. As well it risks destabilizing world order and possibly destroying the credibility of the United Nations itself. It risks destabilizing the Middle East. It risks destabilizing countries well beyond the region, to Pakistan, and with it the efforts that we are making in Afghanistan to recreate peace in that community, Indonesia, India and Malaysia where large Muslim populations watch with concern these developments. The use of force threatens the security of Israel ... Our objective is to rid the Iraqi regime of weapons of mass destruction. There are those who claim that regime change is the only means to this end. If Iraq refuses to co-operate, they may turn out to be right. However, our responsibility to Canadians, to the world community and to the future of the international rule of law is to be certain that we have exhausted all other options and that we so conduct ourselves in this crisis that the international order on which Canada so much depends emerges strengthened and reinvigorated."

At that point Mr. Chrétien preferred to be in the uncommitted middle. His duty – like mine, as foreign affairs minister – was to assert Canada's independent foreign policy without losing sight of the fact that the United States is our most important ally and trading partner. *Realpolitik* compelled him to be very careful about how we dealt with the Americans. No one yet knew which way the United States intended to jump, and if the facts changed, the situation would change, and so public opinion might too. As a result, both the hawks and the doves accused us of sitting on the fence, but as my Cabinet colleague David Collenette once pointed out, that was the smartest place to be because it kept our options open. By way of contrast, Tony Blair, primarily motivated, in my opinion, by his desire to make Britain the closest ally of the United States and himself a confidant to President Bush, got into serious trouble for jumping to the American side too quickly.

In Cabinet meetings and various discussions I had with him, Mr. Chrétien made it clear that *if* Iraq were proven not to be in conformity with its UN obligations, and *if* there were a subsequent UN-authorized mission against Iraq, Canada would be a part of it, because Canadian foreign policy was based on our support of both multilateral action and international law. "If the community of nations decides we have to go, we will have to go," the prime minister told the caucus on October 2, 2002, though he remained confident that Canada's position to seek a UN solution was becoming the default stance of the international community.

At the same time, however, the government left the door slightly ajar to the possibility of Canada going into Iraq, even without another UN resolution. The key would be nearly unanimous support at the Security Council – including the support of our traditional allies – but also, and critically, a clear threat from Iraq. In this way, our position was closer to the one we had adopted during the Kosovo crisis, when the will of most countries on the Security Council was frustrated by Russia's veto power – what some have described as a "capricious" or a "rogue" veto.

I spoke with Colin Powell on October 3 and told him that Canada's position had been consistent: we could commit with the support of the Security Council, but if the UN route failed, there would have to be clear justification for acting without the imprimatur of the Security Council, as there had been in Kosovo. So far, I pointed out, the United States was perceived as more interested in regime change than in disarming Iraq. In fact, just the day before, a White House spokesman had told reporters that Iraqis should assassinate Saddam or push him into exile. As I said to Colin, it seemed that foreign policy was being made in the Pentagon rather than the State Department, and I argued that an invasion of Iraq could have a negative impact on the broader war on terror, alienating potential allies in the Muslim world.

A further complication was the confusion around regime change. What exactly did it mean? I recall one conversation with Colin in which he said, "If Saddam Hussein provides full, open, and transparent co-operation with the weapons inspectors, that in itself constitutes regime change," which was true if you looked at Iraq as a problem of nuclear non-proliferation and not as part of a wider democratization of the Middle East. But it was obvious that the most hardline officials in Washington would be satisfied only with the head of Saddam Hussein. Colin admitted as much when he added, "I've carried the hawks so far – don't make it impossible for me." In other words, there were real constraints on how much farther Powell would be able to nudge George Bush along the path of the United Nations.

In the early days Colin was being a good soldier, while at the same time trying to steer American foreign policy in a direction more consistent with international law and international obligations. In the debate surrounding the first Gulf War, for example, he had been a voice of caution regarding whether to go on to Baghdad and remove Saddam because he understood the difference between conducting a war in which you defeat an enemy and a war in which you take over the running of a country. As he often said, if you break it, you own it, and that's what he wanted to avoid. But he was increasingly isolated by hawks such as Donald Rumsfeld, Dick Cheney, Paul Wolfowitz, and Richard Perle, who were beating the drums for war at any cost. Their position was merely reinforced by Bush's surprisingly successful results in the fall elections of November 2002. I don't think anyone predicted that he would take control of Congress to the extent he did.

The Bush administration was in effect one government with two approaches, depending on whom you were dealing with. I had the easier task, because I liked Colin Powell and understood him. John McCallum, our defence minister, had a tougher time with his counterpart, Donald

Rumsfeld. When Prime Minister Chrétien suggested during a TV interview that 9/11 might have been partly rooted in the wealth, greed, and arrogance of the West, in particular the United States, the US defense secretary was so angry that he cancelled a bilateral meeting slated with McCallum at the Prague summit in November. As inconsistent messages continued to flow out of Washington about the extent to which the United States would go along with the UN, we realized that we were dealing with a tug-of-war in the administration.

All through the fall of 2002 our efforts were directed toward strengthening Colin Powell's hand, which to some extent entailed preventing too much visible distance from emerging between the official positions of Canada and the United States. In fact, all the foreign ministers I dealt with during this period, whether allies of the American position such as Jack Straw or opponents such as Joschka Fischer, had conversations about how we could best protect Colin from the "crazies" around President Bush. It was ironic that we saw a retired four-star general as the one and only dove among all the hawks in the inner circle of the White House. A key element in the strategy of going to the United Nations for a new resolution was structured around helping Colin Powell.

October and November saw weeks of protracted negotiations and discussions as the Security Council worked to come up with a new resolution. The main question – one that would recur again and again during the coming months – was whether the resolution would provide for the automatic use of force in the event of Iraqi non-compliance. The United States and Great Britain were pushing for a single resolution that would include "automaticity." The Russians were ambivalent. As reported by Jim Wright, my assistant deputy minister on global security issues, they didn't like the notion of automaticity, but neither did they want to paint themselves into a corner by taking a strong stand against it. The French wanted at least two resolutions. The first would demand Iraq's co-operation with the inspections regime. If that failed, there would have to be a second resolution authorizing the use of force. In fact, both President Jacques Chirac and de Villepin had spoken against automaticity in such uncompromising terms that it would be very difficult for France to back down. According to a briefing I received from my top advisers on security issues and the Middle East on October 28, the French remained leery of "hidden triggers" in the proposed resolution, and their anti-war stance was "exasperating every-one in Washington," to the point where Powell's own position could be damaged. Evidently his support for the multilateral process was not paying dividends to the Bush administration.

More immediately worrisome, from our point of view, was the belief held by some in the United States that we were on board one way or another. Indeed, the debate over the new resolution was forcing us to wrestle with questions of our own. In the event of an ambiguous resolution or a divided Security Council, Canada would have to chart a dangerous course based on the circumstances and conditions at hand, the global security interests, the stability of the region – and, of course, its own interests. In the mean-time, we could do little more than hope that the inspections would be given a final opportunity to succeed. If this occurred, there would be no need for military action. If it didn't, we would have to assume that Iraq did indeed pose a grave threat to the peace and security of the world, in which case we would need to take whatever action might be authorized by the Security Council or by the international community if one or two outliers on the council prevented effective action.

The uncertainty of the situation led to heightened anxiety in Ottawa and vigorous – if inconclusive – discussions in the Cabinet. Some ministers worried about the unilateralist tendencies in the Bush administration and the possible consequences of a hyper-interventionist American foreign policy. The image of a US general governing a conquered Iraq as pro-consul wasn't very palatable, and, in addition, some ministers questioned Washington's motives for targeting Iraq. "Oil will pay," one of my colleagues stated ominously. Other issues were closer to home. As Finance Minister John Manley pointed out, if we did go into Iraq, we needed to ensure that our security protocols were in order because Canada might become a ter-rorist target, and we would never forgive ourselves if a successful attack were carried out on our watch.

On November 8, 2002, the Security Council unanimously adopted Resolution 1441, which declared Iraq in "material breach" of its disarma-ment obligations under the previous resolution and gave Saddam a "final opportunity" to comply with them or else face "serious consequences." However, this language did not explicitly authorize a military response, and the resolution stopped short of declaring what the serious consequences would be. As a result, it remained ambiguous and could be interpreted in a variety of ways. The French were satisfied that a second resolution would be required to authorize force; the Americans figured that Resolution 1441 gave them the legal cover they needed to act without further wrangling at the UN. Ten days later, the UN inspectors returned to Iraq for the first time in four years to hunt for and eliminate any weapons of mass destruction, whether nerve gas, missiles, or nuclear weapons. "Anything less than full compliance will not satisfy the US," reported Michael Kergin, our ambassador to Washington, though he felt confident that "our economic access is distinct from our military co-operation – there's no direct linkage." He turned out to be right, but that was far from certain at the time.

On November 14 Colin Powell came to Ottawa to talk to me about our joining a "coalition of like-minded nations" to strike Iraq in the event that Saddam refused to comply with Resolution 1441. The next day he sent a letter to Canada and fifty other countries asking about potential military contributions to a future campaign against Iraq. Canada was asked if it might provide a wide range of military assets, including our Joint Task Force 2 special forces. Though Powell assured me that this inquiry was "no ask" – nothing more than a contingency in case of war – and that the United States was still committed to working with the United Nations, it put us in a difficult position. When news of the US list was made public, as soon happened, it significantly increased the political pressure in Canada and elsewhere from both the hawks and the doves.

THE IRAQ SITUATION was on everyone's mind when the NATO leaders met in Prague during the third week of November 2002. The summit was supposed to focus on the enlargement of the alliance, but beneath every discussion were the questions around the true intentions of the United States and the constant attempts by the Americans to draw their NATO partners into a common position on Iraq. The Germans and the French were opposed because of the way in which the position was framed. The British were in favour. We, typically, were trying to steer a way through the arguments so that we could avoid a fracture within NATO – not unlike our position at the time of the Suez crisis, when Britain and France were opposed by the United States and Canada over an important foreign policy issue.

Going into the meeting, the Americans had sent out a draft statement, basically declaring that NATO would take action to ensure immediate and unconditional compliance by Iraq. "Containment doesn't work," Bush told the eighteen others at the Prague summit. "Neither do threats of retaliation. We must be sure that Iraq fulfills its obligations to the UN Security Council." By the final draft, however, the initial American slant had been changed. While calling on Iraq to comply fully and immediately with Resolution 1441, the NATO leaders' statement emphasized assisting and supporting the efforts of the United Nations. Nor was there any indication as to what the "serious consequences" would be if Iraq failed to comply, because the United States hadn't been able to persuade a sufficient number of its allies to support any unilateral approach. It couldn't get a blank cheque. That was a good illustration of the kinds of negotiations that were going on at the time, and it reflected Canada's position regarding the importance of securing a solution consistent with international law.

However, legal arguments are dependent on the facts of the case, and the facts in this case were uncertain, ever shifting, and highly political. There were also different interpretations of Resolution 1441. A number of prominent American lawyers and intellectuals advanced the legal proposition that if the UN Security Council failed to respond to Iraqi non-compliance because of a veto by one of its permanent members, the United States was legally entitled to go to war against Iraq, on the grounds that it was wrong to have a world in which one or two powerful players in the Security Council could prevent the United Nations from acting in the face of atrocity or common danger. Furthermore, as a senior legal adviser at the State Department later put it to me, "We didn't have to ask ourselves the question about the war's legality. Congress authorized it." If the US Congress authorized it, in other words, what's international law got to do with anything? From that perspective, US law supplied the necessary legal justification, and any efforts to build an international coalition revolved around the politics of what the Americans were trying to do.

Others, including the governments of France and Russia, countered with a stricter interpretation of Resolution 1441, according to which intervention in Iraq would be illegal without another Security Council resolution specifically authorizing force. Although we were faced with differing interpretations and implications of international legal norms, it was striking that all governments based their positions on law. As David Kennedy emphasized in his book *Of War and Law,* "law has become a mark of legitimacy – and legitimacy has become the currency of power." I was particularly impressed by the shrewd, experienced way in which Jean Chrétien handled these complex issues at the Prague summit, even while he spent some of the sessions jotting down numbers on a piece of paper trying to calculate how he might balance the next budget. It was through no fault of his own that all hell broke loose when a *National Post* reporter quoted an off-the-record, off-the-cuff aside by his communications director, Francie Ducros, in which she glibly called President Bush "a moron." In response to this classic example of the unexpected in politics, everyone immediately shifted to damage control, and the substance of the summit was completely ignored by the media. David Wright, our able ambassador to NATO, had spent hours briefing the press on the seven Baltic and Eastern European states that were joining the Alliance, but all his hard work went out the window once the "moron" story broke. Eventually, Francie herself felt compelled to resign. It was brutal to watch such a good person be subjected to such treatment.

When I ran into Jack Straw in the gym of our Prague hotel on November 21, we agreed that any intervention would have to be in accordance with international law. But what was the international law at that time? Did it require a Security Council resolution, because only the Security Council was authorized to permit an attack on another state in cases other than self-defence? Or could Kosovo be invoked as a precedent, meaning that an attack would be legitimate even without the authorization of the Security Council? Jack was firmly of the view that Resolution 1441 contained within itself a requirement that Iraq conform to the obligations, and therefore it authorized member states to go ahead and automatically enforce it without need of a subsequent resolution.

A lawyer with a cool, analytical mind, who later became lord chancellor, he was an extremely intelligent person, a concise and forceful speaker, a formidable adversary, but always a pleasure to work with, whether the topic was Iraq, the Commonwealth, NATO, or Afghanistan. If Colin Powell was cast as the heavy in the debate, Jack was the credible counsel. Colin, who wasn't a lawyer, tended to brush aside the legal niceties as irrelevant. (Once, at an ASEAN meeting, when the foreign ministers of Singapore and Thailand and I – all former academics – cornered him on the Responsibility to Protect doctrine, he called out, "Help, I'm surrounded by all these law professors. Save me from law professors.") Jack, by contrast, was highly conscious of where the Security Council resolution fit into international law and what type of language was legally acceptable to justify going to war. He was always careful to frame Britain's position in both a scholarly and a legal way.

As a result, Jack's speeches building the case for war were written with a lawyer's sensitivity to consequences. They argued that his government's actions were acceptable not only in terms of public relations, but also in terms of Britain's legal obligations under the Charter of the United Nations. Britain was also a party to the Rome Statute, which subjected it to the judgments of the International Criminal Court. These were not small, technical, faraway matters. British soldiers and civil servants feared they could be charged if they participated in an illegal war. Admiral Michael Boyce, the British chief of the defence staff, repeatedly asked Blair for advice on the legality of the war, telling the prime minister that his troops deserved the security of knowing that they weren't fighting an illegal war. General Mike Jackson, the head of the army and the commander of NATO ground forces during the Kosovo conflict, proclaimed, "Having played my part in getting Milošević into his cell at The Hague, I've no wish to be his next-door neighbour there."

As we later learned, when British attorney general Peter Goldsmith eventually produced a legal opinion, it was so nuanced that Blair didn't dare show it to his Cabinet. Goldsmith then submitted a second opinion that was much less ambivalent, but Blair still faced major opposition from his own party and government officials. Some Foreign Office lawyers thought an invasion would be illegal, and one of them, a senior legal adviser, resigned over the matter. That again revealed the complexity of international law where one group of experts said yes, there are some circumstances in which you can go to war without the explicit authorization of the Security Council, and another said no, there is no justification. Understandably, the British government wanted to get a new Security Council resolution specifically authorizing force – the gold standard that would help it internationally and at home in its claim that it was acting in accordance with the law.

IMMEDIATELY AFTER THE Prague summit, I flew to Russia for a bilateral with Igor Ivanov on November 25, 2002. I had got to know him at the G8 foreign ministers' meeting in Whistler and elsewhere, though I can't say we ever established as warm a relationship as I had with some of the others. That was partly because we tended to communicate through an interpreter. Though he understood English well enough, he was naturally more comfortable speaking in Russian, so we tended to communicate through a translator.

There were a host of items on the agenda besides Iraq: the Middle East, North Korea, Afghanistan, Kashmir, nuclear waste, clean energy, the Arctic Council, the WTO, the ICC, better commercial ties, and possible high-level visits to Russia by the prime minister and the governor general. We talked at length about the hostage-taking crisis in Chechnya. From Ivanov's point of view, the fight against international terrorism had to extend to what the Russians were trying to do in Chechnya. From our point of view, a solution was more likely to be found through political dialogue than through military action and the type of heavy-handed human rights violations that had been well documented by the Organization for Security and Cooperation in Europe, especially the arbitrary relocation of internally displaced people. In the end we could only agree to disagree.

After lunch Igor surprised me by saying, "Bill, I want to have a private conversation with you about some of these things, just you and me, no officials, no interpreter." Our aides looked at each other nervously. Aides never like their ministers to slip out of their control, lest we say something that isn't in the briefing book or make a commitment we shouldn't, but I trusted Igor well enough to agree. He took me into his private office, which was located in a nineteenth-century nobleman's palace that had been commandeered by the state. It had more the taste of czarist luxury than of Soviet severity, full of ornate French furniture and painted ceilings.

"How private is this conversation going to be?" I asked.

"Are you assuming someone's listening in?" he replied.

"I'd be quite naive if I didn't think that, wouldn't I?"

"Well, certainly, this being my country, people will be listening in. But I want to assure you they're only my people, not other people's people."

"How do you know the Americans aren't listening?" I teased. "They usually know everything before we do anyway." We both laughed, and the

Americans, for all we knew, might have had a full transcript of the conversation within minutes.

Igor mostly wanted to talk about the possible adverse consequences of hostilities in Iraq. In essence he wanted to find out what I knew about Colin Powell's real intentions, whereas I wanted to find out whether the Russians were likely to use their veto in the Security Council if there were a second resolution explicitly authorizing force. We had a frank conversation about the two strains of thought within the US administration and were personally aligned about the need to encourage the Americans to stay within the UN framework. The underlying question was whether Powell planned to go along with the hawks. Neither of us knew what was in Colin's mind at that point, so we restricted ourselves to speculating about the implications for Russia-US relations and Russia-NATO relations if the United States attacked Iraq without UN approval.

My next major opportunity to sound out international opinion came on December 19, when Ottawa hosted a summit on Canada–European Union relations. A number of prominent European political figures attended, including Javier Solana, the Spanish statesman then serving as the senior EU representative for foreign and security policy. I found him uncharacteristically pessimistic. He was convinced that "the US is going the wrong way on everything," I noted at the time, and saw the situation in the Middle East, particularly the Israel-Palestine question, as stagnant. As for Iraq, Solana felt that its government's recently released twelve-thousand-page response to Resolution 1441 was "full of holes and contradictions," and he wasn't alone in being deeply skeptical about its claim that Iraq had completely disarmed.

AT THE BEGINNING of 2003 the Canadian government came under increasing pressure to stake out a position on whether it would support an American invasion if the Security Council refused to authorize force. Every day during this period, we were slammed by the Opposition and the press for not having a clear policy, for or against. "Where do you stand? Where are you going?" we were asked in Question Period and media scrums outside the Commons. The *Toronto Globe and Mail* and the *National Post* demanded that we side with the Americans. The *Toronto Star* and *La Presse* demanded that we stay out of war.

Though Mr. Chrétien sometimes railed about the media in the Cabinet and was furious with the reporter who had betrayed Francie Ducros, he was too hardened by forty years of experience in the spotlight to take press criticism and editorial cartoons as personally as I did. He was also a master at analyzing the political consequences of every decision. If he didn't exactly welcome an attack from the conservative press, he understood how to turn it to his advantage among his natural constituency. If the *National Post* ever applauded him, he would have sensed he was in trouble with his base support. As for the *Globe and Mail,* "it's always against me," he once said in reply to a question of mine, dismissing its editorial arguments as nothing but a matter of his politics or personality. Sometimes he even goaded the journalists. "You guys are preoccupied with this issue," he would tell them in scrums outside the Cabinet room. "Well, I'm not, because I don't read you. It's your problem, not mine, and good luck to you. I'm more concerned about going about my business for the people of Canada." It used to drive them crazy – which was why he delighted in doing it.

I marvelled at the way he deflected the attacks on John McCallum when, after a January 10 meeting with Donald Rumsfeld in Washington, John speculated on the circumstances under which Canada might join the invasion without UN sanction. In fact, I made a similar comment to the media the day after McCallum made his, suggesting that there might be a scenario akin to Kosovo in which Canada would join an action against Iraq without the authorization of the Security Council. For some reason the reporters didn't go after me the way they went after John, perhaps because I hadn't made mine in Washington directly after a meeting with the notoriously hawkish Rumsfeld, and I had been careful to add, "those circumstances don't exist today and we continue to operate in the UN framework."

As the buzz around McCallum's comments grew, there was increasing pressure on the government to issue some kind of clarification. Of the 350 emails and calls that flooded the PMO, 349 were negative, and Mr. Chrétien decided he had to clean up the situation himself. On the evening of January 14, I was attending a dinner hosted by the ambassador of South Korea at the Château Laurier when Dan Costello, my chief of staff, unexpectedly showed up in his overcoat and winter boots. Having failed to reach my aide by phone, he had trudged along Sussex Drive from the

Pearson Building to deliver the message that the prime minister wanted to speak with me immediately. The only private room the hotel staff could find for me to make the call was the manager's office.

The prime minister and I spoke at length about the international legal questions surrounding Resolution 1441, the politics of the Security Council, and the media furor over McCallum's comments. "Tomorrow, I'm meeting with the press to get back on track," Chrétien told me. "We can't move without the United Nations, we're waiting for the inspections, and Chirac will use his veto if there is no substantive proof." The next day, sure enough, Chrétien put the matter to rest. "I don't speculate," he told the reporters. "We're with 1441." Afterward, I made a note to myself, "He is so strong in putting his case he intimidates them completely."

At that point most of the country, most of the Cabinet, most of the Liberal caucus, most of the Commons, and a vast majority in the politically key provinces of Quebec and British Columbia were against sending Canadian troops into Iraq, especially without UN authorization. I didn't need a pollster to tell me that. I heard it in my riding, on my travels across the country, and over the hotline that the Department of Foreign Affairs and International Trade (DFAIT) had set up to allow citizens to phone in with passport problems or consular complaints. During the Iraq debate the calls came day and night, and they were running eight to two against our participation in any invasion. Some evenings I used to go down and answer a few of the calls myself, and I'd get an earful from people demanding that the government stay out.

On the other side were the Canadian Alliance, many business leaders, the right-wing media, the usual gang of academic hawks, a few Liberal ministers and MPs, various senators, much of Alberta, and some Defence Department officials who were tight with the US policy. For them, especially those whose assets and interests were tied to the United States, Canada-US relations trumped every other factor. Whatever the Americans decided, we should stand with them, either because getting rid of Saddam Hussein was the right thing to do or because our trade links and military connections with the United States would be adversely affected if we didn't fall into line. Though these groups weren't yet as agitated and organized as they would become after our decision, the pressure to align ourselves with Washington was tremendous and a lot stronger than people remember today.

I remember one meeting I had with some board members from the Asia Pacific Foundation who told me they wanted to discuss the funding cuts that DFAIT was planning to make to their organization. Instead, every one of them launched into a tirade on how their own businesses would be hurt if Canada didn't go to Iraq with the Americans. "This may be where you are," I said when I had heard enough, "and this may be where your clients are, but it's not where the citizens of this country are, and it's not where this government is. I understand that you're looking out for your bottom line, but we're looking out for the national interest."

THE REASONS FOR the Chrétien government's ambiguity were, in my mind, quite understandable. On the one hand, we did not want to participate in an action that would be both illegal and illegitimate. On the other, only consistent, credible, and global pressure backed by a threat of force would cause Saddam to come around, though it became less clear what "coming around" meant since he didn't appear to have any serious stores of weapons of mass destruction. Not only our policies but the very facts that motivated them were on constantly shifting sands. And yet, with every passing week, it became harder and harder to keep our options open.

On January 15, 2003, the United States formally asked NATO for indirect military assistance in case of a war against Iraq. At the same time we were receiving reports that Defense Secretary Rumsfeld didn't believe that the UN inspection system could do the job of disarming Iraq – largely, it seems, because the inspectors hadn't turned anything up. By mid-February the Americans were in the process of amassing a critical number of troops on the ground.

Canada was facing a delicate task. We wanted to keep our options open with respect to our possible military involvement in Iraq, and that implied participating in American planning for the invasion. But we also wanted to ensure that we didn't signal an unequivocal intention to join the US coalition. In other words, even though our participation was hypothetical, the planning had to be actual, and though I sympathized with the Defence Department's need to prepare for contingencies, that risked, as the expression goes, "the platoon going over the Rhine and the whole army having to follow."

At one point I heard about training exercises that might have been de-signed to tip the balance in favour of our going to war. When I phoned John McCallum to inquire about them, he didn't know any more than I did, and he shared my concern that they would flag to the Americans that Canada was on board no matter what we were saying publicly. It would also make it much more difficult to say no to any subsequent invasion if that turned out to be Mr. Chrétien's decision. In fact, John and I came to suspect that some officials were operating on the assumption that the prime minister would ultimately have no choice but to join with the Americans in Iraq. I cautioned McCallum to be careful, for which he later thanked me.

On January 14, General Ray Henault, the chief of the defence staff, told McCallum that, in the event there was a UN-approved operation or the US decided to go into Iraq unilaterally, he wanted to send some Canadian officers to a planning meeting that was scheduled for the next day at US Central Command in Tampa, Florida. John responded firmly that the Canadians would not be getting on the plane to Tampa. Having expected ministerial approval, Henault and the American brass were startled when it wasn't forthcoming. "I appreciate your position about not agreeing to authorizing early training," John told me when I spoke to him that night. "They would have killed me," he said, referring, I supposed, to the Op-position and the press. "The generals will drive you up the wall." He was, I noted at the time, "really pissed off."

One of the delicate things about the Iraq decision was how tightly Canada and the United States are linked through our joint security operations. That subsequently became the source of confusion and controversy about the true nature of Canada's participation in the Iraq war. Though NORAD has a restricted mandate for continental defence, our military forces are regularly seconded for training with the US Central Command. And though the prime minister made it clear we wouldn't go into Iraq without the UN resolution, that didn't mean we would no longer be involved in the war on terror or fulfill our international obligations in Afghanistan. Even while refusing to participate in a unilateral invasion, we kept our warships on patrol in the North Arabian Sea. In fact, in February 2003, Canada took command of Task Force 151, the international flotilla that was part of

Operation Enduring Freedom, and the Cabinet agreed to provide a battle group and tactical brigade headquarters to the International Security Assistance Force in Kabul for a year. One way or another, we were on the periphery of the Iraq theatre.

If the Defence Department, no doubt influenced by our close ties with the United States over continental defence, was largely in favour of following the American lead into Iraq, John McCallum and I nevertheless saw eye to eye at the ministerial level. We had developed an especially close working relationship and we met on a regular basis, as did our chiefs of staff, Gene Lang and Dan Costello. One night, when the four of us were having dinner together, I got the idea that the major players in foreign affairs and defence should meet on a regular and quasi-institutional basis to be kept abreast of what was going on. The result was dubbed "the portfolio lunch." At first it included McCallum, Pierre Pettigrew (the minister of international trade), and me, and we soon extended an invitation to Sue Whelan, the minister in charge of the Canadian International Development Agency. Next came our chiefs of staff, to speak to the political side of the issues, and before long the deputy ministers showed up too. The group became quite large, functioning almost like a Cabinet committee on foreign affairs.

For the rest of my time as foreign minister, we usually got together for lunch on Mondays in the New Zealand Room, one of the small private rooms at the back of the Parliamentary Dining Room. Those lunches became a great way to avoid conflicts among the departments, get people to understand each other's point of view, and talk informally. They actually made a difference, and I was very proud of them. Amid all the infighting in Ottawa, usually over budgetary issues, they were an opportunity to bring some coherence, cohesion, and collaboration to a process that normally consisted of guys trying to shove a stick into the wheels of other guys. On many occasions I was told, "We really avoided a problem here because we were singing from the same hymnbook." I could also see the advantages of that co-ordination and communication reflected in Question Period. For whatever reason, my successor as foreign minister didn't see the need for the lunches and stopped them. That taught me another lesson about Ottawa: no matter how helpful a change might be to a particular institution, it's not going to last if it's not enshrined in the system and supported at the centre.

JOHN MCCALLUM HAD been given a rough ride because of his press conference in Washington, but his trip was helpful in many ways. It confirmed,
first of all, that the Americans were more interested in our military support
in Afghanistan than in Iraq. I was also struck by his report that they didn't
seem to have any hard intelligence to prove that the Iraqis were hiding
weapons of mass destruction (WMD). I told Jack Straw as much during a
phone call on January 16, six days after John's meeting with Rumsfeld. "I'm
worried that the WMD case hasn't been proven," I said, "but with 150,000
troops in the theatre, it might be impossible to withstand the political
pressure from Washington to strike in February." Yet if we started a war
without authorization from the Security Council and without proof regarding the WMD, there could be terrible consequences. The credibility of the
UN, the war on terror, the peace process in the Middle East, and the reputation of the United States were all at stake. I emphasized that reaching
out to the wider international community would be key to any potential
intervention in Iraq, as the notion of an "Anglo-Saxon" coalition of the
United States, Britain, Australia, and Canada was a political non-starter.

At a Cabinet retreat on January 23, John Manley said, "Our biggest challenge will be how to manage our US relations if they go without a UN
mandate." The prime minister agreed with that analysis, adding, "We can't
be anti-American." He gave the caucus the same message a few days later.
"Bush knows where we stand," he said, "but we won't attack him or the
United States." As for the US intelligence reports, he remained skeptical:
"Security people are paid to see problems; no security problems, no jobs."

Irrefutable evidence of Iraqi non-compliance continued to be elusive,
but the Iraqis weren't making it any easier on themselves by their continued
reluctance to co-operate fully with Blix's UN inspectors. On January 27 I
watched on TV as Blix issued an interim report to the UN Security Council,
and though it was expected to be a decisive moment, he had not found the
"smoking gun." On the whole, he admitted that, though there had been
co-operation on process and access to Iraqi sites, Iraq was still not completely willing to accept the inspections and continued to play games.

The next day I spoke with Mohamed ElBaradei, the director general of
the International Atomic Energy Agency, which was closely partnered with
Blix's UNMOVIC in carrying out the inspections. One of the major priorities of their teams was to interview Iraqi scientists living outside Iraq,

so that they could speak freely without fear of reprisal from Saddam's government. The major problem was guaranteeing the freedom and safety of these scientists and their families. I floated the possibility that Canada could resettle a number of these Iraqis and also thanked ElBaradei for his work thus far, which had been such a credit to the International Atomic Energy Agency and the entire UN system.

I then had a memorable phone conversation with Blix, who admitted that he wasn't confident he could deliver an adequate report in the time frame he had been given, no matter how robust his efforts. When the Iraqi government wasn't being totally unresponsive, it simply brushed away his questions. Moreover, proving to the Americans' satisfaction that Iraq didn't have anything was impossible. "How do you prove a negative?" Blix asked. Iraq's a big country, after all, and he couldn't guarantee that his inspectors had scoured every inch, lifted every rock, and searched every cave. Although he thought there was no reasonable likelihood of Iraq having WMD, he also had to admit to holding little hope for further effective inspections. In that sense, I've always felt that Saddam was the author of his own misfortune. To ward off a possible attack, he pretended to possess dreadful weapons, but the very threat of those weapons gave the Americans an excuse to go after him. Saddam's deliberate ambiguity invited the very military action it had been designed to deter. He would have been far better to come clean.

I was discouraged after speaking with Blix. "I think we just took a big step towards war," I noted at the time. Nevertheless, we were still of the opinion that the UN inspectors were applying Resolution 1441 as best they could and that containment was working according to the current UN process. All the evidence wasn't in; there was no proof one way or another; and the inspectors had to be given the time they needed and wanted. If Blix proved Iraqi non-compliance with 1441, and if the Security Council approved action under 1441 or a second resolution, then we would act. And if there were no second resolution, we would evaluate the situation to determine what action might be legitimate at that time, based on our own independent decision rather than on what might be predetermined by others.

THE FAILURE TO FIND a smoking gun, the confusion of assertions and counter-assertions by the intelligence services, and Iraq's intransigent defiance meant that the debate continued to revolve around the question of whether Resolution 1441 automatically established the right of intervention if Saddam Hussein failed to live up to its conditions. If the United Nations rallied to the American and British position that Resolution 1441 was legally or even politically sufficient, we would have had to accept it. After all, the leitmotif of Canadian foreign policy was to reinforce the instruments of global governance. Mr. Chrétien had emphasized this when he stood in the House and said that because there was no UN sanction, we wouldn't be going to Iraq. Given this, had the UN granted its approval, he would have been hard pressed to say that we weren't going anyway. Even if most Canadians didn't like the idea of war, they remained strong supporters of the United Nations. Recognition by the international community as a whole that Saddam Hussein was a danger to world peace might well have changed the climate of public opinion in Canada. However, the Russians and the French continued to take the position that Resolution 1441 wasn't sufficient authorization and that the evidence of WMD in Iraq was, thus far, inconclusive.

As Jack Straw told me on January 29, the British government was ready to try for a second resolution. Jack thought a more explicit mandate would clearly establish a "material breach" by the Iraqis and bring more countries into a coalition of forces. He didn't say so, but it was obvious that a second resolution would also help sell the invasion to the Labour Party and to the British people. He seemed to think that Russia and China would support a second resolution, and though Germany remained opposed to a war, Straw figured it might be supportive. Perhaps most important, he was convinced that France would not exercise its veto. If he were right and such a resolution were approved by the Security Council, that would tip the scale in favour of Canada's participation.

"He believes that war can still be avoided," I wrote in a memo to the prime minister about my conversation with Straw, "but only if the pressure is kept on and Saddam 'cracks' (what that means was not spelled out – leaves the country?)."

Though the British quest for a second resolution inspired some hope that an open breach in the Atlantic alliance could be prevented, it was now becoming apparent that the Americans were likely to invade with or without a new resolution. How should Canada react to a unilateral move on the part of the Bush administration?

"The United States, the United Kingdom and some others have begun preparing for a potential use of force against Iraq, should this be found necessary," I told the Commons in a major statement on January 29, "and Canada has been engaged in prudent military-to-military discussions with the U.S. in order to be prepared if necessary as well. This credible threat of force has been an essential support for diplomacy, as it keeps the pressure on Iraq to comply. I assure the House, however, that no decision on the use of force has been taken by the government, and we see it as a very last resort."

This was a message I repeated throughout those tense early months of 2003, and one of my proudest moments as minister came when I picked up *Le Droit* and saw on its front-page headline, "Graham: la guerre est le dernier recours." That summed up the feeling of most Canadians at the time, and so far there was no persuasive evidence or clear danger to convince them that the threshold for the use of force had been reached.

ON JANUARY 30 I WENT to Washington to meet with Colin Powell. It had already been announced that he would present the American intelligence on Iraqi WMD to the UN Security Council the following week, and he gave me a brief outline of the kind of evidence he was planning to present. I reiterated Canada's commitment to the UN process and our concerns about unilateral action. When the meeting was over, we went outside to speak to the press. I had been mobbed by reporters before, but nothing prepares you for the sheer number and intensity of the Washington press corps.

"Mr. Minister, is Canada still opposed to using force?" one of them shouted. "It sounds like you're opposed to any coalition using force. What are you waiting for?"

"Resolution 1441 speaks of a process which is going to determine whether or not Iraq is failing to disarm," I replied, "and if that is determined, there will be consequences. We do believe that Iraq has to be disarmed, and we will work with the secretary, with the United States, and with other countries – through the UN – to achieve that goal."

"You're not going to reveal what he told you?"

"Not if I want to get invited back."

After a few minutes, Colin said, "I have to get to a meeting, but the minister has agreed to remain for a few more minutes. Take care, buddy." And then he ambled off, leaving me alone in front of this horde of aggressive reporters and flashing cameras. One of them started to tear a real strip off me about Canada's positions on Iraq, terrorism, and national security until I interrupted him to ask if he were, by any chance, from FOX News. "Yes," he said, sounding a little surprised. "How did you know?"

On February 5, 2003, Colin Powell presented to the United Nations and the world the evidence gathered by US intelligence to justify an invasion. Initially, like many others, I was impressed by the speech and had to ask myself the haunting question, "What if he's right?" He seemed to have shifted the burden of proof from the United States to the Saddam regime. I wrote to Colin shortly afterward to congratulate him. "For a general," I added, "you make a great lawyer." This speech didn't mean, however, that Canada would simply fall in line with the Bush administration. In Question Period that very day, I received a standing ovation from my Liberal colleagues when I told the House, "We are not joining France and Germany. We are not joining the United States. We are representing the voices of Canadians."

Our continued caution was merited. In the days and weeks following Colin's address, experts began to demolish many of the intelligence claims behind his arguments. Ultimately, the episode proved how difficult democratic decision making can be when your information has been politicized. More than a year and a half later, when Colin accompanied Bush on an official visit to Ottawa at the end of November 2004, he asked to see me even though I was no longer foreign minister. During our half-hour meeting I raised the issue of his controversial presentation. I sensed he felt that his good name, his trustworthy image, and his widespread popularity had been used by the Bush administration to bolster its case. His reputation domestically and internationally was sacrificed for the benefit of people for whom he had no respect.

"Bill, you have no idea," he said. "I threw out boxes and boxes of stuff they tried to get me to say. I was briefed by our intelligence people with mountains of crap. That's what I got. I won't be reappointed as secretary of state, but my approval ratings in the United States are something like

80 percent and the president's are around 45 percent, so I'm satisfied most people think I'm doing a pretty good job."

There is still a school of thought that says that only two people could have prevented the war in Iraq: Tony Blair and Colin Powell. But was that fair in Colin's case? If he had quit at that time, his resignation would have crystallized some form of strong opposition against the war within the United States, no doubt about it. However, Bush was going to attack at any cost, and Congress supported him overwhelmingly.

In the wake of Colin's presentation, the United States continued to pitch its intelligence case, offering to send American officials to Ottawa to give us a special presentation on the Iraqi threat. At one point, in fact, Bush offered to come personally to Ottawa to brief the prime minister on secret evidence about the existence of the WMD. Chrétien called me to discuss the matter, and we concluded it wasn't a good idea. "I can say no to Bush on the phone," he explained. "It would be harder to say no to him face to face."

Throughout February, the momentum swung in opposition to war, especially in those European countries whose governments were support-ive of Bush's position on Iraq. "We are having a big problem with public opinion," Spanish foreign minister Ana Palacio told me three days after Powell's UN presentation. Although her prime minister, José María Aznar, was one of the most hawkish of Europe's leaders, many people in Spain believed that the Iraq crisis was a product of US imperialism and its desire to secure Iraq's oil. Despite our differences, Ana and I were united in wanting to prevent an open break at the UN Security Council and to contain further damage to transatlantic relations. She said a second reso-lution would probably be needed and hoped that both Canada and Spain could play a mediating role with France and the United States. When I asked her what a second resolution would look like, she said it would all depend on Blix's report, due February 14.

On February 10 France, Germany, and Russia issued a joint declaration to the effect that the inspection teams were making progress and should be given the time Blix needed, in his own words, "to sweep up these 'crumbs.'" Two days later he told me over the phone that "almost all the intelligence they've been given about the existence or situation of WMD has been erroneous or misleading." No decision, he said, should be based on this "so-called intelligence."

On February 13 Mr. Chrétien gave a major address to the Chicago Council on Foreign Relations. This was an important opportunity for the Canadian government to state our position directly to the American people and to explain why we were holding firm to a UN-based solution to Iraq. When asked for my input, I sat down at my computer and hammered out a rough draft myself. Though it was unusual for a minister to make the time to craft a speech, I thought it was essential in this case for me to set down a number of my ideas and key arguments. I was pleased that Chrétien incorporated many of them into his final speech because it showed that the government had a clear and coherent message.

The day after the prime minister's speech, Hans Blix delivered his much-anticipated report to the Security Council and cast doubt on Powell's case against Iraq. When Dominique de Villepin followed by deploring what he called any "premature resort to force," his intervention was met with applause – a nearly unprecedented event at the UN. On February 15 there were huge anti-war demonstrations in London and other major cities around the world. In Canada thousands of protesters marched in cities across the country. On February 17 the European Union called for the complete and immediate disarmament of Iraq, with force as "a last resort" within a UN framework. However, it remained silent on the difficult question of whether Resolution 1441 was enough of a legal basis for such force or whether another resolution was required. The EU's position wasn't far from Canada's in terms of talking tough about the need for Iraq to disarm, while focusing on the centrality of the UN. We also shared the concern that the United States wanted regime change in Iraq even if it complied fully. When I spoke with Joschka Fischer on February 19, he told me about asking the Americans what they would need to declare victory. "Saddam must be gone," was their reply.

When I spoke with Jack Straw on February 20, he re-emphasized the need to keep the pressure on Saddam, even though we both knew that there was an increasing divergence between what the British public was prepared to accept and the course on which Blair's government was essentially set. More alarmingly, he mentioned the 250,000 troops that the

Americans and the British had been building up, saying repeatedly that it was impossible to keep them on standby indefinitely. "People's patience is running out," he said. "We can't get into an August 1914 syndrome." But wasn't that the problem with amassing a huge military force? How do you back down after you put yourself in that position? At some point you either have to advance or withdraw, and as the tragedy of August 1914 showed, once the troop trains leave the station for the frontier, no political will in the world can hold them back. That was the dilemma the United States and Great Britain had gotten themselves into: deploying troops, ostensibly to provide an incentive for peaceful compliance, had moved them into a dangerous place where they could hardly stand down. Arguably the buildup, which was justified as a measure to avoid war, made the resort to force almost inescapable.

Straw still saw a second resolution as desirable, though he wasn't convinced it was necessary. There was no way the French and the Russians were going to authorize the use of force – they simply didn't believe that the facts as presented by the Americans and the British justified military action. Clearly, though, something had to be done. Not only was there a desire to paper over the split among the major Western powers, especially as Saddam was taking advantage of the divisions on the Security Council to remain defiant, we were also at a critical juncture for the future of the institutions of global governance.

That's when Canada decided to approach the problem from another angle. What if the facts were firmer and more broadly accepted? In other words, rather than focusing our efforts on getting a second resolution, we concentrated on determining what might be sufficient for a second resolution. In mid-February Chrétien instructed our UN ambassador, Paul Heinbecker, to be the spear-carrier for an initiative designed to get clear answers to two precise questions: What specific disarmament tasks remained to be completed, and how much time should Iraq be given to complete them? Our fairly modest hope was to get general agreement about what Saddam had to do and to secure a general acceptance of the principle of a deadline, if not a precise date. It was not a draft resolution. We weren't even a member of the Security Council. We were just circulating an idea that might find favour with everybody. Nor, as rumoured, were we trying to stall for time until summer came to Iraq, making an invasion impossible. Our attempt was a genuine effort to establish the facts.

"In order to spell out clearly to Iraq what is expected of it and within what timelines," Heinbecker told the Security Council on February 19, "we suggest that the Council direct the inspectors to lay out the list of key remaining disarmament tasks immediately and to establish which of those tasks most urgently require evidence of Iraqi compliance. The Council should also establish an early deadline for Iraqi compliance."

At the same time, the prime minister worked quietly behind the scenes, talking to various heads of government and members of the Security Council, especially Mexico and Chile, in an attempt to constrain the United States into operating within the Security Council framework while forcing Saddam to comply with Resolution 1441. We had to tread carefully between two irreconcilable positions. Though the United States and Britain were pushing us to persuade Mexico and Chile to join their camp, we were telling the Mexicans and Chileans that we supported the independent approach they wanted to take in order to preserve the UN system.

It mystified me how badly the Bush administration treated the Mexican government at this critical moment. I used to believe that Bush was the one American president who could have built a decent relationship with the Mexicans. He and Laura spoke Spanish; as a former governor of Texas, he understood the importance of the Hispanic vote; and he worked hard on the immigration issue. But his party strategists chose to play up border security to cater to the prejudices of the Republican right, and the oil interests had their eye on taking over Mexico's energy resources. During lunch at the White House one day, I remember the president going off on a tangent about the Mexicans. "Their politics drive me crazy," he said. "Here they are, sitting on all this oil and gas that would give us security of supply for twenty years, and they won't let us develop it." Damn right we won't, I imagined my friend Jorge Castañeda saying if he had been present.

"If we had a seat in the Security Council," I said to Chrétien one day, "we could have more influence in this matter."

"Bill," he said, knowing what heat Mexico and Chile were getting from Washington, "there are times when you don't want to be on the Security Council."

Indeed, he saw a danger for Canada when a headline appeared in the *Globe and Mail* on February 20, "PM Aims to Broker Iraq Deal." With a wildly fabricated story about weekend phone calls and what my wife, Cathy, read as a pro-US spin, the headline raised expectations and jeopardized success. "If it works, we can take the credit," Chrétien said. "If it doesn't work, no one will be the wiser." In his discussions with Tony Blair, he deliberately called our initiative a "non-paper," less a real document than an amorphous suggestion. The moment it was seen in the media as a major Canadian initiative, he argued, there was every possibility that we would collide with at least one of the huge juggernauts encircling the issue. Given the shameful hounding and vilification of the Mexican ambassador to the United Nations, whom the hawks in the Bush administration ultimately managed to get removed for not supporting the US position, Mr. Chrétien was no doubt right.

"The P.M. is furious at the exaggeration of expectations," I noted on February 21, "so my job is to downplay it but still push it. What a crazy life." That day I spoke with the French, who remained intransigent against including any hint of automaticity in a potential deal, and with the Russians. "We don't have any illusions about Baghdad. We agree that the inspections cannot be limitless," Igor Ivanov explained to me over the phone. "But if Blix says he wants to carry out this plan and needs two months or whatever, there's no need for an immediate war. If we feel that, under certain circumstances, the US wants a political solution, we'll cooperate. But we're getting signals that they don't want disarmament but change of regime. If this policy gets the upper hand in the administration, there's little room for manoeuvre."

Indeed, any remaining middle ground was rapidly disappearing. "It looks like they are determined to go," Chrétien observed on February 24. "There's nothing we can do." Later that day the United States, the United Kingdom, and Spain finally tabled their proposed second resolution, which declared that Iraq had "failed to take the final opportunity afforded it in Resolution 1441." Coming as it did two days before the British government asked for and obtained parliamentary approval for its course of action, despite deep divisions in Blair's own Cabinet and caucus, this new US/UK/ Spanish resolution was generally viewed as a ploy to help rally public opinion in the United Kingdom. As such, it swayed no one and was a complete non-starter for the French and the Russians. I couldn't help but reflect in my notes, "Are we seeing the end of the UN system as we know it?"

Canada continued in our efforts to bridge the divide, but while we were being cautioned by the French not to get too close to the US position, we were perceived by the Americans as trying to put a spoke in the wheel of their war machine. "We're OK with both the French and the Americans," John Manley quipped at the Cabinet meeting on February 25; "as long as they don't talk to one another, we're OK." We suggested a potential deadline of March 28, but Bush immediately shot down the idea in a conversation with the prime minister on February 26. When Colin Powell and I spoke on the telephone that day, he berated Canada for causing trouble. "We are not supportive to the end of the month," he said, dismissing our idea of a late March deadline. Whatever push there had been for a second resolution was Tony Blair's, according to Colin, and the Americans didn't need it. He was convinced that our initiative would be used as an excuse to kick the can down the road forever. The French were being completely obstructionist, he felt, and the Germans would never vote for action under any circumstances.

"We're only trying to establish whether Saddam is in material breach of 1441," I said. "The facts have to be clear if you want everybody on board."

"I understand you're trying to be helpful," Colin replied, "but at this point any further efforts at the United Nations are not helpful. Telling us we can't go without UN approval is not what we want to hear. Being really helpful would be to say, 'Yes, we're on your side, and if you decide to go, we'll go with you.'"

"That sounds to me as if you've made a decision, given the weather and the military conditions in the Middle East, to go on a certain date, and if you get the UN resolution, wonderful, we've been helpful, you appreciate it; but if you don't have it, you're going to go anyway."

"You can draw your own conclusions about that," he replied.

By the beginning of March I was so preoccupied with Iraq that I had to cancel an important and long-planned visit to Sri Lanka, Pakistan, and Afghanistan. I was dealing with the Security Council, a host of foreign ministers, and our military. I was under fire in the Commons and in the right-wing press every day. In addition, I was in the midst of a series of town-hall meetings in cities across the country as a way of involving Canadians in the new foreign policy review that Chrétien had asked me to initiate.

Some officials in my department were reluctant to undertake the review, in part because they feared it would become an anti-war vehicle, in part because they didn't see the point of conducting such a time-consuming effort for a prime minister who was on the verge of retiring. But I felt that the government couldn't be put on hold just because the leadership would change sometime soon. Besides, even if Iraq did dominate the process, wasn't it all the more important for Canadians to feel that their voices were being heard on this vital issue?

In fact, the town halls ended up acting as something of a release valve for public anxiety about the war. Peace activists showed up in Halifax yelling "Keep out of Iraq." A lively crowd in Windsor chanted anti-American slogans so loudly that I could only wonder if they were heard across the river in Detroit. In Montreal, where Iraq was to become a hot issue in the forthcoming provincial election, more than three hundred students crammed into a hall at the Université du Québec à Montréal on a Friday afternoon to discuss their views about Canadian foreign policy. In Victoria almost all the questions and comments were about Iraq, Iraq, Iraq.

Meanwhile, a last, feverish round of diplomacy was being played out at the United Nations. On March 3 I called Jack Straw to make another plea for the UN process. I couldn't think of a more negative result than the Security Council reaching a deadlock or the United States abandoning it. The fallout from such a breakdown would last for years, and other nations with their own ambitions and agendas would take advantage of the precedent set by a unilateral invasion. Yet I also felt that the British and the Americans needed to be sincere in their efforts at the Security Council and had to be willing to negotiate in good faith with the other members. I urged Straw to extend the deadline for Iraq's full compliance to the end of March at least. Though open to the idea, he remained skeptical about the outcome, given Saddam's behaviour pattern in the past.

Canada kept talking with the five permanent and ten non-permanent members of the Security Council to see if a new consensus were possible. By this point, indeed, Chrétien became particularly active with the file, including a quick trip to Mexico where he asked President Fox to take up the Canadian initiative at the Security Council. Nor was he dealing only with other heads of government. On March 2, for example, he was the one who told me about the meetings that Ambassador Heinbecker was having in New York. "Why am I hearing [this] from him?" I wrote in my notes. Though prime ministers often take on important foreign policy decisions at critical moments, discovering that a member of my own department was reporting directly to the PMO put me in a rather awkward position.

On March 7 Hans Blix reported some progress. Under threat from the US and UK military buildup in the region, Iraq was finally making substantial moves toward opening up for inspection and disarming its ballistic missiles. Colin Powell said he was sorry not to see greater compliance, but I suspected he wasn't sorry at all; his orders by this point were to go to war. However, even though the US/UK/Spanish resolution was still on the table, it had no chance of passing, and Britain began working toward some kind of compromise, with benchmarks not unlike the one we had been floating but with a tighter two-week deadline.

Canada's plan was still in play. Chrétien talked to the British and the Chileans to see if the Security Council could come up with a replacement for the doomed US/UK/Spanish resolution. Blix and his team would be given more time to carry out their inspections with Iraq's complete and immediate co-operation; Saddam would undertake the necessary steps toward disarmament within weeks; if he failed to do so, member states would have grounds to use all necessary means to disarm Iraq. The major stumbling blocks were how long or short the time frame would be – fourteen days? thirty days? forty-five days? – and whether authorization to use military force would kick in automatically if Iraq again failed to comply.

Ambassador Heinbecker was scheduled to address the Security Council on March 11 to state Canada's position. In the hours leading up to his speech, I was surprised to read a draft of his statement in favour of a four-week deadline and automaticity. More than surprised, alarmed, for the Americans had made it clear that a four-week deadline was out of the question, and I strongly suspected that automaticity wouldn't fly with the French and the Russians. As a result, I was put in the uncomfortable position of having to call the prime minister to plea for a three-week limit, which he agreed to.

I was later told that some officials had snuck automaticity past Chrétien without calling his attention to it. "They ran this past him," I wrote in my notes on March 12, "and before we saw it, it was too late for us to weigh in on it ('it's already been approved, Minister'). So they misled the boss and then presented it as a *fait accompli* to us!"

We lobbied fiercely with the Latin Americans, the Africans, and the Asians, to rally support for our initiative or for a new one from the "six undecideds" (U6) on the Security Council. But in the end it hardly mattered because the French and the Russians were never going to accept automaticity anyway. In fact, when my upcoming trip to France was suddenly cancelled on the grounds that Dominique de Villepin was "exhausted," the real reason – or so I heard – was that the French were angry with us for even proposing automaticity at the end of what they felt was still too short a deadline. When the U6 proposed three weeks and no automaticity, however, the United States balked. Meanwhile, there was a report that the Americans and Australians had asked Blix to remove their citizens on his team from Iraq by Tuesday, March 18.

The threat of war was close in another way, too, for my son, Patrick, had been posted as a correspondent to Baghdad to report for the *National Post* (ironically enough) and for Global TV. He and I talked fairly regularly in this period, though we had to assume we were being monitored – Patrick by the Iraqi security services, and I by US intelligence. Though it was hard to know exactly what was going on, Patrick thought that the Government of Iraq was feeling a false sense of security that the momentum to war had been stalled. One senior adviser told him that the chance of war was between 60 and 70 percent, and that Saddam was doing everything he could to avoid it. "I'm bored," Patrick said when I spoke to him on February 19, "but that's better than being bombed." Cathy and I were concerned about Patrick's safety, but he was more sanguine. He was being followed all the time, and his driver was an intelligence officer assigned to track his every step. "I'm virtually under their protection," he said, "and if they're worried about the possibility of war, they're not going to take me out and shoot me, because they know there'd be consequences." That didn't give his mother or me a lot of confidence. Now, on March 13, he told me that Global wanted him to get out fast, but he hadn't yet made up his mind. "Don't be concerned," he said. "I will stay with people I trust."

As THE UNITED STATES prepared for an invasion, Canada had to confront the reality that whether we liked it or not, some of our military personnel and equipment were positioned on the edge of the war zone. One of the most pressing questions related to our command of Task Force 151, the international flotilla patrolling the Persian Gulf as part of Operation Enduring Freedom. Now that the Americans and the British were poised to invade, it was unclear whether Canada could remain in command and stay out of the war at the same time. Yet pulling our ships from the task force would mean breaking a commitment and might further aggravate our American allies.

In a conversation I had with John McCallum on March 8, we agreed that the issue was "a bit tricky." If the Americans launched an attack, for example, would we aid them with our ships? How much authorization would we give the commander of our ships, and in fact of the whole international flotilla, to get involved in peripheral actions? What would happen if an American ship were injured? One rather fanciful question considered the possible instructions if a boat came through the Strait of Hormuz with Saddam Hussein aboard, fleeing from Iraq. If we stopped that boat, would we turn him over to the Americans or to the UN, and if we did that, would we be engaged de facto in a war with Iraq, even if not de jure? The dilemma was strikingly obvious. "If it's so obvious," I noted in my journal on March 9, "then why did we take command of 151? We asked at that time what [were] the consequences of taking on 151. Is this a back-door attempt to draw us into something?" Two days later I added, "We are in the worst of all possible worlds – all because we got bad advice."

Nor were we alone. France, Greece, Holland, and New Zealand were in the same legal predicament. France, for example, remained in the task force in the Gulf even while its president and foreign minister were making inflammatory speeches against the United States at the UN. The challenge for all of us would be to maintain our responsibilities to Enduring Freedom and the war on terror without stepping over the line into Iraq. That meant trying to set down a fairly clear-cut division of labour, despite all the command overlaps and naval logistics. How much integration of the forces should there be? What logistical support? What protection of civilian vessels would there be? Could we continue in command of a task force and protect civilians and merchantmen if they were under attack?

On March 12 I met with Prime Minister Chrétien, Defence Minister McCallum, and some of our officials to discuss the problem. "P.M. wants us to stay where we are and to hell with the conflict," I wrote. But the Defence Department's legal advisers kept pushing Chrétien to give them detailed and explicit instructions as to what the Canadians with the task force should and should not do in various scenarios, or else order the ships out of the region altogether. When one of them tried to corner him into answering the precise question "Are we parties to the conflict or are we going to move the ships?" he responded by slamming his fist down on his desk and saying coldly, "We are not parties to the conflict, *and* the ships are staying where they are."

Canada's position was made even more complicated by the fact that we had officers and NCOs on regular exchange programs with the US, British, and Australian militaries, thirty-one of whom were stationed in the Gulf. The most prominent was General Walt Natynczyk, who was to go into Baghdad with the headquarters staff, though McCallum and I didn't discover that until afterward. That was a completely different role from what we had foreseen. When John and I had been informed that everyone would be attached to headquarters and gave our approval, we had assumed they were referring to the HQ in Qatar and not the divisional HQ that could end up in Iraq. My department kept asking the Defence Department for information about these personnel, how many they were, what were their functions, how they fit into the operations, and so forth. We were totally stonewalled and never got a complete list. Nobody claimed to know.

"How long does it take them to come up with these [names], when they've known for months this war was coming?" I noted to myself on March 16 in fury and frustration. I was the one who had to stand in the House of Commons and answer questions about what we were doing in the Gulf, yet Defence wouldn't give me the information I needed to answer the questions properly. Nor did my close relationship and constant communication with John McCallum help. He and I shared the same healthy skepticism about the information coming from his generals. "Defence leaked the info about the ships and the troops attached to the Americans to draw us in!" I speculated privately on March 14.

McCallum and I talked to each other several times a day about our ships in the Gulf, and together we decided to draft a letter of instruction for the prime minister to sign. He was the one who ultimately had to authorize what the Canadians could do on that mission. The early draft from our officials struck me as far too broad, though John didn't think it was as off-base as I did. In particular I questioned the language that would give the task force a mandate to protect military operations "irrespective of their mission," which obviously would include forces and vessels committed to Iraq, as well as to provide airlift with other countries, again "irrespective of their mission." I recommended removing this phrase from the text and specifying that none of our Armed Forces personnel attached to the operational units in the region were to engage directly in any attack. This wording would eliminate any suggestion that we would support military operations other than those that were directly related to Operation Enduring Freedom. When McCallum and I met on the evening of Sunday, March 16, he agreed, and we crafted a final text that satisfied everyone involved. "What a process," I sighed in my notes.

Yet our presence in the Gulf still opened the Chrétien government to charges of duplicity in the House of Commons. "How can you say that Canada is against the war in Iraq when we have troops there?" I was often asked in Question Period by the NDP, whereas the Canadian Alliance criticized me for not boasting about supporting the Americans.

"Just because we don't wish to disrupt Canada's special security relationship with the United States doesn't mean we've decided de jure in favour of the mission in Iraq," I answered.

Continental defence and security, whether through NORAD or in the post-9/11 environment, are too important and too integrated to enable us to pull out of a commitment every time it's politically inconvenient or intellectually inconsistent. I might have managed to have a sophisticated conversation with Colin Powell about why we couldn't keep any Canadians in Iraq whatsoever, but Cheney, Rumsfeld, and probably the American Congress would have regarded this in black-and-white terms as a complete betrayal. By virtue of our reluctance to join the coalition, we were gradually being frozen out of previously shared US intelligence. We couldn't afford to be frozen out of all forms of mutual defence. If Canada is to have allies, we must have that kind of integration. Otherwise, we will destroy any possibility of ever being able to influence the American military or of being involved with it for the good of Canada. Withdrawing the few troops on assignment with US or UK units would have been completely inimical to the interests of our long-term military commitments with those countries. Leaving them there was consistent with our position that we didn't approve of the war. We were participating in Iraq with allied regiments as part of long-standing exchange programs that had continued life in the course of events.

It was a difficult position, but defensible, despite an opinion from the head of the Defence Department's legal team, the judge advocate general, to the effect that we were technically "belligerent" according to international law, even though we hadn't declared war, because we were in command of Task Force 151. I had Colleen Swords, my departmental legal adviser, go over it. Clearly that wasn't a letter anybody in the Chrétien government wanted to carry around in his hip pocket.

I think we made the right decision in respect of the nature of our relationship with the United States. While remaining outside the Iraq conflict ourselves, we respected the previous defence commitments we had made with our allies, and our participation in Operation Enduring Freedom had been legally authorized by the United Nations. More important, the legal question was subsidiary to the political question. That is always at the crux of the nature of international law itself. International law can inform politics, but it's never free-standing.

On Sunday, March 16, President Bush and Prime Minister Blair held a meeting in the Azores with José María Aznar, the prime minister of Spain, and José Manuel Barroso, the prime minister of Portugal, in the run-up to the decision to invade. I spoke the next day with the Spanish foreign minister, Ana Palacio. Though Spain was now committed to joining the coalition under intense pressure from the United States, her tone was the usual one I found in conversations between Canadians and Europeans: a desire to come together whenever we were apart. "We worked hard to ensure that Bush referred to the role the UN would play in any Iraq reconstruction if there is to be a war," she said. "Like Canada, we believe in the importance of the United Nations." In this, she felt, both Bush and Powell were trying to act responsibly, compared with "other departments" of the US government – presumably a reference to Cheney and Rumsfeld. We spoke about the need for Canada and Spain to preserve the North Atlantic relationship, and we made a specific reference to the particularly sensitive position in which Mexico found itself.

At seven in the morning on March 17, while I was exercising in the parliamentary gym, Dan Costello showed up to say that the prime minister wanted to talk. Dan and I went down to Elinor Caplan's office, which was in the same building as the gym. Still dripping in sweat, I called Chrétien. It turned out that the number-two diplomat at the British High Commission had just phoned Claude Laverdure, the prime minister's foreign policy adviser. The United States and the United Kingdom were about to "shock and awe" Iraq, and they wanted answers to four questions by ten o'clock the next morning: Are we with them politically? Will we give them military support? Will we say so publicly? Are we willing to be involved in the reconstruction? Chrétien and I then had a long discussion on the phone, trying to craft the language for the statement he planned to make in the House that afternoon. Finally, at his request, I wrote out a draft in longhand and had it faxed to Claude Laverdure for revision and polish.

John McCallum and I met with Chrétien and some of his key advisers in his office just before Question Period. The only point of contention was between Eddie Goldenberg and me as to whether we should give the Americans advance warning. I thought it was the politic thing to do – a way to take some of the sting out of our decision. Eddie thought it was inappropriate for the prime minister to tell a foreign government before telling Parliament and the Canadian people. I backed down, even though I didn't agree. For months we had been discussing with the US government all kinds of matters pertaining to Iraq that we hadn't first informed Parliament or the Canadian people about, and this final decision was of vital interest to Washington. It certainly would have been appreciated on a personal level by Colin Powell and US ambassador Paul Cellucci.

Nevertheless, we all agreed that the prime minister's statement would take pains not to drive the Bush administration to some extreme reaction. At the insistence of John Manley in particular, part of whose job as finance minister was to keep the Canada-US border open for trade after 9/11, we added a final paragraph that our ships in the Gulf would continue their mission in the struggle against terrorism. John McCallum and I accompanied the prime minister down the stairs from his office and into the Commons, where he used Question Period to give his historic statement.

The moment he uttered the fateful words, "If military action proceeds without a new resolution of the Security Council, Canada will not participate," the House erupted into prolonged pandemonium, whether cheering or jeering, while Manley tried to make sure that the vital last paragraph would be heard.

When I phoned Colin Powell immediately after Question Period, his reaction was one of resigned regret. "Well, Canada is a sovereign nation," he said. "You have made a decision, Bill, and we respect it."

"And it's up to you to make your own decision," I replied. "I frankly think an invasion would be a mistake, because you're going to be trapped in Iraq for years. But even though we've decided not to join, we won't be out leading the charge against you."

March 17 also happened to be my sixty-fourth birthday, and Patrick phoned from Baghdad to wish me many happy returns. All I wanted to hear was when he was getting out of there, but he had decided to stay. In fact, he was on the front page of the *National Post* and on air from Baghdad most days that week, and I didn't think it helped matters that the international media had got wind of the fact that my son and Pierre Trudeau's son Alexandre happened to be there, as was the grandson of former Russian prime minister Yevgeny Primakov. As it turned out, the personal dimension of Patrick's being there gave me a certain credibility with many MPs, particularly in the Canadian Alliance. Myron Thompson, for example, a wild card from Alberta who rarely had a good word for the Liberals, had a son with the American forces in Iraq, and he used to come up to me to share his concern about our boys. Usually fierce political opponents, we actually struck a human chord over the risk our sons were sharing in the heart of battle, one a soldier, the other a reporter.

"The Americans accuse us of killing baby seals," said one of our caucus members from Newfoundland, "and then they go and drop a ton of bombs on hundreds of thousands of innocent people in Baghdad. What irony."

But the prime minister warned everybody not to attack the United States. "I urge you to be careful," he told the Cabinet and the caucus in the days that followed. "We're not anti-American. We just don't agree on this." I learned an interesting lesson in the fickleness of politics, however, when the standing ovation that Chrétien received from the Liberal MPs flipped into a bitter, impassioned internecine fight about his government's gun-control legislation and its significant cost overruns. To him, gun control was like Iraq, abortion, capital punishment, and election financing: ways to build a country different from the United States. "You have to sympathize with the P.M.," I wrote in my notes. "He's exhausted after one of the most difficult couple of weeks he's ever had, the public and caucus are cheering his decision, and now he has to face this crisis."

Unfortunately, some of our ministers and MPs, particularly on the left wing of the party, seemed quite delighted to poke the United States with a sharp stick. Like most of the war protesters, they weren't so much anti-American as anti-Bush. Frustrated with the Bush administration's unilateralism and its wish to impose its views and values on the rest of the world through military superiority, they were angry with Washington's policies, not at the United States of America itself. When Liberal MP Carolyn Parrish participated in a TV comedy show's satirical skit by stomping on a Bush doll, for example, she wasn't stomping on a figure of Uncle Sam. Even so, it was easy to dismiss her as a loose cannon. "So President Bush controls what every Republican wacko in Congress says about Canada?" I asked Paul Cellucci when he complained. "I don't think so."

Herb Dhaliwal's remark that Bush had let down the world "by not being a statesman" was particularly damaging because he was a member of the Cabinet. Although Chrétien no doubt preferred to keep under the radar, he had to treat Dhaliwal with the respect he deserved. In fact, Herb had business interests in the United States and was not, I knew, anti-American at heart. Yet the Americans were annoyed that he wasn't punished like some miscreant schoolboy, and they froze him out at the top.

In general, the Americans never understood the difference between the Canadian and the US Cabinet system. In Washington, Cabinet officers are employees of the president, not independent political actors who have a right to express their opinions publicly. In Ottawa, ministers, though beholden to Cabinet solidarity, have an important constituency of their own in domestic politics. That might be changing, however, as power in Western democracies becomes increasingly concentrated in the Prime Minister's Office. I remember having a conversation about this very issue with Jack Straw after Colin Powell told me that the US Cabinet never meets as a group, just one-on-one with the president. "'President' Blair does exactly the same," said Jack. According to him, the British Cabinet met perfunctorily, with meetings short and only as required to give legal imprimatur to decisions already taken, a situation that was often described in Britain as Blair's "sofa government" – government by the prime minister and a small group of advisors in Downing Street.

On March 25 I invited Ambassador Cellucci to come and have dinner in one of the small dining rooms at the Pearson Building, just the two of us with three aides. It was a really awkward occasion. Cellucci was mad as hell, and he didn't hesitate to tell me so. As a former governor of Massachusetts, an early supporter of George W. Bush, and a political player in the United States, he was a veteran of rough politics and a very tough bird. He certainly wasn't about to exchange diplomatic niceties with me or be intimidated by my position. "You're being politically opportunistic," he said in his thick Boston accent. "To reject the war but keep your ships there is really insulting. You're doing more than the Poles, who are nominally part of the coalition. Yet you won't give us your flag."

"In other words," I said, "you want our symbolic flag more than you want our practical help."

"To some extent, absolutely. Why aren't you with us? We're family."

Talking with him, I realized how misled he had been by his overreliance on the hawks in our Defence Department, his contacts in the business community, and the right-wing press. (Once, when I mentioned to my son that Cellucci had seen him on TV, Patrick replied, "If he's watching Global, he's watching the wrong channel.") He might have taken a more cautious view if he had bothered to talk with me and others, but his lack of familiarity with the full Canadian context, particularly the politics of Quebec, led him to expect that Canada would ultimately come onside – an expectation that he passed on to the president's chief of staff, Andy Card, and other close advisers to Bush in Washington. When those expectations were disappointed, he felt a sense of betrayal. Moreover, having given the White House totally misleading information, he was probably feeling personally embarrassed as well.

"I've got a problem, and you've got a problem," he said. "I've just got off the phone with Andy Card, and he wants to know why we're getting the shit kicked out of us by all these Canadian politicians. And he's given me a message to give to you: The prime minister of Canada needs to say something nice about the president of the United States, in public, soon."

Though too polite to show it, I was furious: Who did they think they were to speak that way about the leader of a sovereign country? Nevertheless, when I met with Mr. Chrétien the following day, I delivered the ambassador's message. When Dan asked me afterward what the response had been, I struggled for a moment to come up with the best image to describe the prime minister's reaction. "He made a face," I said, "like I had reached under the table, grabbed his balls, and turned them eleven times to the left."

The moment a country is at war, it's as though a switch is flicked. The mentality changes instantly. There's no longer as much room for the live-and-let-live attitude of old friends who have agreed to disagree or a generous appreciation of the other person's perspective. That's human nature and completely understandable. What we had to do was find a way of handling that dynamic constructively so that we neither fed it nor got burned by it. A major part of our diplomacy during this period was preoccupied with figuring out how to deal with the Americans in this mood. If we weren't with them, we risked being perceived as against them. Yet we were profoundly worried that, in this bellicose, triumphalist state of mind, they would go on to attack Syria or reshape the geopolitics of the Middle East. Despite Colin Powell's reassurances, my officials kept warning me that Canada had better get ready in the "quite likely" event that the United States began to think it could go anywhere and do anything because it had power and democracy on its side.

It was interesting to see how personal, emotional, and intense the issue of our relationship with the Americans became. Though most members of the public who phoned my department were strongly opposed to the war, some were furious that we were letting down our best friend at its time of need. Some calls came from Canadians whose cars had been attacked in Florida or California, from students who were having trouble getting US visas, and from businesses who had experienced slowdowns at the border. On the upside, America wasn't an abstraction for us, as it could be for the Europeans. It was a matrix of deep, insightful, and extraordinarily complicated personal relationships built up by individuals through daily contact and geographical proximity. Even in the darkest days, Colin Powell and I could have frank, human conversations about what was happening, as could John Manley with Tom Ridge. The members of the Canada–US Inter-Parliamentary Group drew on their close connections to keep the lines of communication open. Business partners spoke to each other by the hour, trying to put out the fires. So did academics and union leaders, families and friends. That whole elaborate nexus of connections and interaction really mattered – and the response was almost like a spontaneous social-action program to help heal the wounds.

When Chrétien spoke to the caucus on March 25, he addressed the issue of Canada-US relations. Though he believed strongly that once the decision was made, the less said about it the better, he worried not that we would lose business because of Iraq but that the Canadian economy would be negatively affected because of the real economic problems the United States was facing. If the States went into a recession, Canada would be hurt as the result of a shrinking American market. In the meantime, the United States still needed our oil, our resources, and our goods. No contracts were cancelled; no boycotts were mounted against our products.

"The United States isn't mad at us," he told the Cabinet, "but the Opposition and the business guys are doing their best to use the press to make sure the Americans do get mad at us, just as they did in 1993 when they yelled and screamed that Chrétien would never ratify NAFTA." Experience told me he was right. For months after the decision, I avoided the lounges at airports because whenever I entered one, I was set upon by every business executive in the room rushing over to scream at me for risking his exports to the United States or making his life uncomfortable in New York City.

In reality, any coalition members who assumed that they could count on an automatic reward from the United States turned out to be very naive. At one point Tony Blair was in deep trouble and needed a favour from the Americans. When he told the president, "You owe me one," the reply came back, "Sorry, but Congress won't deliver, and there's nothing I can do about it." And when the Polish government asked Bush to lift the visa requirement for Poles entering the United States, nothing happened, despite Poland's participation in the coalition. Whether in foreign policy or in business, it's difficult to translate a quid pro quo into a specific action that

26 With Mexican president Vicente Fox.

27 Brian Gable of the *Globe and Mail* captures my experience addressing the Canada-Israel Committee in March 2002.

28 With Israeli foreign minister Shimon Peres in Jerusalem, May 27, 2002.

29 With German foreign minister Joschka Fischer
in Berlin, February 1, 2002.

30 Greeting Russian president Vladimir Putin, Calgary, G8 Summit,
June 26, 2002.

31 With US secretary of state Colin Powell.

32 Hosting the G8 foreign ministers, Whistler, BC, June 2002.

33 Addressing the UN General Assembly, September 12, 2002.

35 A light moment with Igor Ivanov at the UN, September 2002.

34 Hard at work at the UN, September 23, 2003.

36 With UN secretary general Kofi Annan at the UN, September 16, 2002.

37 With Greek foreign minister George Papandreou and Turkish foreign minister Abdullah Gül as they announce their ratification of the Ottawa Treaty, or Mine-Ban Convention, September 26, 2003.

38 With Dominique de Villepin, Paris, September 2003.

39 With George W. Bush at the White House, April 30, 2004.

40 Brian Gable, "The Great Blank Iraq Policy,"
Globe and Mail, February 1, 2003.

41 One of my
proudest moments,
January 23, 2003.

42 With US ambassador Paul Cellucci, May 2003.

43 With Alan Beesley (*right*) on the occasion of Canada's ratification of the Third United Nations Convention on the Law of the Sea.

doesn't have its own benefit. Friendly sentiments are nice, goodwill is nicer, but they're rarely enough to cause people to hurt their own interests.

One evening I met a US senator at a dinner at the Canadian embassy in Washington. "I'm really busy," he said, "but I came tonight because I was in the army side-by-side with your troops in Korea, and we always stood together." I appreciated his words, but I was under no illusion that the conversation would have continued in the same tone if I had asked him to cast a vote in the Senate that his constituents wouldn't have liked. That's not the way the system works.

In the days that followed, the prime minister talked with Jacques Chirac, José María Aznar, Kofi Annan, Gerhard Schroeder, Silvio Berlusconi – but not George Bush. He wouldn't have minded talking to the president, but we weren't sure how to ask. If we tried and failed, we could imagine the headline in the *National Post:* "Bush refuses call from Chrétien." However, the prime minister wasn't worried. The polls showed great support across the country for his decision, and whenever Cellucci slammed us in public, Chrétien said, "The ambassador is giving oxygen to the Alliance, and this is a good thing. We need to keep them alive." I marvelled at how political he was. He could see the strategic advantage in everything.

On March 31 the communications committee of the Cabinet devoted an entire meeting to the issue. A lot of concern was expressed, particularly by its chair, Anne McLellan, that the anti-American statements being made in the media by ministers and backbenchers were muddying the message we wanted to get out. "What the hell is Dhaliwal doing?" she fumed. "Cellucci was right to say he was disappointed." Anne, an Alberta MP who tended to have a positive view of the United States anyway, had to work closely with the Americans on security issues before moving from the Justice portfolio to become health minister, and she worried that what she had achieved with them through friendly contact was going to be jeopardized by her colleagues' comments.

We talked about how to reverse the perception. Perhaps the prime minister could "make nice noises" about Bush, as Cellucci had requested when I met with him for dinner. Or perhaps we could help bring Canada, Mexico, and the United States back to working together by picking up the idea of integrating the Mexicans into NORAD. What struck me in that meeting was how everything related to communications vis-à-vis the United States. Nobody wondered what the Europeans or the Chinese or the Arab nations might think of our words or actions. It was all about Canada's bilateral relationship with the Americans. Again and again, while foreign minister, I observed how a preponderance of our foreign policy concerns had to revolve around the United States. That wasn't unreasonable; it was reality. As Talleyrand said, "La géographie détermine la diplomatie." In twentieth-century Europe, for example, most German and French foreign policy revolved around German-French relations, tragically in the case of the First and Second World Wars, more positively since the formation of the European Community. In North America, given the role of the United States as a world power and the direct economic consequences of our being neighbours, with all the advantages and disadvantages that entails, it's inevitable.

Iraq was a fine illustration of the complexity of the debate between our national values and our national interests. Many people took a black-and-white approach to it. The values side claimed, with reason, that invading Iraq was contrary to international law, bad for the stability of the world, and therefore wrong. The interests side claimed, not without reason, that Canada is totally dependent on the United States, both economically and for our security, and we've got to go with Washington on big decisions. But reality is rarely so black and white. I would make an equally strong argument that it was in our interests as a country to try to persuade the Americans not to invade Iraq, not only because the invasion was illegal and destabilizing but also because it would be bad for the United States. The situation in the Middle East during the years following 2003 would certainly support that proposition.

Trying to divide foreign policy issues into watertight compartments of values and interests is, to my mind, an academic game that practitioners can't afford to play. If we are to serve the best interests of Canada, we must work on the creation of an international system that reflects our values of peace, democracy, and respect for one another, and that encourages the development of human rights throughout the world. This approach in turn will enable us to get along better and guarantee international peace. That is the point where values and interests converge.

Despite all the negative talk in the media, I took pride in the fact that Canada came through this period with our good relations with the United States relatively undamaged. Unlike the French or the Germans, we always tried to remain respectful of the Americans. In fact, there were very few repercussions. At first it was made clear that, as a price for our decision, Canada would be frozen out of the "Five Eyes" – the signals-intelligence-sharing network that included the United States, the United Kingdom, Australia, and New Zealand. But the freeze lasted for only a few months and ended when the United States realized it was depriving itself of vital information from a reliable partner. And a visit by Bush to Ottawa, scheduled for May 5, was cancelled, though Colin Powell publicly emphasized the durability of Canada-US relations and assured us that the visit was merely postponed.

At a NATO foreign ministers' meeting in Brussels on April 3, the serious strains in the transatlantic relationship were evident from the raw nerves around the table. Canada, continuing our traditional role as a linchpin, tried then and during the coming months to bridge the gap between the Americans and those in Europe who were opposed to the war. Luckily Colin Powell was a peacemaker by nature, so the meetings of the NATO foreign ministers weren't nearly as tense as those of the NATO defence ministers, where Donald Rumsfeld heaped scorn on those who had not been supportive. In fact, most of us still felt a lot of goodwill toward Colin personally and wanted to keep strengthening his position in the Bush administration. He retained a lot of credibility, despite his unfortunate presentation at the United Nations, and seemed oddly reinvigorated. He and I even joked about the difficulties each of us had had with Paul Cellucci.

That didn't stop Joschka Fischer from jumping up and saying, in pretty sharp terms, exactly how stupid he thought the war in Iraq was. To which Colin shot back that bashing the Americans was only a convenient tool to boost Joschka's popularity in the polls and that allies shouldn't behave that way with each other for domestic political reasons. Like everything in life, there was a certain degree of truth on both sides. Opposing the war was both sound policy and good politics in Germany, as it was in Canada. Indeed, Colin once turned on me and said, "You're just being political. If people don't support you, you should have the courage to tell them they're wrong."

"Well, I don't think you should go to war unless you've got the support of your population. That's not political courage; it's political craziness," I replied. "Sure, there are times when you have to disagree with popular opinion and try to persuade the population to do what you think is right, but to drag my country into a war that 80 percent of Canadians think is a bad idea is bound to fail." But if popular opinion had some influence on the Chrétien government's decision, as it should have, that was mostly because we thought the Canadian people's judgment was sound on this issue. And it has proved even more so in retrospect. Some of the same business executives and military officers who gave me hell later came up and said, "Thank God you didn't jump when we screamed."

Now that the Americans were in the middle of combat, and certain to win, the talk began to shift toward the future reconstruction and where to go from there. For months we had been asking the Americans about what would happen post-conflict. How did they expect to put the pieces back together after they had broken all the china in the shop? Because the planning for the war was completely in the hands of the US Defense Department, almost no one from the State Department or anywhere else was thinking about it. The military guys seemed to imagine they would defeat Saddam Hussein and be out of Iraq a few weeks later, with everything sweetness and light. It was incredible. They put themselves in a position where they had ownership of this terrible, complicated mess with no idea how to handle it, except to shrug "Oh well, stuff happens in war." From the point of view of global politics and the Middle East, it was totally insane. There were plenty of intelligent people in the American and British foreign services with high levels of experience and sophistication in dealing with post-conflict administrations, yet it seemed as if the people in charge were simply ignoring them.

During a long conversation I had with Igor Ivanov, the foreign minister of Russia, on April 6, 2003, it became apparent to me that, though he felt the Americans had made a terrible mistake, it was not in the Russian interest to see them defeated once they had gone in. "The war brings destruction and destabilization," he said. "It's important to end it soon with as few victims as possible." Igor found the Americans still very militant, even Colin Powell, and very reluctant to make full use of the United Nations.

Once a new government was formed in Iraq, the question of reconstruc-tion inevitably arose. "The U.S. plans to establish an occupation adminis-tration at first," Igor told me, based on meetings he had had with Powell in Brussels and Condoleezza Rice in Moscow. "We believe that, if it does, it will have to accept full responsibility for the occupation. They have an idea that some responsibilities will be given to NATO, the European Union, and the UN, but we disagree. Until the war is over, it's too soon to discuss the precise role of the UN, but they need to make diplomatic contact with Kofi Annan to discuss the generalities, not the specifics. At the same time we must start discussions in the Security Council about its role, inter-national law, and so forth, because this will not be the last crisis. Powell said they won't wage war again, but——." He even suspected that an attack on the Russian ambassador's car, which had occurred in Baghdad that day, was a deliberate provocation by US soldiers.

We also wanted to go the UN route and were troubled by the idea of asking Canadian taxpayers to help clean up the Americans' mess. Never-theless, we had already decided that good relations with Washington were more important than restricting our humanitarian operations to the United Nations out of dogmatic principle. We promised more than $300 million in relief and later joined with other NATO countries in sending military advisers to Jordan to train the new Iraqi defence force.

As the Iraq issue began to fade into the background, I delivered a major speech to the Canada-US Law Institute in Cleveland, Ohio, on April 11, 2003. It tried to set out the general context of Canada-US relations for an American audience in the aftermath of the invasion. "As close friends we can diverge on our approach," I told them, "but that doesn't stop us from being close friends." I justified our opposition to the war not in terms of its craziness but because we felt that "disarming Iraq by force would require the greatest possible international legitimacy," which was diplomatic speak for the United Nations. Then I moved on to talk about what Canada was doing to help – humanitarian aid, reconstruction, governance – even though we hadn't participated in the invasion. But mostly I wanted to remind the Americans why Canada is important to the United States.

If it used to be good to fly under the radar or be taken for granted, that wasn't a workable strategy anymore. Because of 9/11, because of Iraq, the border was thickening every day, and our people and products were having a tougher time getting into the United States. Thanks to distortions from their media and some of their politicians who should have known better, many Americans now saw Canada as a breeding ground for terrorists, and most of them believed that Japan was their largest trading partner. It took effort to let them know that more goods cross the bridge at Windsor than go to Japan. If we spoke before a Chicago audience, we had to remind them that Canada is the number-one export destination for Illinois. If in California, the same was true for California. More than the trade link was the economic interdependence in terms of investment, NAFTA standards, energy, and so forth. And most important of all was the need for Canada and the United States to work together on continental security and international terrorism.

On November 20, 2003, I made a similar argument in a speech to the Chicago Council on Foreign Relations. Afterward, I asked some of the businesspeople in the audience why, in their view, France had paid a price for its opposition to the war, whereas Canada hadn't. "Because you guys didn't rub our noses in it," was the response. Unlike President Chirac, Mr. Chrétien didn't go around stirring up opposition to the invasion in public. On the contrary, he insisted that we keep the level of rhetoric down. The United States would make its own decision as a sovereign country; Canada would do the same; and it has been a constant theme of Canadian-American relations that the less they talk about us, the better off we are. The prime minister certainly shared that view. He also believed that Canadian support of US positions has more credibility if we are seen by the rest of the world as an independent actor rather than a US satellite.

The whole thread of the speech was that we need each other, but we are not the same people. We have shared values of freedom and democracy, and our global goals for peace and prosperity are the same, but we also come from differing political traditions that produce different results, whether health care or gun control, gay rights or official bilingualism. Those differences aren't important enough to destroy our capability to do things together. On the contrary, our different views of multilateralism and interdependence mean that Canada can be complementary to the United States on the global stage, as opposed to being a mere appendage.

As a superpower with unique responsibilities, I pointed out, the United States inevitably looks at the world differently than does a middle power such as Canada. As a result, we approach the international multilateral system with a different emphasis. That isn't a threat or a criticism; it's merely a fact.

The reaction I got from that audience in Illinois was mostly positive, and I'd wager the same would have been true of an audience in Florida or California. There wasn't the same resentment toward Canada as was widely felt toward France, for example, and whatever anger certain people in the White House might have felt at the time wasn't picked up by the population at large. They knew we weren't anti-American. As well, within the United States itself, there was substantial agreement with the Canadian position in opposing the war. "Mr. Graham," a woman said to me after a speech I gave in San Francisco in 2004, "there are more people in California who think the way Canadians do than there are in the whole of Canada."

Any anger that may have existed was soon erased by the deep nature of our intertwined relationship and the broad degree of mutual goodwill that gives cover to disagreements in a way that isn't necessarily true of other countries.

AMONG THE MANY unfortunate casualties of the Iraq war was the public's trust in the integrity of the intelligence services that governments and their people rely on to make sound public-policy choices. For a long time everyone assumed that if the governments of the United States or the United Kingdom vouched for the reliability of their information, we could believe it and act accordingly. But all the subsequent investigations proved that the facts had been invented or manipulated by senior officials to back up their decisions, with no one from the intelligence community standing up and shouting the truth.

When the intelligence community is no longer trusted as an independent source and is seen as merely the mouthpiece of whoever is in power at any given moment, it lacks all credibility – a very unfortunate setback for Western democracy, which needs solid facts to make proper decisions. If you overlay the complexity that Canada was a party to the International Criminal Court as well as the United Nations Charter, and therefore prohibited from using force illegally, the murkiness of the evidence coming out of Washington and London made it much harder to justify going to war.

That was precisely the problem Tony Blair had. He made a decision to go to war without a clear legal justification, without the country united behind him, and without a general trust in the intelligence services or the credibility of their political masters. As a consequence, when David Cameron's government advocated intervening in Syria on humanitarian grounds, its motion was defeated in an August 2013 vote in the Commons, in my view largely because a majority of the British people simply didn't believe what Cameron said were the facts. And the same skepticism existed in the United States, even with a president of the integrity and credentials of Barack Obama. Democracies cannot be led into war very easily. George Bush got away with it, but later American presidents will pay the price. The people have longer memories than is often presumed.

Another consequence of Iraq was reflected in subsequent debates over the Responsibility to Protect (R2P) doctrine. Though R2P had originally been developed to rally the international community to intervene against genocide and other heinous crimes, the whole notion of "humanitarian" intervention was cast in a much more questionable light in the new era of American unilateralism. Nobody was eager to hand another tool to the great powers – particularly those in the West – and let them use it as an instrument to act on their own. Thus, the R2P doctrine, in the version adopted by the United Nations General Assembly at the World Summit in 2005, reaffirmed the role played by the Security Council for the precise purpose of curbing interventionism by the Western powers.

In any event, different facts make different law. Thus, NATO's excursion into Kosovo was legitimate, even though it lacked the legal authorization of a Security Council resolution, both because it was a regional security measure that had been authorized by all the European countries that were involved and because the facts of an unacceptable slaughter of innocent civilians were plain for all to see. In the case of Iraq, if the United States and the United Kingdom had rallied the international community behind them at the Security Council, fine, but that presumed their having facts that could be objectively determined. And if those facts had proved that Saddam Hussein did indeed have chemical or nuclear WMD and the capacity to use them, I think that information would have tipped the balance for us. But, without the proper facts, there wasn't the international support, and without international support on their side, we didn't think they had international law on their side either.

13

PICKING UP THE PIECES

Al-Qaeda's attack on New York and Washington, provoking as it did the Bush administration's figurative war on terror and its literal war against Iraq, broke the progress the world had been making away from absolute state sovereignty toward universal human rights. Suddenly, in the most powerful country on earth, national security took precedence over the security of the individual. Though Canada was caught up in the same pressure to protect our citizenry from internal and external danger, neither our Charter of Rights nor our political culture allowed the Canadian government to go to the extremes we witnessed in the United States.

For more than a year, all through the Iraq crisis, Canada-US relations were strained by the personal tragedy of Maher Arar, a Canadian citizen of Syrian origin. On September 26, 2002, Arar was flying to Montreal from Tunisia via New York City. When he arrived in the United States he was taken aside, interrogated, and sent to the Metropolitan Detention Center in Brooklyn. His family reported him missing three days later, but it took a full week before the Canadian consul was given access to him. A few days after that, he was gone, without any notice to our consul.

The Americans were remarkably unforthcoming, and we learned what had happened only over time and in bits. Eventually it came out that US Deputy Attorney General Larry Thompson had signed off on a report that concluded that allowing Arar to return to Canada was counter to US security interests. Instead, he was ordered to be "removed" from the United

States and rendered to Jordan, where he was beaten before being shipped off to Syria. The Syrians imprisoned him on suspicion of belonging to a terrorist organization, though he was never formally charged with a crime. During his imprisonment, as we later found out, he was brutally treated and tortured by the Syrian authorities.

Once Arar was in Syria, new legal and diplomatic problems arose. We took the position that, because he was a Canadian, international law gave us the right to see him and to assure ourselves that he was being properly treated. The Syrians countered that, because he was also a Syrian citizen, we had no rights to protect him under the Vienna Convention on Consular Relations, which gives countries access to their nationals to assist them and ensure that they are treated in accordance with appropriate humanitarian norms and standards. As with the tragic case of Zahra Kazemi, the Iranian Canadian photographer killed by Iranian prison authorities in 2003, the issue was complicated by their dual nationality. It was further complicated by the fact that, like Kazemi, Arar was a dual citizen of the country in which he was jailed. Syria simply refused to recognize him as a Canadian. "He's our national, in our state," was the implication of their blunt refusal, "and if we choose to torture one of our own citizens, nobody else has any legal status or claim or right to intervene in international law." Though the Syrians were initially willing to grant us consular access as a kind of courtesy, that access ceased after a number of visits.

Meanwhile, I was being attacked in the House by the Opposition for defending a "suspected terrorist" and in the press for failing to defend a Canadian citizen. To make matters even more complicated, the general public tends to assume that if a Canadian is being held in a foreign prison, he or she is either innocent or being mistreated. Neither is necessarily true. In fact, Canada had been burned quite badly some years before when a Canadian couple, Christine Lamont and David Spencer, were arrested in Brazil on kidnapping charges. In Canada, there were widespread calls in the media for their release, and as an MP I was lobbied by a campaign to free these "innocent" Canadians: they had been falsely accused and falsely convicted, the Brazilian police were corrupt and incompetent, their imprisonment was an outrage, and so forth. It wasn't until years later, and after much lobbying activity on their behalf by the Canadian government, that the two admitted that they had been involved in the kidnapping and that they were, in fact, members of an extreme left-wing political group looking to use the ransom money to fund revolutionary activity in El Salvador.

But it was the Ahmed Khadr case that really rankled the RCMP, CSIS, and some officials in my department. Khadr, a citizen of Canada and Egypt, had been arrested by the Pakistanis in 1995 on suspicion of being involved in the bombing of the Egyptian embassy in Islamabad. At the request of Khadr's family, Prime Minister Chrétien personally intervened with the prime minister of Pakistan, asking her to ensure that Khadr received a fair trial. Eventually he was released. It later turned out, however, that Khadr did have links to Osama bin Laden and Ayman al Zawahiri, and he was eventually killed in a firefight with the Pakistani military in 2003.

The Khadr case strongly influenced the views of Canadian security officials about what should be done for Arar. Robert Fry, my senior adviser charged with consular affairs, urged me to take risks in securing Arar's return, but many voices were warning me not to get involved with the case of a suspected terrorist. "Be careful, Minister," they said, "Arar is a person of interest to the Americans, and you may be working to release somebody who's dangerous to Canadian security. You risk looking like a total chump."

"I understand what you're saying from the viewpoint of security," I said. "But my responsibility as minister is consular protection. Whether Arar is guilty or innocent will be determined, but he has to be given the protection of law. He's a Canadian citizen. He has the right to be treated appropriately and not tortured. He has the right to a fair trial. I'm not judging the outcome, but he's entitled to certain rights – and that's what I'm fighting for."

International law itself is a balance between power and principle. Powerful states have always been able to bend it in directions that best serve their purposes. The case of Omar Khadr, son of Ahmed, was yet another example. He was picked up in Afghanistan in July 2002, accused of killing an American soldier during a firefight with American special forces. Some argued he was an innocent bystander. Others claimed he was just a kid who had been shot at and responded in self-defence. Still others saw him as a victim of his family's involvement in al-Qaeda. Whatever the circumstances, Omar was seriously injured, received medical care and, after being detained at the Bagram air base for several months, was transported to the US military prison in Guantánamo Bay, Cuba, where he was held for trial.

There were two incontrovertible facts that brought Omar Khadr to my attention: he was a Canadian citizen, and he had been only fifteen years old at the time of the incident.

Omar Khadr was detained by the United States as an "unlawful alien enemy combatant." The term was used by the Americans to justify the imprisonment in Guantánamo of suspected terrorists picked up in a foreign country, and it was not recognized in any category of international humanitarian law by anybody other than the United States. Had Khadr been regarded as a captured combatant, and thus as a prisoner of war, he would have been entitled to combatant immunity, since killing another combatant in conflict is not a war crime. Had he been treated as a non-combatant accused of murder, he would have been entitled to the due process available under the US criminal justice system. He got neither.

When the Chrétien government requested consular access in August 2002, the Americans said no, and when I raised the case of Omar Khadr with Colin Powell on November 14, 2002, he replied, "Look, he killed a fine young American. He's gone to Guantánamo Bay. He'll be treated by the justice system with the proper American justice – and that's all I'm prepared to say about it." Ultimately, we chose to accept the Americans' word that Khadr was being treated properly under US law and the rules set down by the Red Cross – a judgment I subsequently came to question the more I learned about the conditions and miscarriages of justice at Guantánamo. I regret that I – and the Chrétien, Martin, and Harper governments – were not more aggressive in pushing to get Omar Khadr transferred back to Canada. This failure was compounded by the travel of Canadian officials to Guantánamo Bay to interrogate Omar for intelligence purposes, and by government inaction after Khadr informed these officials that he was being mistreated by the Americans. The Government of Canada should have been – and in the future must be – more clear-sighted and resolute in dealing with cases like Omar Khadr's.

This was the new American reality we were forced to confront in the Arar case. I struggled to determine how his deportation to Syria had occurred in the first place. It was impossible to find out exactly what had been done or who was responsible. I couldn't get a straight story from anybody. Colin Powell and Ambassador Cellucci initially claimed that Canadian authorities knew of the reasons for Arar's deportation and that

Canadian officials had agreed, tacitly or otherwise, to the Americans' plan to deport him to Syria. But neither the RCMP nor the CSIS people would talk to me directly. I had to go through my officials, and the results came back full of ambiguities.

"But my people tell me he's implicated in terrorist cells and they had every right to do what they did," Powell said when I next raised the issue with him at the NATO summit in Prague on November 21, 2002.

"Nothing," I replied heatedly, "gives your people the right to pick a Canadian off the street, throw him in jail, and then ship him off to be tortured in a foreign country. What happened to due process?"

"These are different days," he said, dismissing the whole business.

They were indeed different days if the government of the United States saw fit to behave in this way, as Colin himself experienced. One day, when visiting him in Washington, I found him really upset and asked what was wrong. "This afternoon," he said, "I was supposed to see a leading journalist from Pakistan to discuss foreign policy, but he disappeared this morning. A black car pulled up as he walked out the door from a meeting. He was pushed into the back seat and swept away. My office made some inquiries. Turns out he's been picked up by the Homeland Security guys and is in the slammer somewhere. I'm fit to be tied. Here's an important journalist on his way to meet me, and they grab him off the street and throw him in jail like he's some sort of criminal."

I myself experienced the arbitrary nature of the new reality, in a minor way, when I was Paul Martin's defence minister. One day, I went to check in at the Toronto airport for a flight to Ottawa and found I was on the US "no fly" list that Air Canada had dumped into its system. As a result, a minister of the Crown, travelling in Canada to a Cabinet meeting, had to be cleared by the RCMP. What a bizarre situation. As it turned out, the problem had to do with another Bill Graham, but no matter how many apologies and assurances I received, I was unable to clear my name once and for all. Eventually I had to book my flights as "Hon. William Graham," which struck many ticket agents as either pretentious or oddly Chinese.

Months went by, and we were unable to make any progress on the Arar file. In the spring of 2003 I went to Wayne Easter, the solicitor general, and said I wanted to make representations to the Syrian government to get

Maher Arar released into Canadian custody. That would require, in my opinion, a letter from both of us stating that Arar was totally innocent. "Bill," Wayne said, "I'll never get the police to say that somebody's totally innocent. Do you know what I mean?"

"Okay, but would they lay charges against him here in Canada with the evidence they have?" I pressed.

"No," came the answer, "there's no basis on which charges could be laid in Canada."

"So let's tell the Syrian authorities that." But I couldn't even get that. Eventually, Chrétien agreed to write a letter to President Assad on behalf of the Government of Canada. It asked the Syrians to return Arar to Canada and stated there was no obstacle, from our point of view, to allowing him back in the country.

In June 2003 I met with Arar's wife, Dr. Monia Mazigh, to brief her on what we were doing. She was incredibly impressive, both in terms of her resolve and her effectiveness in drawing attention to her husband's cause. In August we finally got permission for Leo Martel, the Canadian consul in Syria, to meet with Arar again and ensure that he wasn't being mistreated. However, it wasn't a private meeting, so Arar was forced to speak in front of his captors. Though there were conflicting accounts over what he actually said during the meeting, the information I received had Arar denying that he was being beaten and tortured. And that's what I told reporters on August 14 when they asked me.

Because I was under the impression that Arar had been able to speak fairly openly, I put aside my caution and said, "I've just been speaking to my officials in Ottawa, who have been on the phone to Damascus this morning. Mr. Arar has been visited by our consular officials in jail. Our consular officials have assured us that he's in good physical condition. He personally, totally rejects all allegations of torture. He was interviewed independently by our consular officials, and he has stated that his condition is better than it was before we started to intervene on his behalf." Of course, as we later discovered, that information was wrong.

With public support for Arar growing alongside the media coverage, I met with Syria's foreign minister, Farouk al-Sharaa, during the annual meeting of the UN General Assembly and got him to commit to doing his utmost to resolve Arar's case. But the Syrian intelligence officer who was with him suddenly cut in. "The foreign minister can tell you what you like," he said, "but forget it – we're never going to release Arar. In fact, if his wife doesn't stop dragging Syria's name through the mud, it's going to be worse for him."

That made me more cautious, I admit. Now, whenever reporters questioned me about Arar, I simply said, "I'm not prepared to discuss what I know or don't know about this case. You guys want me to give you a quote so you can have your story, but what if that causes more trouble for the guy in jail? The publicity over here isn't necessarily helping him over there."

Grasping at straws, I raised the issue with Amr Moussa, the secretary general of the Arab League, during his trip to Ottawa on October 1. I felt comfortable doing so because of the lunch we had had at the UN the year before – just one more example of how a casual encounter can translate into a diplomatic intervention in international affairs. "Amr," I said, "we have this terrible problem. There's a Canadian in custody in Syria who we fear is being tortured. This is not helpful, it seems to me, to what you're trying to achieve in the Arab League or to the perception of Arab countries around the world." He later told me that he had made representations to the Syrians, and I think his intervention helped.

On October 4, 2003, when I was in Rome for a Canada-EU summit, I was woken up in the middle of the night with the news that the Syrians were going to release Arar. I subsequently called Monia Mazigh to share the good news, and by October 6 Maher Arar was back in Canada and reunited with his family. Shortly afterward, I met with him and his wife, and he shared his disturbing story of his deportation by the Americans, his detainment in Syria, and the defamation of his character. He asked my help in getting the government to dispel the false rumours that had been circulated by the media.

Meanwhile, the Americans were still insisting that Canadian officials had signed off on the decision to deport Arar to Syria. "What is justice in this Kafkaesque situation?" I wrote in my notes. "The most disturbing element is the Americans." On November 5 Chrétien told the House of Commons, in response to criticism from Alliance leader Stephen Harper, "I cannot understand why the Opposition wants to blame the Government of Canada for the actions of the Americans."

The Americans were not pleased. The next day Canada's ambassador to Washington, Michael Kergin, was summoned to the White House to meet with the National Security Council to discuss the Arar case. The affair was taking on all the characteristics of a major diplomatic incident. On November 6 Paul Cellucci invited me to come to his official residence to talk about it over a couple of whiskeys. "I'm going to do something that is actually illegal," he said. "I'm going to share with you information I got from our intelligence services." Though the Mounties had been keeping an eye on Arar, Cellucci told me, they were shocked to learn that he had been deported. In other words, Cellucci confirmed that the Mounties weren't involved in the decision to render Arar to Syria. My esteem for Cellucci rose at that moment, and if we never became close friends, we did develop a new level of trust.

Thanks to the subsequent investigation by Justice Dennis O'Connor, we now know that Maher Arar was not guilty of any offence; nor did he participate in any sort of illicit activity. O'Connor also found that the RCMP had shared highly inaccurate information with US officials, unfairly characterizing Arar as an Islamic extremist and suspected terrorist, information that, O'Connor states, the Americans probably relied upon in deciding to render Arar to Syria. In 2007, Arar received an official apology and a substantial settlement from the Canadian government, though no amount of money could atone for what he had suffered.

During my testimony before the O'Connor commission, I expressed my regret about what had happened to Arar. Knowing what we knew in hindsight, I acknowledged, my officials and I could have done things differently, though we had done our best with the information we had at the time. I shook hands with him on my way out, and he thanked me. "That's the closest a Canadian official has ever come to making an apology," he said.

The Arar incident had consequences for Canada's relations with Syria and for our perceptions of the Arab world, but it also highlighted the new degree of tension in Canada-US relations. Given how tightly bound we are in the security of North America, we don't want to do anything that might stop the Americans from sharing information with us or stop us from sharing information with them. But if we share information, we must be able to trust that it will be handled in an honest way. In September 2004, for example, when the Americans left Canada out of a new tripartite intelligence-sharing committee on terrorism that it created with the United Kingdom and Australia, I noted in my journal, "What a mockery this makes of North American defence! How can the Americans be that narrow-minded and short-sighted?" And, more and more, it seemed that the "war on terror" was being used to justify actions that broke that trust.

One day, I remember, as I was speaking with Colin Powell and Javier Solana, Colin started pressing us about the draconian measures needed to fight terrorism. Javier was furious. "I'm a Spaniard," he said, "and we've had more people blown up in the last twenty years than died on 9/11. The British have had to deal with the IRA blowing up people in downtown London for decades. Typical of you Americans, you think you're the first persons who've ever had to deal with this problem, as if it's never happened before it happened to you, and you've got the only way to deal with it. We've dealt with far worse, and you insist on giving us lessons in how to respond."

ON MAY 14, 2004, before the working meeting of the G8 foreign ministers in Washington, DC, we were invited to go as a group to the White House for a short meet-and-greet and photo op with President Bush. Something was up, we suspected, because it was highly unusual for a president to bother himself with foreign ministers. After breakfast, we were herded onto a bus for the trip across town.

Suddenly my cell phone rang. It was my son, Patrick, who was back in Iraq reporting on the American occupation. Though he had, thankfully, survived the invasion, he had had many close calls. One of the most serious had occurred on April 8, 2003, when a US tank shell hit the upper floors of the hotel where he and hundreds of other foreign journalists were staying. Fortunately, he had taken my advice, which I had once heard attributed to King Hussein of Jordan, to stay near the ground floor in case somebody starts shooting at you. "Where are you, Dad?" he now asked.

"I'm in Washington. In fact, I'm on my way to meet the president in the White House."

"Oh, that's interesting," he said. "When you see your friend Colin Powell, tell him that I'm in Fallujah, and I'm trying to run a humanitarian escape route to get some women and children out of here in the middle of an action. The Airborne are shooting at everything. We can't get anybody across the bridge."

When Colin greeted us as we entered the Roosevelt Room, I said, "I've just been talking to my son. He's in Fallujah."

"Really? Who's he embedded with?"

"He's embedded with the other guys, and your people are shooting at him. You should open a humanitarian corridor to let people out of there."

"I'm not interfering with troop movements, Bill. Tell your son he's crazy." From then on, whenever I came across Colin at some meeting, he would say, "Where's that crazy son of yours now?" He once teased Paul Martin to be careful of me – I had some very suspicious associations.

When President Bush entered the room that day, he was on a full-charm offensive, calling us all by our first names and saying how much he needed our help in these difficult times. But the mood grew solemn when he addressed the recent revelations about the sadistic treatment of prisoners by American soldiers at Abu Ghraib. Colin told us that the photographs that had not been made public were worse than those we had seen. He called the scandal a disgrace to his military and vowed to get to the root of it. "We're a nation of values," he said. For his part, Bush said he was revolted by what had happened in the prison, calling it "an un-American thing to do," as though the soldiers who had participated weren't real Americans. "Evil entered their hearts, their souls," he said, "and they've betrayed America."

Nobody knew how to respond. Then Joschka Fischer, being Joschka, broke the silence by saying, "Surely, Mr. President, something like this could not have happened without orders from the very highest echelons." I don't think he was pointing the finger at Bush himself – more at the Pentagon – but the rest of us were taken aback at this direct challenge to an American president.

In September 2003 I accompanied Chrétien to New York for what he knew would be his farewell speech to the UN General Assembly. At the end of his speech, leaders and diplomats formed a long line to shake his hand, offer their congratulations, say goodbye, wish him well, and thank him for all he had done. He clearly inspired a tremendous amount of esteem and affection in capitals around the world, not least for the experience and values with which he handled the crisis in Iraq.

I got one more insight into how he and his mind worked when, driving back to our hotel with him, I raised an issue that had concerned me for a very long time, first as a law professor and then as chair of SCFAIT: the Law of the Sea Convention. In 1970 the Trudeau government – in which Chrétien was then minister of Indian affairs and northern development – passed the Arctic Waters Pollution Prevention Act, extending Canada's regulatory jurisdiction to a hundred nautical miles off our shores on the grounds that the delicate Arctic Ocean required a particular type of protection against unforeseen threats. An oil spill, after all, is no respecter of national sovereignty, and the consequences in the sensitive Arctic environment would have lasting effects.

However worthy the intent, the act clearly violated the prevailing conception of the law of the sea, which gave us limited jurisdiction off the coast. Though Canadian governments have generally been strong supporters of international law, this extension was a demonstration of its limits. We were in the position of violating the rules-based order we favoured, but we persuaded ourselves we were doing so to make a better rule. At the same time we gave notice to the International Court of Justice that we were withdrawing from its jurisdiction over disputes related to the Trudeau government's new law. We thereby acknowledged tacitly that we were in violation of international law as it was then understood.

International lawyers use the term *de lege ferenda,* "law in the making," meaning law in its emergent state rather than law as actually accepted, and we hoped we could help to facilitate a more effective law of the sea. As it happened, one came out of the Third UN Conference on the Law of the Sea, which ran from 1973 to 1982 and was set in motion by the Maltese ambassador to the UN, Arvid Pardo. Malta was one of a group of states, most of them surrounded by water, that wanted a law of the sea that would protect their continental shelves and regulate the development of mineral resources on the seabed as part of what Pardo called "the common heritage of mankind." Another group, consisting of the traditional maritime powers such as Britain and the United States, looked at the law of the sea mainly in terms of freedom of navigation. They therefore resisted constraints on the movements of their navies, especially through waters like the Malacca Straits and the Northwest Passage.

The Law of the Sea Convention (UNCLOS) that was opened for ratification in 1982 included a regime for seabed resource development, arbitration procedures, and a framework of concentric zones of diminishing degrees of jurisdiction and regulatory authority. These zones ranged from inland waters under almost complete national sovereignty to exclusive economic areas extending two hundred nautical miles from shore or even farther in the case of the continental shelf. UNCLOS reflected Canadian sensibilities in providing a legal and administrative framework for what would otherwise be a free-for-all, but its potential constraints on even the most powerful countries prevented its ratification by the United States. I became familiar with it through my teaching and from participation in the Canadian Council on International Law, which brings together scholars and practitioners, as well as from my acquaintance with Alan Beesley, a legal scholar and our ambassador to the Law of the Sea Conference. We used the Law of the Sea Treaty negotiations as a tool to plug the hole that allowed people to pollute the oceans. There's the Arctic clause (the "Canada clause"), article 234 of UNCLOS, which basically made what we had done legal by giving every state jurisdiction to regulate marine pollution from vessels in ice-covered areas within the exclusive economic zone.

Although Canada had signed UNCLOS in 1982, we still hadn't ratified it by 2003. In the British parliamentary system, the Crown ratifies treaties, not Parliament, and that meant it had to be ratified by the Cabinet. But no one had done so, primarily because of objections from Newfoundland, which was worried that the convention's provisions would weaken our ability to protect our fishing rights in the Grand Banks. That was, in my opinion, a completely wrong interpretation of what UNCLOS was about. Whenever the issue of ratification had come up before, Newfoundland objected. What was particularly egregious was the fact that Newfoundland was developing oil and gas reserves that Canada could own solely by virtue of UNCLOS – which conferred on coastal states jurisdiction over and ownership of the oil, gas, or minerals attached to the continental shelf. Since all the jurisdiction we were claiming in the Arctic was anchored on UNCLOS, Canada absolutely needed it. We had been a principal actor in negotiating it, we had been one of the original signatories in 1982, and yet, when I entered the Cabinet in 2002, we still were not a party to it because of Newfoundland's objections.

"Prime Minister," I said, "I've been talking to the legal department, and they're asking why we haven't ratified the Law of the Sea Convention. It's crazy. We were one of the creators of the treaty, Alan Beesley spent fifteen years of his life working on it, and it was seen as a huge triumph of Canadian foreign policy, yet we still haven't ratified it. Even the Americans are now thinking of signing it, and you know how much they hate signing international treaties. However, they're now realizing that it's dangerous not to be a part of this universal convention." I suggested that ratifying this international instrument would add to his legacy and that it would put us in a stronger position to establish our claims in the North.

"I've tried to get it ratified on a couple of occasions," he said, "but that requires a Cabinet decision – and each time the Cabinet minister from Newfoundland starts an unholy row. I don't like to push things through over their objections, so we don't do it."

"But this isn't just about Newfoundland," I argued. "It's crucial to Canada. One province shouldn't be able to hold up such an important measure."

He agreed with me and, as a lawyer, understood it. "Well, if you're so smart, Professor, why don't you find a way to ratify it?"

In fact, after talking it over with the clerk of the Privy Council, Alex Himelfarb, he found a way himself: he buried it in an annex. The way Cabinet meetings work is you discuss the items on the agenda and then, when all the business is done, you have a chance to talk about the items attached in the annexes to the documents. "Any problems with any of them?" Mr. Chrétien used to ask before ending the meetings at twelve o'clock on the dot. If there were no problems, they were adopted. If someone had an objection to one, it was pulled back for future consideration. Most times no minister even read what was in the annexes unless an official in the department warned us to take a look at them.

"I'm telling you," he said to me before the meeting, "if there's an objection, this isn't going to work."

As noon approached, I was on tenterhooks, barely able to breathe, so anxious was I to see this done. I had promised my department that, after twenty-one years of waiting, now was the moment that would make it or break it. The suspense was excruciating. "Any objections to the annexes?" the prime minister finally asked. No one raised a peep. "None? Fine, they're adopted."

As we left the room he gave me a sly wink and said, "You've got your Law of the Sea, Professor."

"Thank you, Prime Minister, but it's your Law of the Sea – it's Canada's Law of the Sea."

"And you can go sign the instrument of ratification," he added.

I invited Alan Beesley, who had been our principal negotiator. "This is the proudest day of my life," he said as we walked into the Railway Committee Room on Parliament Hill, where the signing ceremony was to take place. Much of his career had gone into UNCLOS, and here he was at this exciting moment after years of effort. As for me, I felt I had done my job as the foreign minister of Canada, which was to advance our country's foreign policy objectives.

When the premier of Newfoundland heard the news, he was furious. The next day the prime minister said, "I got a call from Danny Williams. *You* are going to call him back, not me." So I did.

"What the hell have you been doing," Williams shouted, but after five minutes of discussion he calmed down.

"Seriously," I said, "you're a lawyer. You know Newfoundland is using the Law of the Sea Convention to give you oil and gas – which, by the way, belongs to Canada, not to you." UNCLOS gave the resources to the whole country, not to one province, but that was a different fight.

Ratification was now a fait accompli, and Danny Williams wasn't one to hold a grudge. Indeed, when I later served as leader of the Opposition, I came to know him better and to appreciate his political acumen and his passionate advocacy on behalf of his province.

MEANWHILE, FOR REASONS to which I was not privy, the forces around Paul Martin had manoeuvred to move the leadership convention ahead from February 2004 to November 2003. Although I was not involved in what was a decision of the party executive, I did think that hastening Jean Chrétien's departure was a personal insult to the prime minister. If only in respect for him and what he had accomplished for Canada, the party should have allowed him an orderly transition at his own pace.

In my view, the timing was also a political misjudgment of the highest order. If Chrétien had been allowed to stay another three months, as was his desire, he would have received the highly anticipated auditor general's report on the sponsorship scandal and in all probability would have turned it over to the police for a full criminal investigation. Instead, owing to the early convention, he prorogued the House on November 12, leaving all the issues surrounding the sponsorship program unresolved. In ways that nobody could have predicted, we became the instigators of our own downfall.

PART 4:
FOREIGN LEGIONS

14

CHANGING
OF THE GUARD

On December 12, 2003, Paul Martin took office as the twenty-first prime minister of Canada. Three days earlier, he had asked to see me. "I'm going to be leaving you in Foreign Affairs for now," he said, "but there are no guarantees for after the next election."

"But I've only been there for two years," I protested, "and it takes time to settle into these files. You yourself have been making a lot of speeches about Canada and the world lately, so there's going to be a lot to do in Foreign Affairs if that agenda is to be achieved." He still wouldn't give me a commitment. Later I heard rumours that he had promised the post to Pierre Pettigrew and that I was not exactly popular with certain of his key supporters who were unhappy with my position on Israel.

My conversation with Martin had been cordial, and because my job didn't change in the December Cabinet shuffle, I just carried on with my work. In fact, I was one of only two ministers who retained the same portfolio. But it was far from business as usual. For one thing, Martin had his own distinctive management style. He loved to engage in long, vigorous policy debates in which he grilled his ministers and staff with tough, fundamental questions as a way to generate fresh ideas and new directions. His intellectual curiosity and high standards of excellence made him push everyone hard, but no harder than he pushed himself, and those who knew him well realized that his bark was much worse than his bite. The downside of so much discussion was that his government tended to be less efficient than

Chrétien's, a propensity that was exaggerated by the creation of a host of new committees to give everybody a job. Since I often found my portfolio being carved out from beneath me, I was forced to sit on some of these committees just to keep abreast of key areas of interest to Foreign Affairs. And, of course, the new government immediately got drawn into an almost total preoccupation with the sponsorship scandal and its political fallout.

Nobody asked my advice on how to handle this issue, being neither a minister responsible nor a Quebec MP, so I could only watch with dismay as the prime minister set up the Gomery Commission to investigate his predecessor's actions. Most ministers argued on principle that the law must be upheld and justice done; for political reasons, others wanted to put some distance between themselves and the previous regime; but some of Martin's closest advisers seemed driven by the less laudable motive of getting back at Chrétien for slights they felt they had suffered in the course of their careers. Meanwhile, the Quebec ministers and MPs were horrified by the whole idea of an inquiry into the party's operations in the province, which they feared would lead to an exaggerated picture of what was in reality a limited amount of wrongdoing by a small group of people. I agreed with them that we were in danger of shooting ourselves in the foot. In the end, the concerns of the Quebec caucus were borne out. The Liberals' reputation was severely damaged because of the misbehaviour of a few individuals, and the effect was soon reflected in the deteriorating poll numbers. Caucus became prey to internecine warfare, anger, despair, and panic.

IN THE MEANTIME, amid the travails of the Liberal Party of Canada, I carried on doing my job as foreign minister. On January 10, 2004, I accompanied Prime Minister Martin to a Special Summit of the Americas in Monterrey, Mexico, where Colin Powell and I found time to discuss a number of bilateral issues of concern to both Canada and the United States. The most pressing involved Devils Lake. In 2002, when North Dakota began to build an outlet from Devils Lake to drain its rising water levels, Canada objected because of the large numbers of contaminants and invasive species that would flow from the outlet into Canadian waters. Colin was desperate for a solution because a senator from North Dakota had threatened to hold up all of the State Department's ambassadorial appointments until the issue was resolved to his satisfaction. It was even brought to the attention of President Bush. "That's impossible," he was reported as saying. "Everybody knows that water doesn't drain from south to north." To me, it was another example of how the Americans' domestic politics constantly intruded into their foreign relations.

"They take water seriously out west," Colin reminded me. "It's like a cowboy movie fight where men die for water." That didn't prevent them, he added, from draining the aquifers so that rich men could play on golf courses in the desert. "Go figure," I commented in my notes.

During a breakfast meeting with Bush and Paul Martin, I observed how well the two leaders were getting along. The president was relaxed and at his most charming. When asked what he felt about summit meetings, he said, "They're a colossal waste of time given how they're organized around set speeches. I never know what the other guy is really thinking about anything." He then recounted an argument he had had with Chirac at a G8 summit when the French president suggested that the Western countries had some responsibility for corruption in developing countries. "Not my country! Not the U.S. of A.!" Bush had replied. "Other countries can choose between right and wrong; it's not the fault of the Americans." As he spoke, I thought to myself that his moral certainty, combined with a simplistic and sketchily informed view of things, made him somewhat dangerous. "It's leadership, yes," I noted, "but badly informed leadership is problematic." On the other hand, the president did say that he was at summits to listen, which I found encouraging, and he seemed an intellectual powerhouse beside, say, Hugo Chávez.

At the summit, I had another opportunity to watch Chávez up close – too close for comfort, as it happened. Just before Canada was to present its official statement, Martin called me aside. Something important had come up that required his immediate attention, and so I would have to make the presentation on his behalf. With no time to peruse its content, I simply began to read aloud the pages I was handed when, to my surprise and no little concern, I heard myself launching a tough, almost personal attack on Chávez, who sat glaring at me from a few feet away. I scampered to safety the moment I was finished, only to pass by the hotel restaurant where I saw the prime minister in the middle of his important engagement: what looked like a delicious lunch.

In some ways the best news to come out of the summit occurred when Bush was asked at a press conference about whether Canada-US relations were now out of the "deep freeze." "There was no freeze," he answered. "We can disagree without there being bad blood."

That reality was reinforced when Colin Powell and I worked together on a crisis in Haiti involving Jean-Bertrand Aristide, the charismatic Haitian president who had been elected in 1991, ousted in a military coup, and then reinstalled by the Clinton administration in 1994. Since Aristide's re-election in 2000, he had been increasingly behaving in a corrupt, dictatorial fashion. By late 2003, an armed rebellion against his government had broken out. I began getting worried calls from the foreign ministers of various Caribbean countries, all of whom I knew from Commonwealth or Organization of American States meetings and all of them asking for Canada's assistance. Some hoped that Aristide would simply resign and put an end to the agitation. Others, particularly P.J. Patterson, the Jamaican prime minister and chairman of the Caribbean Community (CARICOM), objected to the overthrow of a democratically elected leader by unelected rebels.

They were also phoning Colin Powell, and he in turn phoned me. "What are we going to do about this trouble in Haiti?" he asked. So much for the argument of those who said the Americans would never speak to us again if we didn't support them in Iraq! If they had been angry with Canada, they couldn't stay angry for long. They even reconciled with France. The history of international relations is a catalogue of ever-shifting alliances, dependent of changing circumstances, and Canada was now an indispensable ally in responding to the crisis in Haiti. We had close diplomatic and personal relationships with the Caribbean leaders; we had extensive business interests in the region; and, more to the point, we had a substantial French-speaking Haitian community in Montreal, represented by important Liberal MPs in the Cabinet and caucus, particularly Denis Coderre, who knew a great deal about the internal politics of Haiti.

In late January 2004 CARICOM suggested a peace plan that would allow Aristide to stay in office but require him to share power with the political opposition. Canada, the United States, and France were supportive, but the plan had yet to gain traction in Haiti. All the while, the humanitarian situation in Haiti was spiralling downward, and the United States was concerned that it would destabilize the entire Caribbean basin. The American government was anxious to avoid a repeat of 1991, when thousands of Haitians had fled the country in boats following the Haitian military's ousting of Aristide. Complicating matters further, the powerful black caucus in Congress was sharply divided between pro- and anti-Aristide factions, and thus between those in favour of or opposed to US intervention.

On February 13 Secretary Powell invited a group of interested foreign ministers and diplomats to an exploratory meeting at the State Department in Washington. The historic significance of the moment was brought home to me as we sat, with portraits of Washington and Jefferson looking down on us, discussing what to do. The concerns of the Caribbean countries were motivated by the large numbers of Haitian refugees landing on their shores. "Haiti needs urgent and immediate action," K.D. Knight, Jamaica's foreign minister, argued. "We can't tolerate the present level of violence." He and St. Lucia's Julian Hunte called for a peacekeeping force to restore normalcy. Colin was noncommittal. The United States, he said, would "only go in if there is something to support," meaning that the Americans weren't going to send in troops unless the Haitians first came up with a political solution. Indeed, after their previous experiences in Haiti, the Americans were less than enthusiastic about the idea of putting boots on the ground. "We're talking hundreds, not thousands here," Colin told us.

At one point he jumped up and said to me, "I have to go and brief the black caucus on this. Come in the car with me and we can talk about it." His refusal to stand on protocol was one of his most commendable attributes, as was his frankness. "You know, Bill," he said during the fifteen-minute drive to Capitol Hill, "in a perfect world Haiti would be put into a trusteeship for ten or twenty years, enough time to bring up a new, educated generation that could run the place, free from the corruption and fallout from the Papa Doc years. Of course, we're not allowed to propose that in public in today's world, but that would probably be the best solution."

"Would the United States be willing to run it?" I asked. I found it an interesting comment, even though a complete non-starter in the realities of the post-colonial world, and I thought of the mess in which the Americans were embroiled trying to govern post-Saddam Iraq.

"Oh, no," he immediately replied, "not us."

As conditions continued to worsen in Haiti, I spent a lot of time working the phones with Powell, Dominique de Villepin, the Caribbean foreign ministers, and the Mexicans, who were also worried about the possibility of a humanitarian disaster unfolding in the region. K.D. Knight and Fred Mitchell, the Bahamian foreign minister, kept advocating for an international intervention; Canada, the United States, and France refused to agree to an intervention that would simply have the effect of propping up Aristide. We were willing to co-operate with a political settlement along the lines of the CARICOM peace plan, but on February 24 the Haitian political opposition rejected the idea of sharing power with Aristide. It was starting to look like a no-win scenario. If the international community intervened, we would be using force to keep Aristide in power, despite all his abuses, and we risked getting caught up in a Haitian civil war. If we didn't intervene, we risked a massacre.

On February 25 I received a call from Powell. "Aristide's time is up," he said. The Americans now saw his resignation as the best possible outcome. I understood and indeed shared the US position, but as one of my advisers pointed out, "The Americans have been undermining Aristide for years. This decision will be perceived as a disguised coup to push him out." His words were prescient, though there were simply no longer any viable alternatives.

On February 26 the United States and France publicly called on Aristide to consider stepping down for the good of his people, and Canada concurred. It was not for the international community to force Aristide out, I told an interviewer on Radio-Canada, but given the failure of the CARICOM plan and the realities of what was happening on the ground, it was perhaps time for him to resign voluntarily. If he did so, I added, Canada would be ready to join with other countries to help restore peace and security in Haiti.

"Aristide won't step aside," Mexican foreign minister Luis Derbez predicted when I spoke with him that day. "There's a bloodbath coming." He lamented that all our possible options were unpalatable.

That afternoon CARICOM approached the UN Security Council requesting an immediate multinational intervention in Haiti. But, though the Security Council deplored the Haitian opposition's dismissal of the

CARICOM plan, it wasn't willing to act until the Haitians had worked out a political blueprint for the country's future. "No one wants to prop up Aristide," Allan Rock, our ambassador to the UN, briefed me the next day. "Once he's gone," he said, "momentum will build for a force." Rock's observations were confirmed in a conversation I had with Colin Powell shortly afterward. "We're not sending in troops," he said. Colin also dismissed the argument that Aristide's departure would represent a blow to democracy in Haiti. "President Nixon left, and it wasn't the end of democracy," he noted.

"Crazy day over Haiti," I jotted down on February 28. "Situation there deteriorating. The US ready to move with 5,000 troops, but not until UN Resolution & Aristide gone. The US and France playing cozy at the UN." When I spoke with Knight, he again asked Canada to be part of an international intervention even if Aristide remained, but I said that we were planning to act in concert with the Americans, fully aware of what their response would be. I then spoke with Kenneth Cook, our ambassador in Port-au-Prince, who told me that we were perceived as having joined with the United States and France in an effort to push out Aristide. That accusation was unfair: Aristide had largely brought this situation on himself, and, given his record, Canada wouldn't risk the lives of our soldiers to keep him in power. "He'll end up being killed," Mitchell told me later that day as he speculated about what a post-Aristide Haiti might look like.

Things came to a head on Sunday, February 29, when I received a call from Powell at seven in the morning. "I've been up all night," he said. "Aristide has resigned." The Americans had warned the Haitian president that he was in danger and that he might face charges related to narcotics and embezzlement if his enemies scized power. According to Colin, reactions in the Caribbean community were mixed: Knight declared that a coup had taken place, whereas Mitchell was more realistic. The chief justice of the Haitian Supreme Court would be sworn in as the interim president, as the country's constitution required, and the political opposition in Haiti was being told to work through the peace plan that CARICOM had proposed earlier in the year. "No thugs will take over," Colin assured me, "but we need to get troops to Haiti as quickly as possible." Interestingly enough, given the Iraqi context, the United States wanted to get an expedited UN

Security Council resolution, even though it wouldn't be strictly necessary under international law once the new Haitian president had invited an international stabilization force into his country.

Later that day I spoke with the Haitian ambassador, who thought that Aristide had been forced out. Now that he was gone, however, the ambassador was already looking to the future. He told me that the creation of a new national unity government was imperative. Aristide still had considerable support in Haiti, and his followers would have to be included in the new political settlement, or there would be problems. He added that Canada would have a special role to play in Haiti, especially as the United States and France were not favourably regarded there.

The UN Security Council met that night to rush through a resolution on Haiti. Because it didn't entail a combat mission, nobody vetoed it. Canada would obviously be playing a role. The prime minister was seriously concerned about the situation in Haiti; it was a traditional mission in our own backyard; our troops were ready and bilingual; there was political pressure from the Quebec MPs to come to the rescue of a poor francophone nation; and the Americans were anxious for Canada to do them a favour. The United Nations approved it. So why then was I later denounced as a war criminal in demonstrations and on websites?

As predicted, many suspected the United States of engineering a coup. Aristide himself quickly claimed that he had been deposed and kidnapped by the United States, though my understanding from Powell was that Aristide had asked for American help to leave the country. (In fact, Colin later told me, when he called US defense secretary Donald Rumsfeld to request a plane to transport Aristide into exile in the Central African Republic, he refused, apparently not caring a fig about the president of Haiti or his fate.) The conspiracy theorists, angered by what they saw as the overthrow of their legitimate president by foreign forces, seized on the fact that the United States and Canada had dropped a small number of troops into Port-au-Prince to secure the airport a few hours before the UN Security Council passed its resolution, and they used that technicality as the excuse to charge Colin Powell and me with launching an illegal war. The fact was, with the security situation in Haiti crumbling, there were concerns over whether any planes would be able to land or take off, including those evacuating Canadian citizens.

Several of the Caribbean leaders, Prime Minister Patterson in particular, were angry with Canada for our position. Little more than a month after Aristide's departure, when Patterson was visiting Toronto, he asked to see me at his suite in the Royal York Hotel for no other reason than to tear a strip off my back for letting down CARICOM and interfering in the internal affairs of Haiti. After sixty minutes of eloquent, erudite recrimination and rebuke, which I accepted without uttering a word, he got up and said, "Well, Bill, enough of that, they're throwing a dinner in my honour downstairs, and I'm here to party!" Then he was off to hobnob with the elite of Toronto's Jamaican diaspora – evidently an important political constituency for him. For me it was yet another reminder that all domestic politics are increasingly global in nature.

The Canadian Forces did a great job in their six-month assignment, and our bilingual, multicultural troops proved particularly well suited to handling the sensitivities of the UN operation. On May 7, only a couple of months after Aristide's departure, I visited them, flying over Port-au-Prince in a little Griffon helicopter with no doors, inspecting their work and meeting with the interim president, the political opposition, and representatives from Fanmi Lavalas, Aristide's party. New efforts at reconstruction and development were under way, but the task remained formidable. A terrible earthquake struck early in 2010, bringing death and devastation to the island, followed by a cholera outbreak that autumn. Lingering animosities, corruption issues, and political intrigues kept getting in the way of fundamental progress, but Canada has never given up on our desire to help the people of Haiti.

On May 23 Prime Minister Martin called an election for June 28, 2004. The term was running out, and he wanted to start again with a fresh mandate from the people. "I'm proud of our record over the past ten years and the last five months," he told the Cabinet on a conference call just before going to the governor general to dissolve the House. "This election is all about the role of government in helping Canadians. If we cut taxes to American levels, we'll end up at their level of social services and health care." Since the call was on an unsecured line, he began by saying hello to all the foreign governments that were listening in and ended by asking, in French, whether any of them had any questions.

Some advisers had wanted him to hold off a while longer, to settle into his role as prime minister and give the public more time to get over the sponsorship scandal, but I suspected that Martin's team in the PMO saw a quick election as an opportunity to firmly establish his own mandate. It was certainly a risk. This was the first election contested by the new Conservative Party of Canada, which had amalgamated the old Tories and the Reform/Alliance under Stephen Harper. Jack Layton had emerged as a popular and effective leader of the New Democrats. The Liberals had been in office for more than ten years, and, the new leader notwithstanding, we were tarred with scandal and had been wounded by internal feuding. "It's very tight; we'll be lucky to keep what we have," I wrote in a note three days before the election call. "It all depends on how we define Harper."

Our initial defence was to be a strong offence, but the party caucus reacted badly to reports in the press about Liberal attack ads against Stephen Harper. During the Ontario caucus meeting on May 5, I was applauded when I warned that adopting the worst of American campaign practices would undercut the values by which we were trying to distinguish our party from the Alliance. However, when our support began to slip after the Liberal premier of Ontario, Dalton McGuinty, broke his promise and introduced a health-care tax, we returned to the confrontational ad strategy by using Harper's own far-right rhetoric against him. Its success forced me to admit how effective negative advertising can be.

As it happened, election day coincided with a NATO leaders' summit in Istanbul, which the prime minister asked me to attend in his stead. I can't say I was happy to be sent out of the country while the voters of Toronto Centre decided my fate, but I was comforted by the knowledge that we had developed a strong base of support in the riding. Though Cathy had always been an excellent campaigner, I owed her extra gratitude for taking my place at the head of our team during the home stretch of this campaign. Nevertheless, no politician ever wants to be sitting an ocean away from his or her constituency on election day. Half the time I was supposed to be concentrating on Afghanistan and NATO-Russia relations, my mind was wondering what was happening back home, and whenever we got a chance, Isabelle Savard and I checked in on the returns. (The thoughts of the leaders of Portugal and Greece were also elsewhere, if the exchange I overheard while sitting between them at dinner was any indication – their only topic of conversation was their nations' rivalry at the European football championship.) My feelings were mixed when the election results came in. I was excited to retain my own seat with more than 55 percent of the vote, winning every poll but one, with the New Democrats in second place and the Harper Tories trailing far behind. However, the Liberals lost seats in Ontario and Quebec, and were reduced to a minority government.

The next day I received warm congratulations from many around the table, including Presidents Bush and Chirac, despite Chirac's earlier complaint to me that Canada wasn't speaking as much French at international meetings under Paul Martin as we had under Jean Chrétien. I also received congratulations from my colleagues Colin Powell, Joschka Fischer, and Sergey Lavrov, the new Russian foreign minister. Such was the sense of collegiality that I felt I had made friends with them after two and a half intense and dramatic years. "Double congratulations on your seat and for your government," Jack Straw wrote in a note. "I felt for you last night. Democracy can be agony."

Perhaps the most surprising reaction came from Tony Blair. At our few previous encounters I found him rather cold and distant, so I was somewhat disarmed when he came over and struck up a conversation about the election results that was relaxed, friendly, and curious. I ended up spending quite a lot of time with him in Istanbul because, according to protocol, prime ministers always followed heads of state, with foreign ministers even lower on the pecking order. As a result, he and I often had to wait at the back of the line to enter a reception or get into our limousines. Blair was infuriated that the president of some minor Baltic state outranked the prime minister of Great Britain, and he regularly grumbled about it. Once, while waiting as usual, I got into a long and amusing chat with Cherie Blair while her husband was busy talking with another head of government. Suddenly we were interrupted when he called out that their car had finally arrived. "Ta, ta," she said as she hurried off. "His master's voice."

IN MID-JULY, Cathy and I were at our country home in the Hockley Valley, north of Toronto, when I got a call from Tim Murphy, my former campaign manager, who was now chief of staff in the Prime Minister's Office. Mr.

Martin was putting together his new Cabinet, Tim said, and it looked as though I would be moved from Foreign Affairs to National Defence. I had heard rumours to that effect, but it still felt like the falling of an axe.

Most of my friends, colleagues, and the media thought I was being demoted, and I probably saw the change as a bit of a demotion myself. Foreign Affairs was a natural fit for me, and I was just starting to hit my stride. I liked the people in the department; they liked me; and I was pleased when one of them said at a social event, "We've got a minister who understands the business of doing what we do." The portfolio lunches I had initiated were proving popular and useful. I had supplemented them with dinners a couple of times a year at which lawyers from the Justice Department met with our lawyers to talk about issues of international law and how we could work more closely together. I was comfortable in the G8 meetings and knew all the players. There was plenty of unfinished work to do. And, to be frank, there is a cachet to being minister of foreign affairs that a defence minister simply doesn't have in Canada, particularly given the low priority and budget cuts that the Department of National Defence (DND) had received in recent years.

When I met with Paul Martin, he said, "Look, Bill, the problem with defence – and I'm as guilty as anyone because I had to make all the cuts when I was finance minister – is that we've underfunded the military budget."

That certainly didn't make the job sound any more attractive, though I agreed with his analysis. "We're like a plane flying on one wing," I said. "We've got the UN and NATO and the Human Security Agenda, but we haven't got the muscle that gives us any credibility. We've got to have both, but at the moment we don't have the capacity to deploy anybody more."

"I'm perfectly aware of that," he said. "That's why I'm going to ask you to rebuild the place."

Perhaps to soften the blow, he added, "Besides, I'll be doing much of Foreign Affairs myself, so maybe you'll be better off in Defence." Of course, prime ministers always end up doing more in the field of international issues than they ever imagined or even wanted. Jean Chrétien was deeply involved in everything from Iraq to the "Turbot War" with Spain. And it was clear that Martin had got a taste for international relations, travelling the world with the G8 finance ministers, hobnobbing with the powerful in London and Washington, and pursuing his lifelong interest in aid to Africa, an area in which he was particularly knowledgeable. Later I watched him wow a conference on foreign aid at the Woodrow Wilson Center in Washington with his knowledge and passion. During the break, I was told, "We never had a head of government who knew this much about development assistance, how it works, and what doesn't work."

Still, Martin's foreign affairs aspirations didn't mean there would be no room for the foreign minister to make an impact. If I'd had my druthers, I would have stayed put. But I was willing to be romanced into believing that Defence would be an opportunity to make a difference, and I was intrigued by the challenges the department faced. Now, whenever I'm asked which was my preferred ministry, I have to pause. Though I was a better fit in Foreign Affairs, I really came to love DND. The issues were exciting, the people were terrific, and the results were mostly gratifying. "Defence is derivative of foreign policy," as John McCallum once put it to me, "but foreign policy is dependent on defence."

On July 20, 2004, I was sworn in as Canada's defence minister. The evening before, a few close advisers and I had had dinner together in Ottawa. The mood around the table had been reflective, even a little melancholy. Though I was honoured to continue on in Cabinet and looked forward to working with incredible people in the Defence Department, it meant saying goodbye to the team I had collaborated with at Foreign Affairs. Of the original group, only Isabelle Savard would be moving on with me to DND. During the dinner, her cell phone began to ring – not an unusual occurrence for a ministerial staffer – but she looked surprised when she answered. She then ushered me outside to take the call. It was Colin Powell. "Bill," he said, "I'm just calling as an old military guy to wish you all the best as Canada's new defence minister." It was a characteristically thoughtful gesture from Colin, and I took it as a good omen for my new portfolio.

For reasons of history, Canada has a bifurcated defence system: a military wing and a civilian wing, presided over by a chief of the defence staff (CDS) and a deputy minister, both of whom report directly to the minister. Its headquarters at 101 Colonel By Drive are even divided into two distinct towers, a real and symbolic separation: North for the military, South for the civilians. That division proved a headache to manage when the two responsibilities overlapped or even clashed. I often had to mediate between the conflicting advice we received from General Ray Henault, the CDS, and my deputy minister, Ward Elcock. I relied on the expertise of Gene Lang, who had served as chief of staff for my predecessor, John McCallum, to help me navigate this complex new environment. I was also very fortunate to work with a highly professional and talented group of young people on my political staff, including Michelle Lobo, Anna Gainey, Roch Charron, and Renée Filiatrault.

Certainly, the learning curve in Defence was steep. I was thrown into a crisis in October, only three months after taking up my new post on July 20, when one of our submarines caught fire at sea, tragically killing a crewman. It was a reminder that, even in peacetime, the men and women of Canada's Forces are always putting their lives at risk in the service of their country. Then, in late December, I found myself leading the initial Canadian response to the massive tsunami that hit south Asia. With Mr. Martin and many of his ministers out of the country or travelling over the holidays, I was one of the few senior members of the Cabinet near Ottawa when the news broke. Every morning my son, Patrick, had to drive me into Ottawa from Montebello, where we were enjoying a family vacation, and I met with the government officials who were working hard to come up with an effective response. Canada ended up sending hundreds of millions of dollars in aid as well as the Disaster Assistance Response Team (DART), a rapid-deployment unit of the Canadian Armed Forces with unique capabilities for delivering medical care, water purification, and engineering expertise. The DART is a sterling example of why our Armed Forces are valued around the world.

One of Prime Minister Martin's first orders on coming into power was to ask for an International Policy Statement that would include a review of diplomacy, defence, trade, and development assistance conducted by each of the four responsible ministries. When I shifted from DFAIT to DND, I obviously switched from the diplomacy review to the defence review, which I found already under way in the department in the wake of the transformative events of 9/11. It was a good introduction to the department because it forced me immediately to get my head around the macro issues as well as the operational issues – NORAD, NATO, Afghanistan, ballistic missile defence, and so forth – both where they had come from and where they should go. Once the review was done, or so I assumed, I would have a better idea of the money I needed to ask for in the budget, and then I could look for the right person to succeed Ray Henault, who was slated to retire in the spring of 2005. That was my order of priority, and I set the process in motion right away.

First we had to deal with the fact that two significant defence reviews had been undertaken in recent memory, both of which had been judged a complete waste of time because their recommendations had never been adequately funded. Everyone I encountered in DND had bitter memories of the work they had done drawing up fresh visions, only to have them thrown into the ashcan the moment they reached the Finance Department. One senior official who had been around a long time told me point-blank, "If Canada wants a place in the world, it's going to have to step up and play, and that is going to cost a lot of money. But the minute you try to get the money, you'll be smacked down, as minister after minister has been before you. I've been through this three times and I can tell you the scenario: it's going nowhere."

Around that time, during a trip to London, I asked Geoff Hoon, the British defence minister, how he had conducted his own recent review. He gave me a copy of their report, and, reading it during my flight home, I was really impressed. Attached to the report outline of strategic objectives was an appendix that listed the equipment the military would need to deliver on the proposed policy: how many ships and what type, how many planes, how many helicopters, how many tanks, how many trucks. That seemed a really smart approach, because if you can't get the procurement, you can't do what you want to do militarily. If you can't procure new double-hulled ships to patrol the Arctic, for example, there's not much point in making grandiose pronouncements about defending our interests in the North. I thought that Hoon's method would help me deal with the demoralized group of people I had inherited in DND.

Meanwhile, the prime minister was calling meetings that would sometimes go to eleven o'clock at night to quiz Pierre Pettigrew, Jim Peterson, Aileen Carroll, and me on our respective reviews of foreign policy, trade, the Canadian International Development Agency (CIDA), and defence. When I told him I was having trouble with mine because I couldn't get anyone excited enough to produce any bold new ideas, he said, "Well, you're a smart guy, you're the one who got the gold medal, why don't you write it yourself?" Paul liked to throw that law-school prize back in my face whenever he wanted to poke me.

"I'm not the Captain Liddell Hart of Canada," I replied, just to annoy him, confident that he wouldn't know the reference.

"Who the hell's Captain Liddell Hart?"

"He was a very famous military strategist in England," I said, driving the knife in a little deeper. "I can write the foreign policy dimensions. But for a military review to be meaningful, it has to be written by somebody who really understands the organizational structure, the personnel requirements, and the equipment that will be necessary to do the job – in particular what tasks call for what equipment, and how to put the pieces together into a working machine. I would be foolish to go in there and just dicker around as an amateur."

Time passed. We made various attempts to get the process under way, but it was clear that nobody's head or heart was in it. The more people I talked to, the more confused I became. We were all going around in circles. I could tell that Mr. Martin was getting very frustrated with me; there was lots of shouting and hair pulling. Suddenly I realized the problem: I had my priorities backward. Instead of review, budget, new CDS, I should put the new CDS in place first, because what I really needed was someone who could kick-start the strategic policy and the procurement element based on actual military experience. Although a defence review would normally have been written by the civilian side with input from the North Tower, I felt I had no choice but to look elsewhere. The same thing happened with the DFAIT review, when the department's inability to come up with a compelling, articulate vision of Canada's role in world affairs led an exasperated PMO to commission a paper from a Canadian scholar at the University of Oxford.

But what to do with General Henault? As fate would have it, NATO was looking for a new chairman of the Military Committee, preferably someone bilingual because France was thinking about rejoining the integrated command. Henault was a perfect fit. He had the experience, he wanted the job, NATO liked him, and so he decided to head off to Brussels, leaving his post open. I interviewed the chiefs of the army, the air force, and the navy, and a few other obvious candidates. Some people suggested that I bring a commander back from retirement, but others were adamantly against it.

The more I learned, the more I kept returning to my meeting with the army chief, General Rick Hillier. My staff and I had been impressed by his grasp of the strategic issues. He had worked closely with the US army in Fort Hood, Texas, and had tested his charts and theories on the battlefields of Bosnia and Afghanistan. He had proven leadership qualities and was popular with his troops, even if that didn't always make him popular with others. And he was a powerful communicator, with a typical Newfoundlander's charm and gift of the gab. Best of all, he came with a very clear concept about the nature and structure of the Canadian Forces at home and abroad in the post-9/11 world.

"I'd love to do the review," he said, "because this place needs to rethink how we can put all the moving parts into place and take them forward."

I took Hillier to see Paul Martin at Sussex Drive one Saturday morning, and the prime minister cross-examined us for about two and a half hours. After the general laid out his strategic vision and what would be necessary to deliver it, I had a short private conversation with Martin in which I said, "This is the right guy. He's by far my preferred candidate." The prime minister agreed without a moment's hesitation, and he offered Hillier the post then and there, with the assurance of full government support for our plan.

With Hillier in place as CDS as of February 4, 2005, the writing of the defence section of the International Policy Statement came more easily. He already had a serious concept that fitted exactly with what we needed as well as the practical experience of how to put it into effect. No one questioned the overarching importance of our bilateral pacts with the United States or our collective membership in NATO. These are integral to the security of both Canada and North America from internal or external attacks. The review aimed to strengthen NORAD by exploring the possibility of giving it new responsibilities in the areas of maritime security. We also set forth our plans to establish a new command headquarters tasked with overseeing the security of Canada. Aside from these efforts to supplement the enduring architecture of North American security, however, Hillier largely focused on how the Canadian military should engage with the new global threats of failed and failing states, non-state combatants, terrorism, and brutal civil wars. Where should we go? What equipment would we need to make a difference? How should we reorganize our Armed Forces to deliver on our foreign policy objective to create peace and stability in conjunction with our multinational allies, DFAIT, and CIDA?

Prime Minister Martin was happy with the drafts we were producing, but I had to remind him that the credibility of the review would depend on its being funded in the next budget. "Otherwise," I told him, "it's going to look like a rerun of all the other reviews. If it's not funded, you can throw the whole exercise out that window, including your foreign policy review, which is dependent on it."

"You're exaggerating," he said.

"No, I'm not. As far as the Defence Department is concerned, and as far as the military families are concerned, if this review turns out to be just another paper exercise, we're going to be total chumps. Just look at what happened to all the previous reviews."

"Oh, okay, absolutely, no problem," he said. "Go and speak to Ralph."

On January 25, 2005, I accompanied a delegation of senior DND officials to see Ralph Goodale, the minister of finance. We sat down for about three hours with him and his deputy minister, Ian Bennett, and went through the whole defence review. Ralph understood it; he agreed it was well done; he saw how it corresponded to government policy, particularly to Mr. Martin's ambitious view of what Canada should be delivering abroad. And yet, though it wasn't articulated at that meeting, I sensed we had run up against Finance's traditional skepticism about military expenditures. Some of that skepticism was justified: DND's record hadn't been entirely successful, particularly in the critically important area of procurement. One infamous computerization system cost several hundred million dollars and turned out to be a complete fiasco. And there were plenty of examples of cost overruns on planes, helicopters, ships, and submarines under Liberal and Conservative governments alike. Procurement is probably the most controversial aspect of the department, not least because it's also one of the most expensive.

Nor is the expense simple to control or even predict. Deployments abroad, whether for NATO or the UN, invariably come with huge and unexpected costs because you have to move troops across great distances with the special type of equipment necessary for the various kinds of armed conflicts in which they will be engaged for who knows how long. For the optimal defence of North America, our military has to be "interoperable" with that of the United States, and that means trying to keep up with the high-tech computer wizardry the Americans are constantly developing. A basic plane, ship, or tank doesn't cost that much. It's just a platform. When you add all the fancy rockets and electronics, the price leaps – and $20 million might become $250 million.

Moreover, the next war is always different from the last one. Most recently, for example, cyber-warfare has introduced unprecedented challenges, and the significance of this new frontier is reflected in our security spending. In 2005, when I signed the cyber-security directive that allowed Communications Security Establishment Canada (CSEC) to monitor and collect the "metadata" of Canadian citizens, its budget was approximately $200 million. Eight years later CSEC's budget had more than doubled to $460.9 million, and then it almost doubled again in 2014 to $829 million, nearly half of which was devoted to building an impressive new headquarters in Ottawa. When I visited the old one, I was as astonished by all the young, long-haired geeks in T-shirts and jeans as by the huge computer screens and surveillance equipment. The work environment, which included a private gym, struck me as "Google-meets-the-CIA."

Then there are the politics. Military spending in Canada, as in most other countries, is as much a matter of regional development and vested interests as of the equipment our Armed Forces require. During my time in DND we were keenly aware of the need to replace the aging C-130 Hercules and Buffalo aircraft we used for search and rescue operations, but when the department identified good American- and Italian-built alternatives, the MPs whose ridings contained aircraft manufacturers resisted the purchase. And when we thought we could save tens of millions of dollars a year by closing down the military base at Goose Bay, Labrador, which was now no longer necessary even as a NATO training centre, we were told we couldn't, because it employed a significant number of people in a strategically important riding. If that were indeed the situation, I proposed turning the problem over to Human Resources Development Canada. "Let HRDC run it as an employment centre," I said, "because it's a job-creation issue, not a military operation."

Instead, the prime minister assigned Anne McLellan and me the task of coming up with a solution. In the process, I got to know the mayor and the people of Happy Valley–Goose Bay well and certainly sympathized with their frustration at seeing what had once been a base with thousands of American troops gradually decline into relative insignificance. I went around Europe begging our NATO allies to continue their training exercises there, but they preferred Cold Lake, Alberta, or a cheaper domestic solution. Raytheon later proposed it as a site for a ballistic missile defence radar facility, but that too went nowhere.

As if regional politics didn't complicate the procurement discussions enough, there was also a constant problem with leaks. I recall one meeting with Hillier and Opposition members on our plans to acquire new long-range transport planes. As we sat down at the table, Claude Bachand, the Bloc Québécois defence critic, pulled out the list of performance requirements. "This is our top secret document not yet taken to Cabinet!" I wrote in my notes. "So much for confidentiality in DND!" The questions posed in the House by Gordon O'Connor, the Conservative defence critic, clearly showed that he had the document as well. With so much supposedly confidential information floating around Ottawa, you never knew when you might be ambushed by the press or in Parliament.

However obvious the importance of our national security and international obligations might be, a number of senior officials in the PMO, the Privy Council Office (PCO), and Finance simply didn't believe that defence priorities were as serious for Canada as were social expenditures. Moreover, several Liberal MPs and many Canadians shared those same doubts about spending a lot of money on weapons and soldiers when governments were cutting back on hospitals, schools, and social services. Once, while I was talking about the military to Jean Chrétien at lunch during a meeting of the Canada-Europe Council in Spain, he said, "It's best to keep the generals out of the country so they can't keep coming around asking for more money." I certainly wouldn't have been the first minister to fail to get more money. "Remember," I joked with Rick Hillier, "the real enemy isn't over there in Afghanistan; the real enemy is here in the Finance Department."

Ralph Goodale was good enough to give my department's request his closest attention. He called in his officials to go over the numbers. He reviewed the prime minister's long to-do list, from a national daycare program to a new health-care agreement with the provinces. He examined the wish lists of all the other departments and considered the political and external pressures to balance the budget. Eventually he came back to me with his conclusion. Although he agreed with my review and the need for new equipment, understood that Canada's commitments in Afghanistan and elsewhere were going to be expensive, and totally supported General Hillier's strategy, he couldn't find the money in this year's budget. "Next year," he said.

I sympathized, but I also had DND's position to protect. "That's the end, Ralph," I said. "I'm telling you if we say next year, nobody's going to believe us. It's just kicking the can down the road again."

But I hadn't been fool enough to think I could get the money simply by walking into Ralph's office and asking for it. "If we're going to get this thing through," I said to Gene Lang, "we better have a game plan. What do we have to do? Who do we have to persuade?" Basically leaving Hillier to reorganize the Forces, I saw my job as getting the resources to deliver on the defence review, and that's where I put about 90 percent of my energy as minister until budget day.

Near the top of the list of the key people I figured I had to persuade was Alex Himelfarb, the clerk of the Privy Council, whom Gene knew well. Not only was Alex the government's most senior civil servant but he was well known as a strong advocate for social programs. "We really have to bring Alex onside," Gene told me, "because he'll be key to persuading the prime minister." Shortly afterward, he and I took Alex to dinner, where we went through the review, the strategy, and the expenditures. "If they come to the PCO," we concluded, "we assume they will get support. Otherwise we're wasting our time." Alex recognized that our budget request was a legitimate and integral part of our foreign policy agenda, and though he had doubts about some specific items, he wasn't entirely hostile. I ticked that box.

Next I tackled the Liberal caucus. I took Senator Colin Kenny to lunch and urged him to come to DND's support. "You've been screaming for years about underfunding," I said. "Now start screaming that we've got to deliver this time." I went to the women's caucus and explained how the plan was essential to Canada's defence and part of our peacekeeping obligations. One by one, I buttonholed members interested in foreign policy and defence.

Moving into Paul Martin's influential inner circle, I arranged to meet with Peter Nicholson, the prime minister's highly respected policy director, and David Herle, a key political strategist. If Herle shot back that his polling results were showing that the public didn't want any more money spent on the military, I would know that our plan was in trouble, if not completely dead. "When you're thinking about the politics of this request," I told him, "think about the fact that we have more than eighty thousand military personnel, making us one of the largest employers in the country. Now add on their spouses, their adult children, their parents, their relations. Then add on all those Canadians who believe in what our military does at home and abroad. The majority of them, I would guess, have been hostile to the Liberal Party for years because they believe we haven't paid attention to their issues. That's a huge constituency in Canada, especially in a lot of critical ridings, and we ignore it at our peril. Here's an opportunity to demonstrate something positive. If we approach it in the right way, it doesn't have to be seen as a negative."

At that point Hillier and I went back to see the prime minister in his office. "Okay," Mr. Martin said after listening to our petition, "I guarantee that you will have two operational task forces of 1,200 personnel each that could be deployed abroad within the framework of our defence policy statement." When the budget was announced on February 23, 2005, the final figure for Defence was $12.8 billion over five years – the largest increase in two decades. In line with our review, the money would increase our regular forces by five thousand troops and our reserves by three thousand; it would improve their training and operational readiness; and it would let DND spend more than $2.5 billion on new equipment. "What a day yesterday," I wrote in my notes on February 24. "A budget that's amazing for the military! In many ways we did it because we had a strategy and followed it." We were also fortunate that our request coincided with a significant increase in the budgetary capacity of the country. The money was there – otherwise no amount of talk would have made any difference.

Unfortunately, that wasn't the end of the story. Allocating the money in the budget did not necessarily mean getting the equipment. For example, in the autumn of 2005 we hoped to make a major four-pronged procurement for the Canadian Forces, including new search and rescue aircraft, helicopters, trucks, and perhaps most important of all, new aircraft that could carry heavy loads long distances. Of the thirty-two old Hercules in the fleet, only twelve could operate at any given time, with the remainder undergoing constant maintenance at considerable expense. We concluded that the best deal was to buy the new generation of US-built Hercules, which meant making a sole-sourced purchase from Lockheed Martin. But when the procurement package went to the Cabinet committee on operations on November 14, there was a chorus of objections, including the usual complaints on behalf of Canadian industry and the more legitimate concern that we should not undertake a big procurement just before an election. Hillier was so livid at the outcome of the meeting that I feared he might resign. I begged Anne McLellan to intervene in her capacity as deputy prime minister, and she and I ultimately succeeded in getting approval for an expedited plan to buy the long-range transport aircraft we so desperately needed. Unfortunately we subsequently lost the election, and the process had to start all over again with the new government. This episode illustrates the sclerotic procurement process that continues to plague Ottawa to this day.

EVERY TIME CANADA tries to rethink its defence policy, we run up against our treaty obligations to NORAD and NATO. The constraints of our military alliances shape what we can and cannot do to a degree that most Canadians – and even many parliamentarians – still fail to grasp. When Pierre Trudeau questioned the need to keep our troops in Europe or to buy new tanks for fighting a land war in an age of nuclear missiles, the Europeans and Americans reminded him forcefully about our commitments to NATO, and in 2001 we had no choice under article 5 but to go to war in Afghanistan. This obligation represents a loss of sovereignty in the sense of freedom of action, but we have consented to it because the benefits in increased security outweigh any of the constraints imposed.

Canadians must be aware of the degree to which our national security depends on close co-operation with our American allies, who have always provided the greater amount of manpower and materiel to safeguard the continent. Every decision made in Ottawa concerning our security is closely influenced by how it might play out in Washington. Since the Ogdensburg Agreement of 1940, Canadian and American governments have acknowledged that the defence of North America is, as our review observed, "indivisible." Our respective armies, navies, and coast guards work closely together to maintain continental security. Our air defence is the most integrated of all, particularly through NORAD, which was formally established in 1958 to monitor and control what was happening in the air space over North America. When US defence strategy shifted from the threat of Soviet bombers to the threat of Soviet missiles, we had to adapt our defence strategy as well. In 1981, in fact, NORAD's official name was changed from North American Air Defense Command to North American Aerospace Defense Command.

NORAD has been an exceptional instrument for Canada because it's an effective bi-national institution in which we have equal say with the United States. That makes it an important political symbol of equality and an article of faith for every Canadian government as well as a unique window into US strategic thinking. With the end of the Cold War, however, its relevance was called into question, and there was talk of developing it as a framework for an emergency response to a cross-border crisis. Just as Canada and the United States exchange personnel and equipment to handle major forest fires in California or British Columbia, could we extend that co-operation to the military in the event of an armed attack or natural disaster on either side of the border? We eventually concluded that having American troops moving into Canada, or Canadian troops moving into the United States, would be far too sensitive.

Then came 9/11, and the whole issue of continental defence was subject to review. Among the changes initiated by the US government were a new military command structure for North American defence (NORTHCOM) and the development of a new ballistic missile defence (BMD) system. In the winter of 2003 Ambassador Cellucci informed John McCallum that the United States wanted Canada to be involved in BMD, or at least to decide on our involvement, and he implied that the future of NORAD itself was at stake. When Paul Martin succeeded Jean Chrétien as prime minister in December, David Pratt replaced John McCallum as defence minister, and on January 15, 2004, Pratt agreed with his counterpart Donald Rumsfeld to begin negotiating a framework memorandum of understanding. However, in February of that year, there were intimations of the problems to come when thirty Liberal MPs supported a Bloc Québécois motion that called for the government to cease our negotiations with the Americans on BMD. This issue was clearly going to be contentious politically, particularly in Quebec. That's more or less where the matter stood on July 20 when I took over from Pratt, who had been defeated in the previous month's election.

As foreign minister, I had been relatively indifferent to our participation in BMD, largely because DFAIT officials were divided between those who feared that a positive answer would alienate the Russians at a time when we were seeking to build greater co-operation, and those who feared that a negative response would infuriate the Americans. But, as defence minister, I came to support it. As I understood the situation, the Americans didn't want anything concrete from Canada; there would be no missiles or bases or radar on Canadian soil; they weren't asking for a financial contribution; and they even held out the possibility of future technological spinoffs for Canadian industry. In the end, they wanted "the flag" – our support – and it seemed to me that saying no so close to the Iraq decision would be badly perceived by the Bush administration. There were also important considerations in favour of participating in the BMD system. Better to have BMD placed under joint NORAD command, I reasoned, than have it housed where we wouldn't have any input or inside information. Above all, I didn't want NORTHCOM to marginalize NORAD, a vital instrument of Canadian security whose agreement was up for renewal in 2006. Indeed, on August 5, 2004, as one of my first acts as minister, I implemented my predecessor's decision by signing a protocol to allow NORAD to provide NORTHCOM with early-warning information for missile defence. Contrary to my intention, the agreement may actually have strengthened the hand of the BMD's critics because it seemed to guarantee NORAD's survival and therefore removed one of the best arguments for Canada's participation in the defence system itself.

In terms of domestic politics, however, it was an emotionally charged issue in which the debate emitted more heat than light. Most Canadians associated BMD with Bush's unilateralist, hawkish policies and viewed it not as a defensive measure but as a tool for an aggressive US foreign policy somehow connected to the invasion of Iraq. It was also linked to Ronald Reagan's "Star Wars" program by a lot of people in Parliament and the press who should have known better. Yet building a defence against ballistic missiles was no more a weaponization of space than the ballistic missiles themselves were. Some argued, with more credibility, that BMD could never work operationally. Others worried that it would lead to a new arms race – a view reinforced by statements out of Moscow – even though the system was designed to be of use against a limited number of missiles from a rogue state or a terrorist organization. Some people wanted the Americans to guarantee that the missiles would never be shot down over Canada in the event of an attack, as though such a guarantee would be possible even if we were partners.

Following a long conversation with Donald Rumsfeld on Friday, November 5, 2004, I recorded in my notes that "he made the point that the US decision to go into space would be made by them alone and that our participation or not in this program would not influence that decision (which was a long way from being taken)." Furthermore, if the weaponization of space were ever to occur, it would probably evolve out of the moon or Mars projects, not BMD. I ended the call by telling him that I had a collection of his somewhat wacky aphorisms, assembled by a satirist as "existential poetry," sitting on my desk. ("There are known knowns; there are things we know that we know," went the most famous one. "We also know there are known unknowns; that is to say we know there are some things we do not know. But there are also unknown unknowns – the ones we don't know we don't know.") "Can you believe I said those things?" he laughed.

When I reported this conversation to the prime minister next day, it became evident that he had shifted his position from leaning toward BMD to leaning against it. The officials had trouble explaining the technology in terms that satisfied his intense questioning, and he thought the benefit to Canada in terms of defence or industrial spinoffs was minimal. Politically, there were no advantages to be gained with the NDP and the Bloc Québécois, and many within the Liberal caucus were strongly opposed. The prime minister also wondered whether we could secure our access to US intelligence by promising to help in other areas. "Can we just say that we support the US's position on BMD without signing on, but by providing NORAD support?" he asked. In other words, it was now a question of managing the Americans, managing the politics, and managing the caucus – a question made more difficult when President Bush went off-script during a visit to Ottawa on November 30 and publicly expressed his hope that Canada would participate in the program. Martin invited me to try to sell it to the caucus, but when he said nothing to support me, I got nowhere.

By mid-February 2005, it was clear to me that the prime minister was going to say no to missile defence. It was now only a matter of how and when to inform the Canadian public and the Americans. There was one final complication, however. On February 22, 2005, shortly before Foreign Minister Pettigrew was to inform Condoleezza Rice that Canada wouldn't be joining BMD, Frank McKenna met with SCFAIT to discuss his new appointment as ambassador to the United States. Asked by the press about BMD on his way out of the meeting, McKenna said that Canada was already participating in the program because NORAD had provided data on incoming missiles. The media took that to mean that Canada was now on board with the BMD program and reported the story accordingly. When McKenna was told to go out and clarify his statement, he was understandably livid. The PMO hadn't told him that Canada was going to stay out of BMD, and Foreign Affairs hadn't briefed him that our indirect involvement through NORAD wasn't the same as full participation. His initial reaction was so intense that I worried he might resign, and I was left with the responsibility of calming him down.

On February 24, 2005, Martin announced his decision: Canada would not sign on. When I discussed the issue with a group of dovish party activists at a Liberal convention the following week, I conceded that I had "lost the war" on the BMD file. The press seized on my words: "Graham loses war on shield," the *National Post* declared in a headline.

Once the prime minister had made up his mind, it was my job to phone Rumsfeld with an explanation, but the defense secretary was ill and I ended up speaking with his deputy secretary, Paul Wolfowitz, instead. I was ready for a rather tense call, but he was surprisingly sanguine about our announcement and stated that the United States would be open to discussing BMD again if Canada ever changed its mind. In fact, he mostly wanted to talk about the movie *Hotel Rwanda* and asked me questions about General Roméo Dallaire. The Americans even renewed the NORAD agreement in perpetuity on April 26, 2006. However, in the years that followed it became clear that the United States regards NORAD as a secondary operation compared to NORTHCOM, to the point where it risks fading away like the Cheshire cat to little but a grin. If so, Canada will lose one of our most important institutions, one that relates not only to our security but to our broader relationship with the United States as well. We have, unfortunately, already lost what voice we might have had in the creation and use of BMD. If a missile is ever directed toward North America, the response will be made in Washington, leaving us to watch from a distance.

SOVEREIGNTY IN MILITARY alliances, sovereignty in global trade, and sovereignty in international law may seem rather abstract, but everyone understands territorial sovereignty. As I always told my students, the European powers laid claim to much of the globe by landing on a few barren rocks and planting a flag on behalf of some monarch far away, even when those lands had long been occupied by other people. Today, that's no longer enough.

Sovereignty is the exercise of power and dominion, and it is exercised differently over different territories. The exercise of sovereignty over New York City is not the same as over northern Canada, because sovereignty is measured in terms of what constitutes a reasonable level of activity and what assets you have at your disposal to conduct that activity. If you don't take active possession, your declaration risks being judged hollow. Our maritime sovereignty in the North was under threat during the early part of the twenty-first century because of new challenges. In the past we had assumed that the Native peoples of Canada had established our possession by their age-old occupation of those vast territories. With the Cold War we had demonstrated our claim with the Distant Early Warning line and the NORAD bases. Now, with climate change and the warming of the Arctic waters, there was the probability of new shipping passages full of international fleets and a tremendous increase in oil exploration and mineral development. The United States began granting exploration licences in waters subject to our claims, and it insisted that the Northwest Passage is international waters – a stance reiterated in a National Security Directive by the Bush administration. Russia, Denmark, and even China were moving in.

The importance of Arctic sovereignty was core to my brief but highly controversial visit in July 2005 to Hans Island, a piece of barren rock not much bigger than a square kilometre in area, midway between Greenland

and Ellesmere Island. Its ownership had been a matter of dispute between Canada and Denmark for decades, even after we agreed on most of the maritime boundary back in 1973. The island itself was of little strategic importance, but there was a principle at issue: Were we willing to make an effort to demonstrate our presence in the face of Denmark's competing claim?

I admit to a bit of cheek in going there without first consulting our Department of Foreign Affairs, but I knew it would have objected. In fact, when I was foreign minister, I probably would have said no for the same obvious reasons: maintaining good relations with a NATO ally and EU member such as Denmark was preferable to causing trouble with a symbolic gesture, and international disputes are usually best handled through quiet diplomacy. However, in this case I felt the symbolism and the media coverage were to Canada's advantage. If the question of Hans Island ever came to the International Court of Justice, my going there as a minister would be a relevant fact. Besides, we don't get many opportunities to advance our claim even a little bit, and a visit by a Canadian defence minister would be a powerful sign of occupation.

After a bone-rattling five-hour flight from Iqaluit over some of the most desolate yet majestic landscape on the planet, Cathy and I set down in Canada's northernmost military base at Alert. It's supplied by Hercules aircraft several times a year and by ship in the summer. In winter the cold and wind are so severe that our troops rarely venture out, and when they do, they often have to hold onto a rope to get from building to building. I saw a wooden sign saying, "Moscow, 4,000 km." At the height of the Cold War, Alert had been an extremely important listening post from which to monitor Soviet activity in the Far North, requiring the presence of several hundred technicians. Once new technology enabled the data to be beamed to Ottawa, the number of communications personnel needed to keep the base operational fell to just a few, though it required the same number of military personnel. At the time of my visit, the base's role in monitoring Russian activity in the circumpolar region had diminished, but it remained an important symbol of Canada's presence in the region, with every possibility of increased relevance depending on Russia's posture in the North.

After a hasty meal with the base personnel, and somewhat exhausted from our trip, Cathy and I were escorted to a helicopter and flown to Hans

Island with the pilots, the base commander, a sergeant, and Jamie Innes, one of my political aides, in the face of seventy-miles-per-hour headwinds. Before long I began to wonder whether coming here in these dangerous conditions had been such a smart idea. Because of the winds, our flight to the island took an hour and forty-five minutes; the return trip, with the wind at our back, took only thirty-five minutes. We stayed about an hour, just long enough to take a brisk walk, snap a few photographs, and check out the Canadian flag that had been raised the week before by a group of visiting Canadian soldiers. When I saw that the last contingent of Danish troops had left behind tinned meats and a bottle of whisky as a sign of occupation, I suggested we should toast our conquest with a swig.

"Minister, I wouldn't do that if I were you," said the sergeant. "You never know what else they might have put in that bottle."

The trip took on a vigorous life of its own in the press and on the Internet, sometimes amusingly. One cartoon suggested we send a hockey player to the island to assert our sovereignty; another had me in a rowboat trying to drive off the Danish navy with a super-soaker. More than a decade later an elderly gentleman approached me at a cocktail party to ask, with a twinkle in his eye, if I thought Mr. Putin had the Hans Island precedent in mind when he engineered the takeover of Crimea. Even my Danish counterpart Søren Gade found some humour in it. At the next meeting of NATO defence ministers, which took place in Berlin in September 2005, he presented me with a Danish flag. "Next time you're up there," he said, "could you plant this and save me the trip?" So though my visit had a serious purpose, it was conducted without rancour or rudeness. Eventually, in 2012, Canada and Denmark proposed to settle the dispute by sharing the island fifty-fifty.

MEANWHILE, OUR disagreements with the United States over the Northwest Passage and the North Slope, where resources of considerable value are at stake, went largely without comment. Some US think-tank analyses predicted a fundamental divergence of Canadian and American interests in the years ahead over resource rights and navigation as the Northwest Passage gradually opened to shipping. These were alarmist scenarios, but the access of American nuclear submarines, the advances in space-based surveillance technologies, and the possible construction of double-hulled naval vessels suitable for employment in the Arctic clearly have serious implications for our sovereignty in the North.

As usual, our best response is to strengthen international law through multilateral instruments and institutions, whether the UN Convention on the Law of the Sea (UNCLOS) or the Arctic Council. We can also draw on the long-standing tradition of discreet co-operation among Canada, Russia, and the United States in search and rescue in the North, which should serve as a model for other kinds of circumpolar co-operation. On my trip to Moscow in 2005, I discussed this topic with Russia's defence minister, Sergei Ivanov – a close confidant of Putin, whom he knew from their days as young KGB officers. Now, with the increasing number of commercial air links over the North Pole, there was an obvious need for Canada, Russia, and the United States to share resources and communications if a jumbo jet carrying four hundred people were to go down in the High Arctic.

In my view, the Americans' wariness of UNCLOS and their insistence on the international character of the Northwest Passage were short-sighted, since this stance would open the passage to everyone. Russia was well along with the mapping of its continental shelf and already used the Northeast Passage for the transportation of goods from Siberia to Murmansk, and its cruise ships were converted icebreakers that could navigate what we claim as our internal waters and visit our northern ports. China was undertaking Arctic research, deploying icebreakers to the region, and had embarked on a worldwide resource acquisition policy. On the other hand, if the Northwest Passage were recognized as Canadian waters, the United States, as a valued ally, would have virtually unrestricted use, subject to environmental controls from which both we and the Americans would benefit. A similar arrangement could meet the EU's interest in free commercial usage, while giving Canada greater latitude to regulate the activities of less benign powers. Moreover, ratification of UNCLOS would put American claims to seabed resources in the North on a sound legal and political footing, forestalling those of rival powers. But if Canada was playing catch-up in mapping our continental shelf in order to submit our claims, the United States was even further behind, and there wasn't enough of a constituency to press for the ratification in Washington.

Though highly publicized trips by various governors general and prime ministers have helped assert our presence in the Arctic, Canadian declarations of sovereignty there had often lacked conviction because they weren't backed by military and other resources in the region. That started to change once our political leaders woke up to the fact that the Arctic accounts for 40 percent of our land mass, 75 percent of our coastline, and an estimated 25 percent of potential world energy supplies. Our 2005 defence review therefore reorganized our command structure along more "Arctic-friendly" lines, with responsibility for all North American operations vested in Canada Command, overseeing six regional sub-commands dubbed Joint Task Forces. One of them, Joint Task Force North, based in Yellowknife, was set up to co-ordinate all operations in the North. As well, the Martin government acted on the principle that Arctic sovereignty required a holistic approach, cutting across departmental boundaries and integrating diplomacy, military activity, environmental protection, scientific research, and law enforcement and border control.

Over time Canada's sizable military presence in the Far North has become more involved with the performance of political, economic, and law-enforcement tasks than with military operations in the traditional sense. It might even be argued that the greatest security problem now is the drug smuggling on ships around Tuktoyaktuk, a border-control issue that has been familiar since 9/11, though it is quite new in the Arctic context. In fact, because the territorial governments lack many of the assets and equipment that provincial governments have in the South, the federal government – and in this respect largely the Defence Department – has had to fill in the gaps. Our Armed Forces play an unusually important role in providing "aid to the civil power" in the North. For many activities we are the only branch of government at any level that has the appropriate resources, even for something as mundane as fire trucks. The "Narwhal" exercises of 2002–07 used scenarios that included satellite and aircraft crashes in the North and threats to the oil and gas infrastructure in the Northwest Territories. The navy and coast guard provided the ships, RCMP officers took part, and health and energy officials participated as well.

Along with the coast guard, the Canadian Forces also play an important role in search and rescue in the North. If a pilot or a hunter goes missing, the military often receives the call as the first responder, launches the patrols that can go on for days at a stretch, and if necessary makes the agonizing decision to call off the search. Of course, economic arguments were made constantly for shifting our search and rescue capacity entirely to Trenton, Ontario, or Cold Lake, Alberta, and sending aircraft north as needed. But I always insisted on basing at least some of the planes in Yellowknife, on the grounds that only a long-term physical presence in the North would confirm to Northerners our interest in their needs.

Because the Canadian Forces rarely have enough regulars, reservists are essential in both foreign deployments and domestic operations. By volunteering their time and contributing their civilian expertise, they are a key component of our Armed Forces, and one that is poorly understood outside of military circles. When I visited Kosovo, for example, I discovered that at least 25 percent of our troops stationed there were drawn from the reserves. Later, during the Afghanistan mission, reservists played an equally indispensable role. Sometimes they served with our soldiers, sometimes in other capacities. For instance, Lieutenant-Colonel Robert Shaw, a former commanding officer of the Governor General's Horse Guards, on leave from his position as a senior officer in the Ontario Provincial Police, was assigned to an American police-training unit. Because he was not bound by US rules of engagement, he was often able to undertake tasks that his American colleagues could not, and his courageous and intelligent work was recognized by a highly valued American military decoration. There are innumerable other examples of the vital contribution made by our reservists, both here in Canada and abroad.

Because of its vast geography, reservists fill an especially important niche in the Far North, where they ensure a Canadian military presence in sparsely populated areas. However, training reservists in Arctic conditions is expensive and logistically demanding, and patrolling the region requires a high level of local knowledge. Consequently, in 1947 Canada set up a permanent reserve unit there – the Canadian Rangers. Most of them are Indigenous people, and their procurement needs are modest, consisting mainly of skidoos, rifles, and ammunition. When I spent a day with the Rangers out on patrol in Nunavut, I was impressed by their professionalism as they dealt with the dangerous weather conditions. They could pitch tents and create a fairly comfortable base with the absolute minimum of supplies and equipment. At Pond Inlet one sergeant, who must have been at least seventy years old, proudly told me about the many excursions he and his Ranger groups had made throughout the area. I also learned about the Junior Rangers program that many Inuit mothers told me is absolutely essential for keeping their adolescents productively occupied and away from the terrible scourges of drugs, alcohol, and glue sniffing that so affect northern communities. The Rangers is a kind of social program for a lot of the communities in the North – one of the few institutions that can provide that sort of leadership and training.

During the 2006 election campaign, the Conservatives made some extravagant and highly impractical claims about how they would do more to defend our interests up north. During a debate at the University of Toronto, Stockwell Day chastised me over the unchallenged presence of American nuclear submarines under our Arctic ice. I replied that I couldn't imagine the scenario in which the armed icebreakers his party supported would fire on an American sub or, for that matter, a Russian one. Nor could I imagine the F-35 fighters the Conservatives subsequently announced they intended to purchase for untold billions of dollars – in part, they claimed, to protect our sovereignty in the Arctic – landing on an ice floe or even detecting anything wrong as they sped overhead. In fact, most of the more expensive Tory proposals for a permanent Arctic presence were shelved for budgetary reasons almost as soon as the Conservatives formed the government.

15

THE 3D WAR

Canada's military involvement in Afghanistan began before I became defence minister and lasted long after my watch was over, but it was front and centre for most of my eighteen months in the job. It influenced our foreign policy and our relations with our most important allies. It shaped the foreign dimension of our defence policy and our procurement needs. It marked our military for a generation and redefined the place of our Armed Forces in the minds of Canadians. It had a profound effect on our aid programs, both in the amount that it absorbed and the manner of delivery. And it had a considerable impact on domestic politics. Yet, at the time, nobody foresaw how large or long a commitment Canada was going to make to a country that was unknown to most Canadians and geographically far removed from any place that touched on our vital interests. It's a cautionary tale that future governments might do well to heed.

There was at the time, and still remains, a school of thought that Canada's extensive commitments in Afghanistan arose from our refusal to join the "coalition of the willing" in the Iraq invasion – a sort of quid pro quo for the Americans. Given the importance of both these theatres to the Bush administration, there was obviously a relationship between the two, and I agree that our significant contribution in Afghanistan helped to soften criticism in Washington about our decision on Iraq. However, our commitment to the rebuilding of Afghanistan by the international community, as reflected in the Bonn Agreement of December 2001, was made more than a year before the US-UK invasion of Iraq and had more to do with our security interests and broad foreign policy objectives than with any need to placate the Americans. In other words, we didn't send troops to Afghanistan as a way to avoid sending them to Iraq or as a specific tradeoff, though the two decisions were complementary in the context of helping the bilateral relationship with our primary ally. Moreover, the International Security Assistance Force (ISAF) sent to Afghanistan was a multilateral, peace-support mission mandated by the United Nations Security Council to create enough stability in Kabul to allow the Afghan Interim Authority to establish a new and legitimate government. It was neither an invasion nor a patchwork coalition of the willing, and therefore it was fully in accord with international law.

On January 8, 2003, John McCallum went to Washington to meet with his US counterpart, Donald Rumsfeld, fully expecting that Iraq would be at the top of the agenda. Instead, eager to free up American troops for an increasingly likely overthrow of the Saddam regime, Rumsfeld was primarily interested in persuading Canada to pick up more of the burden of reconstruction and "nation building" in Afghanistan. In any case, the Pentagon never relished these kinds of tasks. Furthermore, Rumsfeld wanted to take ISAF from the Europeans (who had frozen Canada out of it at first) and put it under NATO's umbrella as a way of securing more troops from more countries, and he hoped that Canada would assume its leadership in Kabul. As McCallum told me on his return, he hadn't committed the government in his response, but he had pointed out to the Americans that the Canadian military was already stretched thin. If we took on a lead role in ISAF, we would have nothing left to contribute to any actions against Iraq. Rumsfeld saw no problem in that regard. As later events confirmed, the Bush administration wanted Canada's *political* support for the course it was to pursue in Iraq more than any specific *military* contribution, something that Paul Cellucci would remind me of regularly.

Rumsfeld's desire to shift American forces to Iraq and away from reconstruction efforts became another argument for those in favour of a greater Canadian participation in Afghanistan. This operation seemed to draw on many of the skills and specialities that the Canadian Forces had employed for decades with the UN. However, reconstruction first required peace and stability, and our military leadership and senior officials in DND, not least General Ray Henault, were reluctant to get involved with ISAF in Kabul. According to one of my officials, Henault was "cautious to a fault." The military brass feared that, without the proper instructions and equipment to engage the enemy, the Kabul mission could be highly dangerous, especially if the Americans weren't there. Nor did they think that Canada would have the resources if – as they fully hoped and expected – we decided to join the US forces in Iraq within a few weeks.

Nevertheless, on February 12, 2003, McCallum announced that Canada would be deploying troops to Kabul for a period of one year beginning the following summer. Nearly two thousand Canadian soldiers were slated to arrive in Afghanistan, making us the largest contributor to ISAF. In April, a month after the Iraq invasion, NATO agreed to assume responsibility for ISAF – its first military campaign beyond Europe – and soon afterward it decided to place Canada in command of the mission for the second half of our deployment. In the meantime, given our prominent role, NATO appointed a Canadian, Major-General Andrew Leslie, as ISAF's deputy commander. In August NATO officially took charge of ISAF in Kabul, where Hamid Karzai had become president of the Afghan Transitional Authority little more than a year earlier.

Although the Americans remained intent on reducing their presence in Afghanistan as much as possible, they did agree to stop short of a complete pullout and to provide assistance if we had to withdraw our forces from Kabul in an emergency. They also agreed not to press the NATO allies to begin operating beyond Kabul at once. So, when I first visited Afghanistan as minister of foreign affairs in September 2003, it seemed that Canada's commitment was limited in time and scope, with the United States backing us. We had a full year in which to find a NATO ally willing to take our place.

OPERATION ATHENA, as the Canadian mission was called, included many experienced officers and troops who had seen extensive service in theatres such as Bosnia, Haiti, and the Golan Heights. They quickly set about building Camp Julien, a multimillion-dollar base situated in a valley below the bombed-out shell of the old royal palace. It was a considerable feat of engineering, which required digging out more than four feet of dirt and putting in special soil to create a sanitized environment to protect the sophisticated computer equipment from dust – and the soldiers from scorpions.

Canada had established diplomatic relations with the new Afghan government in July, so one of DFAIT's early priorities was to construct an embassy and select an appropriate staff willing to serve under volatile and sometimes dangerous conditions. We had already appointed Chris Alexander as our ambassador, a young and dynamic foreign-service officer who had impressed me when I met him in Moscow during his posting there. His fluency in Russian helped him in Afghanistan, and he was much respected by Afghans in general and President Hamid Karzai in particular. (After his government service, he returned to Kabul as second-in-command of the UN mission and subsequently became a Conservative MP and a minister in the Harper Cabinet.) His staff included Nipa Banerjee, who energetically directed our aid program, and Glyn Berry, who later headed up our reconstruction efforts in Kandahar and paid with his life for his willingness to engage in the field when he was killed in the suicide bombing of a convoy travelling to Kabul. On September 5, 2003, during my first visit to Afghanistan since my trip with Patrick Wootten forty-three years earlier, I opened the Canadian embassy in the presence of Abdullah Abdullah, the Afghan foreign minister. Raising the flag over the embassy was a proud moment, even if our people were still sleeping on the floor of the unfinished building.

Major-General Leslie arranged a dinner that included a couple of corporals from Toronto Centre who wanted to talk about local politics. As I discovered, the Canadian army may have been the least class conscious of all the military groupings in Afghanistan. The American officers seemed much more aloof, and the British officers ate separately from their men. Perhaps only the Dutch were more democratic. Their soldiers, many with long flowing hair, even had unions to represent their interests. Our troops were quartered in large tents, with men and women living in close proximity though forbidden to fraternize even if they were married. My communications director, Isabelle Savard, wasn't pleased when she heard that she would have to bunk in with them, so I gave her my cot in the VIP tent that had been erected in anticipation of a visit by Governor General Clarkson, and I had a bed set up for myself elsewhere. "The thing is," I said

44 With Cathy and Prime Minister Paul Martin.

45 With General Ray Henault and General Rick Hillier, February 4, 2005.

46 Meeting Major-General Andy Leslie in Kabul, Afghanistan, September 5, 2003.

47 In conversation with Afghan president Hamid Karzai, October 12, 2005.

48 In Afghanistan
with communications
director Renée
Filiatrault, October
2005.

49 With Donald Rumsfeld, Quito, Ecuador,
November 17, 2004.

50 With Russian defence minister Sergei Ivanov in Moscow, September 2, 2005.

51 Paying a call on Russian foreign minister Sergey Lavrov, September 2, 2005.

52 On Hans Island with Major Rod Sterling, July 20, 2005.

53 With Svend Robinson, Jack Layton, and Allan Rock at the Vancouver Gay Pride Parade, August 4, 2002.

54 "The last hurrah": campaigning with Cathy in December 2005.

55 Leader of the Opposition.

56 With His Highness the Aga Khan, November 2006.

57 Prime Minister Stephen Harper and I dragging newly elected Speaker of the House Peter Milliken to his seat, April 3, 2006.

58 With Justin Trudeau at the 2006 Liberal Party Convention.

59 With Liberal leaders past and present, December 2, 2006. *From left to right:* Jean Chrétien, me, Stéphane Dion, Paul Martin, and John Turner.

60 With Cathy, Patrick, and Katy at the 2006 Liberal Party convention.

to Isabelle, "they put this gizmo beside my bed to press if there's an emergency in the night. You've been saying all day how good-looking the guys in our security detail are, but I don't want you pressing the button at three in the morning to get one of them running in."

Canada's Armed Forces, coming from a multicultural democracy that prizes tolerance and mutual accommodation, brought our national values and experience to the Afghanistan mission. They proved ready and able to fight when necessary but were also willing to reach out to the local population and build their support insofar as the security situation would allow. "What we love about the Canadian troops," a British brigadier once told me, "is that they don't just sit around in Camp Julien." The soldiers of most other nations were kept under strict lock and key, but the Canadians mixed with the community and even volunteered beyond the call of duty. When one of our captains heard about the security concerns around a highly vulnerable girls' orphanage, he assembled a group that took responsibility for protecting it. They drove around it in their spare time, checked in with the matron, and acted like its guards. Soon the message went out not to mess with the girls there, because the Canadians were on the lookout. When Cathy accompanied me to Kabul in 2005, she visited the orphanage and began raising money for it as soon as she returned to Canada.

I met with President Karzai on September 5. Although he would later be criticized by some as a corrupt and incompetent leader, I always found him to be a sophisticated and articulate spokesman for his country. Once, during lunch at 24 Sussex Drive, he told me of the great Persian poets he had read growing up and mentioned that because he had been educated in India, many of his fellow Pashtuns distrusted him. They were allied to Pakistan and saw India as the enemy. At our meeting in the presidential palace, he went out of his way to say that the multilateral NATO presence caused fewer political problems for him domestically than the US-led operation in the south, which had the bad optics of looking too much like an American occupation.

In the months ahead, Karzai returned repeatedly to this point. Indeed, because ISAF had achieved relative success in securing Kabul and its environs, whereas most of the country remained beset by insurgency, Karzai urged NATO to begin spreading its operations into the provinces. When he visited Ottawa a few weeks later, he asked Prime Minister Chrétien to consider deploying Canadian troops outside the capital as part of an expanded NATO presence in Afghanistan. However, on October 18, after continuing his conversations with Karzai back in Kabul, Chrétien announced that we would not be able to send additional troops in the near future. It seemed that Canada's contributions to Afghanistan would begin winding down once our mission in Kabul was over. That was certainly our intention at the time, and the history of our involvement in Afghanistan would have been very different if we had held to that initial purpose.

WHEN PAUL MARTIN became prime minister in December 2003, I think it's fair to say that he wasn't really interested in staying on in Afghanistan. He didn't see it as a crucial foreign policy objective and wasn't even certain why Canada was still there, instead of working to bring peace to Haiti or Darfur. It's true that many voices were calling for an intervention in Darfur, but that mission would have been just as dangerous as Afghanistan, except that the Sudanese government would not have accepted a non-African force on its territory at that time, and the African Union made it clear that a "colonial" presence from Europe and North America was unwelcome. Nor would there have been any well-equipped NATO allies to support us, and we lacked the materiel, particularly helicopters, to mount a campaign by ourselves. In the end, however, once the African Union decided to send troops, we were able to furnish them with armoured personnel carriers.

Traditional peacekeeping, sometimes referred to as "peacekeeping lite," presumes that you're there to help warring parties keep a peace they both want by means of lightly armed troops operating under restrictive rules of engagement. But most peacekeeping these days is peacemaking or "peace-keeping heavy." It often takes place in a combat situation between highly armed opponents, many of whom are non-state actors. As a result, when a Canadian government decides to put our troops into such a dangerous environment, both our military and our civilian leaders must ensure that they are properly equipped, properly trained, and operating under rules of engagement that will allow them to protect both themselves and civilians.

However, peacekeeping heavy isn't the same as old-fashioned warfare. As Roméo Dallaire once put it during an interview, "The era of a general who only knows how to fight is gone, especially with the middle powers ...

Generals who argue that we only go in with clear mandates and time frames – sorry. We're in an era of complexity and ambiguity, and if you can't operate in ambiguity, you've got a problem."

From the beginning, Canada saw ISAF as a "whole-of-government" or "3D" mission, in which defence, diplomacy, and development came together to establish long-term stability by mobilizing the resources of DND, DFAIT, and the Canadian International Development Agency (CIDA). My own thinking had been influenced by Rupert Smith's *Utility of Force,* in which he discussed the demands of the recent complex operations he termed "war amongst the people." The US Marine Corps' concept of the "Three Block War," which evolved from the American experience in failing states such as Somalia and the Balkans, also had a major impact on our vision for the Afghanistan mission. That idea referred to the fact that our Armed Forces were being asked to carry out overlapping missions at any one time. As we described it in our defence review, "Our land forces could be engaged in combat operations against well-armed militia forces in one city block, stabilization operations in the next block, and humanitarian relief and reconstruction two blocks over."

Indeed, the US military in Afghanistan had already pioneered the use of Provincial Reconstruction Teams (PRTs), which brought soldiers together with aid and development specialists to implement projects such as the construction of schools, hospitals, and other fundamental infrastructure. Though the Americans may have used the PRTs to recast Afghanistan as a "nation-building" exercise in order to attract more NATO allies to take some of the burden off their shoulders, they fit well with Canada's values-based conviction that defence should go hand in hand with diplomacy and development.

A growing number of NATO allies were preparing to send their own PRTs beyond the capital region, and it was widely assumed that we would assume responsibility for one as well. Furthermore, because the interests of the global community weren't entirely aligned with those of the United States, many governments shared Karzai's concern that ISAF needed to be perceived as a truly international mission. When you looked at a map of the early fighting, all you saw were a few NATO flags in the north and a lot of American flags everywhere else. That wasn't satisfactory for anybody, including the Americans. Consequently, in October 2003, the UN Security

Council passed a resolution authorizing NATO's ISAF mission to expand beyond Kabul.

As early as spring 2003 we began planning to deploy a PRT of troops, diplomats, development workers, engineers, and legal and medical advisers beyond Kabul as soon as our year-long ISAF commitment ended. But, unlike our NATO allies, we had trouble making up our minds about where and when to go. Prime Minister Martin remained preoccupied with peacekeeping in Haiti and Darfur; David Pratt had to learn the file when he succeeded John McCallum as minister of national defence; everyone in government became engrossed with the election in June, which resulted in an unstable minority government; sharp disagreements within and between DFAIT and DND resulted in conflicting, confusing advice; and, because Afghanistan wasn't a top priority at that time, no one was in any rush to settle the matter. Nothing got resolved for more than a year, though as Prime Minister Martin pointed out in his memoirs, we could not have deployed much earlier, because of the needed "operational pause" that Rick Hillier had recommended for our overworked and thinly stretched forces.

One important consideration was the choice of partners: We wanted to work beside NATO colleagues who shared, in the words of my Norwegian counterpart Kristin Devold, "similar psychological rules of engagement." Though General Hillier was a huge admirer of the United States, he often said to me, "The people I want on my wing are not the Americans, because whenever they get into trouble, they just call in the B52s and bomb the shit out of everybody, and that causes more political problems than they solve with their military stuff. I want the nice, solid Brits and the Dutch, and we're going to go at this in our own way." DND officials concurred, pointing out that working with Britain and the Netherlands would also allow us to build on our previously successful partnership with both countries in Bosnia. We conducted long negotiations with them, and ultimately we all decided to send our PRTs south, with the British going to Helmand Province, the Dutch to Oruzgan, and the Canadians to Kandahar.

By that time, not many options were available anyway: Herat and other proposed locations were either unsuitable for us or claimed by some other nation. But Kandahar also happened to be where President Karzai, the British, General Henault, and Ambassador Alexander were urging us to be. The appointment of Rick Hillier as chief of the defence staff in February 2005 sealed the matter. Having been in command of ISAF from February to August 2004, he understood that the military situation was crying for an international solution in the south, similar to what the British and Germans were doing in the north. Much of the region remained to be pacified. The Taliban and other insurgents were operating there with the specific objective of preventing a return to normal order and civil life. Those forces had to be defeated before a civil society could be established in Afghanistan, even if that involved exposing the Canadian Forces to a violent, experienced énemy in very hostile terrain – just as we had done in our first mission.

On February 8 I travelled to France for a meeting of the NATO defence ministers, where I told my counterparts that Canada would send a PRT to Kandahar the following August and that we were considering a combat deployment in 2006. I repeated this message a few days later when I flew on to Germany to attend the Munich Conference on Security Policy. Held once a year, this international gathering was an important opportunity to meet with many of the key players in security and defence. During dinner on the first evening, I was asked to join Hillary Clinton, an evident policy wonk who drew us into an animated discussion about Iraq reconstruction. "She's lively, engaged, great," I observed in my notes.

The next day Secretary Rumsfeld spoke on the contemporary security landscape. He was in remarkably good humour despite a recent complaint that had been filed against him in a German court on behalf of prisoners in Abu Ghraib. Many jokes were made about his impending arrest, and he laughed off criticisms of his past policies by saying, "Oh, that was the *old* Rumsfeld." During his speech and the subsequent discussion, he often reminded me of his boss, President Bush, with his gunslinger-like personality and forthright approach to issues. Rumsfeld was unequivocal about the challenges faced by liberal democracies in responding to the threat of international terrorism, telling the audience, "We have an enemy with no bureaucracy, no democracy, no inhibitions." Yet he could also be more thoughtful and nuanced than his reputation as a single-minded hawk, as when he emphasized the importance of civil society groups in peace-keeping and post-conflict reconstruction.

The Munich Conference afforded me another opportunity to see my friend and colleague Joschka Fischer, who spoke energetically about the future of the UN. "Joschka is a huge intellectual machine that rattles along sparking off ideas and probably driving the interpreter mad," I noted. "I'd forgotten what he was like at those G8 meetings." That evening at dinner I sat across from Kofi Annan, Hillary Clinton, and Russian defence minister Sergei Ivanov as they discussed the state of the world.

I returned home to continue work on our defence policy review and our plans for the Afghanistan mission. On March 8, 2005, Hillier presented me with a proposal that included sending our PRT from August 2005 to February 2007, along with the Joint Task Force 2 (JTF2) special forces and a fifteen-person Strategic Advisory Team (SAT) to help with governance issues in Kabul. In addition, he was eager for Canada to assume the "region lead" in Kandahar by fielding a brigade headquarters of 320 personnel to oversee operations under the American-led Operation Enduring Freedom and later under ISAF. Finally, he wanted to deploy approximately one thousand combat troops for one year, starting in February 2006, who would fight the Taliban side-by-side with the Americans until NATO took over command, as expected, in 2006.

We had been considering this option for some time, even before his appointment as chief of the defence staff, though once he assumed his new office, he became a particularly effective advocate for a more robust combat role for Canada in southern Afghanistan. Not only would the plan enhance the chances for stability and reconstruction in our area of responsibility but it would have the merit of raising Canada's standing with the Americans and in NATO, as well as meeting Karzai's goal to supplement the American flag in the south with a NATO one. Though unrelated to our decisions not to participate in the Iraq invasion or BMD, it would also have the side-benefit of helping to rebuild whatever metaphorical bridges we might have burned in Washington – never as serious an issue as many had feared. Haiti, NORAD, and my call with Paul Wolfowitz had demonstrated the enduring strength of the Canada-US relationship.

The prime minister, the Cabinet, the Quebec ministers, and the caucus all came on board for a rapid, combat-type mission to supplement the efforts of our PRT in Kandahar and the SAT in Kabul. It fit into our foreign policy objectives and had a clear and realistic mandate; it had adequate resources, international allies, and a multi-stage rollout; and, perhaps most necessary of all, it had a definite exit strategy. No one in any department persisted in pointing out the pitfalls. So, in May 2005, with Cabinet approval, Prime Minister Martin agreed to send an infantry battle group of approximately a thousand Canadian troops to Kandahar for one year, as of February 2006 – but only after Hillier had convinced him that DND could manage and afford another mission that the Martin government might want to undertake, whether in Darfur, Haiti, or even the Middle East. Alongside the battle group, we would also take on responsibility for the Kandahar brigade headquarters for nine months before handing it off to the Dutch in November 2006.

"You'll have to make the miracle of the loaves and fishes," the prime minister once said to us. "You say you can do it all; now I'd like to see it." He kept up the pressure during a four-hour dinner with Rick Hillier and me in a Winnipeg restaurant later that summer, when he grilled us about NATO and Afghanistan, with his usual tough, Socratic questions.

If Iraq had made me suspicious about the advice coming from DND when I was at DFAIT, given the pro-American, pro-war bias I detected in the Canadian military brass, Afghanistan was different, and not just because I was now the minister in charge of the file. It was without question a legal operation according to international law; it fit within DND's policy review and the new budget; and, perhaps most of all, I had complete confidence in Rick Hillier, whose appointment as chief of the defence staff I had advocated. The fact that he had commanded ISAF, knew what was needed to equip Canada's military to do the job, and understood the problems and the players further strengthened my decision to expand our combat role in Afghanistan.

The Kandahar mission appeared on the surface to be a dramatic departure from Canada's recent history of peacekeeping, so I set out to do a series of public speeches during the summer of 2005. Whenever I was criticized for proposing to send heavily armed warriors to Afghanistan, rather than "humanitarian peacekeepers" to stop the massacre of villagers in Darfur, I replied, "Let me get this straight. You don't like Afghanistan because it's a combat mission, but you want us to send Canadian troops into the middle of the Sahara Desert, without the necessary equipment or helicopters, to deal with these *janjaweed* crazies who will be machine-gunning them from every angle? You're dreaming in Technicolor if you think you can just wander around with a blue beret and pat people on the head."

I argued that the Afghan mission was a necessary adaptation of peace-keeping in the new global environment of failed and failing states. We couldn't help bring good governance or humanitarian relief to Afghanistan if we didn't help establish zones of security and stability first. Although the mission certainly entailed a greater combat role than we had had in Cyprus or the Golan Heights, it was still rooted in familiar Canadian values. At its centre was the recognition, as our defence review put it, that "the Canadian Forces will seek to maintain the right mix of military capability to ensure that they can carry out all potential aspects of the three-block war." At least, that was the theoretical framework. It wasn't true, therefore, that combat was unexpected, as some later claimed. We were clearly and deliberately sending our men and women on a peacemaking mission in a dangerous conflict zone. What we underestimated was the scale, intensity, and dur-ation of the fighting that our troops would face.

Educating the Canadian public in the new realities became somewhat complicated after July 14, when Hillier made headlines by calling the Taliban "detestable murderers and scumbags" and telling reporters that the role of a soldier was to "go out and bayonet somebody." Nor did he stop there. "We are not the Public Service of Canada," he went on. "We are not just another department. We are the Canadian Forces, and our job is to be able to kill people." That sounded a discordant note to many Canadians, who are on the whole less comfortable than the Americans with hawkish rhet-oric, and it aroused suspicions that the Martin policy was really about the "Americanization" or "militarization" of Canada's foreign and defence policy. Some of our own MPs, particularly in the women's caucus, were upset. For my part, though it undercut my own message, Rick's use of colourful language and imagery was precisely what made him such a suc-cessful military leader – a quality much needed in the challenging months and years ahead.

CANADA'S PRT, CONSISTING of foreign-service officers, development experts, members of the RCMP, and 250 military personnel – including engineers, medical professionals, and an infantry company – arrived in

Kandahar in August 2005. Its initial focus was to provide security and to help increase the capacity of Afghanistan's own security-related institutions. Later it got involved in the construction of an irrigation dam, education, and the eradication of polio in the province. Combining development and defence ensured that our mission to Afghanistan reflected Canadian values, which were evident in other ways as well. For instance, the Canadian Forces' multifaith Chaplaincy Service, in which one chaplain would often minister to all of his or her comrades regardless of their particular faith, was an effective demonstration of Canadian diversity at work. One can readily imagine the impact that the sight of a Muslim Canadian chaplain, attending to the spiritual needs of Christian or Jewish or even non-religious soldiers, might have on those living in a post-Taliban Afghanistan.

In September 2005 the parliamentary and provincial council elections went ahead with little disruption, thanks largely to ISAF's success in providing security. The following month I paid a fact-finding visit to Afghanistan with a small contingent of military officials, government advisers, and parliamentarians, and my wife, Cathy, chose to join us in Kabul at her own expense. We flew commercial to Dubai, then by military helicopter into the middle of the desert to Camp Mirage, which got its name because no one was supposed to know about it, though in reality its existence was an open secret. It was the forward staging base from which our personnel and supplies were transported into and out of Afghanistan. An enormous amount of military activity has to do with the logistics of moving people, equipment, and food. "Amateurs talk of strategy," goes the old adage, "but professionals talk logistics." In this respect Camp Mirage was key to the Afghan campaign. We stayed overnight and were outfitted with boots, helmets, vests, and desert gear. The Kevlar vest I was given to wear beneath my shirt was a huge improvement over the bulky bulletproof vest I had been forced to wear under my jacket during my first visit, even in my official meetings.

The next morning we were flown to Kabul on board a Hercules transport. Due to the threat of surface-to-air missiles near the airport, the pilots performed their usual landing manoeuvre of going into a steep dive and doing a series of corkscrew circles while dropping like a stone. "Hang on," they yelled, "we're going down." Cathy, sitting up front in the cockpit, just about had a heart attack, but I found it dramatic and actually kind of fun. A more dramatic reminder of the conditions of life in Afghanistan was the rocket attack that occurred just outside of the Canadian embassy the day after we arrived. Our intelligence sources suggested that another of the other embassies and international organizations in the neighbourhood was the target, but two of our security staff were injured nevertheless.

After two days in Kabul, where we stayed at Camp Julien, Cathy flew back to Dubai while I went on to Kandahar. One of my first duties on arrival was to attend a ceremony in which the Canadian headquarters was officially named Camp Nathan Smith, after one of the four Canadian soldiers killed in the Tarnak Farms tragedy. It was a solemn reminder – if any were necessary – of the very real dangers that our troops faced in Afghanistan. While in Kandahar, I discussed foreign aid with our PRT commander, met with the American regional commander and the UN military representative, and spent hours sitting on mats talking to the local governor and elders about their issues and problems. Rick Hillier arrived while I was there, bringing with him a planeload of prominent Canadians, sports celebrities, and Tim Hortons coffee. It was a classic Hillier way of boosting morale at the base and building support at home for the mission – just one more reason why he was such a good commander and so popular with his troops. We all enjoyed a dinner together, and I could see that it lifted the spirits of the troops who had been confined there for months.

However welcome, no amount of good cheer could make up for the dangerous reality of a volatile region under threat from a hardened adversary. Driving along the main street of Kandahar, I thought the city hadn't changed very much since Patrick Wootten and I had come through it in our Land Rover. There were more people, but still the eternally hard and dusty landscape, the same two-story houses, and no glass towers. Perhaps the biggest difference, which would have surprised and amused Patrick, was that I was here now as the Canadian minister of national defence, riding around town in an armoured vehicle. The more important difference was the security situation. As I noted at the time, "Inspirational to see the children running out to wave at the convoy. But we drive through pretty aggressively. What's the security value of our driving around without stopping or interacting with the population & how does that deter IEDs, bombers etc?"

Later, when I accompanied our troops on a patrol to a local village, I asked, "Can we get out and meet some villagers?"

"Oh, no, Minister," I was told. "We're not getting out of this vehicle." They clearly couldn't risk having me shot or blown up.

That's when I learned first-hand that the whole idea of stepping with a light footprint into the villages on a "hearts and minds" mission was becoming less and less feasible. The Taliban had already initiated a series of suicide bombings and attacks using Improvised Explosive Devices (IEDs). However good our troops were at maintaining security, the enemy's change of tactics found us unprepared and ill-equipped, and our PRT was less able to make real human contact with ordinary Afghanis. The more the team members put themselves out there to do good, the more they put themselves at risk of something terrible, as would happen in March 2006 to Captain Trevor Greene, with whom my son, Patrick, had rowed when they attended King's College in Halifax. He was sitting in a village one day talking about its water issues, not wearing his helmet out of respect for the elders, when he was struck by a young assailant with an axe and all but killed. Only the most extraordinary heroism and resilience on his part allowed him to make a gradual though partial recovery. I was proud to present him with an award from the Atlantic Council in 2010.

From Kandahar, General Hillier and I were flown by helicopter to Graceland, a secret base about thirty miles away. It had once been the home of Mullah Mohammed Omar, the Taliban's deposed head of state, but it was now in the possession of the CIA, US Special Forces, and JTF2. Many officials in Kabul were astonished that the CIA was willing to share its base with Canadian troops, but the two groups had established a rapport during earlier joint operations. We spent the night in Omar's old guesthouse, in front of which the JTF2 commander had created a garden of colourful flowers and fruit trees. When I asked him why, he spoke about the psychological benefits for his troops of coming in from the hot, dusty, dangerous desert to a place of beauty and peace. "It restores their humanity," he said. It also provided work for the Afghans – another small, but important, point of local contact. I had dinner with the CIA base chief at the main building, the palace, and he took me to see the large, deep tunnel that Omar had turned into an underground headquarters, reminiscent of Hitler's bunker, replete with electricity and running water. I saw, not far from its entry, where a cruise missile had detonated, narrowly missing the chance to take out the Taliban's military and spiritual leader, and perhaps change the course of history.

I always enjoyed spending time with JTF2 members, some of whom I had previously met when they let me participate in a live-fire exercise at their training camp outside Ottawa. On that occasion, to Hillier's subsequent fury, they had stormed into a room in which I was supposedly being held prisoner, machine-gunned my two dummy "captors," whisked me up to the top of the building, and spirited me away to freedom by helicopter. However intimidating they could look with their pirate-like beards and bandanas, I found them to be brave, skilled, informed, and refreshingly frank. On one occasion at Camp Julien, when I was told by an officer that our Iltis jeeps could be reinforced for patrol use with some stronger armour, one of the JTF2 guys muttered, "Bullshit." And, unfortunately for the Canadian Forces, he was right.

MY TRIP TO KABUL and Kandahar, no matter how fleeting, showed me that all was not well with our strategy. Suicide bombings had increased dramatically in Afghanistan during 2005, and on December 4 a suicide bomber attacked a Canadian patrol in Kandahar, killing two civilians, seriously wounding a third, and injuring a Canadian soldier. On January 15, 2006, another suicide bomber killed Canadian diplomat Glyn Berry and critically wounded three of our troops. Though President Karzai once assured me that suicide bombings weren't an Afghan tradition and therefore must be the work of a few foreign fighters, they became more widespread and common. We had underestimated the Taliban's ability to learn from their defeats or from what was happening in Iraq.

Moreover, flaws in our 3D strategy were becoming apparent even in this early stage of the mission. In terms of money and leadership, defence completely overwhelmed diplomacy and development, and we were not able to achieve the central co-ordination of policy priorities we had envisaged. Instead of DND, DFAIT, and CIDA working in harmony toward common objectives, they often clashed over fundamental differences or petty feuds. Among the casualties was the Strategic Advisory Team (SAT), which consisted of fifteen military and civilian personnel attached to various ministries in Kabul to help build a stable, democratic government.

With their backgrounds in planning, research, and development, SAT members brought skill sets that were in short supply in Afghanistan. Both President Karzai and Foreign Minister Abdullah Abdullah told me on several occasions how valuable they found the team's expertise and how much they appreciated the way it combined unequalled professionalism with sensitivity to the needs of the Afghan people.

But some Ottawa officials – including some in Defence – argued that these functions would be more properly performed by civilian personnel, whether from DFAIT or CIDA, despite all the evidence that few civilians with the necessary qualifications were willing to work in the violent conditions of Afghanistan. They also worried that the SAT had become Hillier's personal "embassy" in Kabul, offering strategic advice directly to Karzai and his government without going through the proper channels, maybe even for the benefit of DND itself. Many who were most familiar with the on-the-ground situation in Kabul saw the closing of the SAT as a significant loss. In my view it was driven by inter-departmental jealousies rather than a genuine disagreement over the best way to achieve our national goals.

Similarly, there were persistent quarrels between my DFAIT officials and the development specialists in CIDA over what kind of assistance programs were appropriate for Afghanistan. I found this unfortunate, because I had been impressed by the contribution Canada was making on my visit in 2005. Nipa Banerjee, CIDA's excellent representative in Kabul, had a keen appreciation of the country's development needs from her vantage point in the capital. But, as I saw it, CIDA was overly prone to strengthening the central government, and some of the NGOs were vociferously opposed to any association of the military with aid delivery. They feared that it would destroy the neutrality they saw as essential to the efficacy of their operations. But CIDA's approach was problematic. Nothing illustrated the difficulty more than how best to pay the local police. If the money were given in Kabul, very little of it actually trickled down to the police themselves. Eventually a solution was found in which the PRT paid the local police directly – a very popular measure.

In Kandahar I had been struck by how knowledgeable the Canadian PRT commander was about development issues. Though he was understandably more focused on how development assistance would contribute to stability in his area of responsibility, he also wanted to advance the operations and credibility of the PRT, which required money to build infrastructure and finance local projects that would directly support our mission in Kandahar. Canadian officers had to call Ottawa to ask DND to fight to get the money from CIDA, in contrast to the US military commanders on the ground, who were given substantial aid budgets under their direct control, allowing them to dovetail their security and reconstruction efforts in the same region. An American general could order the digging of a well or the building of a hospital on his own authority, and the same soldiers who provided security brought tangible proof to the people that their lives were improving.

When I met with the governor of Kandahar and several elders, they all talked about the need for more economic activity. The Soviet invasion and subsequent years of conflict had done tremendous damage to the infrastructure, from schools to irrigation, little of which had yet been repaired. Everybody agreed on the need for crop substitution to replace poppy cultivation and break the power of the drug lords, for example, but that was impossible unless transportation were improved. There weren't enough roads; too few people owned trucks; and a farmer could earn far more from a donkey load of poppies than for a donkey load of wheat. As I had observed at a Paris conference on the "route de la drogue" in May 2003, the Americans were intent on drug eradication by military means, not surprising given their domestic political fixation on the "war on drugs." Both we and the British saw the drug trade as a police issue rather than a military one, and we feared that pitting soldiers against farmers would prove inconsistent with our "hearts and minds" campaign.

Too many of the NGOs delivering aid "had their own agenda," Governor Khalid told me, and they failed to co-ordinate what they did with the local authorities, our PRT, or the central Ministry of Rural Development. Tribal elders in the outlying villages were quick to point out that even the Canadian PRT seemed to be focusing too much of its time and resources in the city of Kandahar. When I met with the British-educated minister of rural development, Hanif Atmar, he talked about the importance of getting more aid into the countryside if we didn't want rural Afghans to lose faith in their national government and in the international community. Yet everywhere I went, I learned how corruption, unaccountability, and inefficiency within the delivery mechanisms clogged our efforts to get development money out of Kabul.

At one Cabinet meeting, my colleague Aileen Carroll, the minister responsible for CIDA, talked about how CIDA had helped Afghanistan avoid a
financial crisis by pumping aid dollars into the central finance ministry.
"That's all well and good," I noted, "but you're not spending money in Kandahar where our young men and women in uniform are risking their lives.
You've got to give them more money so that they can build roads and bridges
down there to give support to troops. Too much is being spent in Kabul."

"We don't do development by building roads and bridges just because
you've got troops there," she said.

"But it's Canadian government money," I replied, "and there should be
a co-ordinated approach to spending it."

"Well, if you want me to give money to your troops down in Kandahar
to build dams and schools in aid of the pacification measures you're taking," she said, "Finance is going to have to give me more money to be able
to do it."

That raised a few eyebrows around the Cabinet table, because everybody
knew that CIDA had received a guaranteed annual increase in its budget
after the 2002 Monterrey Conference on financing international development. Aileen argued, however, with some validity, that a large percentage
of the hike had been pre-committed by Mr. Chrétien to the UN Millennium
Project, aimed mostly at Africa, and that she didn't have the money we
presumed she had. Complicating the issue even more was the fact that,
whereas CIDA technically fell under DFAIT's jurisdiction in those days,
it had its own minister – to demonstrate that aid should be treated separately from foreign policy. However, even the purists agreed that aid is a
component of Canadian foreign policy. CIDA may be in the business of
alleviating poverty, but this fits with security and trade if you take a holistic
view of what our foreign policy is all about.

When Paul Martin ordered the review of development assistance as
well as foreign affairs, trade, and defence, Aileen and her officials argued
in their report that CIDA was overextended. They wanted to concentrate
its money and efforts on a small list of countries that represented some of
the poorest of the poor and on certain projects within those countries. I
didn't like the artificiality of it. Why wouldn't they pick countries where
we had strategic interests and focus on alleviating poverty there? Why
wasn't Afghanistan on the list? What would happen to the important legal

program that CIDA was funding in China when China didn't make the list? Nor did I think that the policy was sustainable. "The first trip you take to West Africa or Brazil," I said to Prime Minister Martin, "someone's going to ask Canada for a well or a hospital, and are you really going to tell them, sorry, but your country isn't poor enough to get on our list? And if you say yes, who has the money other than CIDA? Within a year, I promise you, this policy will be in tatters."

In 2013, then, I welcomed the Harper government's decision to integrate CIDA back into DFAIT. Though there's a risk that the pendulum will swing too far, with CIDA becoming little more than a tool for furthering Canada's trade and commercial interests, it made sense to me to integrate our aid program into a broader strategy even while it keeps its coherent integrity. The CIDA story was another interesting example of the debate that always takes place in foreign affairs between values and interests. CIDA may be a values instrument, but as with human rights or peace, promoting economic development and social justice around the world is in Canada's long-term interest. Similarly, putting troops into Afghanistan was a mixture of values and interests. It was in our interest to contribute to NATO and protect our security; it was in our value system to build peace and come to the aid of the Afghans.

ONE PROBLEM THAT continued to preoccupy me as we prepared to send our battle group to Afghanistan was the proper treatment of captured prisoners. This was a classic issue in international humanitarian law and especially important since the creation of the International Criminal Court, of which we were a party and a principal advocate. Rick Hillier often used to emphasize that Canadian soldiers operate within a concept of a rule of law, and his successor, General Walt Natynczyk, reiterated that the rule of law governs how Canadian troops behave as soldiers. Whenever Canadian Forces deploy, legal officers are present to advise them that their use of force must be proportional to the military objective so that their actions fit within the constraints of international law. The rule of law gives legitimacy to our operations in the field.

As a former law professor, I took a particular interest in the relationship between Canada's military operations and our international legal responsibilities. After one of my speeches on this theme, a distinguished

American jurist who happened to be present told me how impressed he was that a minister of defence gave such attention to these issues. "No one ever heard Rumsfeld talking about international law," he said.

Indeed, I remember having a discussion with Donald Rumsfeld at a September 2005 NATO meeting in Berlin during which he complained about the "caveats" that kept the Germans from being more active militarily. "You've got to remember that they've got a constitution," I said. "They're governed by certain things that you may think a caveat but, for them, are political, legal, and sometimes constitutional limits." Though I occasionally shared Rumsfeld's frustrations with our NATO allies, I accepted the fact that some NATO members were always going to be constrained by those types of limitations. At that time, for instance, our soldiers didn't do crowd control, because they hadn't been properly trained for that task. The Canadian Forces didn't want to be used as a substitute for a local police force. Eventually, we relaxed the prohibition, largely because we were pushing other countries to scale back on their caveats, but only after ensuring that our troops received specialized training in dealing with civil disturbances.

The rights and welfare of detainees were a real test for our mission. The issue had first arisen in January 2002 when a newspaper photograph showed handcuffed Taliban fighters being transferred by Canadian soldiers into American custody in Afghanistan. From there, some of the prisoners were later relocated to the US base in Guantánamo. The Americans labelled them "unlawful enemy combatants," which is not a classification used in international treaties, and claimed that the Geneva Convention protections relating to prisoner-of-war status did not apply. When the Bush administration declared that such protections would nonetheless be extended to them as a matter of policy rather than law, Prime Minister Chrétien welcomed this declaration as providing the reassurances Canada required. However, subsequent press reports of the torture and suicide attempts of detainees, followed by accounts of the degrading treatment of prisoners at the Abu Ghraib facility in Iraq, made the transfer of detainees to American custody problematic after we assumed the lead role in ISAF and prepared for the move to Kandahar.

Proper treatment of prisoners has always been a concern of the Canadian Forces – a reflection of our values and our commitment to humanitarian principles. Moreover, any mistreatment of prisoners would alienate Afghans and undermine the mission's very purpose. Still, we faced serious practical constraints. Neither the Canadian Forces nor NATO had the capacity for building and operating prisons.

Ultimately, we became convinced that the Afghans were our only logical partners. We were operating in their sovereign territory, at the invitation of their government. It made sense that Afghanistan would be responsible for the prisoners we had taken in the course of military operations on its behalf. If we could be assured that the Afghans would treat the prisoners properly, the appropriate action was to turn them over to the local authorities. In conversations I had with the leaders of Amnesty International Canada, they were emphatic that the right approach was to transfer detainees to the Afghans.

Not everyone agreed. There were legal arguments from within the Defence Department that we would still meet our legal obligations if we continued to transfer prisoners to the Americans. After all, the US government had sought to investigate and punish any abuses, and its official policy was to treat detainees humanely. Essentially, this argument ran, the abuses at Bagram, Abu Ghraib, and Guantánamo Bay were isolated incidents, and continuing to transfer prisoners to the Americans was the option that best minimized future legal liability.

This was not my view. At the time, the US government's interpretation of international laws regarding the treatment of detainees and suspected terrorists had become increasingly erratic. Every day in the press we heard more and more about black sites, "enhanced interrogation," and extraordinary rendition. I felt it would be morally abhorrent to transfer detainees into this legal black hole. I also felt that continuing to transfer prisoners to the Americans was something that the Canadian public would not accept. In op-ed pages and other media outlets, commentators and activists voiced concerns about Canadian complicity in the torture of detainees and suspected terrorists by the Americans or by proxies such as Syria. These sentiments were echoed in the take-note debate on the Afghanistan mission that was held in the House of Commons on November 15, 2005.

After decades of occupation and civil war, Afghanistan was still in the midst of developing essential institutions, including its police force, army, judiciary, and legal system. The Karzai government was also facing challenges in its attempts to assert authority outside of Kabul. There were, therefore, legitimate concerns about whether the new Afghan government would be willing and able to assume responsibility for the prisoners and ensure that they were treated according to international legal standards. However, we believed that if we could reach an agreement with Afghanistan that guaranteed detainees the protections found in the Geneva Conventions, it would be safe and responsible to transfer them to the Afghan authorities. Indeed, ensuring the existence of robust safeguards against any kind of mistreatment was the entire purpose of negotiating the agreement.

I discussed negotiation of an agreement with Foreign Minister Abdullah Abdullah when he visited Ottawa on May 31, 2005, and when I was in Kabul the following October, I raised the issue with Karzai. I mentioned that Denmark had recently signed a detainee agreement with Afghanistan and that Canada was hoping to complete a similar agreement with his government soon. During my subsequent meetings on that trip, I discussed the issue in greater detail with Abdullah and Defence Minister Abdul Rahim Wardak, who, as the minister responsible for prisons, was in a good position to know the limits of the Afghan prison system. "This is a very important issue," I told them. "There should be some responsibility here for detainees. The whole question has a direct impact on the credibility of the mission."

Abdullah was supportive. "Yes, yes, yes," he said, "this is something we should be doing. Absolutely. We should proceed with this right away."

Wardak was more reticent, though he did admit that President Karzai liked the idea. In his view, the Afghan forces didn't yet have the capacity to deal with detainees. These were still early days for the retraining of the Afghan army, and this new initiative would be a major distraction. "We don't have anybody to do this task," he said. "I don't want to be responsible. There's no way that our troops are properly prepared to do it. The president may have said he's going to give me a trained team, but we don't even have enough people to sweep the streets at the moment."

Later, I met with Sima Samar, the head of the Afghan Independent Human Rights Commission, and she agreed that her commission would be willing to assume responsibility for inspecting the well-being of any prisoners, not least because such a mandate would help strengthen her organization as a national institution.

Officials in DND took the lead in drafting an agreement, and I met on many occasions with two of the lawyers in the office of the JAG. We wanted to make sure that all detainees enjoyed the Geneva Convention protections; that none would be subject to the death penalty; that the Red Cross could visit them and assess their treatment, and would be notified when they were transferred to a third party and could visit them and assess their treatment; and that the Afghan Independent Human Rights Commission would have monitoring responsibility. Going over the detainee agreement that Denmark had signed with the Afghans, my staff and I found a follow-up provision that gave the Danes the right to inspect how the prisoners were being treated. I raised this matter with my department, but the DND lawyers told me, "We don't think it's appropriate. The Danish agreement is too paternalistic. Our own is better." We kept the pressure on Kabul and presented a final version to the Afghan government, which it agreed to sign on an appropriate occasion. I remember getting assurances from our lawyers that the agreement contained the best language possible for the protection of the detainees.

Subsequently, the Martin government lost a confidence vote in the House of Commons, and an election was called for January 23, 2006. On December 18, in the midst of the campaign, Rick Hillier and our ambassador, David Sproule, met with Wardak to sign the agreement. Wardak, a former chief of the defence staff in Afghanistan, knew Rick from ISAF in Kabul, and they had become good friends. With Sproule looking on, the two men signed the agreement. Later, questions were raised about why a general, and not the official representative of the country, had signed for Canada. As far as I was concerned, it didn't make the slightest difference to this particular agreement. Sproule was in the room; Wardak was ready to sign; and everything else was incidental.

In fact, that detail proved a relatively minor technical matter compared to the substantive issue in the agreement. In the aftermath of our defeat at the polls by the Harper Conservatives, various human rights groups reported that prisoners in Afghan custody were being tortured and in some cases killed. When the matter came up in the House in April 2006, Defence

Minister Gordon O'Connor made the mistake of saying that it wasn't a problem, because the Red Cross, which had the right to see the prisoners, would have reported problems. What O'Connor didn't know or understand was that the Red Cross reports only to the detaining authority, not to anybody else. That was the problem with Guantánamo Bay as well: the Red Cross could report only to the Americans. The system is designed that way; otherwise, the Red Cross wouldn't get any access at all.

As it turned out, our initial focus on the problems associated with transferring detainees to the Americans had obscured the fact that the Afghan system simply could not manage this issue. Whereas the monitoring provisions in the British and Danish agreements were stronger than ours, the distinction made little difference in practice, without an Afghan capacity to fully implement them. International and Afghan laws against torture did little to prevent the widespread abuse of detainees by members of the Afghan National Police and the National Directorate of Security, Afghanistan's intelligence agency. In Canada, the prisoner issue became a major problem for the government, the department, and the mission. We were committed to help bring the rule of law to Afghanistan, and now we were in danger of being branded as hypocrites or worse. Think of how the Abu Ghraib scandal damaged the credibility of America's mission in Iraq, or of how Canada's reputation suffered after two members of the Airborne Regiment were found to have participated in the torture and murder of a teenaged boy while on a UN peacekeeping and humanitarian mission to Somalia in 1993.

Controversy over the issue revived in November 2009 when Richard Colvin, previously the second-ranking official at our embassy in Kabul, told a parliamentary hearing that Canada had largely failed to monitor the treatment of detainees after transfer and that NGOs had little access to Afghan prisons, where torture was routine. Clearly our agreement was insufficient, and in retrospect we were all naive to believe that the Afghan system could handle the prisoners. Our agreement had been drafted in anticipation of events, on the basis of imperfect knowledge, and with limited foresight. If the Liberal Party had won the 2006 election, it too would have been confronted by the defects of that agreement and would have had to fix them quickly. In May 2007 the Harper government concluded a new agreement that tightened the monitoring process so that Canada could assess how prisoners were being treated, and it committed both countries to the improvement of Afghanistan's justice and prison systems.

The detainee discussion was just the tip of the iceberg as to why a new approach to these types of operations continues to be so important, and why the same problems will dog future NATO missions. The mistreatment of prisoners by Afghan security officials diminished the legitimacy of the mission in the eyes of Afghans and Canadians, yet our troops lacked the capacity to deal with detainees. The role of Canada in Afghanistan wasn't only to win battles; it was also to aid the country in creating a civil society. In that sense, it was a political operation in which the military had a defined function. In my view, if NATO intends to mount more missions of this sort, it must make the question of detainees part of its advance planning. A member state that doesn't want to provide combat or patrol troops could perhaps provide a corrections contingent, in the way that Iceland had run Kabul International Airport on ISAF's behalf. Regardless of the solution we come up with, NATO has to recognize that in this type of theatre we will always have to respond to the issue of detainees.

The British, primarily because of their experience in Northern Ireland, already have a highly sophisticated view about the relationship between the military operation and the civilian dimension. The Europeans also tend to take a broader view of what "security" entails by incorporating development, capacity building, and constabulary components to their operations abroad. Even in my day, Canada usually deployed police as well as military personnel on a regular basis to train and work with local forces. That was part of the purpose of the PRT in Afghanistan, and it was a feature of other missions as well. The fact that we could send bilingual RCMP officers was of enormous benefit in Haiti. Moreover, our high-ranking female police provided a model for women's rights wherever they served.

WHEN I STEPPED DOWN in January 2006 as minister of national defence after the Liberals lost the election, Canada was on the cusp of engaging in a combat mission in Afghanistan that would last almost six more years, exceeding the duration of the First World War, bringing heavy casualties, and involving the deployment of troops in many different capacities at a cost of more than $15 billion. Moreover, the combat mission was only one part of a significant Canadian presence that entailed reconstruction and development spending of almost $2 billion from 2001 to 2011 – by far our largest aid contribution to any single country during that period. And yet, with each passing year, a secure and democratic Afghanistan remained beyond our grasp.

As a result of the Conservatives' victory, neither Prime Minister Martin nor I were in government when approximately one thousand Canadian Forces troops arrived in Kandahar in February 2006 to do battle alongside the American troops in Operation Enduring Freedom. The following September, under the command of General David Fraser, Operation Medusa defeated the Taliban in a large-scale battle that saved Kandahar and perhaps the whole country. If the war had stopped at that point, everybody might still be congratulating us on our intelligent and triumphant policy. However, as a consequence of their losses, the Taliban returned to their original use of guerrilla warfare, shifting from conventional combat back to insurgency. We had to reassess both our strategy and the tactics to make it work while the war was raging. In fairness, our American and British colleagues had to do the same. Our initial planning had failed to take into full account how easy it was for the Taliban to find refuge by slipping into Pakistan's Northwest Frontier region, though there were early indications that it would be a problem. "The solution to Afghanistan is still Pakistan," I had been told in a briefing as early as July 2005. "A secure border is key." Yet our policies continued to deal with Afghanistan as primarily a management problem within NATO, and as a result they failed to focus sufficiently on the regional dynamics.

The conflict in Afghanistan could not be geographically insulated from outside developments, as our counterinsurgency models tended to assume. Many of the insurgents were recruited from Pakistani madrassas, and because Pakistan's foreign and defence policy was largely determined by the military and intelligence services, there was a great deal of sympathy for the Taliban and al-Qaeda in those quarters as potential allies against their "real" enemy, India. Not just sympathy, but even practical assistance. Every time the Taliban took a pasting, they crossed the border and came back refreshed and rearmed with the latest generations of IEDs. As their operations in Kandahar increased, it became clear that we couldn't deal with the military situation in Afghanistan unless we also dealt with Pakistan and the porous border. However, according to international law, our forces couldn't pursue and destroy them across the border, even if that made perfect military sense. The Americans eventually resorted to drones, which sometimes managed to kill selected adversaries but at a high civilian-casualty and political cost.

Whenever Canada and our allies pressed Pakistan to do more to control its border, we were told that the Northwest Frontier had always been an uncontrollable no man's land, though the fact that Pakistan had about ten times as many troops on its Indian frontier was a telling statement of its priorities. I had raised this issue as early as September 2003 during the private, forty-five-minute discussion I had with President Pervez Musharraf when I met with him in Rawalpindi. Because he was also the head of the army at that time, I pointed out that he should deploy more troops along the border with Afghanistan. He responded that the Northwest Frontier provinces, as far back as Alexander the Great, had never been subdued. He also emphasized that the Durand Line between Pakistan and Afghanistan, drawn by the British and Afghans at the close of the nineteenth century, wasn't a defined, formal border but a vague and contested line of demarcation, with Pashtuns on both sides of the boundary.

This conversation, though disquieting, hardly foretold the degree to which the permeable border would make the Kandahar mission so much more difficult than our early strategies had envisaged. Nor did we know at the time the actual degree of support the Taliban were receiving from Pakistan's Directorate for Inter-Services Intelligence. The bitter truth was that we had undertaken a 3D operation in a political environment involving regional players whose motives we couldn't rely on and over whose conduct we had little influence.

As the security situation deteriorated throughout 2006, Canadian troops increasingly began operating as a heavily protected force, which insulated them from the civilian population and inhibited Canada's PRT efforts. Even our embassy staff in Kabul worried constantly about the possibility of rocket attacks. Nor were we able to achieve a centrally co-ordinated balance of defence, diplomacy, and development in Ottawa. In 2008 the Manley Report gave the Harper government political cover to adopt some of the ideas we had favoured, but which were otherwise out of bounds by virtue of being Liberal. They included another push to break down the departmental silos that prevented integration of the 3Ds, a stepped-up CIDA effort, and a modest increase in support from other NATO members as a condition of our continued presence.

If I were being crassly political about it, I could blame everything that went wrong on the fact that the Liberals lost the election, and the Tories mismanaged our best-laid plans. In all honesty, however, I have to admit that some of the seeds of our disappointment should have been evident at the start. We knew much less about Afghanistan and the politics of the region than we should have. Many Canadians resisted a combat role for Canada and believed that it was better equipped for traditional peace-keeping operations – despite the fact that such missions were largely a thing of the past. It was unrealistic of us to expect that we could construct a truly effective government and civil society in the midst of the ongoing carnage. Moreover, our efforts to create an accountable, corruption-free, and efficient police force capable of providing basic security for the population met with only modest, highly localized success, and the Afghan army was certainly not ready to shoulder enough of the weight. As a result, public support for the mission, which had been considerable in the wake of 9/11, eroded in the face of mounting casualties, an apparent lack of progress, and a perception that we were carrying an unfairly heavy share of the burden.

A large part of the criticism was related to the fact that we got into an extended conflict from which we couldn't extract ourselves. Though NATO remains Canada's most important international security instrument, the Afghan experience did not boost its reputation with the Canadian public, our political leadership, and the military itself. Canadian participation in combat missions such as Kandahar is predicated on their being multilateral – in this case under a UN mandate and NATO command. In my view, we would not have suffered the number of casualties we did if NATO had been able to provide the appropriate "operational tempo," rotating our troops in and out every year or two with significant breaks for training and the reconstitution of our forces. The problem was, though every NATO member is entitled to vote in favour of going to war, each is free to choose what assets it will provide for that war, and few are capable of exceeding the commitments they have already made. In effect, the secretary general has to go around like a beggar with a bowl, pleading for a tank or an aircraft.

In this case, NATO failed to get other partners to take their turn in a full combat role. After Afghanistan, public regard for our troops has never been higher, but public support for NATO has never been lower. Yet, for all NATO's faults, other than hemispheric operations like the 2004 peacekeeping deployment in Haiti, it is difficult to envision Canada engaged in an international combat mission in which NATO is not involved.

If our overall approach – using the military to create a space in which reconstruction and development could occur – proved disappointing, it wasn't a complete failure. The Taliban didn't regain power; democratic elections were held; and new rights and opportunities were secured for women and girls. Furthermore, whatever doubts outside observers might have about the political wisdom and ultimate success of the mission, the men and women of our Armed Forces who risked their lives day after day saw it almost universally as a positive one. Canadians can only be proud of the highly professional, highly skilled, and ultimately humane manner in which they performed their responsibilities and sought to better the lives of the Afghan people. These men and women brought honour to Canada. And the competence and experience of today's Canadian Forces vastly exceed what they were when we first deployed in Afghanistan. No doubt the lessons learned from the Afghan mission will inform policy makers and military planners for some time to come – or, perhaps more realistically, until the next experience imposes its own unforeseen exigencies.

16

HOME FIRES

On the domestic front, the main problem facing the Martin government wasn't a lack of good programs; it was dealing with the distractions of a contentious minority Parliament. A huge amount of our energy was expended on mere survival, and the most intense part of many Cabinet meetings was the report from the House leader: Would we manage to survive the next confidence vote, or could we delay it to give ourselves some breathing room to govern? The Opposition was intractable. Its MPs often refused even to "pair" on a vote so that ministers could attend international meetings essential to Canada's interests. Given that fraught situation, it's remarkable that the Martin government accomplished so much, including the health-care and daycare agreements with the provinces, the historic Kelowna Accord with five national Aboriginal organizations, and the important cities' agenda, which recognized the role that our largest metropolises play as engines of national economic growth. I firmly believe that, with a majority government and more time in office, Paul Martin would have emerged as a great and truly transformative prime minister.

Of all his accomplishments, none resonated more in Toronto Centre or gave me greater satisfaction as a citizen than the full recognition of equal rights for gays and lesbians in Canada. It was the culmination of a long struggle that had been picked up by the Chrétien government and pushed forward by the courts. And it was the fulfillment of a cause I had fought for from my earliest days at party conferences, as a caucus MP, and in the

Cabinet. As far as I was concerned, equal rights for homosexuals was both a matter of principle and a personal issue. Perhaps because of the discovery of my parents' secret history or perhaps because of my own experience of life, I came to know the complexity of adult sexuality and of the human heart. I hold a firm conviction that we should resist being judgmental about what law-abiding adults choose to do and should respect their right to privacy, just as we want our own privacy to be respected. No one should be subjected to shame or discrimination because of sexual orientation.

I was more fortunate than many MPs in that gay rights was neither a moral anathema to the majority of my constituents nor a political liability to me. Along with Vancouver Centre, my riding had the largest gay community in Canada. When I first entered politics, policing, harassment, and the scourge of AIDS were recent and much-publicized problems. "It's something we are going to have to deal with when we get into government," I said to Mr. Chrétien as we were campaigning past the gay restaurants and bars on Church Street during the 1993 election.

"Bill," he said, "you can talk about those things, but I will not talk about those things." He was typical of most Canadians in those years. Having been educated by the Roman Catholic Church in a hinterland region of Quebec before the Quiet Revolution, Chrétien had grown up with the belief that homosexuality was a sin, a crime, and not to be discussed in polite society. However, in spite of his origins, he was remarkably non-judgmental, and like most Canadians, he underwent an extraordinary evolution in his thinking during the next ten years.

The issue of gay rights was emotionally difficult and electorally charged. It was also a good lesson in politics. Each small victory at a party policy convention felt exciting and important. It boosted morale in my riding association, stimulated debate among Liberals, and brought in newer, younger members who had never been involved in politics before. Whenever there was a major setback, I urged them not to be discouraged or give up. "We'll win the next time around," I said. "I can feel it moving in the right direction." When you make progress, take it and don't hold out for perfection. As the French say, "le mieux est l'ennemi du bien" – perfection is the enemy of the good.

In 1995 a modest but controversial amendment to the Criminal Code, Bill C-41, made gay bashing a hate crime. Then Allan Rock, the minister of justice, supported by his Cabinet colleague Hedy Fry, pushed for an amendment to the Canadian Human Rights Act to include sexual orientation in the list of prohibited grounds of discrimination. At that point the prime minister felt we had already done enough for one term. He was concerned that going further or faster would hurt the Liberal MPs who were already in trouble in their rural ridings over C-41 and gun control. That might have been canny politically, but producing one minor reform every four or five years was hardly the pace of change we wanted. A small delegation from the women's caucus went to see Chrétien to argue that the issue of equality for gays and lesbians was similar to the issue of equality for women. "We think it has got to be done for the sake of the party," they said. "It's a fairness issue." And a number of us followed up with group and individual petitions, urging him not to listen to "a few hate-mongering, narrow-minded members of caucus" who weren't, in our opinion, "Liberal voices."

The issue also spoke to the credibility of the Liberal government and its willingness to keep the promises we had made in the 1993 election campaign, which included reforming the Human Rights Act to better protect gays and lesbians. Many individuals in my riding, such as Brent Hawkes at the Metropolitan Community Church, and several organizations deserve credit for keeping up the pressure – in particular, the Canadian Human Rights Commission, Parents and Friends of Lesbians and Gays (PFLAG), the Campaign for Equal Families, Liberals for Equality, and Equality for Gays and Lesbians Everywhere (EGALE). "If the commitment is not fulfilled in this mandate," I wrote the prime minister on February 20, 1995, "no one will believe any undertaking we make concerning what will be done after the next election." He came round, though first throwing a sop to the dissenters by making it a free vote.

Once Mr. Chrétien had decided to introduce the legislation, I got a call from my former chief of staff, Bill Charnetski, who was now working for Allan Rock, the minister of justice. Rock wanted to ensure there would be enough supportive voices on the committee that would examine the bill, and he requested that I be one of them. I agreed immediately. At one point a delegation from the Canadian Conference of Catholic Bishops showed up and claimed that the proposed reforms might lead to the legal recognition of same-sex relationships and thereby damage the institution of marriage. That didn't make any sense to me. Once upon a time, for example, the law hadn't recognized illegitimate children on the grounds that doing so would harm the institution of marriage, but the law changed and marriage survived. Besides, we already recognized common law partnerships between heterosexual couples. Was the church saying we should stop doing that? "How will discriminating against gays and lesbians or making people's lives more difficult preserve the matrimonial institution you say you're here to protect?" I asked. "I'm not attacking the church. I'm just trying to understand. We're all reaching out to one another to understand these profoundly troubling and important issues." After two days of charged and sometimes combative committee meetings, Bill C-33 was sent back to the House of Commons. On May 9, 1996, the bill was approved overwhelmingly by the Commons, 153 to 76, even though the Reform Party MPs and 28 Liberals voted no.

The next major struggle was over the question of equal benefits for same-sex couples as for heterosexual couples with regard to pensions, immigration, income tax, and other areas of federal responsibility. Though many conservatives were adamantly opposed, I knew of at least one right-wing tabloid that was already paying same-sex benefits to its own employees. When I asked why, I was told, "Because we need to hire the best employees we possibly can, and if they happen to be gay, that's what we have to do to get them." In other words, the economic argument in favour of same-sex benefits was stronger than the economic argument against, and the actual costs were nowhere near the billions that our opponents had predicted.

As far as I was concerned, equal benefits were a constitutional issue. In that sense, the Modernization of Benefits and Obligations Act, Bill C-23, which was introduced in February 2000, simply brought us into conformity with the Charter of Rights and Freedoms. It was hard to argue that gays were so evil that we should deny them pensions. Nevertheless, to appease the angst of some MPs in our own caucus and to defuse potential criticism from the Reform Party, Justice Minister Anne McLellan agreed to insert a provision that defined marriage as the "lawful union of one man and one woman to the exclusion of all others." By adding this unnecessary amendment, I protested in a letter to her on March 23, 2000, she "would be giving government approval to the position taken by the Reform Party." I also raised the issue heatedly in caucus. "This is crazy," I argued. "Why are we larding this bill with something that has nothing to do with it? This is a constitutional obligation." But Chrétien came to Anne's defence. "Calm down, Bill," he said. "She's right. We all have to put some water in our wine to get this one through."

When the bill came before the House, Svend Robinson of the NDP moved an amendment to strike out that provision, but to no avail. Normally, on the spectrum of party rogue to team player, I was a team player. For reasons of loyalty and efficiency, I often had to vote on matters that I didn't entirely agree with or entirely understand. Even Cathy sometimes wondered why I didn't just stand up and say so. "We got elected on a set of promises," I would explain. "The government has to deliver on its program." In this case, however, of the twenty-six MPs who supported Svend's amendments, I was one of only seven Liberals. Though many of my colleagues gave me hell or thought me nuts, Mr. Chrétien never said anything about it. In the end, though the benefits bill passed, seventeen Liberals voted against it.

At each step of the way our opponents argued that Canadian society was on a "slippery slope" to same-sex marriage – and eventually their worst fears did come to pass. But those of us who favoured full equality for all citizens before the law weren't sure that same-sex marriage would ever be achieved in our day. The closer we came to the marriage issue, the closer we got to bedrock convictions and religious dogmas that were much more difficult to answer with reason and facts. With the sanctity of marriage threatened, the Catholic bishops weighed in with threats of excommunication and political attacks from the pulpits. They were not alone. Even within the party and the caucus, there were explosive debates in which a few of our MPs always sprang to the defence of what they called "family values." As Carolyn Bennett used to joke, "Why is it that the family values people are always the ones who get divorced?"

But, like the party and the country, the caucus evolved. In December 2003 Scott Brison crossed the floor to join the Liberals because, as the first openly gay Progressive Conservative MP, he didn't believe he had a place among his colleagues in the new Conservative Party, who used family values as "code words for prejudice and bigotry." It was a very tough statement. To be fair, the Conservative MPs were not uniformly opposed, and though the NDP and the Bloc were overwhelmingly in favour, their support wasn't unanimous either. That's why the process took so long. It required a matrix of various developments moving in tandem at the national and provincial levels, in the political parties and particularly the courts, to shift political and social opinion over time.

Then, all at once, on June 10, 2003, a decision in the *Halpern* case by the Ontario Court of Appeal, presided over by Chief Justice Roy McMurtry, blew everything apart. Previously, whenever the question of same-sex marriage had been tested in lower courts in Quebec and British Columbia, the rulings were heavily tilted toward equality. Barring couples of the same sex from obtaining a legal status that was available to heterosexual couples was clearly discriminatory under the Charter of Rights and Freedoms – and it could not be demonstrably justified under section 1 of the Charter. But in the absence of a definitive ruling by the Supreme Court of Canada, the lower courts stopped short of demanding instant remedial action. They preferred to give governments and elected officials time to figure out a workable solution, just as a Supreme Court decision in 1985 had given the Manitoba government five years to bring its legislation into conformity with the constitutional requirement to offer bilingual services. Everyone expected the Ontario Court of Appeal's ruling to follow the same pattern. Instead, the court took a giant leap forward. Like the other courts, it said that the traditional definition of marriage violated the Charter's guarantee of equality. But it went beyond this, judicially correcting the common law definition and ordering immediate relief. The court changed the definition of marriage by substituting the words "two persons" for "one man and one woman." And this decision, the court said, was to have immediate effect. Officials were ordered to perform and recognize the marriages. Same-sex couples were suddenly eligible to get married in the province of Ontario. And they immediately started to do so.

In the aftermath of the *Halpern* ruling, I was invited by Mayor David Miller to say a few words at a celebration at which dozens of gay marriages were performed at Toronto's City Hall. Just as I rose to speak, a young man jumped on the platform and said to the huge crowd, "I've come here with my partner from Boston. We've been fighting for this right in the United States for a long time, and we've never got anywhere. Now Canada has done it, and we've come here to get married. For me, the Statue of Liberty has moved from my country to Canada as we come here today to celebrate our individual and collective liberties." The whole place went wild, which made it a somewhat difficult act for me to follow.

The decision of the Ontario Court of Appeal dramatically shifted the debate over same-sex marriage. People were stunned, not least the Chrétien Cabinet. Many called on the government to take the decision to the Supreme Court, but the prime minister was given clear advice by Martin Cauchon, the minister of justice, that the government could not win an appeal. "Prime Minister," I remember weighing in at the Cabinet, "if the chief legal officer of the Crown is advising the Cabinet that this appeal is not winnable, I think it would be an abuse of the process for the Cabinet to order the chief officer of the Crown to take an appeal that you know you're going to lose just because we're trying to buy time."

He came to the same conclusion. "If the justice minister says it's not appealable," he announced on June 17, "it's not appealable."

There's no doubt that the Ontario Court of Appeal's decision strengthened the hand of gay-rights supporters in the Cabinet and the Liberal caucus, though the role of the courts also drew criticisms over so-called judicial activism. The Reform Party liked to rant about the power of unelected judges "usurping" the power of Parliament. However, this ignores our constitutional history. After decades of federal-provincial conferences and the negotiation of the Canada Act, 1982, the legislatures of Canada deliberately surrendered part of their sovereignty to a Charter that forbids them from legislating in areas that violate the basic rights of citizens. Protecting the rights of minorities from abuses by the majority doesn't make Canada any less of a democracy. Quite the contrary. Some MPs, Liberals among them, urged us to use the notwithstanding clause, which permits legislatures to override the Charter with certain conditions, but many more understood that this would be like resorting to the nuclear option: once used, it would be used again and again with dreadful consequences. Even if they didn't like the court's decision in the *Halpern* case, they were averse to undermining the Charter of Rights.

Whatever Mr. Chrétien's personal views might have been, he set them aside once the courts ruled same-sex marriage a Charter issue. After all, as minister of justice in 1982, he had been a co-author of the Canadian Charter of Rights. He remembered from personal experience when the question of including sexual orientation had been discussed in public hearings and at the constitutional conferences. At the time, it was felt that sexual orientation had not achieved a level of acceptability in Canadian society as a right or a freedom, and therefore it was left out. But there was always a notion that, through the courts, the Charter would gradually evolve with society, which was exactly what happened. In other words, the courts created the intellectual environment in which politicians and citizens were forced to discuss a highly emotional issue and deal with it. They served as the catalyst to make us work out same-sex marriage in the context of the Charter, and that took the issue beyond our personal belief in right and wrong to the root of our concept of Canada and of what is just in a modern democratic society. Should we compel others to comport themselves in the ways we approve? What are the limits of the state's role in taking that approach?

In Chrétien's case, it meant putting individual liberty ahead of his church's strictures. He had a precedent, as he told the caucus. His grandfather had been refused Communion by the Catholic hierarchy because of his liberal political views, and he didn't believe a prime minister who represented all Canadians should impose his particular values on those who didn't share them. Gilles Duceppe once expressed the same view well in the House of Commons: "The religion of some should not become the law for others." Once same-sex marriage was put in that framework, the prime minister really opened himself to the issue. At a key caucus meeting in North Bay in August 2003, he listened to a heartfelt appeal from Senator Laurier LaPierre and a beautiful speech by Elinor Caplan. "Prime Minister," she said, "I was discussing this issue at a family dinner the other night. My mother couldn't believe we were talking about it at all. My kids couldn't believe we were *still* talking about it." It was a perfect way to describe the generational shift that was taking place about gay rights, and it made an impact. At the end of the meeting, the prime minister summed up the debate by saying, "The Charter of this country does not permit us to discriminate against individuals on this basis. That's the nature of the country we live in."

The closer you get to people's cultural roots, the more difficult it is to ask them to vote against their community. I'm sure there were times when some of the Quebec members had to wonder about how far they could go in opposing the Catholic hierarchy, and one Calgary bishop even suggested that Mr. Chrétien's soul was in peril. Many Muslim leaders in Toronto Centre disapproved of same-sex marriage, but when my provincial counterpart, George Smitherman, and I met with them to discuss the issue, we placed it in the broader context of the Charter of Rights and Freedoms. Our argument was basically, "Just as the Charter protects you, so it should protect gay people." It was noteworthy that both of us continued to receive significant support from the Muslim community.

I was particularly struck by the courage of Liberal MPs such as Navdeep Bains, Omar Alghabra, and Nancy Karetak-Lindell. They knew that same-sex marriage would be a tough sell among their constituents and their cultural communities. Standing up and voting against their party's leadership, whether for the sake of principle or to save their seat in the next election, demands a certain measure of courage from backbenchers, but sometimes it takes even more courage to vote with the party when they know that the majority of their constituents disagree. Because the same-sex marriage bill was a free vote, in which the MPs could vote according to conscience rather than the will of the government, there was no hiding behind the excuse of party solidarity. The Canadian people would get their chance to respond at the next election.

The government, fearing it might lose a bill allowing same-sex marriage if it proceeded too quickly, chose a slower course of action in hopes of persuading the dissenters in the caucus and the country. It would draft a bill redefining marriage for civil purposes as "the lawful union of two persons to the exclusion of all others," test its constitutionality by putting three questions to the Supreme Court, and only then put a court-sanctioned version to a free vote in Parliament. In some ways, just as the judiciary had caused the Cabinet to change direction, the Cabinet now hoped that the judiciary would have the same impact on the caucus, the Commons, and the general public. The court would begin hearings on the reference in April 2004, several months after Paul Martin had been sworn in as the new prime minister.

Thus, the Martin government inherited the issue and had to scramble to figure out what to do. Some people wanted the Parliament of Canada to get out of the marriage business altogether. In January 2004 Justice Minister Irwin Cotler complicated things by adding a fourth question, which asked whether the opposite-sex requirement for marriage for civil purposes was consistent with the Canadian Charter of Rights and Freedoms. I thought this was ill-advised and opposed it vigorously, though Irwin insisted that he wasn't trying to dodge the government's commitment. Ultimately the justices refused to answer his question and declared on December 9, 2004, that the government's plan to define marriage as "the union of two persons" was "consistent with the Canadian Charter of Rights and Freedoms."

With the Supreme Court reference behind us, it was now up to the Martin government to steer the bill through Parliament. On February 21, given only three hours' notice with which to prepare one of the most significant speeches of my life, I rose to talk about the issue in the House. I decided to focus on diversity, tolerance, and the Charter. "I know something about multicultural societies," I said. "I happen to live in a riding which has a very rich mixture. I happen to know many of the people in that riding, many of whom have cultural hesitations about this matter, who feel it is not part of their religious tradition, who would not wish to see it as a part of their family. However, those same people know they have had the privilege of coming to this country and living in a society with a constitutional protection such that, while it might apply in this circumstance as something they disagree with or would not practise themselves, they know that those same rights will protect them when the time comes. That is the essence of what the Charter protection is all about. It protects all equally."

The speech was well received; it may even have benefitted from the fact that I hadn't had a week to fuss over it. I couldn't help but feel, however, as I noted in my diary, "a great sense of disappointment" at how few people were in the House to hear it and how indifferent many of my own staff and friends were to the occasion. After all, this bill was the victorious culmination of a battle many of us had been fighting for more than a quarter-century. I couldn't help making a wry comment during the congratulatory attention I received the next day for a statement I made about ballistic missile defence. "What a funny place and life," I observed. "So what you want to have an effect [on] drops like a pebble into the well, and something unforeseen has an effect totally out of proportion."

On June 28, 2005, the Civil Marriage Act passed third reading on a free vote, with thirty-two Liberal MPs opposing, and became law on July 20,

2005. I kept a copy signed by many of the key players, including Prime Minister Martin.

When the Martin government fell and the Harper Conservatives were elected, the whole issue surfaced again. Would they bring in a bill to revoke the previous one, as the vast majority of their caucus wanted to do? Now leader of the Opposition, I had quite a few conversations about it with Conservative Cabinet minister John Baird, who had taken a keen interest in the file. Baird said, "Leave it with me. We'll bring this up at the right time, and you'll have plenty of notice." In the end, Harper allowed a free vote in the House, and Baird along with 5 of his fellow Cabinet ministers as well as 169 other MPs voted in favour of maintaining the status quo. So too did a fair number of Liberals who had opposed the original measures. However much I had disagreed with their initial position, I respected their integrity. Homosexuality remained a difficult moral issue for them, even after they accepted defeat on the legal and political fronts. "The battle's over and lost," one socially conservative MP explained to me, "and we don't want to keep these social wars going any longer. The sooner they're finished, the better for everybody." Judging from his actions, that seems to have been Stephen Harper's view as well.

On the evening of December 7, 2006, I threw a celebration party for many of the dedicated workers who had come from Toronto to watch the vote from the gallery of the House of Commons. We had just experienced one of the most dramatic days of our lives. We had fought for decades for this moment, had lost friends and colleagues to AIDS, and had taken a lot of verbal abuse on the street and in the media. Although we knew how emotionally difficult the issue had been on both sides, we felt proud to have fought and won for justice.

There was no turning back – the change in societal values was too profound. When I first ran for public office in 1984, for example, the early Gay Pride Parades in my riding were really protest marches against police raids and persecution. Eleven years later Barbara Hall became the first mayor of Toronto to march in the parade. I'll never forget the moment when, walking with her and several other politicians, we came around the corner of Yonge and Wellesley and saw hundreds of thousands of people filling the streets, hanging out of windows, and chanting Barbara's name.

It was one of those great personal and historic moments that will remain in my memory for the rest of my life. Now, of course, the parade has become a massive community celebration at which people of all ages, backgrounds, and orientations show up for a summer party.

My annual Pride party became something of a tradition of its own. We originally held it at our home in Toronto, but as it grew from year to year, I had to rent space to accommodate all the guests. It drew a diverse and lively crowd, including the comedian Rick Mercer, the musician Ashley MacIsaac, and the skater-turned-artist Toller Cranston. John Tory, then leader of the Ontario Progressive Conservative Party, made a point of dropping by, as did many other prominent figures from all parties and levels of government, and even the German foreign minister, Joschka Fischer, showed up during one of his visits to Canada. But, as fun as the party always was, its serious purpose was to provide an occasion for politicians and gay and lesbian activists to meet. The two communities had had little previous contact with one another, especially in the years when the struggle for gay rights was essentially a protest movement that had few spokespeople in party politics. I felt that, if real change were to occur, we needed to build more and better lines of communication, and I truly believe that those kinds of social events helped further the advance of same-sex rights in Canada.

Participating in the struggle for equality for gays and lesbians was one of the great privileges of my political career. I never felt more honoured than when, thanks to the efforts of activists Bonte Minnema and Mathieu Chantelois, I was awarded the Pride Toronto Lifetime Achievement Award in 2007. Recognition came in other, sometimes less formal ways. Once, when I was defence minister, I was invited as the MP for Toronto Centre to officiate at the annual Dykes on Bikes event, in which hundreds of women, most dressed in heavy leather outfits, roared around town on big, loud motorcycles as part of the Gay Pride festivities. When a rather tough-looking rider introduced me to her friend from Detroit as Canada's Donald Rumsfeld, the American looked me up and down and said, "I don't think Rumsfeld would ever lead off the Dykes on Bikes."

No MATTER WHAT THE Martin government did, it could not escape from the dark shadow cast by the Gomery Commission, which inquired into the sponsorship scandal. Its hearings had garnered huge television audiences as a kind of daily soap opera, particularly in Quebec, and they created a poisonous atmosphere for the Liberal Party. One of our ministers told me of being spat on in the streets of Montreal. Ultimately the entire scandal boiled down to a few bad apples and a fraction of the sponsorship program's budget. Nevertheless, the Liberal brand was badly damaged when Gomery released his preliminary report on November 1, 2005.

Four weeks later, on November 28, the NDP decided to pull the plug on our government by joining the Conservatives in support of a non-confidence motion. Though I respected Jack Layton as a person and understood he had his own agenda, I also thought he had acted for crude partisan purposes. He chose political expediency over what he believed was sound public policy, even while knowing that his decision would probably elect Stephen Harper, kill the landmark Kelowna Accord, and destroy the national daycare program that had finally been crafted after years of effort by educators, social workers, provincial governments, and our minister Ken Dryden. It was a bitter pill to swallow, and only the extremely naive could claim he had done it for the good of the country. The next day Prime Minister Martin called a general election for January 23, 2006.

At first it appeared that the Liberals would be returned to office despite the scandal. My own seat looked safe, and the riding events passed without a glitch, but midway through the campaign I could feel the national party was in trouble – for a variety of reasons. We couldn't escape the general impression that the Liberals were tired and corrupt after too many years in power; the frequent flip-flopping around issues and the sense that policy was being made on the fly reminded people of the disastrous elections under John Turner; and our desperate attack ads, designed to scare voters away from the Conservatives, completely misfired. The worst of them, which was widely leaked but never officially broadcast, showed armed soldiers patrolling the streets of Canada while a voice of doom intoned, "Stephen Harper actually announced he wants to increase military presence in our cities." That probably cost us the military vote we had worked so hard to get. Even the mother of Major-General Andrew Leslie, a lifelong Liberal, told me she wouldn't be supporting us this time.

What doomed us was an announcement on December 28 that the RCMP was investigating a possible leak from Ralph Goodale's office about taxing income trusts – an accusation that was later proved not to be true. The NDP finance critic had made the charge in a letter, and the RCMP decided to add Ralph's name to the press release regarding the investigation. I can't think of a more egregious example of direct interference by police officials in the middle of an election. I was astonished and totally lost faith in the leadership of the RCMP. From that moment the Liberals plunged in the polls and the Conservatives took the lead – and they went on to win a minority government. For the first time as an MP, I was on the Opposition side.

AFTERMATH

On February 1, 2006, Paul Martin announced that he would be stepping down as leader of the Opposition effective immediately, and he called for a party convention to choose his successor. Who would replace him in the meantime? He left that decision to the caucus, with two obvious conditions: the candidates had to be bilingual and had to promise not to join in the leadership race. That eliminated a number of possibilities, and the choice quickly came down to Lucienne Robillard, a very popular Quebec MP, or me. Lucienne and I agreed that whoever was chosen would ask the other to be the deputy leader. The caucus chose me, I asked Lucienne to serve as deputy, Ralph Goodale became our House leader, and away we went.

The next question was whether Paul Martin would remain the party leader until the convention, as John Turner had done. I was of two minds on that, but if forced to make a choice, I probably would have preferred that he stay on. Though I had always attended the conventions and worked on dozens of resolutions, I had never been much of a party person. My dual focus on international affairs and constituency work meant that I didn't know a lot of the party's national players or internal machinations. That independence was neither good nor bad – it was simply a fact.

"You worry about the party problems, and I'll worry about the House problems," I said when Martin and I talked about it. "That would be a nice division of responsibility."

If everyone had urged him to stay, I think he would reluctantly have agreed out of a sense of duty, but the people in the party with the longest memories were against it. Dividing the leadership into two hadn't worked very well in the past, they warned, and it would simply lead to all sorts of unnecessary problems. As well, many Liberals were concerned that Martin's closest advisers were encouraging him to hold onto the party leadership in the event that the Conservatives called a snap election. But he sincerely wanted to resign, and as a result, on March 18, 2006, I became the interim leader of the Liberal Party of Canada as well as the official leader of the Opposition. When one of Mr. Martin's assistants was informed of our decision, he said, "But the board hasn't discussed that yet." Apparently the prime minister's inner circle still thought they had more influence than they actually had.

IT TURNED OUT TO BE the right decision. I forged a good working relationship with our party president, Mike Eizenga, and the national director, Steven MacKinnon, both of whom did a superb job in making sure that the leadership race was properly conducted and the convention organized without a hitch. At the same time we made overdue reforms that helped modernize the Liberal Party. I learned a great deal about the inner workings of the party. And my position as head of the party forced me to get out of the House of Commons. I travelled to Yellowknife, Quebec City, Montreal, Halifax, Vancouver, and all over the country, attending Liberal functions, making speeches, and meeting old friends and lifelong partisans. I found many of them in a demoralized state after our defeat, particularly in Quebec, but we set to work to organize the leadership convention in December. Rather than being bored or discouraged, I found sparks of genuine excitement and even moments of pure fun everywhere I went.

Instead of focusing on a government's priorities, I now had the chance to better understand the priorities of our party members and the Canadian public generally. They weren't always the same or easy to reconcile. Nor were they necessarily consistent. At one town hall in my riding, I encountered a vocal lady with strong opinions about almost everything. When we came to Aboriginal rights, she recounted how badly Canada's Aboriginal peoples had been treated, the horrible history of the residential schools, and the dreadful statistics of unemployment and substance abuse. "Give them what they want," she concluded. "Be generous." Everybody applauded. A half-hour later, when we came to gun control, she sprang to her feet and yelled, "Nobody should be allowed to have guns!"

"Well, you've got a problem there," I said. "Earlier you wanted us to give Aboriginal peoples whatever they want. But some want guns, because they need them to hunt for their livelihood." She was adamant, however: no guns, anywhere. It was a classic example of the complexity of making policy in a country as diverse in interests and ways of life as Canada.

Though my visits to the Arctic now tended to be about party politics rather than departmental business, I continued to learn from its inhabitants about the problems of the North, whether the lack of social programs or the challenges of education. Opportunities for higher education, in particular, remain scarce in the region, though there have been innovative attempts to address the inevitable "brain drain" to the South. During a visit to Iqaluit as defence minister, I had met with seven impressive law graduates from a special program run by Nunavut Arctic College, the University of Victoria Faculty of Law, and the Akitsiraq Law School Society. Premier Paul Okalik told me how happy he was, finally, to be advised by lawyers who spoke his own language and shared his cultural background. On that same trip, I had also gained a greater appreciation of the growth and influence of the evangelical churches in the North. Nancy Karetak-Lindell, for example, felt the wrath of her constituency for voting in favour of the gay marriage bill. It was yet another example of how the politics of the South can clash with the politics of the North in ways that are hard, if not impossible, to reconcile. With only three MPs, Northerners have very little clout to affect the decisions that control their lives.

As the mood in the party improved, some people were kind enough to say that I should throw my hat into the leadership race. There was even a brief moment of insanity when some Liberals, uncomfortable with keeping the Tories in power, talked about trying to bring down the government and force an early election. Mike Eizenga came to me and said, "If we have an election, you're going to have to take charge." Fortunately, that was a very remote possibility. I had accepted the job on the absolute understanding that I wouldn't be a candidate, not least because I believed we needed a younger leader with the time and energy necessary to rebuild the party over the next five to ten years. Frankly, although I was proud of my career in politics, I wasn't sure that I had the toughness of character and clarity of purpose it takes to be a successful prime minister, something Donald Macdonald once called "the royal jelly."

I was so certain of my decision that I hesitated about moving into Stornoway, the residence for the leader of the official Opposition. Moving there for less than a year seemed rather immodest and impractical, and Cathy and I liked our apartment near the ByWard Market. I soon realized, however, that the house and its staff were useful tools whose costs were being covered whether we lived there or not. With my position came a constant need to entertain people at dinners and receptions, some official, some unofficial. In the spring, for example, there were the traditional parties for the parliamentarians and the press. And I started hosting a Thursday night dinner at Stornoway for our MPs who had to remain for House duty on Friday. They were stuck in Ottawa – and in Opposition to boot – with little to do other than simply being there, so the dinners proved a special and relaxed way for us all to get to know each other better, to vent any problems and issues, and to establish a sense of comradeship.

Once Cathy and I saw how often we were using the house, we decided to move into it full-time. Our only regret was that we hadn't done it sooner. It made a comfortable home, not overly large and surprisingly informal. Though we weren't allowed to change much in the "public" rooms on the main floor, I managed to get a fine portrait of Wilfrid Laurier hung in the library, and Josh Drache looked after us as if we were family. Cathy, of course, was an active and charming hostess to the parade of strangers and friends who came through the door, as busy a doyenne as an ambassador's wife, and even when the insider talk turned more tedious than most mortals could bear, she usually found a kindred spirit with whom to share a laugh. If we'd been there longer, I would have used the house more ambitiously to host think-tank discussions or invite community leaders in for a lunch, but my days in the position were limited and they rushed by in a blur of activity. Few people were around town in the summer, and by fall the leadership convention loomed near.

THE FIRST THING I discovered when the House reconvened in April 2006 was that asking a good, snappy question in Question Period was much harder than giving a good, snappy answer. After being briefed by their officials, ministers can be fairly spontaneous with their answers as long as they know their facts and don't say something stupid. Perhaps my lowest moment came when Elsie Wayne accused me of being a useless defence minister because of problems with our submarines. "Your submarines don't even float," she yelled in the House. After a brief pause, I replied rather weakly, "Perhaps the member should be aware that submarines are designed not to float." But Opposition members have to be more strategic. I always admired the clever way Joe Clark, for example, used to approach Question Period almost like a trial lawyer. He would ask a question one day, then come back to it three days later, then again five days after that, until he eventually caught a minister in a contradiction or painted us into a corner.

But when I suggested following his example, I was dissuaded. "Oh no, you can't do that," my advisers told me. "You'll never get your question on the evening news that way. And if you don't get your question on the evening news, you're useless as an Opposition leader."

Some people's idea of a better question was for me to go after the hottest issue of the day and demand the prime minister's resignation. They saw Question Period as all about the tactics of politics. In that respect the news cycle drove Question Period into the grandstanding it has become, which is why few Canadians have much respect for it. It's no longer an intelligent exercise in trying to figure out what's happening or how to improve a government's performance. It's all about making instant political hay. And the tacticians usually win out over the strategists. No matter how hard I tried to change its tone or behaviour, nothing made a bit of difference. The moment Question Period began, it was as though the fox had been let loose and the hounds went barking in pursuit.

As a result, preparing for Question Period could be wildly time consuming and very stressful. Day after day I spent much of my morning working on and arguing about my allotted three questions, trying to decide on the theme of the day and the thrust of our attack. If I didn't agree with my advisers, it became a fight, with lots of back-and-forth. My job was to frame my questions, test them on my staff, and practise them right up to the moment I had to head to the Commons. I can't say I ever became very effective at it.

Then there was the added problem of a question in French. It is a matter of great concern for national unity that the Quebec press isn't much interested in many of the issues that relate only to the rest of the country. The fact that I could speak French made me accessible as an MP, but little that I said was reported until I became a minister. As a result, we had to find an angle or issue that grabbed the attention of Quebec journalists. For a while I had a bright young assistant, Mylène Dupéré, who helped me with the French question. She often came up with really funny Québécois expressions that had the Bloc MPs rolling in the aisles, especially when I mangled them with my accent. The francophone press started to pick up on them, and I got on a bit of a roll. Unfortunately she took a better job, and that was the end of that. I could never convince anybody else to give me anything funny. After about a month of glory, it was back to banalities.

Another challenge was to cram my questions into the thirty-five seconds I was allowed. I soon learned to watch for the little wiggle the Speaker made in his seat before he stood to cut someone off or the quirky smile he gave to push you to get to your point. I found it a very difficult exercise. I'm too long-winded by nature to have been good at it, and even doing it successfully struck me as a rather bizarre talent. By way of contrast, Ralph Goodale remained calm under pressure and loved jumping into the fray, and Lucienne Robillard was equally unflustered. But I hated the whole business, especially when one of my colleagues started screaming into my ear with her foghorn-like voice. "Can't we all just calm down?" I used to beg whenever our own MPs behaved like a pack of hyenas, but I couldn't actually order them to shut up. The argument that subdued behaviour would win us the respect of the public over the long term lost any force once Question Period began and the blood lust was up.

EVERY LEADER OF THE Opposition I ever talked to, federal or provincial, agreed that it's the worst job in any parliamentary democracy: no power to accomplish anything, no role but to be negative, and little authority over the caucus. Every Wednesday morning I met with my Liberal colleagues and gave them the same message about party unity that previous leaders had given us, but I suspected they would do whatever they wanted anyway.

That already dismal situation was worsened by the fact that we were in the midst of a leadership race. The contenders who were MPs were rarely in the House, since they were out campaigning across the country. Though I had few problems with the candidates themselves, they naturally held conflicting views on many of the major issues, and their supporters backed them regardless of the party line. There were vicious but completely irrelevant fights for empty titles about who would be the government critic for this or that. And forget about any semblance of cohesion on sticky issues such as the gun registry or the war in Afghanistan.

On July 18, 2006, for example, when Cathy and I arrived in Vancouver after riding the train from Calgary with two of our grandchildren, William and Claire, I was surprised to see about two dozen reporters waiting at the station to pounce on me. "What do you think about Harper's statement about Israel's invasion of Lebanon?" they shouted. "What's your party's position?"

"Israel has a right to defend itself against attacks, but I think an invasion will be counterproductive if its purpose is to get back the Israeli soldiers who were captured by Hezbollah," I responded. "It will look like a punishment mission, bring a lot of destruction, and destabilize Lebanon even more." I just couldn't see how bombing the hell out of downtown Beirut was going to help protect Israel or lead to long-term peace.

Of course, that and similar remarks I made later in the day at a press conference at the Hotel Vancouver were spun as being anti-Israel, which translated into huge problems inside the Liberal caucus itself. We had an enormously complicated debate that was reflective of the debate within the country and around the world. Some Liberal MPs argued that Israel should have a totally free hand to do what it decides is needed for its security. Others argued that the killing of civilians was a crime against humanity. In my opinion, the invasion of Lebanon wasn't an illegal use of force; it was an act of self-defence. But the question remained whether the bombing of Beirut had gone beyond self-defence to the point of being counterproductive. As was said of Napoleon when he executed a royalist rival, "It was worse than a crime; it was a mistake." In fact, a subsequent Israeli inquiry described the decision to use force as poorly conceived and the military campaign itself as rife with errors in judgment.

Caught in the middle, denounced by both sides in private, I formed a caucus committee to come up with a coherent and nuanced party position. The idea was to put all the differing points of view in the same room and let everyone hear the legitimate arguments on all sides. The committee had a good balance of perspectives and a mandate to arrive at the most constructive and reasonable conclusion possible. Although it couldn't satisfy the extremes, it worked out well enough in the end.

Nor, of course, was Stephen Harper averse to setting the cat among the pigeons. I was chairing a caucus meeting at 10:45 on Wednesday morning, November 22, 2006, when I was handed a note saying that the prime minister wanted to see me in the hall outside his caucus room. When we met, he presented me with a piece of paper and said, "I'm going to introduce this motion in the House this afternoon." The resolution he handed me declared, "That this House recognize that the Québécois form a nation within a united Canada."

His purpose was to pre-empt a similar resolution from the Bloc and to signal English Canada's goodwill to the "soft" nationalists in the province, while also including the reference to Canadian unity. In my opinion the debate could and should have been avoided, and I don't think the Conservatives would ever have put forward that motion if they had been in the majority in Parliament. It was another example of the madness that can overtake a government in a minority situation. The Tories were driven to do something they normally would have avoided at all cost, and as a result, the Liberals had to support it too.

Harper must also have known that the resolution would add fuel to the flames that had engulfed the Liberal Party's leadership battle after Michael Ignatieff came out in support of just such a recognition and was opposed by other Liberal candidates who asserted that it would open the door to future trouble. It was Meech Lake and the Charlottetown Accord all over again. I returned to the caucus, which was in fact discussing this very issue, and told them what had happened. "We have just been handed a bomb," I said. Then Ralph Goodale, Lucienne Robillard, and I adjourned to the next room for half an hour to consider a response.

Perhaps Pierre Trudeau could have got away with saying, "Over my dead body," but I wasn't in a position to do that, even though I understood his intellectual argument. Once you open the door to a special status or distinct recognition of Quebec, you risk not being able to close it to incremental separatism or inevitable independence. Still, a strong case could be made that the French-speaking majority of Quebec did indeed constitute a nation in the sociological sense. The motion wasn't ideal, but it was defensible.

"I know we are divided on this issue," I told the caucus, "but in my view we can't oppose this motion. Not only would opposing it mean the death of the federal Liberal Party in Quebec but defeating it would be highly problematic for the unity of the country." Harder still, I then had to run the gauntlet of media. I don't think I had ever seen so many reporters and cameras, all shouting at me about our position. In the end, the vast majority of our caucus voted to support the resolution, despite some reservations about its wisdom, for the sake of national unity.

I NEVER DEVELOPED a close relationship with Prime Minister Stephen Harper. We met a few times in his office on the third floor of the Centre Block when he needed to consult with the leader of the Opposition out of politeness or for the sake of business. He always began by joking that he preferred my office upstairs; I always responded by joking that I'd be willing to trade at any time. The meetings, which rarely lasted more than half an hour, were cordial and efficient. Mr. Harper wasn't the warm and cuddly type, but I treated him with appropriate respect, both for his position and his formidable skills.

He was a smart opponent, though sometimes I think he outsmarted himself. In May 2006, for example, the Tories had proposed a resolution that the House support the government's two-year extension of Canada's diplomatic, development, civilian police, and military personnel in Afghanistan as well as the provision of funding and equipment for this extension. Although the constitutional responsibility for deploying our Forces abroad clearly rests with the government of the day, the role of the House of Commons has evolved in recent times to include discussion of this issue within the committees of the House and non-binding votes in the Commons itself. In 1991, for instance, the Mulroney government held a vote regarding the commitment of Canadian Forces to the first Gulf War, though only after our Forces were already in the theatre. In 1994 the Chrétien government held a debate to sound out opinion in the House about Canada's participation in peacekeeping operations in the former Yugoslavia. In such debates, a motion asks the House to "take note" of a proposed course of action. Though it seldom comes to a recorded vote, it gives MPs an opportunity to express their opinions on an important question of policy, and it serves as a barometer by which the government can gauge the mood of the country.

According to Prime Minister Harper, a vote on Afghanistan was necessary in order to send two messages: one to our troops, who deserved to know that they commanded the support of their elected representatives, the other to the Taliban, who needed to learn that our mission had broad national support. When I met with General Hillier on May 16, he explained that a two-year extension would coincide with the end of Karzai's mandate as president and would therefore serve as a good benchmark to assess progress in establishing democracy in Afghanistan. As well, he said, if the Taliban thought we were talking about exit strategies, they could just hold on and wait us out. A two-year extension would also allow Canada to take on the leadership of ISAF. Though I was concerned that much of the impetus for the extension stemmed, as I noted at the time, "from the desire of the military to take a lead position," my conversation with Rick assured me that it was the right thing to do.

The problem, from the perspective of parliamentary procedure, was that we were given only two days' notice. Moreover, the defence committee would not be allowed to consider the resolution and question Defence Minister Gordon O'Connor, despite the emphatic desire of all parties for a serious debate. In my view, the motion would have been more easily supportable with a one-year extension, but the Tories wanted this issue off their political agenda. The Bloc Québécois, despite the fact that opposition to the mission was more widespread in Quebec than in most of English Canada, offered to vote for the resolution if the defence committee were given time to hold hearings to quiz the defence minister about what was going on. After intense negotiations, the government made a single concession to allow the House as a whole to debate the resolution, but only for six hours on one afternoon.

The debate had to be strictly curtailed, Harper insisted, because the longer it went on, the greater the incentive for the Taliban to engage in attacks on our Forces in order to erode Canadians' support for the mission. Under the doctrine of "propaganda of the deed," often employed in wars of insurgency and counterinsurgency, public opinion becomes as much a target of enemy operations as traditional military objectives.

The already testy debate became even testier when we learned in the middle of it that the seventeenth Canadian casualty in Afghanistan, and our first woman, had been killed not far from Kandahar. The prime minister framed the issue in narrowly partisan terms by insisting that a vote against the resolution was nothing less than a vote against our troops in the field. The NDP argued just as vehemently that a vote against the resolution was in fact a vote *for* the troops, because it was a vote against prolonging their participation in a misguided and doomed mission. It came as no surprise when all the New Democrats voted no, given their preference for reserving our military for traditional peacekeeping operations. The Bloc MPs also voted no, blaming Mr. Harper for short-circuiting the debate and claiming, as Gilles Duceppe put it, that "he has placed party politics ahead of government policy. That is unforgivable on the part of a prime minister."

The Liberals were put in a particularly difficult position, as Harper no doubt intended. The vote would force us either to reaffirm our support for an undertaking that had commenced on our watch or appear to be playing partisan politics with the lives of our troops by reversing ourselves. Voting yes would give political cover to the Conservatives' decision to extend the mission; voting no would give the appearance that we were playing partisan politics while the lives of our troops were at risk. In addition, should Liberal MPs not all vote in the same way, the divisions in our ranks could be used as evidence of our unfitness for power. In fact, the Liberal caucus was split, not least because we were in the midst of a leadership campaign in which the various candidates and their partisans had different views on the matter. Some of our MPs had long-held doubts about the mission. Others felt we simply couldn't support a government motion, particularly in the context of a minority parliament in which any concession to the government was viewed not on the merits of the particular issue but in the light of an imminent election call.

"But we created this mission, we're responsible," I argued. "We were the ones who sent our soldiers to Afghanistan in the first place. Are we now going to say that we don't want them to finish the job simply because the Tories are proposing it? What kind of credibility will we have if we do that?" On the other hand, I did have some reservations about the way in which the mission was being conducted, and I told the caucus that we should hear the government's response to those concerns before making our final decision.

"You don't understand anything about politics, Bill," the opponents said. "Harper needs at least twenty-four of our votes to pass this thing. We have to be against it because we're now the official Opposition."

"Well, I may not understand the politics, but I do understand one thing: if we vote against this motion, Canadians are going to look at us and wonder what kind of chumps would flip-flop on such an important issue involving the lives of our troops just because we don't happen to be sitting in the same seats as we were a few months ago."

I thought I had persuaded the caucus until some of my MPs, who had supported the mission and were favourably disposed toward the resolution, changed their minds because they were offended by the manner in which the prime minister had introduced it, the stringent restrictions on debate he had imposed, and his stated intention to go ahead with a one-year extension no matter which way the House voted. By the time he finished his opening statement, several of my colleagues from the Maritimes, all strong military proponents and all members of the defence committee, came up to me and said they would not vote for the resolution. No matter what I said, I probably lost another ten votes at that point, and I lost even more every time a Tory MP made needlessly provocative and partisan attacks upon us.

During my own speech, which the prime minister didn't stay to hear, I laid out four major questions that the government needed to address to gain the support of the House. What was the government's commitment to aid? Would we continue to address governance and other development issues? How would the government involve Parliament as the mission unfolded? Finally, echoing Paul Martin's concerns in 2005, I wanted to know if extending the Afghanistan mission would preclude Canadian involvement in other global trouble-spots. "We will take part in this debate," I concluded. "We will listen to the government's arguments, and each of our members will vote according to the information we receive from the government."

Part way through the debate, Foreign Affairs Minister Peter MacKay called me into the corridor. "I've just spoken to the prime minister," he said. "He told me to ask you what you want and to make sure you get it."

I reiterated the four questions that we needed answered; he agreed to address all of them, and I reported back to my MPs that, in my opinion, we now had no reason to oppose the resolution. In the end, much to the anger of many of them, I voted for it along with twenty-three other Liberal MPs, including Michael Ignatieff and his team, and it passed by a narrow margin of 149 to 145 – hardly the overwhelming support Mr. Harper claimed to have sought in the House. The Conservatives' highly partisan approach and constraints on parliamentary participation had not created the conditions to ensure success and ultimately turned the signal to the Taliban into a failure. If anything, the vote tended to undermine, rather than reaffirm, public support for the mission.

If Harper's purpose had been to use the debate as a political wedge issue to keep the Liberals divided, he was successful. In terms of demonstrating that Canada was strongly united behind our troops, however, he behaved in a way that proved utterly self-defeating. The Tories could have had the Bloc MPs and more of the Liberals on their side if they hadn't structured the debate to make consensus impossible.

As THE RESULT OF THAT experience, I came to the conclusion that asking the House of Commons to vote on questions of troop deployment risks enmeshing the issue too deeply in political considerations, whether inter- or intra-party, long or short term. Even non-binding votes are highly problematic. Although obviously more democratic than no vote at all, they often confuse the military and strategic goals with conflicting political motives. Parliamentary approval of a decision to go to war is both appropriate and politically essential, but authorizing the specific deployment of troops, in my view, is not. Ministers are responsible for the conduct of our foreign and defence policy. They have access to all the relevant information about the rationale for a given mission and the capabilities and preparation of our Forces to perform it. MPs are at a disadvantage in this respect. Ultimately, the Cabinet should take the responsibility for its decisions, rather than abdicating them to the House of Commons.

To those who argue that, in a democratic country like ours, such a highly important decision should be supported by a vote of the elected representatives, I would argue, yes, provided that the vote in the House of Commons is sure to be taken on the merits of the initiative and based on an informed opinion. But we can't assume that MPs will jump out of their partisan shells and suddenly become objective, no matter how important the decision. That's not the way the system works. Perhaps a majority government, which has control over its members, might get away with it, but putting the decision to send troops to an international war zone into the hands of a fragile minority parliament is a roll of the dice. The outcome is a reflection of a whole host of political and personal considerations that may have nothing to do with the issue.

Besides, votes in the House are not the only means of ensuring parliamentary input. The standing committees on defence and foreign affairs can bring in specialized expertise when given the opportunity to consider certain questions in depth. True, these too are political bodies, but raw partisanship tends to be moderated in their deliberations. When they are well constituted and well run, they generally subordinate personal and ideological differences to broader considerations. They can also perform a vital educative function, as was our experience with the televised committee hearings we held during NATO's bombing campaign over Kosovo in 1999.

The committee system runs well only if the people at the top allow members of Parliament to work on issues and achieve results even if that means a messier process. I think Jean Chrétien and Paul Martin maintained a better balance between efficiency and flexibility, though they didn't have to sit quite so hard on quite so many members of the lunatic fringe as Stephen Harper had to do with his caucus. When I was chairing SCFAIT, I was involved with people from every party who, like myself, were totally engaged in the issues. All of us around that table thought we were doing something meaningful for Canada as well as something interesting. My friends on the defence committee or the justice committee felt the same way, regardless of party.

In other words, Parliament had a framework that allowed us to participate in the life of our country and our riding, and to advance any agenda we wished, whether co-op financing, same-sex marriage, or military procurement. If you suck all the independence out of the committee system by control and manipulation, as the Harper government was accused of doing, you lose the constructive input of MPs to find common ground. Whether intentional or not, for example, the consequence of the Conservatives' use of omnibus bills, in which all sorts of matters were dumped into the budget legislation, was to deprive the relevant committees of having the input that the system was designed for them to have. SCFAIT, for example, held no cross-country hearings on any aspect of international policy once Harper took power in 2006.

More serious, in my view, was the decline in mutual recognition and respect. Increasingly, for all kinds of reasons, the parliamentary system has become less collegial. Modern transportation meant that MPs don't hang out together in Ottawa for months at a time, as they used to do. Television encouraged more adversarial, less rational behaviour in the Commons. The election of Reform and Bloc MPs sent a new type of representative to Parliament – the former convinced they had come to Ottawa to tame a corrupt and venal institution, the latter contemptuous of Parliament's authority to act as the national meeting place. Instead of working to make the system function well, they actually tried to undermine it. But how can MPs accomplish anything if fanatic partisanship and rigid ideology get in the way of human beings willing to come together and collaborate for the common good?

ON DECEMBER 2, 2006, the leadership convention was held in Montreal. To the surprise of many, Stéphane Dion came from third place when the support for Michael Ignatieff and Bob Rae froze. I delivered a farewell speech, but it was overshadowed by the speeches my children gave in French and English by way of introducing me. People came up to me for months afterward asking when Katy and Patrick were going to run for office. Though that wasn't ever likely to happen, it was indeed time for some new blood in the Liberal Party. Six months later I rose in the House for the last time to announce my resignation as an MP, effective July 2, 2007. I was delighted when my friend Bob Rae, the intelligent and eloquent former NDP premier of Ontario who became a Liberal in 2006, was nominated and elected to succeed me.

It was an emotional moment for me to say goodbye to my colleagues in Parliament and to what I called the "sacred" place itself. I thanked the electors of Toronto Centre for giving me the privilege of serving them. I thanked the parliamentary staff for their help over the years. I thanked our foreign-service representatives and our military for their selfless contribution to the country. And I thanked Cathy and our two children for their sacrifices and support. Without them I would never have dared public life or been able to contribute half as much. But I mostly wanted to leave with a message that might also be a good concluding thought for my memoirs.

"In closing," I said, "I want to say one thing about the civility of this place. There has been a lot in the press recently about the lack of civility in the House. It may be attributable to the minority situation we are in, and it may be attributable to a lot of causes, but surely we owe it to ourselves to disagree without being disagreeable. We do not need to do that. I believe everyone in the House carries within him or her the desire to serve our country and, whether one has that desire or not, the capacity to affect the future lives of every citizen of this great land, and to some extent others around the globe. Let us treat each other with the respect that thought brings. In what we bring to this place, let us respect one another and, in so doing, I believe our fellow countrymen will respect this institution and respect us for the work we do."

What I said about our Parliament, I could say about the world. Empathy is one of the most important tools in the conduct of diplomacy and an invaluable resource in international commerce. I strongly believe that the Canadian experience, as a bilingual, bi-juridical culture, makes us particularly sensitive to the need to see the other's point of view. As a middle power, we have a clear interest in living in a rule-based world, and it has to be our task to work to persuade the superpowers that it is in their long-term interest as well. That has been a consistent theme in Canadian foreign policy, and we can succeed only if there is the mutual understanding that comes with multilateral associations.

In that regard, Canada's foreign policy in the decade following the defeat of the Martin government was a profound disappointment. I say that not as a partisan but as a citizen. In fact, many of my concerns have been expressed by two former Conservative prime ministers, Joe Clark and Brian Mulroney. Whether to pursue an ideology or simply to save money, the Harper Conservatives turned away from the constructive internationalism and multilateralism that had been the bedrock of Canadian foreign policy since the Second World War. They snubbed the United Nations. They boycotted the Commonwealth Heads of Government meeting in 2013, simply because it took place in Sri Lanka, and then, in a further demonstration of pique, cut funding to the Commonwealth itself. They pulled out of the Kyoto Accord and withdrew from the UN Convention to Combat Desertification. They made Canada the only NATO member not to sign the Arms Trade Treaty on conventional weapons. They disregarded the Arctic Council. They abandoned our role as honest brokers in the Middle East and closed our embassy in Iran during a time when engagement with that country has become increasingly vital. Surprisingly for a party that once accused the Liberals of jeopardizing Canada's economic interests on a matter of principle with regard to Iraq, the Tories permitted their own ideology to get in the way of good trade relations with China. They failed to resolve the visa issue that has been such a long-standing irritant to our close friends and trading partners in Mexico.

Perhaps most important of all, they needlessly allowed Canada-US relations to stagnate. Indeed, the Harper years must be regarded as a period of missed opportunity for constructive partnership with an outward-looking and multilateralist administration in Washington. Under Stephen Harper, the Canadian government was unhelpful on files of vital importance to President Obama, especially those involving the environment and the Middle East. The Canada-US relationship is resilient and will certainly endure these errors in judgment, but the pro-Americanism of Stephen Harper's Conservatives revealed itself for what it always was: a simplistic admiration for the right-wing of the Republican Party coupled with an inability to understand the complex and diverse constituencies represented by the Democratic Party and moderate Republicans.

Wherever I went in Canada or around the world during the Harper years, I got the impression that many people shared my concerns about Canada's deteriorating reputation on the international stage. And I believe that became an important factor in the minds of Canadian voters during the federal election of October 2015, when the government's lack of a serious plan to deal with the Syrian refugee crisis or climate change surfaced as major issues. The result was a mandate, I believe, to Justin Trudeau and his Liberal government to re-engage in international affairs wisely, energetically, and with heart.

RECENTLY MY SON, Patrick, said to me, "Dad, you have to pick out three or four issues and make them highly controversial. Then people will attack you, you'll get media attention, and people will buy the book." He may be right, but Patrick has been a war correspondent, whereas my whole life has been about diplomacy, always trying to reduce the heat and increase the light. Even my high-school yearbook described me as "a diplomatic line between two points."

Though never officially a diplomat, I have been concerned as a lawyer, an academic, and a politician with promoting Canada's place in a system of international co-operation. International law is an important component of that structure. For the most part, rule-based diplomacy serves the world better than power-based diplomacy. States ought to accept the long-term benefit of constraints on their actions even when they view binding international instruments as detrimental to their interests in the short term. But great powers in particular often hesitate to cede a portion of their sovereignty and lose even a small part of their freedom of action. Perhaps they see extensive regulation and collective decision making as obstacles to meeting their regional and global responsibilities; certainly they differ strongly at times in their interpretation of international law and its obligations.

Today we have a body of international law, but not always the rule of international law. Power-based diplomacy remains the norm all too frequently, and many states continue to flout international law or simply refuse to acknowledge some of the obligations that it requires of them. Ultimately, however, President Clinton put the proposition best when he said, "The US has two choices about how we use the great and overwhelming military and economic power we now possess. We can try to use it to stay top dog on the global block in perpetuity. Or we can use it to try to create a world in which we will be comfortable living when we are no longer top dog on the global block." My experiences have borne out the wisdom of that remark.

I am not naive about the challenges. As a student of European Community law and a believer in the European Union, I watched the recent Greek financial crisis with concern and have listened with dismay to all the talk of Great Britain pulling out of the EU. But the EU is a relatively young experiment – far younger than the Canadian federation – and like Canada it constantly suffers from the growing pains associated with efforts to find the right balance between central authority and local autonomy. As imperfect a model as it may be, the EU still holds many lessons for the rest of the world in two major respects: the interaction between international and domestic legal norms; and the way in which certain states can craft institutions and legal systems that result in a "pooled" sovereignty designed to enhance their collective well-being.

I am certainly not a world federalist, and, just as I have no desire for our Canadian provinces to disappear into a unitary government, I do not advocate that states totally submerge their sovereignty in some idealistic world government. However, some global issues – such as climate change, terrorism, or cyberspace – require global solutions. Canada, having played an important role in creating the international institutions and norms after the Second World War, must remain proactive in crafting a new system for the ever-increasing nexus between domestic and international political and legal factors. If it neglects this role, the rules developed by other states will impose consequences on Canadians without our being able to shape the outcomes. We neglect our capacity to influence the world at our peril.

The development of international law is a matter for states, obviously, but it is also a matter for people. Individuals can make a difference in history, as I witnessed whenever I was sitting at the Cabinet table or attending summit meetings. That is why I constantly urge young people to engage in politics, whether as professionals or as volunteers. It's also why I took the lead in funding a centre for the study of contemporary international history at the University of Toronto, with the hope that its teaching capacity, conferences, and internships will enrich the lives of our students and help prepare them for the global challenges that future Canadians will face.

Political action, domestic and international, creates much of the framework of the societies in which we prosper or perish. Bad leadership can have far-reaching, negative results; a few rotten apples can spoil the whole barrel. Conversely, good leadership can produce long-lasting, positive effects; a few good individuals can improve the lives of multitudes. And public service is not just an essential realm of human endeavour: it is, as I had the privilege of discovering first-hand, an honourable and fulfilling life.

ACKNOWLEDGMENTS

I am not a historian, so these memoirs are largely the result of my recollections from my own perspective. Some of these memories have been corroborated by the notes I took at the time or by external sources, but they are largely personal nonetheless. As a result, as my wife, Cathy, pointed out, there's a lot of "me" in here when, in fact, many other important actors and events have been left unmentioned or underplayed. This is perhaps inevitable given the nature of a memoir, and I must leave it to others to tell their own stories.

It was never my intention to write a scholarly work, and I beg the forgiveness of any academics and experts among my readers for some fairly sweeping generalizations.

That said, I was encouraged to recount my experiences by two historians whom I respect greatly: John English, himself a former parliamentarian, and Bob Bothwell, a prominent member of the History Department of the University of Toronto. In their view, historical research in Canada lacks the depth of personal reminiscences by political players that have featured prominently in the political cultures of the United States, Great Britain, France, and elsewhere. Our national understanding of the historical context in which decisions are made is the poorer for that.

The idea was one thing; the execution quite another. I probably wouldn't have persevered if not for the encouragement and literary abilities of Ron Graham, a highly accomplished author and journalist who also happens to be my nephew. Ron's deep knowledge of our country and its political personalities is unrivalled, and he brought to the task the editorial skills he had previously used to assist Prime Ministers Trudeau and Chrétien in their writings. The story may be mine, but the telling of it must be credited to him.

Nor could this work have been accomplished without the dedication, long hours, good-humoured patience, and Oxford-trained historian's eye that Joe Dunlop brought to researching the materials, fact checking, and shaping the wording of key passages. Joe's efforts are reflected on every page, as is his passion for the history of Canada. I have no hesitation in predicting that he will make his own significant contribution to the field in the future.

Early drafts owed much to the scholarly and highly professional work of Jack Cunningham, now the program co-ordinator at the Bill Graham Centre for Contemporary International History, who worked with me on preparing materials for the course we teach at Trinity College; conducted hours of interviews; and drafted speeches, articles, and the initial versions of some of the chapters of this book. He was aided by the considerable organizational skills of Daniel Grubb.

Assembling the voluminous number of files produced by years of parliamentary life was a considerable task. Michelle Lobo generously spent weekends in Toronto sorting and organizing the 124 boxes of material. She was helped by Dilys Williams, who has been the indispensable person in my office for many years, the force that brings order to my business and family affairs.

Many people were generous with their time and recollections, reading chapters and providing valuable insights. Diplomats with whom I had the privilege to work – Michael Bell, Marc Lortie, David Mulroney, and Michel de Salaberry – commented on areas with which they were familiar. For guidance and wise counsel, I owe much to Dan Costello, Gene Lang, and Andy Mitchell, my chiefs of staff, respectively, when I was in turn minister of foreign affairs, minister of national defence, and leader of the Opposition. And I had the opportunity of consulting once again with many of the young people who brought their idealism and energy to Ottawa: Jeremy Broadhurst, Bill Charnetski, Robert Fry, James Innes, Suh Kim, Michelle Lobo, Warren Mucci, Brian O'Neil, Earl Provost, Isabelle Savard, Amanda Sussman, and Lillian Thomsen. Mike Eizenga added his knowledge of the Liberal Party, and John McCallum his ministerial experience, as did John Baird, from across the floor. Gerry Schmitz's comments enriched the sections on parliamentary diplomacy and SCFAIT, and Professor Karen Knop from the Faculty of Law at the University of Toronto cast her knowledgeable eye on the many passages discussing international law. Her close reading of the manuscript improved this book immeasurably. Professor Mayo Moran, the provost of Trinity College and former dean of the Faculty of Law at the University of Toronto, contributed to our discussion of the *Halpern* ruling, while Professor Audrey Macklin, also of the Faculty of Law, shared her knowledge of the Omar Khadr case. Life-long friends, including George and Martha Butterfield, John Campion, Bryn Matthews, Rosemary McCarney, and Elizabeth and Tom Wilson, all helped with memories and insights. Of course, this book could not have been completed without my supportive family: my wife, Cathy; my children, Katy and Patrick; and my sister Helen and cousin Carol, who read drafts, shared stories, and generally helped set the record straight.

I was also fortunate that one of Canada's great editors, Rosemary Shipton, agreed to comment on the text and polish the prose. UBC Press was ably represented by Melissa Pitts and Emily Andrew, both of whom encouraged me to undertake this task. Although they recognized that my book would not be a scholarly publication in the traditional sense, they insisted that it had social and historical value nonetheless. Lesley Erickson oversaw the complex task of the production and actual publication of the book, ensuring that the final product conformed to the high professional and aesthetic standards that are such a hallmark of this very fine publishing house. Deborah Kerr greatly improved the text itself through her skillful copy-editing and careful fact-checking, and Roger McConchie lent his expertise to the legal review.

It would be impossible in this limited space to thank the many talented photographers who have worked with me over the years, but I would like to make special mention of Jean-Marc Carisse, who took a number of the photos that appear in this book, and whose consummate professionalism and skill went into ensuring that his images were of the highest quality possible. I would also like to thank France Bureau at the Department of National Defence, who gave generously of her time and expertise in securing photos from DND, as well as Joanne Guillemette of Library and Archives Canada, whose advice and assistance is greatly appreciated.

A previous version of the chapter on Afghanistan appears as "Afghanistan – Some Lessons Learned: A Personal Political Perspective," in Jack Cunningham and William Maley, eds., *Australia and Canada in Afghanistan: Perspectives on a Mission* (Dundurn, 2015). Some material dealing with the Arctic also appears in "The Arctic, North America and the World: A Political Perspective," in Dawn Berry, Nigel Bowles, and Halbert Jones, eds., *Governing the North American Arctic: Sovereignty, Security and Institutions* (Palgrave Macmillan, 2016), reproduced with permission.

One of the major reasons I entered public life was because I felt Canadians were unaware of the extent to which their lives and their country's sovereignty were being shaped by global institutions largely beyond our control. And that remains one of the major reasons why, after my retirement from politics, I have continued to travel to conferences and symposia around the world, chair organizations such as the NATO Association of Canada and the Canadian International Council, and work closely with the faculty and students at Trinity College, where I have the honour of serving as chancellor. I have also been able to continue my association with the Canadian Forces. In 2010 I was proud to receive an honorary doctorate from the Royal Military College of Canada, and since 2012 it has been my privilege to serve as an honorary colonel in the Governor General's Horse Guards, a storied reserve regiment based in Toronto.

As active as I am, I have delighted in having more time and more adventures with my family. Because Katy and Matthieu still live in Paris, I have the perfect excuse to make regular visits to France, including prolonged stays at our house in Corsica. Cathy and I take joy in spending time with our grandchildren. Claire is at university in the United States, William attended McGill and has recently graduated from the prestigious IE Business School in Madrid, and Thomas, still in high school in France, visits with us when he shows up every summer to go to camp in Ontario. Meanwhile, Patrick and his wife, Naomi, have blessed us with a new grandchild, Audrey. Among the many virtues of having Naomi and Audrey arrive into our family is their hold on keeping Patrick from going off to war zones.

And, of course, so much of my happiness and zest for living comes because I am able to share them with Cathy, my invaluable partner and the love of my life. From our days at Trinity together, through my absences as an international lawyer, through the joys and vicissitudes of my political career, during my travels and work schedule as a minister, right up to her comments on early drafts of this book, she has been my best friend, my most loyal companion, my most valued and honest adviser, and my comfort. To her, I dedicate this book with the same love I declared in Paris more than half a century ago.

ILLUSTRATION
CREDITS

Every effort has been made to identify, credit appropriately, and obtain publication rights from copyright holders of the material reproduced in this book. Notice of any errors or omissions in this regard will be gratefully received and correction made in subsequent editions.

SECTION 1 (AFTER PAGE 56)

16 Family photo, ca. 1970s. Photographer Hubert de Santana, courtesy of Susan de Santana.

SECTION 2 (AFTER PAGE 184)

17 Black-and-white family image, 1984. Photographer Michael Mahovlich.
20 On election night with Tom Wilson and Jack Layton. Photographer Peter Power/GetStock.com.
21 With Prime Minister Chrétien, 1995. Photographer Jean-Marc Carisse.
22 With Cathy and Jean and Aline Chrétien, 1995. Photographer Jean-Marc Carisse.
23 With King Hussein of Jordan. Photographer Andy Shott, HOC/CDC.
25 With John Ralston Saul, Cathy, and Adrienne Clarkson. Photographer Diana Murphy.

SECTION 3 (AFTER PAGE 312)

26 With Mexican president Vicente Fox. Courtesy of the Department of Foreign Affairs, Trade, and Development.

27 Canada-Israel Committee cartoon. The Canadian Press, Brian Gable, *Globe and Mail.*

28 With Shimon Peres. Photographer Nir Elias, Reuters.

29 With Joschka Fischer, 2002. The Canadian Press, AP Photo, photographer Fritz Reiss.

30 With Vladimir Putin, 2002. The Canadian Press, AP Photo, photographer Elaine Thompson.

31 With Colin Powell at Whistler. *Globe and Mail,* photographer John Lehman.

32 Whistler group portrait. Photographer Brad Kasselman/Coastphoto.com.

33 Speaking at the UN, 2002. The Canadian Press, AP Photo, photographer Richard Drew.

34 Yawning at the UN. The Canadian Press, AP Photo, photographer Gregory Bull.

35 With Igor Ivanov at the UN, 2002. Photographer Shawn Baldwin.

36 With Kofi Annan at the UN, 2002. Photographer Shawn Baldwin.

37 With George Papandreou and Abdullah Gül, 2003. Photographer Shawn Baldwin.

39 With George W. Bush at the White House, 2004. Photographer Tina Hager, courtesy of the George W. Bush Presidential Library and Museum/NARA.

40 Great Blank Iraq Policy cartoon, 2003. The Canadian Press, Brian Gable, *Globe and Mail.*

41 Front page of *Le Droit.* The Canadian Press, photographer Tom Hanson, courtesy of *Le Droit.*

42 With Paul Cellucci. Photographer Patrick Doyle, Reuters.

43 With Alan Beesley on Canada's ratification of UNCLOS. Photographer Jean-Marc Carisse.

SECTION 4 (AFTER PAGE 376)

44 With Cathy and Paul Martin. Teckles Photo Inc.

45 With General Henault and General Hillier. Courtesy of the Department of National Defence.

46 Meeting Major-General Leslie in Afghanistan. Courtesy of the Department of National Defence.

47 With President Karzai. Courtesy of the Department of National Defence.

48 In Afghanistan with Renée Filiatrault, 2005. Photographer Master Corporal Ken Fenner, courtesy of the Department of National Defence.

49 With Donald Rumsfeld. Associated Press, photographer Dolores Ochea.

50 With Sergei Ivanov. The Canadian Press, AP Photo.

51 With Sergey Lavrov. Courtesy of the Department of National Defence.

52 On Hans Island with Rod Sterling. Photographer Jamie Innes.

55 Leader of the Opposition. Photographer Jean-Marc Carisse.

56 With the Aga Khan, 2006. Photographer Jean-Marc Carisse.

57 With Stephen Harper and Peter Milliken. The Canadian Press, photographer Tom Hanson.

58 With Justin Trudeau. Photographer Jean-Marc Carisse.

59 With the Liberal leaders, 2006 convention. Photographer Rene Johnston, GetStock.com.

60 Family photo, 2006 Liberal Party convention. Photographer Jean-Marc Carisse.

ABBREVIATIONS

ABCD	atomic, biological, and chemical warfare defence
AFTA	ASEAN Free Trade Area
APEC	Asia-Pacific Economic Cooperation
ASEAN	Association of Southeast Asian Nations
BMD	ballistic missile defence
CARICOM	Caribbean Community
CARP	Canada AIDS Russia Project
CDS	chief of the defence staff
CIA	Central Intelligence Agency
CIDA	Canadian International Development Agency
CMHC	Canada Mortgage and Housing Corporation
COPA	Parliamentary Confederation of the Americas
CPAC	Cable Public Affairs Channel
CSEC	Communications Security Establishment Canada
DART	Disaster Assistance Response Team
DFAIT	Department of Foreign Affairs and International Trade
DND	Department of National Defence
ECJ	European Court of Justice
ECSC	European Coal and Steel Community
EEC	European Economic Community
EGALE	Equality for Gays and Lesbians Everywhere
EU	European Union
FIPA	Inter-Parliamentary Forum of the Americas
FLQ	Front de libération du Québec

FTA	Free Trade Agreement (Canada-US)
FTAA	Free Trade Area of the Americas (proposed)
GATT	General Agreement on Tariffs and Trade
G7	Group of Seven
G8	Group of Eight
G20	Group of Twenty
HRDC	Human Resources Development Canada
ICC	International Criminal Court
ICJ	International Court of Justice
IED	improvised explosive device
IMF	International Monetary Fund
IRA	Irish Republican Army
ISAF	International Security Assistance Force
ITO	International Trade Organization (proposed)
JTF2	Joint Task Force 2
LTTE	Liberation Tigers of Tamil Eelam (Tamil Tigers)
MERCOSUR	Mercado Común del Sur
NAFTA	North American Free Trade Agreement
NATO	North Atlantic Treaty Organization
NDP	New Democratic Party
NEPAD	New Partnership for Africa's Development
NGO	non-governmental organization
NORAD	North American Aerospace Defense Command
NORTHCOM	Northern Command (US)
OAS	Organization of American States
OPEC	Organization of the Petroleum Exporting Countries
OECD	Organisation for Economic Co-operation and Development
OSCE	Organization for Security and Co-operation in Europe
PCO	Privy Council Office
PFLAG	Parents and Friends of Lesbians and Gays
PMO	Prime Minister's Office
PRT	Provincial Reconstruction Team (in Afghanistan)
RCMP	Royal Canadian Mounted Police
R2P	Responsibility to Protect doctrine
SAT	Strategic Advisory Team (Afghanistan)
SCFAIT	Standing Committee on Foreign Affairs and International Trade

3D	defence, diplomacy, and development
UCC	Upper Canada College
UN	United Nations
UNCITRAL	United Nations Commission on International Trade Law
UNCLOS	United Nations Convention on the Law of the Sea
UNESCO	United Nations Educational, Scientific and Cultural Organization
UNMOVIC	United Nations Monitoring, Verification and Inspection Commission
UNTD	University Naval Training Division
U6	six undecided countries on UN Security Council (at time of possible US invasion of Iraq)
WMD(s)	weapon(s) of mass destruction
WTO	World Trade Organization

INDEX

Please note: (i) For abbreviations used in the index, please see the Abbreviations list that precedes this index. (ii) The term "riding," in entries and subentries, refers to the riding of Rosedale, later Toronto Centre; the riding itself has been indexed as "Rosedale/Toronto Centre." (iii) Except for "al-Qaeda," which has been alphabetized as spelled out, all Arabic surnames prefixed by "al-" have been indexed under the element following the particle (for example, "Assad, Bashar al-").

Abdullah, Crown Prince of Saudi Arabia, 219–20
Abdullah II, King of Jordan, 248
Abdullah, Abdullah, 270, 376, 389, 395
Abel, Albert, 39
Abu Ghraib prison (Iraq), 331, 381, 393, 394, 397
Afghanistan, 132, 145, 238, 254, 280, 282, 287, 299, 324, 348, 352, 374, 396, 397; and border with Pakistan, 35, 252, 399–400; Canadian embassy in, 376, 386, 397, 400; development assistance to, 270, 388–92; drug trade in, 390; Graham-Wootten travels in, 30–31, 95, 376; Martin's lukewarm interest in, 378, 380; police in, 389, 390, 394, 397, 401. *See also entry following;* Taliban
Afghanistan, Canadian mission in, 225, 235, 252, 270, 287–88, 289, 373–
402, 423; background to, 373–75; budget for, 358–59; casualties of, 252, 386, 388, 398, 401, 427; combat role of, 252, 382–84, 386, 388, 398–402, 427; and detainees, 392–98; development assistance by, 388–92; extension of, 425–29; local outreach by, 377, 386–87; and move from Kabul to Kandahar, 380–90, 393; NATO and, 181, 224–25, 361, 374, 375, 377–94, 398–402; vs peacekeeping, 225, 252, 378–79, 383–84, 401, 427; reconstruction by, 273, 373–75, 379–92, 398–99; reservists and, 371; and suicide bombers/IEDs, 376, 386–87, 388, 399–400; "3D" approach to, 379, 388–92, 400–1
Africa, 68, 96, 133, 159, 302, 346; CIDA and, 391, 392; Graham's legal work in, 26, 61–65, 73; Martin and, 351,

378; NEPAD initiative in, 253, 260, 268. *See also specific countries*
Aga Khan IV, 65
AIDS, 93, 97, 103, 107–8, 148–49, 205, 404, 413
air traffic control bilingualism in Quebec, 58–61, 64, 88
Alderdice, John, 134
Alexander, Chris, 376, 380–81
Alghabra, Omar, 411
Alliance Française, 66–68
al-Qaeda, 223, 224, 252, 266, 322, 324, 399
Annan, Kofi, 186, 187, 260, 270, 271, 313, 317, 382
Arafat, Yasser, 164, 240, 248–49
Arar, Maher, 322–30
Arctic Council, 143, 282, 369, 433
Arctic sovereignty, 332–33, 366–72
Arctic Waters Pollution Prevention Act, 49, 332
Aristide, Jean-Bertrand, 342–47
Armenia, 95, 148, 243
Arms Trade Treaty, 433
Arrell, Tony, 101
Ashworth, Gordon, 263
Asia-Pacific Economic Cooperation (APEC), 237, 259
Asia Pacific Parliamentary Forum, 166
Asian Infrastructure Investment Bank, proposed, 175
Asper, Israel "Izzy," 242
Assad, Bashar al-, 327
Association des jurists d'expression française de l'Ontario, 69
Association of Southeast Asian Nations (ASEAN), 165, 175, 256–57, 280–81
Athlone School for Boys (Vancouver), 7, 11
Atmar, Hanif, 390
Avro Arrow, 16
Axworthy, Lloyd, 124, 145, 146, 150, 173, 182, 186, 235; as appointed foreign minister, 140–41; and landmines treaty, 190; and SCFAIT nuclear weapons review, 156, 177
Azerbaijan, 145, 148
Aznar, José María, 294, 306, 313

Babb, Glenn, 102
Bachand, Claude, 358
Bagram Air Base (Afghanistan), 324, 394
Bailey, Arthur (half-brother), 5, 6, 10, 14, 19, 36
Bailey, Helen. *See* Graham, Helen (mother)
Bailey, Loring, 5, 10, 36
Bailey, Loring, Jr. (half-brother), 5, 6, 7
Bains, Navdeep, 411
Baird, John, 413
Balfour, Lisa, 21
Balkans, war in. *See* Bosnia and Herzegovina; Kosovo; Yugoslavia, former
Ballenger, Cass, 167
ballistic missile defence (BMD), 352, 358, 362–66, 382, 412
Banerjee, Nipa, 376, 389
Barak, Aharon, 248
Barcelona Traction, Light and Power Company, case of, 48–54, 55, 189
Barlow, Maude, 169
Barrington, Jack, 21
Barrington, Josephine, 21
Barroso, José Manuel, 306
Bassett family, of Toronto, 85
Bastedo, Tom, 23
Bastide, Suzanne, 58
Beatty, David, 101
Beaumier, Colleen, 144
Beesley, Alan, 80, 333–35
Begin, Menachem, 224
Beil, Charlie, 13
Beirut, 27, 34, 61, 240, 423
Bell, Max, 84

Bell Canada, 58
Ben-Gurion, David, 250
Bennett, Carolyn, 247, 407
Bennett, Ian, 356
Benson, Ezra Taft, 13
Bergeron, Stéphane, 140, 141
Berlusconi, Silvio, 251, 273, 313
Berry, Glyn, 376, 388
Bhabha, Homi J., 13, 33
Bhagan, Ken, 103
Biggar, "Piff," 15
bilingualism, 58–61, 65–70, 398
Bill Graham Centre for Contemporary
    International History (University
    of Toronto), 435
bin Laden, Osama, 324
Bissell, Claude, 39
Black, Conrad, 242
Blackmore, David, 103
Blaikie, Bill, 141
Blair, Tony, 260, 267, 306, 310, 349;
    and US invasion of Iraq, 269, 274,
    281, 294, 295–96, 298–99, 306,
    312, 320
Blix, Hans, 267, 269, 289–90, 294–95,
    298, 301, 302. See also UN Monitor-
    ing, Verification and Inspection
    Commission
Bloc Québécois, 80, 117, 216, 358, 422,
    424, 426–27, 429, 431; and BMD
    program, 362–63, 364; and same-
    sex marriage, 407–8; and SCFAIT,
    140, 141, 144–46; and separatism/
    Quebec on world stage, 80, 144–46,
    155, 165–66
Board of Broadcast Governors, 85
Boehm, Peter, 166, 167
Bolivia, 154
Bonn Agreement (2001), 225, 373
Boreal Institute for Northern Studies
    (Edmonton), 143
Bos, Maarten, 50
Bosnia and Herzegovina: Canada's
    involvement in, 178–80, 355, 375,
380, 425; and commission on inter-
    vention, 186
Bouchard, Lucien, 123–24, 165, 199–201
Boudria, Don, 139, 165, 184
Bourassa, Robert, 69–70
Boyce, Michael, 281
Brazil, 60, 154, 162, 164, 165–66, 168,
    257, 270, 323–24, 392
Bretton Woods Conference, 76, 156,
    159–60
Brewin, John, 39
Brison, Scott, 407
Broadfoot, Dave and Diane, 103
Broadhurst, Jeremy, 198
Burjanadze, Nino, 145–46
Bush, George H.W., 247
Bush, George W., 168, 221, 257, 260,
    266–69, 275, 297–98, 330, 341,
    349; on Abu Ghraib scandal, 331;
    Blair and, 269, 274, 306, 312; on
    BMD program, 364–65; Canadian
    criticisms of, 280, 309, 313; 9/11
    anniversary reception of, 271–72;
    personality/moral certainty of, 251,
    341, 381. See also entry below
Bush, George W., administration of:
    and Afghan detainees, 324–25, 331,
    381, 393, 394, 397; and Arar/Khadr
    cases, 322–30; and Arctic sover-
    eignty, 366, 368–69; and BMD pro-
    gram, 362–66; and Canada's stance
    on Iraq, 273, 289, 291–92, 294, 299,
    307–8, 310–19, 342, 373–74; hawk-
    ishness of, 274–78, 283, 284, 298, 306,
    363, 381; and ICC, 189, 190–91; and
    Israel, 243–44; and Mexico, 297–98,
    306–7; and Spain, 294, 306–7. See
    also Iraq, US invasion of; specific
    topics
Bush, Laura, 271, 297
Bustamante y Rivero, José Luis, 53
Butterfield, George, 21, 35
Butterfield, Martha (née Robinson),
    21, 35, 169–70

Cabbagetown, 93, 94, 103, 108, 163, 203, 209

Cable Public Affairs Channel (CPAC), 211

Caccia, Charles, 124

Cadieux, Marcel, 80

Cameron, David, 320

Cameron, Donald, 13

Cameroon, 64

Camp Julien (Kabul), 375–77, 386, 388

Camp Mirage (near Kabul), 385

Camp Nathan Smith (Kandahar), 386

Campaign for Equal Families, 405

Campbell, Barry, 133, 159

Campion, John, 88, 89–90

Camplin, "Nurse," 7, 14

Canada AIDS Russia Project (CARP), 148–49

Canada and the Circumpolar World (SCFAIT report, 1997), 143–44, 156

Canada-China Joint Committee on Human Rights, 174–75

Canada-Europe Parliamentary Association, 150

Canada-Israel Committee, Graham's speech to, 238–48; Goldenberg's suggested changes to, 239–40, 246, 247

Canada-Mexico Parliamentary Association, 166

Canada Mortgage and Housing Corporation (CMHC), 204–5

Canada-US Inter-Parliamentary Group, 151–55, 162, 222, 232, 312

Canada-US Law Institute, 317

Canada-US relations: Arar case and, 322–30; as asymmetric, 106; border issues and, 155, 221–22, 307; free trade and, 104–7, 136–40, 158, 165, 167, 238, 312, 318; under Harper, 433; Khadr case and, 324–25; after 9/11 attacks, 221–25; parliamentary democracy and, 151–55; softwood lumber dispute and, 137, 153, 255–56;

US invasion of Iraq and, 273, 310–19, 342, 373–74

Canadian Airborne Regiment, 397

Canadian Alliance (formerly Reform Party), 214–15, 285, 305, 308, 313, 328, 348

Canadian Charter of Rights and Freedoms, 39, 78, 223, 248, 322, 406, 408–12; Chrétien and, 92, 127, 222, 409–11

Canadian Conference of Catholic Bishops, 405–6

Canadian Council on International Law, 80, 82, 189

Canadian Forces 180, 346–47, 352, 370–72, 385; equipment needs of, 357, 360–61, 388; Hillier on, 355, 384; and issue of detainees, 392–98; Parliamentary votes on, 425–31. *See also* Afghanistan, Canadian mission in; peacekeeping

Canadian Human Rights Commission, 405

Canadian International Development Agency (CIDA), 170–71, 174–75, 288, 353, 356; under Harper, 392, 401; and "3D" war, 379, 388–92

Canadian Radio-Television Commission, 58, 85

Canadian Rangers, 371–72

Caplan, Elinor, 234, 307, 410

Cappe, Mel, 231

Card, Andy, 310

Cardoso, Fernando Henrique, 154, 166, 168

Careless, J.M.S., 20

Caribbean Community (CARICOM), 342, 344–45, 347

Carroll, Aileen, 353, 391

Carter, Jimmy, 243

Carvajal Moreno, Gustavo, 166

Casey House (Toronto), 148

Castañeda, Jorge, 137, 167, 297

Castel, Jean, 43, 79

Castro, Fidel, 163–64, 164–65
Catterall, Marlene, 152, 235
Cauchon, Martin, 409
Cavalier, Scott, 90
Cellucci, Paul, 307, 309, 310–11, 313, 315, 325–26, 329, 362, 374
Central Intelligence Agency (CIA), 357, 387–88
Centre francophone de Toronto, 68
Chad, 62, 64
Charnetski, Bill, 198, 405
Charron, Roch, 352
Chávez, Hugo, 167, 168, 341
Chechnya, 149–50, 282
Cheney, Dick, 275, 305, 306
Chicago Council on Foreign Relations, 295, 318
Chile, 154, 164, 168, 238, 297, 301
China, 65, 67, 82, 150, 159, 161, 187, 189, 220, 271, 291, 314, 392; and Arctic sovereignty, 366, 369; and Falun Gong, 173–74, 256–57; Graham's teaching of civil servants from, 170–71, 172; Graham's visits to, 171–75; Harper government and, 151, 433; and international trade community, 77, 162, 170–76, 257; as represented in riding, 91, 93, 109, 171, 173–74
Chirac, Jacques, 67, 276, 285, 313, 318, 341, 349
Chouinard, Julien, 59
Chow, Olivia, 204
Chrétien, Aline, 126, 213, 252
Chrétien, Jean, 100, 112–17, 132, 138, 141, 150, 157, 166, 186, 195, 251–52, 253, 358, 362, 391, 425, 430; and Afghanistan mission, 225, 377–78, 393; Catholic upbringing of, 222, 404, 410; and Charter, 92, 127, 222, 409–11; and deficit reduction, 157, 201, 202; election of (1993), 114–17; election of (1997), 211; election of (2000), 213–15; and gay/lesbian rights, 403, 404–7, 409–11; govern-

ment style/policies of, 339–40, 349, 350–51; and Graham as SCFAIT chair, 136, 216; and Graham as foreign affairs minister, 225–28, 231, 234, 235, 238; and House of Commons, 124, 126–28; international respect for, 166, 260–61, 331–32; and international trade, 170, 172–73; and Israeli-Palestinian conflict, 244, 245, 250; and Khadr/Arar cases, 324, 325, 327, 328; and Law of the Sea convention, 332–35; and media, 71, 115–16, 124, 173, 280, 283–85, 298; and parliamentary democracy, 133–34, 166, 168, 169; and Quebec, 71, 92, 199, 200–1; and rivalry with Martin, 128, 212–13, 261–64, 335–36, 348; on roots of 9/11 attacks, 276; and Sampson case, 218–21; UN farewell speech by, 331–32; and US invasion of Iraq, 267–68, 274, 280, 284–85, 286–88, 291, 294–319
Christian Leadership Council of Downtown Toronto, 203
Christie, Keith, 228
Civil Marriage Act, 405–13
Clarity Act, 201, 216
Clark, Joe, 99, 242–43, 421, 432
Clarke, Frank, 198
Clarkson, Adrienne (née Poy), 21, 91, 97, 228, 231–33, 259, 376
Clarkson, Stephen, 14, 21
Clement, Tony, 102
Clinton, Bill, 138, 150, 188–90, 216, 243, 251, 267, 342, 434
Clinton, Hillary, 221–22, 381, 382
Coderre, Denis, 342
Cohen, Shaughnessy, 247
Cold Lake (Alberta), military base in, 358, 371
Collenette, David, 274
Colvin, Richard, 397
Combating Terrorism Act, 223

commercial arbitration, international law of, 81, 82

Commission of Inquiry into Bilingual Air Traffic Services in Quebec, 58–61, 64, 88

Commonwealth, 236–38, 270, 280, 342, 432–33

Commonwealth of Independent States, 148

Commonwealth Youth Movement, 18, 19

Communications Security Establishment Canada (CSEC), 357

Comuzzi, Joe, 152

Conference of Parliamentarians of the Arctic Region, 143, 150

Conservative Party of Canada, 348, 407–8

Convention on the Prohibition of the Use, Stockpiling, Production and Transfer of Anti-Personnel Mines and on their Destruction (1997), 190, 218, 237

Cook, Kenneth, 345

Cools, Anne, 89, 97–98

Cooper, Jim, 111, 211

Copps, Sheila, 112, 113, 262–63

Corsica, 25, 179; Graham-Wanklyn home in, 56, 74, 101, 157

Costello, Dan, 234, 263, 284–85, 288, 307

Cotler, Irwin, 192, 411–12

Council of Europe, 157–58, 225

Cournoyea, Nellie, 144

Crane, David, 247

Cranston, Toller, 414

Crédit Lyonnais Canada, 101, 139

Creighton, Donald, 20

Crimea, 185, 186, 368

Criminal Code, 191–92, 404

Crombie, David, 98–100, 102–3

Cuba, 95, 152, 163–64, 185. See also Guantánamo Bay (Cuba), prison at

Curry, Cathy. See Graham, Cathy

Curry, Hugh, 21–22

Dallaire, Roméo, 186, 365, 378–79

Dang Quan Thuy, 195

Darfur, 378, 380, 383–84

Davies, Hal, 23

Davis, Bill, 69

Day, Stockwell, 213, 214–15, 372

Dayan, Yaël, 241

daycare, national, 358, 403, 415

Dayton Peace Accords, 179–80

Dean, Howard, 134

Debost, Claire, 423

Debost, Denis, 25

Debost, Matthieu, 108, 259

Debost, William, 423

deficit, federal, 201–7

Delacourt, Susan, 247

Delille, Lionel Armand and Diane, 55

Demirel, Süleyman, 213

Denmark, 143, 366–68, 396

Derbez, Luis, 344

Devils Lake (North Dakota), 340–41

Devold, Kristin, 380

Dhaliwal, Herb, 309, 313

diaspora politics, 94–96, 243, 347

Dickie, Anna (aunt), 6, 14, 15–16, 20

Dickie, Bill (uncle), 6, 15–16, 20, 39

Diefenbaker, John, 16, 84–85, 86

Dion, Stéphane, 200–1, 431

Diori, Hamani, 62, 63

diplomacy, 53, 187, 255–60, 366–67, 432–34; food as factor in, 62–63, 171–72, 248, 258; parliamentary, 133–55; and "3D" war, 379, 388–89; and US invasion of Iraq, 268–69, 292, 300, 311. See also parliamentary diplomacy

Disaster Assistance Response Team (DART), 352

Dixon Hall (Regent Park), 193, 203

Doucet, Gerry, 88, 104

Downe, Percy, 226–27

Downer, Alex, 236, 256–57

Drache, Josh, 420
Dreier, David, 153
Drew, Chris, 198
Dryden, Ken, 415
Duceppe, Gilles, 410, 427
Ducros, Francie, 280, 284
Duncan, Sir Val, 47, 49
Dunn, James, 48
Dupéré, Mylène, 422
Dyer, Ainsworth, 252

East Jerusalem, 34, 250
Easter, Wayne, 326–27
Eaton family, of Toronto, 85
Edmonton Bulletin, 84
Egbo-Egbo, Thompson E. (doctor), 193
Egbo-Egbo, Thompson T. (musician), 193
Eggleton, Art, 224–25, 252
Eizenga, Mike, 418, 419
ElBaradei, Mohamed, 289–90
Elcock, Ward, 352
election campaigns. *See* Rosedale/ Toronto Centre, *and entries following*
Elizabeth II, 13
English, John, 130, 131
Equality for Gays and Lesbians Everywhere (EGALE), 405
Erekat, Saeb, 241
Essaye, Joe, 19, 27
European Economic Community (EEC), 44–45, 70–71
European Commission, 44, 157–58, 253
European Convention on Human Rights, 73
European Council, 180, 253
European Court of Justice (ECJ), 43, 44–45, 73, 138
European Union (EU), 44, 104, 130, 137–38, 148, 160, 179, 253, 328, 367, 369; membership in, 181; and state sovereignty, 157–58; and US invasion of Iraq, 283, 295, 317; as world model, 434–35
Evans, Gareth, 186
Evans, John, 87
Export Development Act, 156
Export Development Canada, 101, 169

Fahd, King of Saudi Arabia, 219
Fairview Corporation, 42
Falun Gong, 173–74, 256–57
Farris, Haig, 7
Fasken, Calvin, MacKenzie, Williston and Swackhamer ("Fasken's"), 41, 58, 73, 101, 117; Graham as articling student at, 41–43; Graham's European/international work for, 45–54, 55, 61
Filiatrault, Renée, 352
Finance, Department of, 147, 352–53, 356–61, 391–92
First Gulf War, 275, 425
Fischer, Joschka, 254, 258, 270, 295, 331, 349, 382, 414; vs US invasion of Iraq, 272–73, 276, 315
Fisher, Barry, 171
519 Community Centre (Toronto), 108, 209
Flanagan, Bill, 148–49
Fogel, Shimon, 241
Foreign Affairs and International Trade, Department of (DFAIT), 285, 354, 363, 367, 376; and CIDA, 356, 379, 388–92; and DND, 379, 380, 383, 388–89. *See also entry below*
Foreign Affairs and International Trade, Department of (DFAIT), Graham as minister of, 96, 231–336, 339–49, 363, 383; Chrétien's appointment of, 225–28; and fellow foreign ministers, 236–37, 254–57, 272–73, 349; first days on job for, 233–37; first speech by, 238–50; international meetings attended by, 250–60; and Law of the Sea convention,

331–35; and Liberal Party leadership rivalry, 260–64, 335–36; portfolio lunches held by, 288, 350; town halls held by, 299–300; and US invasion of Iraq, 264–65, 266–321; and "War on Terror," 322–31

Fortier, Yves, 58, 59, 70, 72, 100, 113, 199

Fowler, Robert, 184

Fox, Paul, 20

Fox, Vicente, 301

FP Publications, 84

France, 10, 24, 44, 46–47, 56, 135, 150, 163, 166, 168, 224, 253, 314, 354, 381; former African colonies of, 61–65; and French language/culture, 59, 65, 66–68, 270; Graham's law studies in, 43–45, 54, 57–58; Graham's legal work in, 45–54, 55, 61; Graham's recognition by, 67–68; Grahams' island home in, 56, 74, 101, 157; and Haiti crisis, 342, 344–46; and US invasion of Iraq, 95, 276–77, 278, 279, 291, 294–95, 296, 298–99, 301–2, 303, 315, 318, 319, 342

Franco, Francisco, 48, 51, 52, 53

La Francophonie, 62, 66, 150, 237, 270

Frank magazine, 227

Fraser, David, 399

Fred Victor Mission, 203

free trade. *See entries below;* globalization/free trade; North American Free Trade Agreement

Free Trade Agreement (FTA), 104–7, 136

Free Trade Area of the Americas (FTAA), proposed, 156, 165

Fried, Jonathan, 234

Friedman, Milton, 201

Fry, Hedy, 405

Fry, Robert, 234, 324

Gade, Søren, 368

Gagliano, Alfonso, 205

Gainey, Anna, 352

Gardiner, George, 101

Gardiner, Helen, 21

Gardiner, Percy, 21

Gaulle, Charles de, 24, 46–47, 56

Gauthier, Jean-Robert, 129, 130, 136

Gaviria, César, 166

gay/lesbian community, in riding, 93, 103, 404–5, 412–14

gay/lesbian rights/equality, 403–14; early initiatives of, 404–8; same-sex benefits, 406–7; same-sex marriage, 405–13

General Agreement on Tariffs and Trade (GATT), 76–77, 79, 104, 105, 158, 162, 170, 175

Geneva Conventions, 188, 393, 395, 396

Georgia (country), 145–46, 181

Germany, 44, 45, 73, 134–36, 150, 152, 180, 182, 231, 253, 314, 381, 393; and US invasion of Iraq, 272–73, 276, 278, 291, 294, 299, 315

Gil-Robles, José María, 52–53

Gillies, Jim, 101

Gilman, Ben, 152–53, 155

Giscard d'Estaing, Valéry, 135, 253

globalization/free trade, 156–76; in China, 170–76; in EU, 157–58; in Latin America, 163–66; and national sovereignty, 157, 159; parliamentary diplomacy and, 160–70; protests against, 157–58, 160, 162, 169–70, 257–58; subnational involvement in, 162–63, 165–66. *See also* World Trade Organization

Globe and Mail, 283, 284, 298

Godfrey, John, 122

Godsoe, Gerry, 104–5

Golan Heights, 241, 375, 384

Gold, Neil, 78

Goldenberg, Eddie, 126, 136, 169, 239–40, 246, 264, 307

Goldman, Berthold, 43–44, 73

Goldsmith, Peter, 281

Gomery Commission, 340, 414–15

Goodale, Ralph, 356, 358–59, 415–16, 417, 422, 424
Goose Bay (Labrador), military base in, 357–58
Gossage, Pat, 21
Grafstein, Jerry, 152
Graham, Al (Canadian senator), 133
Graham, Ann (sister), 6
Graham, Bill: birth/childhood of, 5–13, 36–37; as cyclist, 209–10, 258; education/early travels of, 7, 11, 14–35, 38–43, 121, 217; at Fasken's law firm, 41–43, 45–54, 55, 58, 61, 73, 101, 117; French law studies of, 43–45, 54, 57–58; French legal expertise of, 57–65, 68–70; international law expertise of, 26, 45–54, 61–65, 70–77, 79–82, 94–96, 170–71, 350; journal-writing/note-taking by, 24; as law professor, 70, 73–80, 83, 100–2; as law school gold medallist, 40, 41, 42, 117, 353–54; as law teacher to Chinese civil servants, 170–71, 172; and Liberal Party/first election campaigns, 68, 87–117; marriage/family of, 35–36, 39–40, 43, 55–56, 74, 88; and media, 91, 94, 112, 113, 140, 211, 234, 246–47, 248, 308, 367–68, 422, 425; as member of Parliament, 121–225; as minister of foreign affairs, 96, 225–28, 231–336, 339–49; as minister of national defence, 349–98; naval training of, 23–26; as Opposition leader/interim Liberal leader, 417–31; and Quebec culture/politics, 56–61, 65–72, 79–83; recognition of, 67–68, 196, 206, 414; resignation of, 431–32; and Rosedale/Toronto Centre riding, 68, 87–100, 102–11, 115–17, 126, 193–212, 348–49, 403–14; and SCFAIT, 128–99, 204, 212, 216, 220–25; as Trinity College chancellor, 16; and Trudeau, 56, 86–87. See also Rosedale/

Toronto Centre, and entries following; entries for specific persons, organizations, and topics
Graham, Bob (US senator), 153, 154–55
Graham, Cathy (née Curry), 16, 57, 69, 73–74, 85, 101, 112, 153, 157, 171, 196, 259, 298, 302, 407, 420, 423, 431–32; background of, 21–22; and election campaigns, 88–89, 97, 108, 109–10, 210–11, 348; and Graham's defence appointment, 349–50; and Graham's foreign affairs appointment, 225–28, 231–33; and house in Corsica, 56, 74, 101, 157; at international functions, 233, 257, 270, 271–72; marriage/family of, 35–36, 39–40, 43, 55–56, 74, 88; at riding activities, 195, 203, 232; and visit to Alert/Hans Island, 367–68; and visit to Kabul, 31, 377, 385–86; volunteer activities of, 56, 74, 88, 203, 263
Graham, David (brother), 7, 10, 11, 16, 85, 115
Graham, Francis Ronald (father), 5–13, 16–17, 19, 21, 23, 26, 27, 34, 36–37, 84–85, 98, 240, 404
Graham, Francis Ronald, Jr. (brother), 6
Graham, Fred (uncle), 98
Graham, Helen (mother), 5–13, 15–17, 27, 34, 36–37, 98, 240, 404
Graham, Helen (sister), 5–7, 10, 11, 14, 36
Graham, Jane (sister), 6, 36–37, 92
Graham, John (brother), 6, 12, 14, 19
Graham, Katherine (Washington Post), 154
Graham, Kathleen (sister), 6
Graham, Katy (daughter), 40, 43, 55, 431; education of, 56, 74; election campaigning by, 97, 108–9; marriage/family of, 19, 25, 259
Graham, Leona (cousin), 98
Graham, Margie (sister), 6

Graham, Marguerite Phelan, 5, 8

Graham, Mary (sister), 6

Graham, Mimi (sister-in-law), 6

Graham, Patrick (son), 43, 52, 55, 102, 259, 352, 431, 433–34; education of, 16, 56, 74, 116, 387; election campaigning by, 97, 98; at Global TV, 302, 308, 310; at *National Post*, 183, 242, 302, 308; as trapped by US fire in Iraq, 330–31

Graham, Peter (brother), 6

Graham, Philip (brother), 6, 136

Graham, Sheila (sister), 6

Grandmaison, Nicholas (Nicky) de, 13

Grassley, Chuck, 162

Gray, Herb, 129, 228, 234

Graymont (Graham family investment firm), 10, 101

Great Britain, 18–19, 34, 51–52, 75, 150, 157, 267, 330, 400, 434; in Afghanistan, 376, 377, 380–81, 390, 397, 398, 399; and law of the sea, 332–33; traditions/culture of, in Canada/abroad, 15, 17, 18, 21–22, 32, 86; and US invasion of Iraq, 274, 276, 278, 280–81, 289, 291–92, 295–96, 298–99, 300, 301, 306–7, 312, 319–21. *See also* Blair, Tony; Straw, Jack

Greece, 158, 303, 348–49, 434

Greene, Trevor, 387

Group of Eight (G8) meetings, 237, 257, 260, 341, 350, 382; of foreign ministers, 252–54, 272–73, 282, 330

Group of Twenty (G20), 257

Grubel, Herb, 123

Guantánamo Bay (Cuba), prison at, 324–25, 393, 394, 397

Gunn, Charlie, 23

Gürsel, Cemal, 29

Haaretz (Israeli newspaper), 240

Haiti, 178, 237, 375, 378, 382, 383, 398; Aristide crisis in, 342–47; Canadian Forces in, 343, 346–47, 380, 402

Hakim, Peter, 153–54

Hall, Barbara, 413–14

Halpern v. Canada (Ontario Court of Appeal), 408–9

Halton, David, 21

Hamilton, Lee, 151–52, 186

Hans Island, 366–68

Harder, Peter, 233

Harper, Elijah, 113

Harper, Stephen, 151, 325, 328, 349, 376, 392, 400, 413, 423, 424–33; and Afghan detainee issue, 396–98; and extension of Afghanistan mission, 425–29; Liberal attack ads against, 348, 415

Harris, Alan, 15

Harris, Mike, 205–6

Hawkes, Brent, 405

Hayden, Salter, 23, 40–41

Heald, Darrel, 59

Heinbecker, Paul, 296–97, 301–2

Henault, Ray, 183, 287, 352, 353, 354, 375, 380

Henning, Doug, 116

Herat (Afghanistan), 30, 380

Hercules transport aircraft, 357, 361, 367, 385–86

Herle, David, 360

Hervieux-Payette, Céline, 199

Hickman, Alex, 86–87

Hilchie, Janice, 143, 161

Hill, John, 21

Hillier, Rick, 355–56, 358–61, 380–89, 392, 393, 396, 426

Himelfarb, Alex, 334, 359

HIV/AIDS. *See* AIDS

Hoffmann, Ron, 234

Homeland Security, US Department of, 221, 326

Hoon, Geoff, 353

Hošek, Chaviva, 126

Houghton, Amory (Amo), 153

House of Commons, 121–28; attendance in, 122–23, 124; caucuses of,

124–26; Chrétien and, 124, 126–28; committee work in, 129–32, 141–42; office choices of, 121–22, 235; positions for MPs in, 128–29. *See also* Question Period; SCFAIT *entries*

housing co-operatives, in riding, 93–94, 204–6

Howard, John, 135, 256

Howe, C.D., 21, 84

Hoyer, Steny, 152

Human Resources Development Canada (HRDC), 202–3, 357

human security, 177–92; and acknowledgement of genocide, 188–89; and Balkans/Rwanda crises, 178–80, 180–86; and ICC, 189–92; and R2P doctrine, 187; and SCFAIT's nuclear weapons review, 177–78; and state sovereignty, 184–87

Human Security Network, 190, 270

Hunte, Julian, 343

Hussein, King of Jordan, 330

Hussein, Saddam, 217, 264, 266, 275, 285, 291, 303, 316, 320–21

Husseini, Faisal, 241

Hutchison, Bruce, 12

Iacobucci, Frank, 73, 78, 105

Ignatieff, Michael, 14, 83, 186, 424, 429, 431

immigration issues, in riding, 196–98

improvised explosive devices (IEDs), 386–87, 399

India, 12, 13, 26, 27, 28, 31, 32, 164, 236, 273; economic issues of, 159, 162, 163, 257, 270; vs Pakistan, 95, 254, 377, 399

Innes, Jamie, 368

intelligence-sharing groups, 315, 329–30

Inter-American Dialogue, 153–54

International Atomic Energy Agency, 289–90

International Commission on Intervention and State Sovereignty, 186–87

International Court of Justice (ICJ), 49–54, 189

International Criminal Court (ICC), 175, 188–92, 237, 268, 281, 319–20, 392

International Criminal Tribunal for the former Yugoslavia, 180, 189

international law, 20, 39, 90, 145, 154, 217, 218, 237, 253; and Afghanistan mission, 374, 383, 392–93, 399–400; and Arar/Khadr cases, 322–30; and Canadian politics, 94–96, 104, 138–40; and global politics, 170–76; Graham's education in, 40, 43–45, 54, 57–58; Graham's expertise in, 26, 45–54, 61–65, 70–77, 79–82, 94–96, 170–71, 350; and Haiti regime change, 345–46; and ICC, 188–92; and Israeli-Palestinian conflict, 238, 242, 249–50; and Law of the Sea convention, 332–35, 369; vs power-based diplomacy, 434–35; and R2P doctrine, 186–87; and state sovereignty, 184–87, 366–68, 369; and US invasion of Iraq, 264–65, 267, 274–81, 303–6, 314, 317, 319–21

International Monetary Fund (IMF), 31, 76, 130, 156, 159, 160, 253, 257

International Policy Statement reviews, 352–61

International Security Assistance Force (ISAF), 225, 252, 288, 374–84, 385–86, 393, 396, 398, 426

Internationale Handelsgesellschaft case (ECJ), 73

Inter-Parliamentary Council against Anti-Semitism, 248

Inter-Parliamentary Forum of the Americas (FIPA), 167–70, 225–26, 238

Inter-Parliamentary Union, 150, 161, 163

Inuvialuit Regional Corporation, 144
Iran, 29–30, 32–33, 217–18, 220, 266, 269, 270, 323, 433
Iraq, 27, 32, 33, 217, 266, 275, 425. *See also entries below*
Iraq, UN inspections in, 266–67, 269, 275, 276–78, 285, 286, 289–90, 294–95, 297, 298, 301, 302; as finding no evidence of weapons, 269, 286, 289–90; as refuting Powell's claims, 293–95
Iraq, UN Security Council resolutions concerning: on Iraq's destruction of weapons/UN inspections, 266–67; on Iraq's destruction of weapons/UNMOVIC inspections, 267, 269, 275, 276–78, 285, 286, 289–90, 294–95, 297, 298, 301, 302; on Iraq's "material breach" of obligations, 276–83, 285, 290–92, 295–99; and question of automaticity, 276, 280, 290–91, 298, 301–2; and second resolution, 276, 278, 283, 290, 291, 294, 296, 298–99, 301; and sanctions for non-compliance, 267, 269
Iraq, US invasion of, 266–321; as based on faulty intelligence, 269, 289, 293–95, 319–20; and Canada-US relations, 273, 289, 291–92, 294, 299, 307–8, 310–19, 342, 373–74; Canada's attempts to prevent, 296–302; and Canada's commitment to UN, 273–75, 276, 277, 284–86, 290–93; and Canada's nearby sea patrol, 287–88, 289, 303–6, 307; Canada's refusal to join, 291, 307–16, 373–74; by coalition of US/allies, 264, 269, 278, 279, 286, 289, 291, 305, 306, 310, 312–13; as following 9/11 attacks, 95, 266, 322; hawks vs doves on, 274–78, 283–85, 294, 298, 310–11; legality of, 273–74, 278, 279–81, 285, 286, 290–91, 295, 319–21; public opposition to, 294, 300, 311, 319; and regime change,

273, 274–75, 295; vs US position on Haiti, 343, 345–46. *See also entries for specific countries*
Ireland Fund of Canada, 74, 110
Irish Republican Army (IRA), 224, 330
Islam, 30, 217, 218, 220; Sharia law of, 81–82
Ismay, Lord Hastings, 180
Israel, 20, 34, 95, 134, 150, 189, 218, 252, 273; Graham's official visit to, 248–49, 251; invasion of Lebanon by, 423–24
Israeli-Palestinian conflict, 238–51, 283; Graham's speech on, 238–50; two-state solution to, 240, 249–50
Istanbul, 12, 28–29; summits/meetings in, 149–50, 348–49. *See also* Turkey
Ivanov, Igor, 254, 272, 282, 298, 316
Ivanov, Sergei, 369, 382

Jackman, Hal, 7
Jackson, Mike, 281
Jagan, Cheddi, 164
Jerusalem, 241, 242, 248
Jerusalem Post, 240, 242
Jewett, Mark, 80–81
Jewish community in Canada, 95, 238–48, 339
Jiménez de Aréchaga, Eduardo, 50
Johnson, Lyndon B., 56, 177
Johnson, Mora, 198
Johnston, Don, 92
Johnstone, Vaughan, 260
Joint Task Force North, 370
Joint Task Force 2 (JTF2), 225, 382, 387–88, 393
Jordan, 34, 243, 245, 248, 270, 317, 323, 330
journalists/media, 46–47, 251–52, 326; Chrétien and, 71, 115–16, 124, 173, 280, 283–85, 298; Graham and, 91, 94, 112, 113, 140, 211, 234, 246–47, 248, 308, 367–68, 422, 425; on US

invasion of Iraq, 283–85, 298, 313, 315, 318. *See also* Graham, Patrick

Junior League of Toronto, 56, 110

Justice, Department of, 198, 313, 350, 406–7, 411–12

Kabul (Afghanistan), 30–32; Canadian embassy in, 376, 386, 397, 400; development assistance in, 389, 390–91; governance problems outside of, 377–78, 395; Graham's visit to, 377, 385–86, 388, 395; ISAF base in, 225, 252, 288, 374–84, 385–86, 393, 396, 398; and move to Kandahar, 380–90, 393; orphanage in, 377; SAT deployment in, 382, 388–89

Kananaskis (Alberta), G8 meeting at, 252, 253–54, 257–58, 260

Kandahar (Afghanistan), 30–31, 376, 380–90, 393; combat missions in, 252, 382–84, 386, 388, 398–402, 427; JTF2 deployment in, 225, 393; PRT deployment in, 380–81, 384–87, 389–90

Karetak-Lindell, Nancy, 411, 419

Karzai, Hamid, 31, 375, 376, 377–80, 382, 388–89, 395, 426

Kazemi, Zahra, 323

Kelowna Accord, 403, 415

Kennedy, David: *Of War and Law*, 280

Kennedy, John F., 39, 76, 177, 185

Kenney, Jason, 142

Kenny, Colin, 359

Kergin, Michael, 222, 278, 329

Keynes, John Maynard, 201

Kfoury family, 34

Khadr, Omar, 324–25

Khalid, Asadullah, 390

Kilgour, David, 123

Kim, Suh, 198

King's College, University of (Halifax), 74, 387

Kirsch, Philippe, 189

Kleinwort Benson (British merchant bank), 49

Knight, K.D., 343, 344, 345

Korean War, 29, 183, 313

Kosovo, 146; Canada's involvement in, 182–86, 274, 284, 371; NATO air strikes on, 183–86, 187, 209, 274, 280, 281, 284, 320, 430

Kountché, Seyni, 63–64

Kuperwasser, Yosef, 241

Kyoto Accord, 433

Laanemäe, Erna, 7

Laanemäe, William Mart, 7–8

Lalonde, Francine, 141, 145–46

Lambsdorff, Otto Graf, 134, 135

Lamido, Sule, 236

Lamont, Christine, 323–24

landmines treaty (1997), 190, 218, 237

Lang, Eugene, 288, 352, 359

LaPierre, Laurier, 410

Laprès, Daniel, 234

Larijani, Ali, 218

Laskin, Bora, 38–39, 248

Latin America, 133, 135, 153–54, 159, 187, 227, 238, 302; OAS and, 163–70. *See also specific countries*

Laurier, Wilfrid, 104, 420

L'Aventure, Linda, 35, 100, 109

Laverdure, Claude, 307

Lavertu, Gaëtan, 233

law of the sea, 74, 80; UN Convention on, 332–35, 369

Law Society of Upper Canada, 38, 128

Laws, Mrs. ("Lawsie"), 7, 14

Layton, Jack, 116, 204, 348, 415

Le Droit, 292

Lebanon, 12, 24, 27, 32, 61, 240, 243, 423–24

Lee, Jim, 143

Legion of Honour (France), 67–68

Leslie, Andrew, 375, 376, 415

Leung, Sophia, 171

Lévesque, René, 57, 68, 69

Li Zhaoxing, 175, 257
Liberal International, 133–36, 147, 214, 240
Liberal Party, 124–28, 140, 183, 223, 340, 342, 348, 359, 364–65; Chrétien-Martin rivalry in, 128, 212–13, 261–64, 335–36; Chrétien's leadership/handling of, 124, 126–28, 133, 136, 169, 202, 213, 216; and combat mission in Afghanistan, 382, 384; and gay/lesbian rights, 403–14; Graham's leadership of, 417, 422–29; and Israel, 247–48, 423–24; and Quebec, 200–1; and US invasion of Iraq, 274, 285, 289, 308–9, 312; women's caucus within, 125, 359, 384, 405. *See also specific persons*
Liberal Party leadership conventions: (1968), 56; (1984), 92, 100, 128; (1990), 111–14; (2003), 335–36; (2006), 417, 422–23, 431–32
Liberals for Equality, 405
Liberation Tigers of Tamil Eelam (LTTE, or Tamil Tigers), 195, 224
Libya, 132, 186, 187
Liquor Control Board of Ontario, 77
Lobo, Michelle, 352
Lockheed Martin (US aircraft manufacturer), 361
Lukin, Vladimir, 182, 186
Lynch, Denis, 24–25

MacDonald, David, 103–4, 115, 116, 117, 151, 212
Macdonald, Donald, 87, 97, 104, 420
MacDonald, Melvyn, 219
Macdonald, Ronald St. John, 39, 80
Macdonell, Harry, 46
MacEachen, Allan, 130, 132
Macedonia, 178, 182–83
MacGuigan, Mark, 39, 92
MacIsaac, Ashley, 414
MacKay, Peter, 428–29
MacKenzie, Bryce, 42

MacKenzie, Norman, 11, 13
MacKinnon, Steven, 418
MacLaren, Roy, 126
MacMillan, Margaret, 127, 134
Maier, Joe, 259
Mandela, Nelson, 102, 224
Manley, John, 235, 262, 277, 289, 299, 307–8, 312, 400–1
March, Juan, 49, 51–52, 53
Marchand, Jean, 59
Marcos, Ferdinand, 194
Martel, Leo, 327
Martin, Paul (Jr.), 107, 124, 132, 325, 326, 331, 370, 378, 380, 383, 384, 396, 399, 428, 430; and Africa, 351, 378; and BMD program, 362–66; election victory of, 347–49; and gay/lesbian rights, 403–14; Graham as defence minister of, 349–98; Graham as foreign minister of, 339–49; as Graham's law school classmate, 29, 112, 212, 263, 353–54; and G20 concept, 257; International Policy Statement reviews of, 352–61, 391–92; Liberal Party convention defeat of, 112–14; and non-confidence/election defeat, 414–16, 432; as Prime Minister, 339–40, 378, 411; resignation of, 417–18; and rivalry with Chrétien, 128, 212–13, 261–64, 335–36, 348; and sponsorship scandal, 336, 340, 348, 414–15
Martin, Paul (Sr.), 114, 212
Martin, Sheila, 263
Mashhad (Iran), 29–30, 217
Matthews, Bryn, 18–19
May, Elizabeth, 169
Mazigh, Monia, 327, 328
McCallum, John, 252, 284–85, 287–88, 303–5, 307, 351, 352, 362, 380; and Rumsfeld, 275–76, 284, 289, 374
McCarney, Rosemary, 90, 171
McCarthy and McCarthy ("McCarthy's"), 23, 40–41, 42

McDonald, David, 61
McFadden, John, 103
McGill University, 21, 74, 79, 101
McGuinty, Dalton, 348
McKeen, Stanley, 11
McKenna, Frank, 365
McKinnon, Don, 236, 237
McLellan, Anne, 313, 357, 361, 406–7
McLeod, Young, Weir, 23
McMurtry, Roy, 68–70, 408
McNamara, Robert, 177–78
McWhinney, Ted, 192
media. *See* journalists/media
Meech Lake Accord, 112–13, 424
Meighen, Michael, 103
Merafhe, Mompati, 236
Mercado Común del Sur
   (MERCOSUR), 165
Mercer, Rick, 215, 414
Mercy Centre (Bangkok), 259
Mestral, Armand de, 79
Metropolitan Community Church
   (Toronto), 405
Mexico, 12, 17, 101, 150, 156, 165, 166,
   168, 225–28, 270, 313, 340, 344, 433;
   and NAFTA, 137–38; and US border
   issues, 155; and US invasion of Iraq,
   297, 298, 301, 307
Michel, Louis, 250
Mies van der Rohe, Ludwig, 42
Miller, Billie, 236
Miller, David, 408
Milliken, Peter, 53
Mills, Bob, 141, 184
Milošević, Slobodan, 178, 182, 183, 281
Mitchell, Fred, 344, 345
Mitterrand, François, 67
Model Law on International
   Commercial Arbitration, 81, 82
Modernization of Benefits and
   Obligations Act, 406–7
Mohammad Reza Pahlavi, Shah of
   Iran, 29, 217, 218
Montenegro, 27–28, 150, 178

Moore Park, 92–93, 97
Morin, Jacques-Yvan, 80, 82
Moss Park, 93, 97, 98
Moussa, Amr, 249–50, 270, 328
Mubarak, Hosni, 248
Mucci, Warren, 198
Mugabe, Robert, 236–37
Mulroney, Brian, 68, 100, 110, 112, 115,
   130, 164, 178–79, 425, 432; and free
   trade, 104, 105, 106–7, 136–37
Multilateral Agreement on Invest-
   ment, 156
Munich Conference on Security
   Policy, 381–82
Murkowski, Frank, 153
Murphy, Tim, 107, 263, 349–50
Musharraf, Pervez, 35, 236, 400

Napolitano, Janet, 221
Nasser, Gamal Abdel, 34
National Defence, Department of
   (DND), Graham as minister of, 349–
   98; and appointment of Hillier, 355,
   381, 382–83; and BMD program,
   362–66; and citizen metadata collection, 357; and Goose Bay base,
   357–58; and International Policy
   Statement review/DND budget,
   352–56; and military-civilian bi-
   furcation, 351–52, 354. *See also*
   Afghanistan, Canadian mission
   in; Canadian Forces
National Democratic Institute (US),
   134
National Post, 183, 231, 242, 248, 365;
   and Ducros incident, 280, 284; and
   US invasion of Iraq, 280, 283, 284,
   302, 308, 313
NATO, 53, 130, 132, 145, 147, 152, 177–
   82, 196, 217, 354, 433; and Afghanistan mission, 181, 224–25, 361, 374,
   375, 377–94, 398–402; air strikes on
   Bosnia/Kosovo by, 179, 180, 183–86,
   187, 209, 274, 280, 281, 284, 320,

430; Canadian training centres of, 357–58; and NATO treaty, 224–25, 361; Parliamentary Assembly of, 150, 160; and Russia, 180–86, 251, 283, 348

Natynczyk, Walt, 304, 392

Nayef, Saudi prince/minister of the interior, 219–20

Netanyahu, Benjamin, 242

Netherlands, 134, 135–36, 270, 303, 376, 380, 383

New Democratic Party (NDP), 117, 155, 183, 305, 348, 364, 407, 427, 431; and Martin government, 415–16; in riding, 106, 107, 116, 204, 207, 209–12, 215, 349; and same-sex marriage, 407–8; and SCFAIT, 140, 141, 161

New Partnership for Africa's Development (NEPAD), 253, 260, 268

Newfoundland, 39, 86–87, 158, 221, 308, 333–35, 355

Newman, Don, 247

Nguyen Thi Binh, 195

Nicholson, Peter, 360

Niger, 61–65, 73, 172

Nikitin, Alexander, 149

Nigeria, 193–94, 236, 270

Nixon, Richard, 76, 345

Non-Aligned Movement, 164

non-governmental organizations (NGOs), 130, 149, 168, 177, 182, 245; in Afghanistan, 389, 390, 397; anti-globalization protests by, 160–61, 169–70, 258

North American Aerospace Defense Command (NORAD), 235, 287, 305, 313, 352, 355, 361–66, 382

North American Free Trade Agreement (NAFTA), 136–40, 158, 165, 167, 238, 312, 318

North Atlantic Treaty (1949): article 5 of, 224, 361

North Atlantic Treaty Organization. See NATO

North Korea, 95, 266, 282

Northern Command, US (NORTHCOM), 362, 363, 365–66

Northern Ireland, 73, 74, 134, 224, 243, 398

Northwest Passage, 332–33, 366, 368–69

Noyek, Arnold, 245

nuclear submarines, 149, 368, 372

nuclear weapons, 24, 132, 185, 203, 206, 218, 254, 275, 361, 409; Iraq and, 268, 269, 278, 320–21; SCFAIT review of, 156, 177–78

Nuremberg Trials, 45, 188, 190

Nye, Joseph, 131

Obama, Barack, 320, 433

Obasanjo, Olusegun, 236

O'Connor, Dennis, 329

O'Connor, Gordon, 358, 396–97, 426

Ogdensburg Agreement, 361–62

Okalik, Paul, 419

Oliver, Spencer, 152

Omar, Mullah Mohammed, 252, 387–88

O'Neil, Brian, 198

Operation Apollo (Canada), 225

Operation Athena (Canada), 375–76

Operation Desert Fox (US/UK), 267

Operation Enduring Freedom (US), 225, 287–88, 303–6, 382, 399

Operation Medusa (Canada), 399

Orbán, Viktor, 134, 135

Organisation for Economic Co-operation and Development (OECD), 156

Organization for Security and Co-operation in Europe (OSCE), 146–50; Parliamentary Assembly of, 147–50, 152, 181

Organization of American States (OAS), 130, 163–64, 168, 342; inter-parliamentary organization of (FIPA), 167–70, 225–26, 238

Organization of the Petroleum Exporting Countries (OPEC), 74
Origo, Iris: *The Merchant of Prato*, 75
Osgoode Hall Law School, 38, 43
Ouellet, André, 140
Owen, Iris, 98

Pakistan, 32, 164, 236, 273, 299, 324, 326; and border with Afghanistan, 35, 252, 399–400; vs India, 95, 254, 377, 399
Palacio, Ana, 294, 306–7
Palestinians, 34, 239–51; displacement of, 239, 240, 245, 246; Second Intifada of, 244; and West Bank barrier wall, 249–50. *See also* Israeli-Palestinian conflict
Pan Ocean Minerals, 61–65
Papathanaskis, Spiros, 103
Pararajasingham, Joseph, 196
Pardo, Arvid, 332
Paré, Philippe, 144
Paredes Rangel, Beatriz, 166
Parents and Friends of Lesbians and Gays (PFLAG), 405
Parizeau, Jacques, 199, 200
Parkinson Foundation, 74
Parliamentarians for Nuclear Non-proliferation and Disarmament, 177
Parliamentary Confederation of the Americas (COPA), 165–66
parliamentary diplomacy, 133–55, 432; by Canada-US groups, 151–55; and globalization issues, 160–63; by Liberal International, 133–36; by OSCE, 146–50. *See also* SCFAIT *entries*
Parliamentary Spouses Association, 232
parliamentary system, Canadian, 87, 333–35, 429–31
Parrish, Carolyn, 309
Parti Québécois, 57, 59, 70, 165, 200, 216, 237

Pasteur, Louis, 66
Patten, Christopher, 175
Patterson, P.J., 342, 347
peacekeeping, 132, 177, 359, 381, 397; and Afghanistan mission, 225, 252, 383–84, 401, 427; in Bosnia, 178–80, 425; in Darfur, 380, 383–84; in Haiti, 343, 346–47, 380, 402; in Kosovo, 183; "lite" vs "heavy," 378–79; vs "peace enforcement," 180; in Rwanda, 186
Pearson, Frederick Stark, 48
Pearson, Lester B., 56, 130
Peers, Michael, 231
Pelletier, Jean, 126, 226
Penson, Charlie, 139, 141
Peres, Shimon, 245, 248
Perle, Richard, 275
Petersen, Jan, 196, 224
Peterson, Jim, 353
Petit, André, 66–67
Pettigrew, Pierre, 161–62, 163, 288, 339, 353, 365
Philip, Prince, Duke of Edinburgh, 36, 85
Pickering College (Newmarket, ON), 6
Pietersma, Philip, 198
Pinochet, Augusto, 191
Pitsuwan, Surin, 259
Plavšić, Biljana, 179–80
Poland, 310, 312
Porter, Dana, 42
Porter, Julian, 41
Portugal, 40, 94, 306, 348–49
Powell, Colin, 167, 169–70, 257, 280–81, 299, 301, 305–12, 316–17, 330–31, 340–41, 349, 351; and Canada's stance on Iraq, 308; as dove, 274–78, 283, 305, 306; at foreign ministers' meetings, 254–56, 270, 272, 315; and Haiti crisis, 342–46; on ICC, 190–91; on Khadr/Arar cases, 325–26; UN presentation by, 292–95, 315

Poy, William, 91
Pratt, David, 362–63, 380
Prichard, Robert, 100
Pride Parade and festivities (Toronto), 413–14
Primakov, Yevgeny, 308
Prime Minister's Office (PMO), 124, 128, 234, 284, 301, 354, 358, 365; and Chrétien-Martin rivalry, 212, 263, 348
Princess Patricia's Canadian Light Infantry, 252, 386
prisoners/detainees: at Abu Ghraib, 331, 381, 393, 394, 397; Afghani, 225, 392–98; Arar and Khadr as, 322–30; at Bagram Air Base, 324, 394; Canadian citizens as, 323; at Guantánamo Bay, 324–25, 393, 394, 397; journalists as, 326
Progressive Conservative Party, 84–86, 117, 407; of BC, 115; of Ontario, 69, 414; in riding, 211, 215
Provincial Reconstruction Team (PRT), 379–81, 384–87, 389–90; and development assistance money, 388–92; and local police, 389, 398; as supported by combat troops, 382–84, 400
Provost, Earl, 263
Putin, Vladimir, 251, 260, 272, 368, 369

Qasim, Abd al-Karim, 33
Quebec, 56–61, 65–72, 70–71, 79–83, 86, 215, 224, 234, 237, 264, 349, 363, 382, 418, 422, 424–25, air traffic control in, 58–61; in bilingual Canada, 58–61, 65–70; Chrétien's upbringing in, 222, 404, 410; and gay/lesbian rights, 404, 408, 410; and Haiti crisis, 342, 346; and international law, 79–82; Quiet Revolution in, 56–57; referendums in, 70–72, 199–201; sponsorship scandal in, 336, 340, 348, 414–15; vs US invasion of Iraq, 285, 300, 310
Question Period, 124; Graham's Opposition experiences of, 420–22; and US invasion of Iraq, 283, 288, 293, 305, 307–8

Rabin, Yitzhak, 240, 241
Rae, Bob, 431
Rae, Kyle, 411
Ramsay, Angus, 180
Raytheon (US defence contractor), 358
Reagan, Ronald, 156, 363
Rebick, Judy, 169
"Red Book" of Liberal campaign promises (1993), 114, 116, 201
Red Cross, 12; and war detainees, 325, 396, 397
Reform Party, 117, 123, 135–36, 139, 141, 151, 184, 194, 210, 406, 409, 431; and "perks"/travel, 142–44, 153; in riding, 116, 211–12; and right-wing mergers, 197, 214–15, 348. See also Canadian Alliance
Refugee Working Group, of Middle East Peace Process, 245
Regent Park: demographics of, 93, 94–95, 193–94, 195, 202; election campaigning in, 96–99, 107, 209, 211; Mandela school in, 102; social supports for, 103, 193–94, 203, 206
reservists, of Canadian Forces, 371–72
Responsibility to Protect (R2P) doctrine, 187, 190, 260, 320
Reuter, Paul, 51
Reza, Ali al- (Imam Reza), 29–30
Rice, Condoleezza, 317, 365
Ridge, Tom, 312
Rièse, Laure, 66
Roberts, Ed, 39, 86
Roberts, John, 92
Robertson, Lord George, 181
Robertson, Ron, 41–42

Robillard, Lucienne, 417, 422, 424
Robinson, Sidney, 21
Robinson, Svend, 141, 161, 183, 407
Rock, Allan, 41, 128, 198, 345, 404–5
Rolin, Henri, 52–53
Rolls, Ron, 41
Roman Catholic Church, 8, 21–22, 86, 98, 178; Chrétien's upbringing in, 222, 404, 410; and same-sex marriage, 404, 405–6, 407, 410–11
Rome Statute of the International Criminal Court (1998), 189, 190–92, 281
Rose, Elliot, 20
Rosedale (neighbourhood), 40, 93, 94, 97, 206
Rosedale/Toronto Centre (riding): description of, 92–94; Graham's nomination battles in, 87–92, 103, 110–11; Graham's resignation as MP for, 431–32; international politics in, 149, 173–74, 193–99, 203–4; local office/staff in, 197–99, 200, 234; Martin supporters in, 261–63, 264; social cutbacks as factor in, 201–7; town halls in, 418–19. *See also entries below*
Rosedale/Toronto Centre, campaigns in: (1984), 68, 94–100; (1988), 102–10; (1993), 110–11, 115–17; (1997), 207–12; (2000), 213–15; (2004), 348–49
Rosedale/Toronto Centre, canvassing in, 92–100, 103, 106, 209; in AIDS era, 103, 107–8; in apartment buildings/condos, 96, 207–8; with Chrétien, 115–16; against Crombie, 98–99; enumeration problems of, 107; free trade as factor in, 104–7, 108; by Graham family members, 97–98, 108–11; in housing co-ops, 93–94; international impact on, 94–96; against Layton, 116; and plastic record giveaway, 106–7; among sex trade workers, 97–98

Rosedale/Toronto Centre, demographics of, 92–94, 103; Canadian soldiers, 376; gay/lesbian community, 93, 103, 404–5, 412–14; in housing co-ops, 93–94, 204–6; immigrants, 93, 94, 103, 196–98; north of Bloor Street, 92–93, 97, 98, 103, 106–7, 110, 116, 117, 197; south of Bloor Street, 93, 94–95, 97–99, 102–3, 107, 110, 116, 117; students, 93. *See also specific neighbourhoods*
Rosedale/Toronto Centre, ethnic/religious groups of, 94–96; Aboriginal, 93, 202; African, 68, 94, 96; Chinese, 91, 93, 109, 171, 173–74; Filipino, 103, 172, 194, 197–98; Muslim, 222–23; Nigerian, 193–94; Portuguese, 94; Serbian, 95, 209; Somali, 103, 194, 197–98; Tamil, 103, 195–96, 224; Vietnamese, 194–95
Ross, Frank, 92
Roth, William V., 162
Rothschild family, 46, 47, 55–56
Rouhani, Hassan, 218
Royal Canadian Mounted Police (RCMP), 60, 61, 102, 260, 326, 370, 384, 398, 415–16; and Khadr/Arar cases, 324, 326, 329
Royal Commission on Banking and Finance, 42
Royal Commission on the Economic Union and Development Prospects for Canada, 104
Rubinstein, Amnon, 134, 240
Rumsfeld, Donald, 191, 286, 289, 346, 362, 364–65, 374, 393, 414; hawkish stance of, 275–76, 284, 305, 306, 315, 381
Russia, 143, 148–50, 187, 189, 219, 220, 231, 233, 242, 253, 258, 270, 272, 282, 363; and Arctic issues, 366, 367, 369, 372; and Chechnya, 149–50, 282; and NATO, 180–86, 251, 283, 348; and Ukraine/Crimea, 132, 147, 182,

185, 186, 368; UN veto of, 274, 283; and US invasion of Iraq, 276, 279, 282–83, 291, 294, 296, 298–99, 301–2, 316–17
Rwanda, genocide in, 178, 186, 188–89, 365
Ryan, Claude, 70

Sabri, Naji, 269
Sadlier, Dick, 15
Sahnoun, Mohamed, 186
Salaberry, Michel de, 217–18
Samar, Sima, 395–96
same-sex marriage, 405–13
Sampson, William, 219–21
Sandoval, Oswaldo, 166
Saro-Wiwa, Ken, Jr., 193–94
Sastre, Antonio Rodriguez, 49–53
Saud Al Faisal, Saudi prince/foreign minister, 219
Saudi Arabia, 218–20, 257, 270
Saul, John Ralston, 131, 231–32, 259
Sauvé, Jeanne, 87
Savard, Isabelle, 234, 249, 348, 351, 376–77
Saywell, John (Jack), 20
SCFAIT: Graham's appointment as vice-chair of, 128–30, 133; Graham's roles/impact as chair of, 95–96, 136–40, 145–46, 161, 164, 168–69, 171, 195, 197, 199, 204, 212, 216, 232, 238, 246–47, 332, 430; under Harper, 430–31
SCFAIT reviews, 136–46, 191–92, 238, 241, 243, 267, 332, 365; Balkan conflict, 179–86; Bretton Woods institutions, 156, 159–60; Canadian Arctic, 143–44, 156; NAFTA, 136–40; nuclear weapons, 156, 177–78; South Caucasus/Central Asia, 145–46, 156, 220; WTO, 156, 160–63, 165
Schmidt, Helmut, 253
Schmitz, Gerry, 143, 161
Schroeder, Gerhard, 272, 313
Schwartz, Laurent, 13

Scott, Ian, 91, 106, 108
Scott's Hospitality Inc., 101
September 11, 2001 terrorist attacks, 132, 155, 217, 221–25, 238, 243–44, 252; Chrétien on roots of, 276; first anniversary of, 271–73; military implications of, 235, 305–6; and US invasion of Iraq, 95, 266, 322. See also Iraq, US invasion of
Sewell, John, 39
Sharaa, Farouk al-, 327–28
Sharon, Ariel, 248, 249
Sharp, Mitchell, 227
Shaw, Robert, 371
Shead, Bill, 23
Sinclair, Bill, 59
Singh, Yashwant, 236
Smallwood, Joey, 86–87
Smith, Brian, 81
Smith family, 17–18
Smith, Nathan, 386
Smith, Rupert: The Utility of Force, 379
Smitherman, George, 206, 411
Smoot-Hawley Tariff Act (US), 75
Société québécoise de droit international, 82, 83
Solana, Javier, 272–73, 283, 330
Somalia, 178, 379, 397; as represented in riding, 103, 194, 197–98
Sopinka, John, 41
Soros, George, 159–60
South Africa, 94, 102
South China Sea, 175–76
Soviet Union, 82, 180, 282, 362, 367; in Afghanistan, 31, 390; collapse of, 132, 146, 148, 156, 177, 181, 254. See also Russia
Sowby, C.W., 15, 16
Spain, 18, 48–54, 55, 168, 350, 358; and US invasion of Iraq, 283, 294, 298–99, 301, 306–7
Special Joint Committee of the Senate and the House of Commons

on Reviewing Canadian Foreign Policy, 130–32, 133, 182
Spencer, David, 323–24
sponsorship scandal, 336, 340, 348, 414–15
Sproule, David, 396
Srebrenica (Bosnia), massacre in, 179
Sri Lanka, 93, 95, 195–96, 224, 270, 299, 432
Srpska, Republic of, 178, 179–80
St. Clement's School (Toronto), 21, 74
St. James Town, 110, 203; demographics of, 93, 94–95, 194, 202; election campaigning in, 107, 115–16, 207–8, 209
St. Jamestown Youth Centre, 103
St. Laurent, Louis, 21, 84
Standing Committee on Foreign Affairs and International Trade. See SCFAIT entries
Stanfield, Robert, 85–86
state sovereignty, 131, 184–87, 322, 332–33, 366, 394, 434; in Arctic waters, 366–72; and Canada's stance on Iraq, 308, 310–11, 318; in globalization/free trade era, 77, 104, 105–6, 108, 157, 159; and international agreements, 71, 75–76, 166–68, 361
Stornoway, 420
Strategic Advisory Team (SAT), in Afghanistan, 382, 388–89
Straw, Jack, 236, 254, 270, 349; on Blair, 309–10; and US invasion of Iraq, 276, 280, 289, 291, 295–96, 300, 349
Stronach, Frank, 90–91
submarines, 352, 356, 421; nuclear, 149, 368, 372
Summers, Lawrence (Larry), 257
Summits of the Americas: (2001), 168–70; (2004), 340–42
Supreme Court of Canada, 41, 59, 73, 82–83, 408–9, 411–12
Sussman, Amanda, 242

Swackhamer, J.W., 42, 47
Swords, Colleen, 234, 306
Syria, 34, 311, 394, 433; Arar's imprisonment/torture in, 270, 322–23, 325–30; civil war in, 132, 186, 243, 320

Taiwan, 151, 161, 171
Taliban, 31, 220, 381, 382, 384, 385, 393, 402, 426, 429; overthrow of, 224, 252; suicide/IED attacks by, 376, 386–87, 388, 399–400
Talleyrand-Périgord, Charles Maurice de, 314
Tamil Tigers, 195, 224
Tanaka, Makiko, 256
Tang Jiaxuan, 173–74
Tarnak Farms incident (Afghanistan), 252, 386
Task Force 151, 287–88, 303–6, 307
Thatcher, James, 107–8
Thatcher, Margaret, 156, 172
Thompson, Larry, 322
Thompson, Myron, 308
Thomsen, Lillian, 234
Thomson, Roy, 84–85
Thornton, A.P.: The Imperial Idea and Its Enemies, 20
"three-block war," 379, 384
Tobin, Brian, 227
Toronto Centre (riding). See Rosedale/Toronto Centre entries
Toronto Council Fire Native Cultural Centre, 93
Toronto Dominion Bank, 42–43, 61, 240
Toronto East Downtown Residents Association, 205
Toronto French School, 56
Toronto Star, 247, 263, 283
Toronto Telegram, 40, 85
Tory, John, 414
Townshend, Charlotte, 115
Tran, Luong, 194–95

Travers, Jim, 247
Treaty of Paris (1951), 44
Treaty of Rome (1957), 44–45, 51, 157
Treaty on Conventional Armed
  Forces in Europe, 146
Tremblay, André, 79
Trilateral Commission, 154
Trinity College (University of
  Toronto), 16, 34, 35–36, 61, 88, 89,
  93, 231; Graham's education/
  activities at, 19–23, 35, 40, 96
Trudeau, Alexandre (Sacha), 308
Trudeau, Justin, 433
Trudeau, Pierre Elliott, 8, 21, 39, 59,
  49, 62, 89, 94, 99–100, 104, 126, 130,
  146, 308, 332, 361; death of, 214;
  Graham and, 56, 86–87; Liberal
  Party farewell to, 92; and Quebec,
  56–57, 71–72, 112–13, 424
Tuktoyaktuk (NWT), 144, 370
Turkey, 28–29, 30, 32, 95, 147, 213, 220,
  270. See also Istanbul
Turner, John, 92, 99–100, 104, 105,
  108, 112, 128, 415, 417
Turp, Daniel, 80, 82, 169, 191–92

Ukraine, 132, 182, 243, 270
UN, 24, 76, 101, 130, 141, 150, 161, 237,
  244–45, 271, 382, 391, 432; Bush's
  address to, 268–69, 272; Canada's
  commitment to missions sanctioned
  by, 179, 183–87, 225, 274, 284–85,
  287, 291, 292, 401; Graham's address
  to, 268; Powell's presentation to,
  292–95, 315. See also entries below;
  Iraq, UN inspections in; Iraq, UN
  Security Council resolutions concerning; peacekeeping
UN Charter, 49, 184–85, 281, 319
UN Commission on International
  Trade Law (UNCITRAL), 80
UN Convention on the Law of the
  Sea (UNCLOS, 1982), 332–35, 369

UN Convention to Combat Desertifi-
  cation, 433
UN Educational, Scientific and
  Cultural Organization (UNESCO),
  80, 147, 244–45
UN Genocide Convention, 188–89
UN Millennium Project, 391
UN Monitoring, Verification and
  Inspection Commission
  (UNMOVIC), 267, 269, 275, 276–
  78, 285, 286, 289–90, 294–95, 297,
  298, 301, 302
UN Security Council, 189, 237, 245,
  253, 255, 297; and Afghanistan, 374;
  and Balkans, 178, 183, 184–85, 187;
  and Haiti crisis, 344–46; and R2P
  doctrine, 187, 320. See also Iraq, UN
  Security Council resolutions concerning; Iraq, US invasion of
Union Internationale des Avocats,
  66, 73
United Nations. See UN, and entries
  following
United States, 51, 53, 56, 64, 66, 81,
  95, 131, 134, 156, 178, 185, 187, 190,
  206, 238, 253, 340–41, 408–9; in
  Afghanistan, 379–80; and Arctic
  sovereignty, 366, 368–69; and
  Canada-US parliamentary group,
  151–55; and continental defence,
  361–66; and evolution of GATT,
  75–77; and FTA, 104–7, 136; and
  Haiti crisis, 342–46; and Iran, 217–
  18; and Israel, 242–45; and NAFTA,
  136–40, 158, 165, 167, 238, 312, 318;
  and OAS/FIPA, 163–64, 167; and
  trade disputes with Canada, 255–
  56. See also Bush, George W., and
  entry following; Iraq, US invasion
  of; Powell, Colin; September 11,
  2001 terrorist attacks
Université de Montréal, Graham as
  professor at, 79–80, 83, 101

Université de Paris, Graham's doctoral studies at, 43–45, 54, 57–58; thesis written for, 43–44, 45, 58
Université du Québec à Montréal, 300
University Hill School, 11
University Naval Training Division (UNTD), 23–26
University of British Columbia (UBC), 10, 11, 12, 19, 92
University of Oxford, 20, 51, 354
University of Toronto, 87, 90, 102, 372; Bill Graham Centre at, 435; St. Michael's College, 74, 93; Victoria College, 66, 93. *See also entry below*; Trinity College
University of Toronto Law School, 38–40; Graham as gold medallist at, 40, 41, 42, 117, 353–54; Graham as professor at, 70, 73–80, 100–2
University of Victoria, 78, 419
Upper Canada College (UCC), 6, 74, 103; Graham as student at, 14–19, 20, 21, 38, 41, 121

Vanclief, Lyle, 163, 262
Vancouver, Graham homes in, 6–7, 10–11, 12–13, 14, 16
Vegh, Tom, 110
Victoria Times Colonist, 12, 84
Vienna Convention on Consular Relations, 220, 323
Vigneault, Gilles, 57
Villepin, Dominique de, 270, 273, 276, 295, 302, 344
Volcker, Paul, 159

Wade, Mason: *The French Canadians*, 9
Wadia, Phiroza, 13
Waldock, Sir Humphrey, 51–52
Wanklyn, Fred and Vicky, 55, 56
"War on Terror," 238, 250–51, 326; and Abu Ghraib prison abuses, 331, 381,

393, 394, 397; and Arar/Khadr cases, 322–30; and US invasion of Iraq, 250, 275, 287, 289, 303, 322
Wardak, Adbul Rahim, 395, 396
Warren, Jake, 76
Watson, Andrew, 34
Watson, Gordon, 20
Wayne, Elsie, 421
weapons, 358, 433; biological/chemical, 24, 218, 254, 268, 269, 320; landmines as, 190, 218, 237. *See also entry below*; ballistic missile defence; nuclear weapons
weapons of mass destruction (WMDs), in Iraq, 266–67, 269, 273, 275, 276–78, 285, 286, 289–90, 292–95, 297, 298, 301, 302, 319–20
West Bank, 241, 243, 249–50
Weston, Hilary, 74
Whelan, Susan, 288
White, Arthur (grandfather), 6, 15
White, Elizabeth (grandmother), 6, 8, 15
Williams, Danny, 335
Williams, Jody, 190
Willis, John, 39
Williston, Walter, 41–43, 52, 58, 83
Wilson, Doug, 107
Wilson, Elizabeth, 90
Wilson, Tom, 21, 89–90
Wolfensohn, James, 159
Wolfowitz, Paul, 275, 365, 382
Wong, Greg, 91
Wootten, Patrick, 20, 22, 26–35, 95, 217, 240, 376, 386
Wootten-Wootten, Patrick William, 26–27
World Bank, 76, 130, 156, 159, 253
World Trade Center (New York), 95, 132, 221, 224, 271–72. *See also* September 11, 2001 terrorist attacks
World Trade Organization (WTO), 76–77, 79, 137, 156, 157, 159, 164–65,

282; membership rules of, 174, 220; parliamentary assembly proposal for, 160–63; protests against, 160, 162, 257

Wright, Cecil "Caesar," 38, 39, 54, 73
Wright, David, 280
Wright, Jim, 183, 255, 276

Xtra! magazine, 210–11

Yad Vashem memorial (Jerusalem), 241
Yellowknife (NWT), 112, 143, 144, 149–50, 370, 371, 418

Yeltsin, Boris, 149–50, 253
Yugoslavia, former, 27–28, 178, 180, 182, 189, 425. *See also* Bosnia and Herzegovina; Kosovo

Zarif, Mohammad Javad, 218
Zawahiri, Ayman al-, 324
Zeng Jianhui, 171
Zhou Enlai, 171
Zimbabwe, 164, 236–37, 270
Zussman, David, 227

C.D. HOWE SERIES IN CANADIAN POLITICAL HISTORY

Series editors: Robert Bothwell and John English

This series offers fresh perspectives on Canadian political history and public policy from over the past century. Its purpose is to encourage scholars to write and publish on all aspects of the nation's political history, including the origins, administration, and significance of economic policies; the social foundations of politics and political parties; transnational influences on Canadian public life; and the biographies of key public figures. In doing so, the series fills large gaps in our knowledge about recent Canadian history and makes accessible to a broader audience the background necessary to understand contemporary public-political issues.

The series originated with a grant from the C.D. Howe Memorial Foundation and is further supported by the Bill Graham Centre for Contemporary International History.

The Call of the World: A Political Memoir is the second volume in the series. The first was *Grit: The Life and Politics of Paul Martin Sr.,* by Greg Donaghy.

C.D. Howe Series in
Canadian Political History